Preaching the tradition

Preaching the tradition

Homily and hermeneutics after the exile

Based on the 'addresses' in Chronicles, the 'speeches' in the Books of Ezra and Nehemiah and the post-exilic prophetic books

Rex Mason
Regent's Park College, Oxford

The right of the
University of Cambridge
to print and sell
all manner of books
was granted by
Henry VIII in 1534.
The University has printed
and published continuously
since 1584.

Cambridge University Press

Cambridge
New York   Port Chester
Melbourne   Sydney

Published by the Press Syndicate of the University of Cambridge
The Pitt Building, Trumpington Street, Cambridge CB2 IRP
40 West 20th Street, New York, NY 10011, USA
10 Stamford Road, Oakleigh, Melbourne 3166, Australia

First published 1990

Printed in Great Britain at the University Press, Cambridge

British Library cataloguing in publication data

British Library cataloguing in publication data
Mason, Rex, 1926–
Preaching the tradition: homily and hermeneutics after
the exile.
1.   Bible. O.T. – Critical studies
I.   Title
221.6

Library of Congress cataloguing in publication data

Mason, Rex. 1926–
Preaching the tradition : homily and hermeneutics after the exile
based on the 'addresses' in Chronicles, the speeches in the Books of
Ezra and Nehemiah and the post-exilic prophetic books / Rex Mason.
     p.   cm.
Includes bibliographical references.
ISBN 0 521 38304 8
1. Bible.   O.T.   Chronicles–Criticism, interpretation, etc.
2. Preaching–Biblical teaching.   3. Bible.   O.T.   Ezra–Criticism,
interpretation, etc.   4. Bible.   O.T.   Nehemiah–Criticism,
interpretation, etc.   5. Bible.   O.T.   Minor Prophets–Criticism,
interpretation, etc.   6. Judaism–History–Post-exilic period, 586
B.C.-A.D. 210.   I. Title.
BS1345.6.P69P74   1990
222'.606–dc20   89-27943   CIP

ISBN 0 521 38304 8

FOR AUDREY

Contents

Abbreviations

OTL	Old Testament Library (SCM Press, London)
OTS	*Oudtestamentische Studiën*
RSV	Revised Standard Version
SBL	Society of Biblical Literature (Monograph and Dissertation Series)
SBT	Studies in Biblical Theology, SCM Press & Allenson, Naperville, Illinois
SJT	*Scottish Journal of Theology*
SVT	Supplements to *Vetus Testamentum*
Syr. Vulg.	Syriac Peshitta and Latin Vulgate
TBC	Torch Bible Commentaries
VSS	Versions
VT	Vetus Testamentum
WMANT	*Wissenschaftliche Untersuchungen zum Alten und Neuen Testament*
ZAW	*Zeitschrift für die alttestamentliche Wissenschaft*

Introduction

In 1934, Gerhard von Rad wrote an article entitled 'The Levitical Sermon in I & II Chronicles'.[1] In it, he noted that the Chronicler gives a number of speeches to some of his characters which do not appear in parallel passages in Samuel–II Kings, the so-called 'Deuteronomistic History'. These speeches seldom fit the historical context in which they are placed, and all tend to use similar vocabulary to express similar truths. They share the characteristics of citation of, or at least allusion to, earlier legal and prophetic sayings, a general parenetic nature, and have many features of style in common. Von Rad claims that they 'evince a distinct form-category of later origin, that of the "Levitical Sermon"'.[2] This way of understanding the 'speeches' in Chronicles has commanded a great deal of support, which is still evident in many of the recent commentaries on Chronicles.[3] Nevertheless, it has also received some strong criticism.[4] On the other hand, some writers have claimed to find material similar to the 'Levitical Sermons' elsewhere in the post-exilic literature, especially in the prophetic books.[5] In order to take the discussion further, it seems appropriate to base it on a fresh examination of the main speeches in Chronicles.[6] In Part I, therefore, after a brief mention of some of the critical issues affecting the approach to the Chronicler's work which occupy contemporary scholarly debate, we shall in Chapter 2 consider each of the speeches in turn. This examination will not be limited to those passages used by von Rad in his study (see n. 2 above). We shall look at all the significant addresses given to his characters by the Chronicler which are not found in Samuel/Kings. This will be followed by a special note on II Chr. 36:15f. In Chapter 3, we shall attempt to draw some conclusions from that examination respecting contents, style and form of the speeches, asking whether von Rad's claim that they represent a *Gattung* or 'genre' of 'Sermon' can be upheld in general, and how far they might be held to be 'Levitical Sermons' in particular. In Part II some other post-exilic literature will be considered to see how far we may find material similar to, or in any way related to, the 'speeches' in Chronicles and what conclusions can be drawn from such similarity as may be found. Chapter 4 will deal with the Books of Ezra and Nehemiah, since here, whatever the relationship of their authorship to that of the Books of Chronicles, we might expect to find some continuation of the 'Chronicler tradition'. In following chapters attention will be given to the post-exilic 'prophetic tradition', represented by the Books of Haggai, Zechariah 1–8 and Malachi. Clearly, there is much more post-exilic literature which might be examined. However, it is hoped enough is represented in this study to show what 'trends' may be observable in some post-exilic traditions. I hope to test and develop conclusions reached in this book with reference to other post-exilic traditions and literature in a later work.

The general conclusion reached here is that, while it is difficult, if not impossible, to make a case for a *Gattung* or precisely identifiable form-structure of 'sermon', and certainly not possible to say that such was the exclusive prerogative of Levites, the material does reflect and encapsulate something of the 'preaching' that must have gone on in the second temple. Of course, the term 'preaching' must not necessarily or exclusively conjure up pictures of present-day sermons. A recent scholar has referred to the post-exilic tradents as 'rhetors'.[7] By 'preachers' we must think of those who preserved, developed and taught the traditions which must have been becoming increasingly enshrined in Israel's 'Scriptures'. The activity of such tradents must have been both literary and rhetorical and have taken place in the study and the classroom as well as in more formally 'liturgical' settings. We lack the precise and detailed information to be more exact. But the written material itself may be found to indicate by its very nature an origin in the activity of those who were consciously interpreting and teaching the 'traditions'. As it became more fixed in form it must itself have acted both as a guide for the development of that tradition and as a basis for continuing interpretative and exegetical practices.

Viewed in this light the literature may be seen to afford an illuminating window into the life, beliefs, doubts, fears and hopes of the post-exilic community of faith, and especially into the cares and concerns of their spiritual mentors. This community, from which the literature sprang, and among whom it was preserved, expounded, reinterpreted and applied to ever-changing situations, have thus left in their 'Scriptures' a vivid and living witness to their brave attempts to interpret the ways of God in difficult circumstances.

It is difficult to find the right term for the passages in Chronicles to be examined. To call them 'sermons' begs the question of their form. 'Speeches' is hardly an appropriate term, for some of them are too short to be that, and some are directed to one person only. Perhaps 'addresses' is the most suitable description since this can be used of any spoken communication, and yet, in English, carries overtones of a religious context in which the faithful are encouraged, instructed, warned or exhorted.

Part I

The '*addresses*'
in the Books
of Chronicles

I Introduction to Part I

As we turn to examine the 'addresses' in the Books of Chronicles, on any count an important feature of the total work, we find that a number of critical questions concerning the work of the Chronicler remain unresolved in contemporary scholarship. These must at least be noted where any discussion of the books takes place. Broadly they fall into four categories:

(1) the unity of I & II Chronicles
(2) the relation of I & II Chronicles to the Books of Ezra and Nehemiah
(3) the date of the 'Chronicler'
(4) the text of Samuel/Kings used by the Chronicler.

These questions overlap since the answer given to one will affect the answers given to others. They are 'unresolved' in that there is no general consensus of scholarly opinion about them and because, at least and especially with (4), insufficient evidence is available to provide a clear solution. Before we begin our discussion of the addresses in Chronicles some brief outline of these issues needs to be given.

There is certainly little agreement as yet concerning the unity of I & II Chronicles. As long ago as 1927 J. W. Rothstein and J. Hänel argued that, while the original Chronicler wrote soon after 432 BCE, a redactor, working about 400 BCE, revised his work, while various further additions were made even later.[1] In 1954, K. Galling took the view that there were two separate authors, the second Chronicler being as late as the second century BCE.[2] More recent writers have also found I & II Chronicles to be of complex composition. Rudolph found Rothstein and Hänel's approach too simplistic. The Chronicler, he argued, is not all of one piece. The 'additions are much too varied and contradictory for them to be attributed to one compiler or redactor'. There was an original Chronicler who worked about 400 BCE, but 'his work was expanded in the course of time, even up to the Maccabaean period, by a whole series of additions with differing viewpoints'.[3] Some have seen all the genealogical lists of I Chr. cc. 1–9 as later additions to the work.[4] Some have found considerable interpolations in I Chr. cc. 10–29, especially in those passages in which David is shown to be giving detailed instructions concerning the temple, its personnel and its worship.[5] Others, noticing some tension between an apparently pro-priestly point of view (e.g. II 24:5) and an apparent pro-Levitical apologetic (e.g. II 29:34), have argued either for a pro-Levitical or a pro-priestly editing of Chronicles.[6] F. M. Cross proposed three editions of the Chronicler's work. The first, about 520 BCE, served as the programme for the restoration of the kingdom under Zerubbabel, its enthusiasm for the temple reflecting the call to the community by the prophets Haggai and Zechariah to rebuild the temple, and the equal enthusiasm for David showing that a hope for the restoration of the monarchy was entertained. This ended in Ezra 3:15 (= I Esd. 5:65) with the report of the completion of the rebuilding. A second edition, c. 458 BCE, extended the work to include all that is now contained in I Esdras, that is to the reading of the Law by Ezra and the subsequent covenant by which it was adopted. A third edition, c. 400 BCE, added all that is now contained in the Books of Ezra and Nehemiah, together with I Chr. cc. 1–9. This view has more recently been endorsed by S. L. McKenzie.[7] In the face of all these, and many other, attempted analyses of different redactional processes, perhaps the balance of probability belongs with J. R. Porter:

The whole process may indeed have been part of a continuing Chronistic circle, which we have postulated as the setting for the Chronicler's activity and for which the rebuilding of the temple would have provided a new home and impetus, and this would account for the links which undoubtedly exist between 1 and 2 Chronicles and Ezra and Nehemiah, while freeing us from over hypothetical speculations about a number of redactions of, or additions to, already existing compositions.[8]

Whether we agree or not with his belief that the 'Chronicler' process started as early as 520 BCE (see below), his scepticism over some of the elaborate reconstructions of the alleged processes by which the work achieved its final form is a healthy one. It is shared by P. R. Ackroyd:

Furthermore, while it is clear that the original work – if indeed such a term is entirely appropriate – has been added to, I am both doubtful of the degree to which certainty can be established in regard to additions, and also doubtful of the supposition that the additions have radically altered the trend of the work.[9]

The attempt to show the separate authorship of Chronicles and the Books of Ezra and Nehemiah is not new. A. C. Welch argued for it in 1935.[10] More recently it has been vigorously championed by S. Japhet,[11] and H. G. M. Williamson.[12] Their arguments have rested mainly on variations in vocabulary, style and theology. Among the points they make are that there is nothing of the Chronicler's emphasis on David and the Davidic Covenant in Ezra/Nehemiah. There it is the Exodus tradition which is stressed, a tradition virtually ignored by the Chronicler. The Chronicler is tolerant towards the mixed marriages of Solomon to a degree which would have been impossible for one who recorded the abhorrence shown by Ezra and Nehemiah towards intermarriage with foreigners. Ezra/Nehemiah shows none of the stress on immediate retribution which is so marked a feature of the Chronicler's theology. The Chronicler's emphasis on prophecy is not shared in Ezra/Nehemiah. R. L. Braun has also argued for marked ideological differences between Chronicles and Ezra/Nehemiah.[13] All of these, and the other arguments advanced, are open to discussion. They have been questioned by S. L. Croft[14] and Menahem Haran,[15] while R. Polzin[16] and M. A. Throntveit[17] have challenged Japhet's arguments on linguistic grounds. Neither Cross nor McKenzie accepts them, as has been shown above (see n. 7). They attribute the differences to three successive editions of the whole work I Chronicles–Nehemiah.

Nevertheless, the realisation that, one way or another, the date of the 'original Chronicler' need no longer be tied to the date of the latest name in the genealogical lists in Ezra/Nehemiah[18] has opened the way for much earlier dating than was once customary. D. N. Freedman suggested that the Chronicler belonged to the time just after the exile:

The parallel between the first building of the temple under the direction of David (and Solomon), and the second building under Zerubbabel is too strong to be accidental, and must have formed part of the original structure of the work.[19]

In this, as has been shown, he has been followed by Cross and McKenzie. The quotation from Porter above showed that he too favoured this date for the beginning of the process which he described as the work of a 'continuing Chronistic circle'.[20]

A further difficulty in discovering the message of the 'Chronicler' stems from the questioning, not only of the extent of his work, but the precise nature of his sources. Traditionally it has been accepted that he had before him the Books of Samuel and Kings and that, by marking the differences between these and the account in Chronicles, one could detect the special interests and concerns of the Chronicler by 'subtraction' and 'addition', so to speak. However, the evidence from Qumran suggests that the text of Samuel/Kings which the Chronicler used was different from that of the MT, resembling more an early Palestinian type. This might suggest that where, in some places at least, the Chronicler diverges from MT, the divergences may be due, not to the special interests of the Chronicler or his own conscious reinterpretation of MT, but to the text he had before him.[21] This has been investigated most recently by S. L. McKenzie (see n. 7 above), who conducts a detailed comparison of the text of Chronicles with that of the 4Q Sam[a] fragments. Where 4Q Sam[a] is extant (and the fragments represent about 10 per cent of the whole text), McKenzie finds only six cases where a variant can be seen as due to the Chronicler's special interests. So, speaking of I Chronicles, he concludes:

The appearance of the 4Q Sam[a] fragments has shown that the evidence for tendentious change on the part of the Chronicler in the synoptic passage is very slight. *(p. 72)*

Nevertheless, by omissions and by the inclusion of some special matter he has introduced his own interests, including 'his pan-Israelite interest, his idealised view of David and Solomon, and his concern with Levites and the cult' (p. 72). For II Chronicles 1–28, 'The conclusions . . . are very similar to those reached for I Chronicles' (p. 113). (There are greater differences from Kings in II Chr. 29–35, but these, while partly due to the Chronicler's tendency to periodise monarchs' reigns, McKenzie attributes as much to the special concerns of the first editor of the Deuteronomistic History.) However, we have to note that 'the evidence for the text of K from Qumran is far less extensive' (p. 83). Of special interest for the present study is his comment:

He [i.e. the Chronicler] does compose most of the speeches and oracles, but some of them may also be based on other sources. *(p. 113)*

So, omissions and variations show here also, as for I Chronicles, that the special interests of the Chronicler concern the Davidic monarchy, the cult and its personnel, especially the Levites and his view of all-Israel. Further, he strengthens the impression of the immediacy of Yahweh's retribution in the way he structures narratives, often periodising a king's reign. By such means he presents history as a 'prophecy–fulfilment' schema. McKenzie's work is extremely useful, especially since the Qumran material has not always been readily available to scholars without easy access to Harvard. It certainly suggests that extreme care is needed before pressing details of textual variations between MT Samuel/Kings and Chronicles into exegetical service. Nevertheless, the general impression is that the broad aims of the Chronicler do become apparent and, certainly as far as the addresses are concerned, we are justified in looking for the Chronicler's own beliefs, either because he composed them, or because he saw fit to introduce them from sources which were not utilised in Samuel/Kings.[22]

These are some of the issues which need to be borne in mind in any discussion of the Chronicler's work. However, it is not our intention to pre-determine answers to them at this stage and so, to some extent, pre-pro-gramme our interpretation of the addresses. They must figure in the discussion where one answer or another would affect that interpretation. On the other hand it may be that the examination of the addresses which follows will be found in places to have its own light to throw on these very issues.

2 The addresses in Chronicles

[1] 1 12:18 (19)* *Amasai to David*

Yours,ᵃ O David,
And with you,ᵇ son of Jesse.
Rich prosperityᶜ be yours,
and prosperityᶜ to those who help you;
For your God helps you.†

Text

ᵃ LXX vocalises the Hebrew consonants to give an imperative, 'Go forth.' MT
is to be preferred, however. It may be that a word has dropped out meaning
'we' or 'all of us are yours', but it is implicit in the terse, vivid style of the text as
it stands.

*Verse numbers in brackets, or following /, refer to MT where that differs from the
EVV.
†Translations of the addresses are mine. Elsewhere, except where specifically stated,
quotations are taken from RSV. The discussion of the 'addresses' centres on their
major themes and is not intended to fulfil the role of a commentary in detailed
treatment of specific issues. For this reason textual notes are confined only to matters
which affect the translation offered.

b LXX vocalises the Hebrew consonants to read 'Go forth, O David, *and your people . . .*' Again, however, MT 'and with you' gives the better sense in this affirmation of loyalty in reply to David's questioning of their motives (v. 17/18).

c The Hebrew word is שָׁלוֹם (*shalom*), often translated 'peace'. It means much more than the absence of strife, however, and includes all the physical, moral and spiritual elements that make for 'well-being'.

General description

The address is in the form of a poetic blessing, affirming loyalty. It is introduced by a brief narrative formula conferring prophetic inspiration and authority, 'And the spirit clothed itself with Amasai, chief of the thirty' (v. 18/19).

Contents

The setting for this address is the period of David's exile in the face of Saul's hostility. I Sam. 27:1–7 tells how he found refuge among the Philistines (who doubtless saw his threat to the royal house of Saul as a factor working in their interest). Achish, king of Gath, gave him Ziklag as headquarters. The Chronicler's description of those who came to join him is rather different from the impression given in I Sam. 22:2, where we read, 'And every one who was in distress, and every one who was in debt, and every one who was discontented, gathered to him . . .' It suggests something of a raffish band. Here, those who come are skilled warriors and army officers led, significantly, by people from Benjamin (Saul's own tribe, v. 2) and Judah (v. 16/17). Yet, already, the 'all-Israel' theme is being represented in an expression of loyalty in this early stage of David's career, for there came some from east of the Jordan (v. 8/9, 15/16) and some from the northern tribe of Manasseh (v. 20/21). Thus David's later rule of all Israel is anticipated. Indeed, those who come to his support here are described by the Chronicler as being 'great, like an army of God' (v. 22/23). The Hebrew idiom 'X of God' can express the superlative and so means here, 'A very great army'. Nevertheless, its use by the Chronicler is significant, for this army itself is seen as a work of God who 'helps' David, as Amasai's blessing affirms.

Amasai is not mentioned elsewhere. He is described as a 'chief of thirty', which was evidently some recognised office of military rank.[1] There were no doubt several of these in the various sections of the armies which defected to David, and so there is no need to identify him with Ishmaiah (v. 4). His real significance is to be a mouth-piece for the Chronicler's theology.

It is possible, however, that the choice of name is deliberate. It may well recall the name of 'Amasa', who was appointed leader over troops by Absalom (II Sam. 17:25), but to whom David appealed, successfully, for support:

Are you not my bone and my flesh? God do so to me, and more also, if you are not commander of my army henceforth in place of Joab. *(II Sam. 19:13/14)*

Joab had slain David's rebellious son, Absalom (II Sam. 18:14). Indeed, the themes of loyalty and disloyalty run throughout the story of Amasa, for II Sam. 20 tells how David summons him to call the men of Judah together to meet the threat posed by the revolt of Sheba. Later in the chapter, Joab treacherously assassinates Amasa (vv. 8–13). Yet that same chapter opens with the cry of treachery and disloyalty by which Sheba sought to rally support for his rebellion:

We have no portion in David, and we have no inheritance in the son of Jesse; every man to his tents, O Israel! *(II Sam. 20:1)*

These words fatefully anticipate the similar cry with which, later, Jeroboam will summon the people of the North to rebel against the house of David (II Chr. 10:16). Ackroyd has suggested that the address of Amasai is intended to be a deliberate repudiation of these very words of treachery.[2] That would be all the more appropriate if the whole incident was seen by the Chronicler as in some way an exegesis of the incident involving Absalom, David, Joab and Sheba recorded in II Samuel. It is clear from v. 17 that the Chronicler has incidents in the same narratives in mind (although he does not mention them) when he records David as warning those who come to him, 'If [you have come] to betray me to my adversaries . . . then may the God of our fathers rebuke you.' It must be to such episodes as those recorded in I Sam. 23 (esp. vv. 12, 19) that allusion is being made. We might add that the name Amasai occurs more than once in Chronicles of priestly figures (I 6:25; 15:24; II 29:12). It would, thus, be doubly suitable for the Chronicler's purpose.

In any event, Amasai's words fit so clearly into the theme of the chapter that it is clear they are either the composition of the Chronicler, or he has shaped the narrative in such a way as to elaborate their content. One form or another of the verb 'help' (עזר) occurs no fewer than six times in the chapter. In v. 1 we read that there came to David warriors who 'helped' him. In v. 17/18 David asks if they have come in 'peace' (שָׁלוֹם) to 'help' him. In vv. 21/22f. the service of those who fought for David is again described as 'helping' him. This, as we have seen, is strongly contrasted with its alternative of 'betrayal' (v. 17/18), the kind of betrayal seen in the revolts led by Sheba and Jeroboam. So Amasai blesses David's 'helpers' by wishing them 'peace'. All who 'help' in this way are identifying themselves with God's purposes and concerns, for 'your God helps you'. The opening formula of this address by Amasai gives prophetic status and authority to the words with its description of God's spirit 'clothing itself' with him. Soldier as he is, he speaks God's word as truly and, as it proves, with as much creative power, as any prophet. It is not coincidental that the first of the addresses in Chronicles thus speaks of the divine choice of David from well before the time of his kingship. It acts as a summons to all true 'Israelites' to align themselves with the well-being of the Davidic line by showing that active support which places them within the divine purpose. Equally significantly, it associates 'peace' with David, that peace which later will characterise his continuing line and the temple. All God's purposes for peace, prosperity and success centre on David. Amasai is the herald of this theology which is to be at the heart of the Chronicler's interpretation of history.

[2] I 13:2f. *David to all the assembly of Israel*

[2] *And David said to the whole assembly of Israel, 'If you think it is good and of Yahweh, our God, let us strike out [boldly]ª and send to our brethren who remain in all the territories of Israel together with the priests and Levites in the towns and their surrounding districts, in order that they may assemble here with us.³ And let us bring back the ark of our God, for we did not consult itᵇ in the days of Saul.'*

Text

ª The Hebrew verb is / פרץ, 'to break out'. There may be a significance in its use here since v. 11 shows that God can 'break out' in judgement against those who transgress while, on the other hand, 14:11 shows that he can also 'break out' against the enemies of those who obey him. I have retained it unamended, taking its meaning to be 'Let us strike out from the dangerous situation we are in on a bold new course of obedience' (the Chronicler's account, unlike that in

I Samuel, has not yet recorded the defeat of the Philistines: that is to follow the people's obedience, not to create the conditions where such obedience would be easy).

b The Hebrew verb / סבב echoes I Sam. 5:8f., but, as Williamson has pointed out (*1 and 2 Chronicles*, p. 115), its use here does not seem to be so much spatial as evocative of the idea of repentance, of 'turning back' to God. While the Chronicler usually employs some form of the Hebrew / שוב to indicate such 'turning', this verb may carry such overtones in I 10:14 and 12:23, and the opposite, certainly, in II 29:6.

General description

This 'address' does not have quite the form of any of the others. It is too 'democratic' to be a 'royal decree', being virtually an appeal. It marks a call for repentance by the whole community in showing a new attitude towards the ark and so towards the worship of Yahweh, and a call for action to show that repentance by bringing up the ark.

Contents

We would expect the first words given to David to have a special significance. The Chronicler highlights their importance by attributing them to him the moment he has been crowned at Hebron as king by 'all Israel' (he records no 'two-stage' accession to such a position like that found in the Deuteronomistic History – see n. 4 below – and these words have no parallel in I Samuel). They reveal that the first action of David as king is to show concern for proper cultic worship. This can be correct only if the ark is central, for it is the place where Yahweh may be 'consulted' (v. 3, the Heb. root / דרש), and so the community live under the constant direction of Yahweh. It is thus the first instance the Chronicler gives of the proper purpose of the choice of David and the Davidic line. It shows an immediate expression of the loyalty and obedience which will find its full outlet in making provision for, building and maintaining the temple and its worship. It is not to be purely a 'political' or 'nationalist' rule. David addresses the whole 'assembly' (Heb. קָהָל, the term used of a religious congregation) of Israel. All are to be involved, priests and Levites as the proper leaders of this community and all the people, acting in an ideal unity of concern and obedience in matters cultic. The totality of the participation is stressed in that it is not only those present at Hebron who are to act but those 'who remain in all the territories of Israel' (v. 2). The Chronicler goes on to record the unanimous and faithful response of this congregation (v. 4).

This 'address', then, like an overture, sounds some of the themes which will be heard in fuller chorus in the more major addresses to follow.

[3] I 15:2 *David (to all Israel?)*
I 15:12f. *David to the leaders of the divisions of the Levites*

2 Then David said, 'Only the Levites shall carry the ark of God, for Yahweh has chosen them to carry the ark of Yahweh and to serve him for ever.'

12 And [David] said to them, 'You are the leaders of the divisions[a] of the Levites: sanctify yourselves, you and your fellows, and bring up the ark of Yahweh, the God of Israel, to the place[b] which I have prepared for it.13 Because you did not do it at first[c] Yahweh has broken out against us since we did not consult him as the commandment required.'

Text

[a] Lit. 'the heads of the fathers of the Levites'.
[b] Inserting 'the place' with the VSS.
[c] The Hebrew word is uncertain, but an explanation of the previous disaster (13:9–12) is apparently being offered.

General description

The first statement by David is worded more in the form of a royal decree than the more deferential form of his address in 13:2f. There is no explicit indication of those to whom it was addressed. Perhaps it is intended that we should understand it to be to 'all Israel' whom, the next verse indicates, he assembled at Jerusalem. The words of vv. 12f. appear most naturally to address the Levites, the names Zadok and Abiathar in v. 11 probably being additional. The statement takes a form to be met with frequently in the addresses of an 'Encouragement for a Task' (see pp. 24f.), which includes a call to a specific enterprise, a reason for undertaking it and/or grounds of encouragement which make the task a hopeful one.

Contents

These two 'words' given to David by the Chronicler are of relevance here only for three things. First, they show David to be a model king who acts strictly in accordance with the law (see also Deut. 10:8, 18:5) and, secondly, they show his exemplary concern for the ark, proper provision for sacral worship and so the central place of Yahweh in the life of the community. Thirdly, they show the importance of the 'sanctification' of those leaders who exercise special responsibility in the worship of the community. Thus they continue and strengthen the function of the first address assigned to David in 13:2f. and anticipate notes which will find stronger voice in the addresses to come.

[4] 1 22:6–16 *David's charge to Solomon to build the temple*

⁶*Then David summoned Solomon, his son, and charged him to build a sanctuary for Yahweh, the God of Israel.* ⁷*And David said to Solomon, 'My son,ᵃ as for me, it was my intention to build a sanctuary to the name of Yahweh, my God.* ⁸*But the word of Yahweh came to me, saying, "You have spilled much blood and fought fierce battles. Because you have spilled so much blood on the ground before me you shall not build a sanctuary for my name.* ⁹*But a son shall be born to you. He will be a man of rest and I will give him rest from all the enemies who surround him. His name shall be Solomonᵇ and I will give Israel peace and quiet in his time.* ¹⁰*It is he who will build a sanctuary to my name. He will be a son to me and I will be a father to him. I shall establish his royal dynastyᶜ for ever."* ¹¹*Now, my son, may Yahweh be with you so that he may give you success. Build a sanctuary for Yahweh, your God, even as he has predicted for you.* ¹²*But may Yahweh give you insight and understanding so that, when he gives you authority over Israel,ᵈ you may follow the teaching of Yahweh your God.* ¹³*You will succeed if you take care to observe the statutes and the decrees which Yahweh imposed on Moses for Israel. Be strong! Be resolute! Do not be afraid! Do not be discouraged!* ¹⁴*See, even in my own difficult circumstancesᵉ I have provided for the sanctuary of Yahweh one hundred thousand talents of gold, a million talents of silver, and more bronze and iron than can be weighed. I have provided timber and stone as well. To all this you must add more.* ¹⁵*You will have a host of people engaged in the work to help you, wood-cutters, stone-masons, joiners and men skilled in every kind of craft.* ¹⁶*There will be incalculable gold, silver, bronze and iron. Rise to the task, and may Yahweh be with you.'*

Text

a The consonantal text, the Versions and a number of MSS read 'his son'. The Massoretes, by their vocalic pointing, however, intend us to read 'my son' as the opening of the direct address to Solomon.

b The name 'Solomon' (Heb. שְׁלֹמֹה) comes from the same root as the word for 'peace' (שָׁלוֹם) – hence the NEB rendering 'man of peace'.

c Lit. 'the throne of his kingdom'.

d Or 'may he instruct you [in your position] over Israel'. LXX renders, 'May he strengthen you over Israel both to keep and to do the teaching . . .' The syntax is a little awkward, but Williamson points to parallels in similar contexts: Deut. 31:14, 23 and Josh. 1:9. The sense is taken up in Solomon's prayer recorded in II Chr. 1:10. Emendation of the text seems unnecessary.

e This could also be rendered, 'by my own toil', but in a majority of instances the noun עֳנִי means 'affliction' or 'poverty'. It may refer to the difficulties David had experienced in gathering all these resources when engaged in so many battles. The king in Zech. 9:9 is said to be עָנִי, and, since a form of the same verbal root is used of the Servant in Isa. 53:4, one wonders whether in some lines of post-exilic tradition the picture of the king as the humble, faithful, even suffering, servant of God and his people arose.

General description

The description of 'Installation to Office' has been used by some to designate as a particular genre such injunctions as those found in vv. 13b and 16b. Perhaps a better term would be 'Encouragement for a Task' (see the discussion below). The address is introduced by a brief narrative phrase, 'Then David summoned Solomon, his son', and, if the MT vocalisation is followed, it opens with the vocative address 'My son'. It includes admonition in vv. 12, 13a.

Contents

The address of Amasai served to show that David and his dynasty were the objects of God's grace and that 'peace' would be the hallmark of that dynasty. The theme of 'peace' is now taken up in the first major address attributed to David himself. It is likely that these words are the Chronicler's version of

David's dying charge to Solomon recorded in I Kgs. 2:2–4. If so, the differences are instructive. In Chronicles the words are spoken while David is still very much alive, cc. 23–7 showing how, although he was 'old and full of days' (23:1), he appointed all the orders and divisions of the Levites, Aaronites and other temple personnel such as singers and gate-keepers together with the more general administrative orders of judges and military leaders.[3] More important is the different theme of the address. Only the command to be loyal to the law of Moses (v. 13) and the call 'Be strong!' are common to both passages. I Kgs. 2:2–4 has often been understood as one of three *loci classici* in which the Deuteronomistic Historian[4] aims to bring the Exodus/Sinai and Davidic covenant traditions together, making conditional (v. 4) the alleged 'unconditional' nature of the Nathan covenant (II Sam. 7:1–17).[5] But, thereafter, the main thrust of the charge in Kings is a call to Solomon to take vengeance on the two sons of Zeraiah, Joab and Shimei, who had opposed David's interests, and to reward the faithful Barzillai. The Chronicler, in any case, could not have kept these references since he had not mentioned the historical incidents in which these characters figured, although, as we shall see, he may make a subtle and indirect allusion to them. In the Chronicler's version the main purpose seems to be to achieve Davidic authority for the temple, that focal point for the whole life of Israel as the people of God.

The address begins with an explanation by David of why he did not himself build the temple, an obvious question for later generations since both the Deuteronomistic History and the Chronicler try to answer it. Whereas, however, in I Kgs. 5:3 it is suggested that David could not build because of the many wars in which he was engaged, the implication being that they were too demanding on time, attention and, perhaps, resources, in the Chronicler's version (vv. 7f.) these wars are said to have made David cultically unfit to be the temple builder. Here, possibly, is an allusion to the Kings version of the charge with its reference to Shimei who pursued David as he fled from Jerusalem on the Jericho road with stones and the taunt, 'Begone, begone, you man of blood, you worthless fellow. The Lord has avenged upon you all the blood of the house of Saul . . . See, your ruin is upon you; for you are a man of blood' (II Sam. 16:7f.). David's restraining of Abishai from killing Shimei seems to be based, according to the account in Samuel, on his tacit acceptance of Shimei's reproach as a word from Yahweh (vv. 12f.), and this could have been the quarry whence the Chronicler extracted the material to construct his theory.[6]

The prediction of the birth of his son, Solomon, which he recalls (v. 9), is interesting for the contrast with himself. Solomon is to be a 'man of rest', and so the theme of Amasai's address is taken up. There is word-play on the name of Solomon later in the verse. 'His name shall be Solomon (שְׁלֹמֹה) and I will give Israel peace (שָׁלוֹם) and quiet in his time.' This word-play is also found in the use of the noun 'rest' (מְנוּחָה) at the beginning of the verse, followed by the Hiph'il of the verbal root, 'I will give him rest' (וַהֲנִחוֹתִי לוֹ). Ackroyd rightly draws attention to this second word-play, complaining that it has been missed in most recent English Versions.[7] He also draws attention to the fact that, for the Chronicler, it is only of Solomon that the promise is given of 'rest from all his enemies round about'. That which is emphasised in the Deuteronomistic History as the fulfilment of Deut. 12:9f., the 'rest' in the land of promise,[8] is associated by the Chronicler with the 'rest' which comes to the people of God because of the presence of God in his temple. This is borne out by the vocabulary used here. 'Rest' is associated with two elements in the Deuteronomic literature, the gift of the land to the people and the 'presence' of God with his people. So in Josh. 1:13 Joshua reminds the Trans-Jordan tribes of the promise of God communicated through Moses, 'The LORD your God is providing you a place of rest (מֵנִיחַ), and will give you this land.' (See also v. 15, Deut. 3:20, 12:9.) Similarly, the loss of land results in loss of 'rest' (Deut. 28:65; see also Ps. 95:11). There is in the Deuteronomistic literature a very close connection between 'land' and 'temple' (see, e.g., Deut. 12:9–14, where the two are brought into close relationship).[9] This leads directly, therefore, to the other concept associated with the divine gift of 'rest', that of the 'presence' of God. So, in Exod. 33:14, God says to Moses, 'My presence will go with you, and I will give you rest.'[10] Possibly the reference there is to the ark. Certainly the thought is of an accompanying 'presence' for the pilgrim people, but the Chronicler associates the concept quite clearly with the temple where God's presence among his people is effected and realised, and to which the ark was brought (II Chr. 5:2–10).

This is made explicit in the very interesting I Chr. 23:25 in a passage dealing with the duties of the Levites: 'For David said, "The LORD, the God of Israel, has given peace (הֵנִיחַ) to his people; and he dwells in Jerusalem for ever."' There is no need any longer, therefore, for the carrying of the ark. That which it symbolised in the days of the tabernacle is now given permanent expression in the temple.[11]

We now see why the Chronicler finds such contrast between David's reign which, unlike the Deuteronomistic description of it (II Sam. 7:1, contra I Chr.

17:1), could know no 'rest' because the temple had not been built, and the reign of Solomon. With Solomon's accomplishment of the task of temple building the way was open for the fulfilment of those promises of 'rest' which had earlier been associated with the gift of the land. The two are firmly cemented together by the linking of the building of the temple in v. 10 to the promise of 'rest' in v. 9.[12]

There is a logical progression, too, in David's wish for the presence of God with Solomon in his task (v. 11), for only the divine presence can make human effort fruitful and effective, a truth in projects both of peace and war which is reiterated many times in these addresses.

Not only is Solomon encouraged by the assurance of God's presence, but by the fact that his divinely appointed task and its fulfilment are the subject of divine promise spoken through the prophets, 'as he has spoken concerning you' (v. 11b). The reference is to the promise spoken through Nathan in II Sam. 7 which the Chronicler recorded in I Chr. 17. Here he takes up the idea of history seen as divine 'word' and its fulfilment, a concept prominent in the Deuteronomistic History. This suggests that, for the Chronicler, the prophetic word is not only and always admonitory and paraenetic. He sees it as conveying power to accomplish the divine purpose, to bring about that which it promises and of which it warns.[13] It is interesting that in the context of a passage which some have seen as furnishing a model for the Chronicler's account of the commissioning of Solomon by David, namely the commissioning of Joshua by Moses,[14] the same promise of encouragement is made to the people concerning him: 'The LORD will go over before you . . . so that you shall dispossess them; and Joshua will go over at your head, *as the LORD has spoken*.' Again, the Chronicler carefully records the fulfilment of God's promises concerning which David has spoken (II Chr. 5:1, 6:10).

These emphases on the grace of God which lie behind every effective human action, his presence, his promise of rest and the prophetic word of promise, are further combined with the reminder, already known in the earlier Solomonic tradition, that God gives those very qualities of mind, spirit and character which make faithful human response possible. David's prayer that God will *give* (v. 12) 'insight' (שֶׂכֶל) and 'discernment' or 'understanding' (בִּינָה) stresses this. It is picked up from I Kgs. 3:9, 11, 12, where Solomon prays that God will grant him the ability 'to discern' (לְהָבִין) between good and evil (v. 9), to which God responds by promising that, in addition to this, he will give him a 'wise and discerning mind' (לֵב חָכָם/נבון, v. 12). The Chronicler is concerned to show how this promise was fulfilled. In II Chr. 2:12/11, Hiram of Tyre blesses the God of Israel and acknowledges that it is this God, the creator of heaven and earth, who has given king David a 'wise' (שֵׂכֶל) son who knows 'discretion' (חָכָם) and 'discernment' (בִּינָה),[15] thus adding to the *Vorlage* of I Kgs. 5:7 the exact words of David's prayer in 22:12. Thus, while David exacted acknowledgement from the nations by force of arms, Solomon achieves acknowledgement of himself, and, above all, of Israel's God, by 'wisdom'. It is interesting to note that the Chronicler can see one form of שֵׂכֶל as manifesting itself in the proper worship of God (II Chr. 30:22).

Here it is strongly connected with the proper observance of the law given through Moses, and in this passage the Chronicler lets echoes of the Kings passage sound. Both refer to the 'law of Moses' and both use the term 'statutes' and 'decrees' or 'judgements'. Where in Kings, however, this will result in the fulfilment of the divine promise concerning the Davidic dynasty (I Kgs. 2:4) as well as Solomon's 'prospering' (שכל/), in Chronicles it is Solomon's 'success' (צלח/) perhaps generally, but specifically in the task of building the temple, that is referred to. This is shown by the link between the Hebrew root / צלח ('succeed') in the temple-building context in v. 11 and what follows in vv. 14ff. All the promises to David are now focussed on the temple and its worship.

The command 'Be strong!' (חֲזַק), linked with its parallel term 'Be resolute!' (וֶאֱמָץ), recalls in general the exhortation in I Kgs. 2:2 (וְחָזַקְתָּ). Such exhortations have been the subject of a good deal of discussion recently. Together with the negatives which sometimes accompany these verbs, 'Fear not!' (אַל־תִּירָא) and 'Do not be discouraged!' (אַל־תֵּחָת), it has been urged that they constitute a genre to which the name 'Installation to Office' has been given.[16] Certainly the form does occur a number of times, although with several variations, most often in the Deuteronomic literature. It characterises Moses' commissioning of Joshua (Deut. 31:7, 23; Josh. 1:6, 7, 9, 18). We may, however, also note its use in a context of war (II Sam. 10:12), although, perhaps, the Joshua references might be included in such a context since he is being commissioned to lead the people in the conquest of Canaan. Perhaps it is also worth noting that the imperative 'Be strong!' can be used in a cultic context (Deut. 12:23, rendered in the RSV as 'Be sure'). Possibly its use in Ps. 27:14 could suggest a cultic context, although here too it might be argued that this Psalm has some reference to battle (v. 3). Nevertheless, the variety of the forms and contexts in the few examples we have of these 'commissioning' words makes talk of a 'genre' perhaps a little too precise. It would seem better to speak more generally of an 'Encouragement for a Task'. Such a formula would link the varied uses in the Old Testament sufficiently well, and this is the term which will be used in this study. Williamson's more general suggestion of a conscious parallel between this passage and the commissioning of Joshua by Moses is well made, however.[17] Certainly there seems little doubt that the Chronicler saw David as a second Moses, especially as he receives and transmits the divine instructions for building the temple/tabernacle. We might see even a further parallel, as Williamson argues,[18] for David, like Moses, was not permitted to complete the task given to him. However, we cannot press this to suggest that he saw Solomon as a second Joshua. The reverse is the truth. He has already shown that, in contrast to David, Solomon is to be a man of peace, achieving God's purpose not by force of arms but by the wisdom which expresses itself in obedience to God's law and by faith in his power. While the Chronicler can use what might be termed the 'Be strong!' formula in a context of war (I Chr. 19:13), the greater number of instances of his use of it relate to the building of the temple (e.g. I Chr. 28:10, 20). Its use in a similar context in Hag. 2:4 shows how, in the circles among whom the oracles of Haggai were preserved and passed on, it was natural to relate all the promises and lessons of the first temple to the second, and how closely akin to the views of the Chronicler they were.

The final charge with its call 'Rise to the task!' (קוּם) reminds us of the call to Joshua in Josh. 1:2 with its summons to the holy war (see also Josh. 7:10, 13, Judg. 4:14, 5:12, 7:9, 8:20f., 9:32f., I Sam 23:4 etc.). Again, however, it is now employed in a call to 'work' (עֲשֵׂה) on the temple. The Chronicler here might well be influenced by its apparent use as a formula in a prophetic call, e.g. I Sam. 16:12).[19] The conclusion of the charge to Solomon in v. 16b, by the repetition of the formula of v. 11a, 'The LORD be with you!', highlights the concept of God's 'presence' as a cardinal theme of the address.

[5] I 22:17–19 *David's call to the leaders of Israel*

[17] *And David charged all the leaders of Israel to help his son, Solomon.* [18] '*Is not Yahweh, your God, with you? He has given you*[a] *peace on every border, for he has delivered the inhabitants of the land into my power. The land has been brought into subjection to Yahweh and to his people.* [19] *Now, give heart and soul to seeking Yahweh, your God. Stir yourselves to build the sanctuary of Yahweh, your God, so that you can bring the ark of Yahweh's covenant and the sacred, divine vessels into the temple which is to be built to the honour of Yahweh.'*

Text

a If the rules of classical Hebrew still applied, the *waw* consecutive with the perfect of the verb would give a *future* sense to these verbs, 'he *will give* you peace and the land *will be* brought into subjection . . .' (so NEB). However, the context suggests that here, as elsewhere in later Hebrew, these rules are being followed more loosely. The obvious sense is that David is acknowledging what God *has already done* in his reign to make possible the building of the temple in 'peace'.

General description

This short address might best be described as an 'Assignment of a Task' (v. 19), together with an 'Encouragement Formula' (v. 18). It is introduced by a brief narrative formula (v. 17). The Encouragement Formula makes use of a rhetorical question, 'Is not Yahweh, your God, with you?'

Contents

The theme of God's 'presence' continues in this address of David to the leaders of Israel, with its opening words, 'Is not Yahweh, your God, with you?'[20] The 'rest' (וְהֵנִיחַ) which has been granted them is based on the victories, ostensibly won by David, but in fact given by God, and this forms the basis of the call to the leaders to help Solomon in the task of building the temple. It demonstrates that the proper task of God's people is to 'seek' him (v. 19). This they do by building the temple and, then, by inference, worshipping him in it once place has been made for all the sacred implements of worship, especially for the ark, which symbolises the presence of God. God's giving of 'rest' to the community through David's victories thus sets the people free for their true calling as a theocratic community.

It seems, then, that a real modification of the Davidic covenant theology is taking place. It has often been said that the Chronicler's picture of David not only obscures all reference to his sins, but changes him from a military to an 'ecclesiastical' figure. This is not wholly true. Details of some of his wars and campaigns are given (I Chr. cc. 18–20), and the previous address has frankly recognised that he was a 'man of blood' who 'waged great wars'. But, in this version of God's promise to the Davidic dynasty, military prestige is not its goal. Its goal is what might be called 'theocratic'. It realises that it is God who gives 'rest' by himself giving victory over enemies. The wish for David expressed by Amasai has been realised. The goal of the purpose which runs through David and his line is that Solomon now concern himself with the temple and its service so that the people may know that deeper 'rest' which is marked by the presence of God in their midst. Later Davidic kings will have to wage wars, which they can do successfully by reliance upon God. But, as we shall see, their real business also is to secure that obedience to God's laws which shows itself in concern for the temple and its worship. We have here a call away from concern with militaristic and nationalistic policies, all of which can be safely left to God to realise, and towards 'theocratic' ones.

In this we may very possibly hear a call from the Chronicler to his post-exilic contemporaries. Indeed, the addition of these three verses to David's charge to Solomon, extending the call to the leaders, may well fulfil the function of relating the call for concern for the temple to the later post-exilic community. It is the kind of call we hear closely echoed in the Books of Haggai, Zechariah cc. 1–8 and Malachi. Prosperity and true 'rest' are God's gifts to the faithful. In the changed circumstances of the Persian rule the people are to look for the fulfilment of the promises to David in this way, and not in hopes for some political and military renewal of the Davidic dynasty.

[6] I 28:2–10 *David's call to the leaders and to Solomon*

 ² *Then David, the king, stood and said, 'Hear me, my brothers and my people. It was my intention to build a sanctuary as a resting place for the ark of the covenant of Yahweh and as a footstool for our God. I have even made all the preparations for building.* ³ *But God said to me, "You shall not build a sanctuary in my honour, for you are a warrior and you have spilled blood."* ⁴ *Nevertheless, Yahweh, the God of Israel, chose me among all my father's family to be king over Israel for ever. He chose Judah as leader and, from the tribe of Judah, my father's family, and among my father's sons it was I he was pleased to make king over all Israel.* ⁵ *And from all my sons (for Yahweh has given me many sons) he chose my son Solomon to sit on the throne of Yahweh's kingdom over Israel.* ⁶ *And to me he said, "It is your son, Solomon, who shall build my sanctuary and my courts, for I have chosen him as my son, and I will be a father to him.* ⁷ *I will found his kingdom for ever if he remains as resolute in keeping my commandments and my decrees as he now is."* ⁸ *So now, in the sight of all Israel, Yahweh's congregation, and in the hearing of our God, remain loyal! Search out all the commandments of Yahweh your God so that you may inherit this fair land and bequeath it to your children after you for ever.*

⁹*Now, Solomon, my son, know the God of your father and serve him with your whole mind and with an enthusiastic heart. For Yahweh searches out every mind and discerns every motive. If you seek him he will be found by you. But if you forsake him he will reject you for ever.* ¹⁰*Take care, for Yahweh has chosen you to build a temple for him[a] as a sanctuary. Be resolute! Begin work!*

Text

[a] Adding 'for him' from LXX. Without this the somewhat pleonastic addition of the MT, 'a temple for the sanctuary', makes little sense.

General description

Introduced by a narrative formula (vv. 1, 2a) the main thrust of the address to the elders is an exhortation to keep God's commandments (v. 8a) based on a declaration of the action of God in choosing the Davidic line to build the temple (vv. 2–7). This is followed by an assurance that obedience will secure enduring possession of the 'land' (v. 8b). It opens with a call for attention, 'Hear me . . .' Rhetorical devices include inversion (v. 9b), play on the word 'seek' between vv. 8 and 9, and allusion to earlier biblical material (vv. 8, 9). The words to Solomon in vv. 9f. take the form of an admonition and a call to undertake the task of building.

Contents

This passage in some ways parallels the two addresses in 22:6–19 and echoes several of their themes. Indeed, if, as many believe, cc. 23–7 are to be seen as secondary insertion, this would directly continue what was initiated there.[21] Nevertheless, the passage introduces one or two further elements which merit attention. It has no counterpart in Kings other than the very general relation all these Davidic addresses may be said to have to I Kgs. 2:1–14.

The account of the assembling of the leaders in v. 1 which introduces the address seems to go out of its way to be comprehensive. Indeed, it may be the result of an attemp to knit cc. 23–7 into the text by introducing all the classes of people mentioned in those chapters.[22] But it serves the further point of stressing the 'all Israel' theme,[23] which is re-emphasised in v. 8a. Further, it is interesting to note that the charge to Solomon is to some extent universalised when it is said that Yahweh searches out 'every mind' (v. 9). As in 22:17–19 address to Solomon is linked with address to the representatives of the wider community, although in this instance the two are so closely related that it seems better to treat them as one address. But the extension of the address to 'all Israel' again indicates that a wider reference is intended than that suggested merely by its supposed original historical, religious and political context.

At the beginning of the address the same reason for David's failure to build the temple is given as in 22:7f., and the same association of the temple with 'rest' is made in v. 2. But now, to show that David was nevertheless in line with God's will, we are introduced to a particular theme of this passage, namely that of the divine choice. God chose Judah from the tribes, Jesse's house from the tribe of Judah and David from within his family of brothers. Now, from David's sons, God has chosen Solomon as 'son' to sit on the throne and, especially, to build the sanctuary (v. 10). Such choice was implicit in 22:6–19, particularly with the idea that Solomon was the object of the predictive promise of prophecy. Here, however, this is made explicit. Again, the grace of God is stressed before the faithful are charged with their responsibility. It is in the light of this God-directed choice that the representatives of Israel are addressed in v. 8, the plural of the Hebrew showing that this is no longer God's address to David but David's call to them. They are to set themselves, not only in the sight of the whole nation, but, even more awesomely, in the hearing of God, to 'seek' the commandments of God. But, here again, there is reference to a much later situation. By their faithfulness they will ensure that the land comes to their successors as their due inheritance, those successors whom the Chronicler is really now addressing. That he is envisaging the later situation is shown even more clearly by the striking phrase in v. 5, for there we hear that the throne on which Solomon is to sit is 'the throne of Yahweh's kingdom over Israel'. That is the real truth behind the historical monarchy, and it remains the truth when the historical incidence of the monarchy has passed away. The people are still God's 'kingdom'.[24] The kingdom is eternal and survives all changes of fortune and outward forms of history.[25] The same truth can be expressed poetically:

Thy kingdom is an everlasting kingdom. *(Ps. 145:13)*

The address to Solomon is clearly linked with the charge to the elders and leaders. As they have already been commanded (22:19), they are to 'seek God' and 'seek his commandments', two closely related realities for the Chronicler. Now Solomon is reminded that this is a two-way process. God 'seeks' (the same Hebrew verb is used) 'all hearts', and he, from whom Solomon sought 'discretion', 'discernment' and 'insight', himself 'discerns' the forming of all thoughts, or 'motives', as the Hebrew phrase can be rendered. The same phrase occurs in Gen. 6:5 and 8:21. The plurals here certainly extend beyond Solomon, generalising it as a theological truth for all people of all times. The allusion to the Genesis texts reinforces this. Again, the charge is really to the Chronicler's contemporaries. The succession to Solomon and the historic monarchy lies in the theocracy, and its members must show a response like his.

There then follows one of those striking inversions which form such a prominent feature of the addresses:

If you seek him he will be found by you.
But if you forsake him he will reject you for ever. *(v. 9)*

This illustrates another feature of many of the addresses, namely the allusion to, if not direct citation of, other scriptural passages. We have seen in v. 9 the echo of two passages from the Genesis flood narrative. Now, as Williamson has pointed out,[26] at least two prophetic texts seem to be recalled, Jer. 29:13f., and Isa. 55:6. By this device also the original address to Solomon is extended to later generations, to present them with the prophetic call and challenge, but also to assure them that they are to experience the fulfilment of the prophetic promises. Although there is no play on words in the inverted statement of v. 9, such an aphorism in so memorable a form is an effective rhetorical device. The lesson that God will be found by those who seek him, but will reject those who turn from him, is repeated several times in the addresses in Chronicles. It would have relevance far beyond the immediate context of urging obedience in building the temple. Further scriptural allusion occurs in the promise that, if they set themselves to obey Yahweh's commands, they will 'inherit the land' which is God's gift to them. This takes up a theme prominent in the Deuteronomic literature (e.g. Deut. 4:5, 5:31, 10:11). Yet the stress in this address is not so much on entry into or conquest of the land, but on the fact that obedience will earn it as an inheritance for their descendants 'for ever'. The phrase 'for ever' is not used in the Deuteronomic literature in connection with the land. By such means the Deuteronomic promises also are given especial relevance for later generations. The words call for obedience in all ages as the only ground for continuance as God's people in God's land.

Again, in v. 10, call for response is found in the imperatives, 'Be resolute!' (חֲזַק), 'Begin work!' (עֲשֵׂה), to which is now added 'Take care!' or 'See to it!' (רְאֵה). Here, as in 22:1–16, theology and proclamation of God's past acts issue in urgent pastoral call for response on the part of the hearers.

[7] I 28:20f. *David's renewed charge to Solomon*

[20] *And David said to his son, Solomon, 'Be resolute! Be determined! Get on with the work! Do not be fearful or discouraged, because Yahweh my God[a] is with you. He will not let you down or desert you until all the work in the service of Yahweh's sanctuary is complete.[b] [21] Look at the divisions of the priests and the Levites, ready for all the service of God's sanctuary. And in all the work every man of good-will with skill in every kind of craft, all the leaders and all the people will be with you, waiting for all your commands.'*

Text

[a] With LXX omitting the unnecessary reduplication of the word 'God' in MT.

[b] LXX has a long addition to the text at this point, repeating much of vv. 11, 12a.

General description

This address again takes the form I have described as 'Encouragement for a Task'.

Contents

This address of David follows his handing over to Solomon the plan for the temple, its vessels and ornaments which, it is stressed in v. 19, he had received in writing from God. So here also a parallel is seen between David and Moses, Solomon's temple and the tabernacle. To drive home the point, Exod. 25:9, 40 is recalled by the use of the word 'plan' (Heb. תַּבְנִית). Indeed, if the LXX is right to include at this point the substance of vv. 11, 12a, then the link with Moses is made explicit in this address. In the Exodus passage תַּבְנִית is used both of the tabernacle itself and of its vessels.[27] The injunction to Solomon recalls closely that of Moses to Joshua, thus strengthening the parallels already noted.[28] However, with André Caquot, we should note the assurance that God will not forsake Solomon 'until all the work in the service of Yahweh's sanctuary is complete' (v. 20).[29] Of course, we must not interpret this with a heavy-handed literalism to mean that God would abandon him once that work was completed. This is not borne out by the Chronicler's narration of Solomon's reign with its achievements and acknowledgement of its glory after the dedication of the temple (II Chr. c. 9). But it does need to be taken in conjunction with the emphasis we have already seen on the choice of Solomon by God for just this purpose (I Chr. 22:9f., 28:7f., 10). Indeed, the suggestion is that all David's exploits were really the 'pains' necessary to make possible the building of the temple (22:14ff.), a sort of Mosaic self-abnegation (Deut. 4:21f.), which rendered him unfit for the task himself (22:8). We have seen that the purpose of God's choice of David from among all the tribes and from among all his brothers was that Solomon might be chosen from among all his sons (28:4–6). This suggests that the Chronicler's main interest was not so much the Davidic dynasty *in itself*, but the temple, for the sake of which the dynasty was called into being and in which it found its fulfilment.

It is in this connection that we ought to note the several instances where expressions of God's concern for the line 'for David's sake' in the Deuteronomistic History are omitted by the Chronicler.[30] Rather, as we have seen, it is stressed that Solomon will be protected for the sake of his divinely appointed task. This suggests caution in accepting the views of those who see a 'messianism' in the Chronicler's writings based on his concern for the Davidic line.[31] We must heed Caquot's words when he says of I Chr. 28:20f., 'for the Chronicler, the task of the Davidic dynasty has been achieved once the Temple is built'.[32] Again, speaking of the variations in the Chronicler's ending of Solomon's prayer of dedication of the temple when compared with that of Kings (I Kgs. c. 8), he says, 'If there is a future perspective in these verses, it is concerned, not with dynasty issuing from David, but the lasting soteriological function of the Temple.'[33] This may be why the Chronicler can show that later Davidic kings are judged for their attitude to the temple and why he appears little concerned with the long-range issue of the dynasty itself. The temple survives the exile by its rebuilding, and the divinely appointed function of the dynasty finds itself fulfilled in the emergence of the temple community. Over this community God now reigns, exercising through priest and cult personnel the rule which once was exercised through Davidic kings, although seldom perfectly. The Chronicler would have seen those later temple leaders as descendants of the very people whose help is held out now as an encouragement to Solomon in the task of building the temple.

[8] I 29:1–5, 20 *David to the assembly of Israel*

[1] *Then David, the king, said to the whole assembly, 'My son, Solomon, is the one God has singled out.[a] He is young and inexperienced, but the task is immense. It is*

to be a palace, not for man, but for the LORD *God.* [2] *I have provided gold for the sanctuary of my God to the limit of my resources: to the gold I have added silver, to the silver, bronze, to the bronze, iron, to the iron, timber, and to the timber, a great amount of onyx and stones for setting, antimony, embroidery and linen.*[b] [3] *Further, in my concern for the sanctuary of my God, I have given gold and silver from my private wealth for the sanctuary of my God, in addition to all that I have already provided for the holy temple.* [4] *I have given three thousand talents of gold, gold from Ophir, and seven thousand talents of refined silver to cover the walls of the buildings.* [5] *All this has been added*[c] *to the gold for the gold work, silver for the silver work, and for all the work executed by the craftsmen. Who among you*[d] *today will volunteer for the ministry of Yahweh?'*[e]

[20] *And David said to the whole assembly, 'Bless Yahweh, your God.'*

Text

[a] We should not replace the rather pleonastic אֶחָד, 'Solomon, my son, *one*, God has chosen him' with the relative pronoun on the basis of LXX. The omission of the relative pronoun is a feature of the Chronicler's style,[34] and the construction here strengthens the divine choice of Solomon as the basis of the call to everyone to support him in the light of that choice. 'God has chosen him, one . . .' suggests the idea of 'singling out'.

[b] רִקְמָה is used almost always of cloth. שֵׁשׁ is also a word for 'fine linen'. Curtis's suggestion that the word for 'stones' has crept in as gloss in a misplaced attempt to explain פּוּךְ is therefore a plausible one.[35]

[c] MT literally reads, 'To the gold, to the gold, and to the silver, to the silver and to/for all work by the hand of the craftsmen'. Each translator must do what he can with such awkward and turgid prose.

[d] Adding 'among you' from LXX.

[e] The Hebrew reads literally, 'offer himself for the filling of the hand this day to Yahweh'. This is often a technical term for consecration to the Levitical priesthood (e.g. Exod. 32:29, II Chr. 29:31), and I have sought to catch this overtone in its more general extension of a call to everyone to engage in the 'service' of the temple.

General description

This address takes the form of an exhortation to share in the building of the temple, based on God's choice of Solomon who, by virtue of his youth, needs the support of the whole community, and the sacrifical example of David himself. V. 20 is a call to worship.

Contents

Again, to the charge to the monarch-to-be is added a charge to the representatives of the whole community. Partly the function of this is to encourage Solomon by assuring him that his obedience and zeal will be matched and supported by that of the priests and Levites and all who have 'good-will' and who have 'skill in every kind of craft' (28:21, 29:5).[36] So again the fact is stressed that the temple and its service call for loyal support and participation by the whole theocratic community. The Chronicler does not portray it as a royal prerogative alone. In this he closely echoes the Priestly Writer's account of the construction of the Mosaic tabernacle (Exod. 35:5, 22, 29, 36:1-7). That is why the addition of the words of I Chr. 28:11, 12a by the LXX in David's address after 28:20 looks authentic. It reinforces the parallels between this and the roles of Moses and the people in the construction of the tabernacle. If secondary, it shows how the role and work of David could be interpreted at an early stage in the development of the text and represents remarkably penetrative exegesis. Others seem to have seen a parallel between the construction of the tabernacle, the building of Solomon's temple and the rebuilding of the second temple after the exile. As we shall see in more detail later, the editorial framework of the Book of Haggai clearly has the Priestly account of the building and ornamentation of the tabernacle in mind when it describes, not only the encouragement of the prophet to the two leaders, but also the response of the whole people (Hag. 1:12-14). From all this it is difficult to avoid the impression that the Chronicler sees the whole people of the theocracy inheriting the responsibility for the temple, once entrusted to the Davidic dynasty. If so, it would be a kind of 'democratisation' of the Davidic role not altogether dissimilar to that found in Isa. 55:1-5. It does not seem fanciful to believe that in these addresses to Solomon and the leaders of his time, the Chronicler is bringing a charge for zeal and loyalty to the temple to his own contemporaries after the exile. Whether this represents a literal concern for the rebuilding of the temple, thus placing the Chronicler as a contemporary of the rebuilding energised by Haggai and Zechariah and carried out by Zerubbabel, or shows a later and more general concern for support and upkeep of the temple now standing, is an issue which cannot be decided from this one passage alone (see pp. 9f. above). But whatever the

historical context of this call, the example of their forefathers, further elaborated in I Chr. 29:6–9, is held up to them as one to follow. Indeed, this address
shows that David himself set a perfect example of the kind of whole-hearted,
sacrifical concern for the temple that the community which inherits his calling
should follow.

It is wholly in keeping with this that the last words of David (29:20) form a
call to 'all the assembly' to worship God, just as the first words attributed to
him had shown a like concern with true worship (see pp. 16–18 above). The
worshipping temple community are his true descendants and successors.
They fulfil their true calling when they worship God, with all that entails in
terms of care for the temple and zealous obedience to its service.

[9] II 12:5–8 *Shemaiah the prophet to Rehoboam and the Judaean leaders*

⁵ *Then Shemaiah the prophet came to Rehoboam and the leaders of Judah who had
gathered at Jerusalem for defence against Shishak and said to them, 'This is what
Yahweh is saying. You abandoned me. Now I, for my part, have abandoned you to
the power of Shishak.* ⁶ *Then the leaders of Israel and the king were contriteᵃ and
said, 'Yahweh is just.'* ⁷ *And when Yahweh saw that they were contrite his word
came to Shemaiah, 'Since they have shown themselves contrite I will not destroy
them. I will grant them some respite.ᵇ My wrath will not vent itself on Jerusalem by
means of Shishak.* ⁸ *But they shall be subject to him so that they may experience
both my service and service of the kingdoms of this world.'ᶜ*

Text

ᵃ Lit. 'humbled themselves'. For a discussion of the implications of this verb
see Williamson, *1 and 2 Chronicles*, pp. 225f.
ᵇ Or, 'I will grant them deliverance in a short time.' This is favoured by Curtis,
The Books of Chronicles, p. 371, and suggested by Williamson, p. 248.
Nevertheless it does not seem to fit the context of announcement of imminent
judgement as well.
ᶜ Lit. 'the kingdoms of the lands'.

General description

V. 5 opens with an historical introduction to a prophetic threat of judgement.
This consists of the opening messenger formula, grounds of accusation and

announcement of judgement. V. 6 records the people's submission to the divine word, followed in vv. 7f. by the announcement of modified judgement. The rhetorical device of play on words occurs in v. 5 with the verb 'abandon' and in v. 8 with the noun 'service'. In each instance the word is used contrastingly of divine and human activity.

Contents

With the words of Shemaiah the prophet to Rehoboam and the leaders of Judah at the time of Shishak's invasion we hear the first of the 'prophetic' addresses of Chronicles. It occurs in the context of the end of the reign of Solomon and the division of the kingdom. The Chronicler has already mentioned Shemaiah (II 11:2–4), but the words he spoke there almost exactly parallel the address ascribed to him in Kings (I Kgs. 12:22–4). There are interesting variants in that the Chronicler describes those addressed as 'all Israel in Judah and Benjamin' while the Kings phrase 'your kinsmen, the people of Israel' has become simply 'your brethren' (II 11:3f.; see also Kgs. 12:23f.). Our concerns here, however, are with those addresses which have no counterpart in the Deuteronomistic History. The detailed account in Kings of Judah's sin under the reign of Rehoboam (I Kgs 14:22ff.; the LXX has Rehoboam as the subject rather than Judah) is expressed simply by the Chronicler with the verb 'Rehoboam *forsook* (Heb. /עזב) the law of the LORD, and all Israel with him' (12:1). This links with the verb used in the address of Shemaiah, 'you *abandoned* me' (Heb. עֲזַבְתֶּם) (v. 5). The use of the verb 'to show contrition' (Heb. /כנע) also links the address with the historical context (v. 6; see also v. 7). Like the addresses of David, then, this also is fitted well into its alleged context. Like those addresses also it is characterised by play on words (the verb 'abandon' in v. 5 and the noun 'service' in v. 8). One purpose of the address seems to have been to make explicit what may been implicit in Kings, that Shishak's invasion was divine judgement for the sin of the community.

In the second part of the address (vv. 7f.) another parallel with the addresses of David appears. It is said that the judgement is to be tempered by 'some deliverance' or 'respite', as I have rendered it. They will become 'servants' to Shishak, and yet they will also know Yahweh's 'service' as well as the 'service' of 'the kingdoms of this world' (v. 8). This last phrase, with its plural form, in a way similar to the addresses of David, appears to extend the range and significance of the address far beyond its precise historical context at the time of Shishak's invasion. Its exact force is not altogether clear. A number of modern Versions (e.g. NEB, JB) take it that the two forms of service indicate separate contrasting states. They thus render the final phrase, 'that they may know the *difference* between my service and that of the kingdoms of the lands' – the people so learning that it is better to obey Yahweh. While that note may well be present, the Chronicler in no way emphasises the difference between the two states but shows them as contemporaneous realities in the experience of the people. What is ostensibly announcement of tempered judgement on the people in Shemaiah's own day becomes an apt description of their life in the post-exilic community when they live both as the people of Yahweh and yet a people subject to the overlordship of other powers. The word 'service' (Heb.עֲבוֹדָה) is used frequently, especially in the Pentateuch, both of the bondage in Egypt, of the 'work' on the tabernacle which the people undertook so willingly,[37] and also, more generally, of the 'worship' of God.[38] Ackroyd is surely right in seeing here a theme of 'exile and restoration'.[39] Yet can we not also note something more finely perceptive? It would be easy to say that the people of God *either* know 'service' to God *or* find themselves in the forced 'service' of the oppressor nations. Shemaiah's address, however, shows that the Chronicler recognises that the community of faith have to live in both worlds at once. No doubt their loss of political independence under the Persians is seen as due to sin, past and present, as the prayers in Ezra 9:6–15 and Neh. 9:6–37, esp. vv. 30, 36f., show (whether these are from the Chronicler or not).[40] But the experience of the people of God is to know always only a measure of deliverance (12:7; see also Neh. 9:31). They must live always in the tension of 'service' in two realms (v. 8). The call of this address to the wider and later congregation of the post-exilic community is to remain faithful to God's service even while they have to live under the service of 'the kingdoms of this world'.

The style of the address which, like those of David, is fitted into its context and marked by such a rhetorical device as word-play,[41] and the use of the plural to make the reference to the original historical situation more general,[42] together with its absence in Kings, must lead us to suppose that we are dealing with a passage of the Chronicler's own composition.[43] We have here not primarily interest in the story of Israel's history, but theological explanation of a situation so as to relate it to a congregation and make it the basis of a call to that congregation for response in the present. This is the practice of what may be termed, in the broadest of senses, the 'preacher'.

[10] II 13:4–12 *Abijah, the Judaean king, to Jeroboam and all Israel*

⁴*Then Abijah stood on the top of Mount Zemaraim in the hill country of Ephraim and said, 'Hear me, Jeroboam and all Israel!* ⁵*Should you not know that Yahweh, the God of Israel, has given the kingdom over Israel to David and his successors for ever by an immutable covenant?ᵃ* ⁶*And Jeroboam, the son of Nebat, servant to David's son, Solomon, rose in rebellion against his master.* ⁷*And worthless, evilᵇ men gathered round him and set themselves against Rehoboam, Solomon's son, while he was still immature and inexperienced and unable to control them.* ⁸*Now you intend to fight against the kingdom of Yahweh entrusted to David's descendants. You are a large army and you have with you the golden calves which Jeroboam made as gods for you.* ⁹*Yet have you not dismissed Yahweh's priests, the Aaronites and Levites, and appointed priests for yourselves just like the people of other nationsᶜ? Anyone who has offered to consecrate himself with a heifer or seven rams has become a priest – but a priest serving non-gods.* ¹⁰*But, as for us, Yahweh is our God. We have not abandoned him. We have Aaronites and Levites ministering to Yahweh as priests in hisᵈ service.* ¹¹*Morning and evening they offer to Yahweh whole burnt offerings and sweet incense offerings; they arrange the showbread on the pure table and the golden Minorah with its lamps for burning at evening. So we keep the commandment of Yahweh our God. But you have abandoned him.* ¹²*Know, then, that God is with us at our head, and his priests with their trumpets summon us to battle against you. Israelites, do not fight against Yahweh, the God of your fathers, for you can never succeed.'*

Text

ᵃ Lit. 'a covenant of salt'. It is sometimes maintained that this phrase originated in the idea that those who have eaten together are bound to each other by a solemn covenant. Whatever its origin, it certainly signifies an enduring covenant. See discussion below.

ᵇ Lit. 'sons of Belial'.

ᶜ LXX has the interesting variant, 'You have appointed priests *from among the people of the land*', meaning from those who were not entitled to be given priestly status. Either LXX or MT would fit the context well and be equally forceful as an expression of contempt.

ᵈ Adding 'his' to make better sense. Since the final suffix meaning 'his' and the conjunction which is the first letter of the opening word of the next sentence are the same Hebrew letter (*waw*), the likelihood is that the first dropped out by the copyist's error known as haplography, writing only once something which should be repeated.

General description

This address is cast in the form, not of a prophetic oracle, but of what might rather be termed a 'royal proclamation'. Its opening call 'Hear me!' is used also to introduce addresses of David (e.g. I 28:2), Jehoshaphat (II 20:20) and Hezekiah (II 29:5). However, the same formula can also characterise words of a non-royal speaker such as Azariah (II 15:2), whose address is described later (v. 8) as 'the prophecy' (see discussion in Chapter 2). It is an exhortation not to resist God by resisting the divinely sanctioned rule of the House of David with its consecrated temple and priesthood. It employs the device of rhetorical question (vv. 5, 9) and play on words ('with', vv. 8b, 12a, 'abandon', vv. 10, 11b, 'fight against' (/חזק), vv. 7, 8).

Contents

This is the first address attributed to a king other than David. Throntveit and Williamson both stress the importance of this speech in the overall structure of the Chronicler's history. Throntveit argues that it introduces the second major division of the history of the monarchy, that of the divided monarchy. He accepts Plöger's description of it as an *Umkehrreden* ('Call to return') addressed to the northern kingdom[44] and sees it, with the 'Call to return' of Hezekiah (II Chr. 30:6–9) as marking off the parenthetic period of the divided kingdoms which interrupted the united monarchy, lost after Solomon's death but resumed with Hezekiah.[45] The historical note about the beginning of Abijah's reign is taken from I Kgs. 15:1f. with a different form of his name (Abijam in I Kings). The names of his mother and father are also different, but comparison of the Chronicler's text with that of the LXX shows there was some confusion over this.[46] Interestingly, the adverse verdict given on him in the Deuteronomistic History is omitted. If he is to be the bearer of exemplary theological truths to the apostate North he can hardly merit such a judgement by the Chronicler.[47]

Significantly, again, the interesting statement of the Deuteronomistic Historian that God spared him as a lamp in Judah 'for David's sake' (I Kgs. 15:4) is also omitted. This is doubtless also partly due to the fact that it belongs to the adverse judgement on him in the earlier work, yet it also shows how the Chronicler tends to play down the note of promise of an 'everlasting' line of royal successors to David, or, as in this address, give it a new significance.[48] Taking up the note in Kings that 'there was war between Abijam and Jeroboam' (I Kgs. 15:6), not only does the Chronicler give us a detailed account of a battle and its successful outcome for Abijah and Judah (vv. 12–22),[49] but he attributes to Abijah this long address pleading with the king and people of the apostate northern kingdom to repent and return to God, and so to the Jerusalem temple cult. This theme is to be repeated in the Chronicler's writings. He gives Hezekiah just such an appeal, which on that occasion, however, is delivered in written form (II 30:6–9).[50]

Abijah's address has been described as his 'sermon on the mount'. Why Mount Zemaraim in the hill country should have been chosen is not clear. The form and contents of the address make it unlikely that the Chronicler had access to some otherwise unknown historical source of information concerning King Abijah, unless he knew of this area in the territory of Benjamin (Josh. 18:22) as the site of an encounter in the war between North and South at this time.[51]

Abijah addresses 'Jeroboam and all Israel' with words of reproach culminating in an exhortation not to fight against Yahweh (v. 12). The unusual form of opening reproach, 'Should you not know . . .?', underlines the fact that they cannot plead ignorance. Micah, the prophet, had used the same form of address to the 'leaders and rulers of Israel' (Mic. 3:1). Whereas, however, Micah told them that they should have known 'justice', characteristically the Chronicler has Abijah chiding the North with defection from Jerusalem and the Davidic line. By this defection they have refused to acknowledge that God had made an eternal 'covenant of salt' with David. It is interesting that the only other reference to a covenant of salt in the Old Testament occurs in the Priestly Writing (Num. 18:19, cf. Lev. 2:13), where it is concluded with the Aaronic priesthood. All the offerings of Israel are given to Aaron and his sons and daughters as a perpetual due. It is a 'covenant of salt' for him and for his descendants for ever. Does this suggest that the Chronicler saw the promise to David as being fulfilled in the priestly line as they administered the theocracy, and so is it a re-interpretation of the Davidic covenant theology, just as we see another such re-interpretation in Isa. 55:1–5? Certainly, all that follows relates to *cultic* apostasy rather than to its political aspects. The reference to Jeroboam in the third person (vv. 6, 8) when he is ostensibly the one being addressed shows that this is no actual speech spoken in the particular historical circumstance of the disruption of the kingdom, but that the real address is to those, much later, for whom that division is long since past history, but for whom the Chronicler believes cultic loyalty to be an urgent imperative against all the divisions which threaten the people of God at that later time.

We may note further some of the stylistic features we have met already in the addresses. There is play on words, and words which figure in such a device elsewhere. Rehoboam is to some extent excused in that he was the inexperienced dupe of 'sons of Belial'. We have seen how the Chronicler, while not entirely exculpating Rehoboam for the division, sought to present him in a favourable light in contrast to Jeroboam. The fact that we have already been told that he was forty-one years of age when he came to the throne (12:13) is hardly consistent with the picture of him given by the Hebrew text which reads literally 'an immature youth'! Yet there we are told he 'could not withstand' (Heb. הִתְחַזַּק) such sons of Belial. Now Jeroboam and the Israelites plan to 'fight against' (לְהִתְחַזֵּק) the kingdom of Yahweh by their actions (v. 8). This offers a play on the Heb. root (חזק) which has appeared frequently in the royal addresses. There it has been said that one can 'strengthen oneself' or 'take comfort' by trust in Yahweh. Such courage will always be effective. The brazen foolhardiness of that 'courage' which opposes God rather than trusts him is destined to frustration and failure. This address also, then, offers strong links with its context. Again, it offers a play on the word 'abandon' (עזב/). Abijah can say, 'We have not abandoned him' (v. 10). Their opponents, however, for all the size of their army, cannot hope to win, for they have 'abandoned' Yahweh (v. 11). Finally, the Israelites have 'with' them the golden calves which Jeroboam made (v. 8). By contrast, those from the South can say, 'God is *with* us at our head' (v. 12).

We should not miss the significant description of the Davidic dynasty as 'the kingdom of Yahweh entrusted to David's descendants' (v. 8). Not only is the Davidic line not an end in itself but, as divinely appointed agent of God's own kingdom, the practical outworking of its faithfulness is the obedient observance of cultic purity. The northern kingdom have rid themselves of the true Aaronic priesthood (v. 10), and those who do act as priests officiate at an empty and ineffective altar in the service of a 'non-god' (v. 9). By the use here of the phrase 'Anyone who has offered to consecrate himself . . . has become . . . a priest serving non-gods', the address apparently recalls the Deuteronomistic Historian's account of Jeroboam's act in consecrating as priests of the high places 'any who would' (I Kgs. 13:33), just as the reference to the 'golden calves' (v. 8) alludes to I Kgs. 12:28 and Jeroboam's call, 'Behold your gods, O

Israel!' The address of Abijah, indeed, might be described as exegesis of the Kings account of the division of the kingdoms. There might also be an overtone of allusion to the warning of social anarchy given by the prophet Isaiah as one sign of the dissolution of the kingdom (Isa. 3:1–8) in which they will ask desperately the least fitted to act as their leaders. That this is the Chronicler's own style can be seen by reference to II Chr. 15:3, where it is said that for many days Israel had 'no true God'. By contrast, Judah has true priests, Aaronites and Levites, who minister to Yahweh (v. 10). As Exod. 29:10ff. makes clear, when Aaronic priests are consecrated[52] they are consecrated to serve Yahweh (see also Exod. 29:44) and become the effective means by which all the people know God's presence and covenant relationship with him (v. 45). The description of the service of the temple and the sacred objects which these priests administer (v. 11) is pure Chronicler. It fulfils the Aaronic role instituted by David (I Chr. 16:39f.). Failure to fulfil these tasks brought judgement on the community (II Chr. 29:7f.), and true reforming kings like Hezekiah and Josiah always saw to it that these Davidic institutions were put into operation again (II Chr. 29:18ff., 35:12ff.). The whole concept of the cultic purity of the Jerusalem temple, its personnel and its worship, is closely paralleled by the Chronicler's variations introduced into Solomon's words to Hiram (II Chr. 2:3–10, cf. I Kgs. 5:3–6).

All this meant that Judah and Jerusalem knew God's 'presence', and this, in turn, meant that however great the military threat, it would not avail against them, as the subsequent narrative (vv. 13–20) makes abundantly clear. We are thus introduced to a theme which recurs frequently in the addresses, that of the 'holy war'. Always the enemy has impossible numbers. Yet God fights for those who submit in trust and obedience to him and who, especially by their faithful observance of the cult, are open to his presence. It is always God who defeats the enemy (v. 15b). He 'gives' their enemies into his people's hands (v. 16). For all this emphasis on victory in battle, the Chronicler is a quietist. The people's task is cultic faithfulness and obedience. Where these qualities are shown, God looks after their military defence. The thrust of this lesson for the Chronicler's contemporaries, a lesson so often repeated in these addresses, is not hard to find. They are subject to the impossibly greater military might of the Persians. They are neither to plot rebellion nor to despair. Let them keep the faith. God is able to deliver them and will do so in his own good time.

Finally, we may return to the question of why this address is given to a king, when such similar sentiments are also to be found in the prophetic addresses. It is, surely, the main emphasis of this address to show that the real role of the

Davidic dynasty is to ensure the proper functioning of the temple cult under the Aaronic priests and the Levites. In this way its role is self-effacing. The priestly theocracy is its true goal. Who can make such a pronouncement more effectively than a royal representative of the Davidic line himself? By doing so he is showing himself a true descendant of the David who, in the addresses attributed to him by the Chronicler, makes this point abundantly clear. Indeed, we see that Abijah here, like the later royal figures who are assigned addresses, are really mouth-pieces for David, showing themselves by what they say to be true Davidides and by their actions to be behaving in a David-like way. Yet this emphasis on David in Chronicles is not a sign of a traditional 'messianic' eschatological expectation but, in a way, of the very reverse. It is to make clear that the divinely appointed restoration of the line *has* taken place in the priestly temple theocracy.

[11] II 14:7 (6) *Asa, the king, to Judah*

⁷And he said to Judah, 'Let us build these cities and encircle them with a wall, with towers, gates and bars. The land is still ours. Because we have sought Yahweh, our God, he has sought us[a] and given us peace on all sides.'[b]

Text

[a] LXX reads a pointing of the Hebrew verb giving a play on words which is so characteristic of these addresses that it is to be preferred to the repetitive 'We have sought' of MT.

[b] LXX makes part of the reported speech of MT 'So they built and prospered' a continuation of Asa's address, 'and he has caused us to prosper'.

General description

This brief address takes the form of a 'Summons to a Task' for which the grounds of encouragement are found in Yahweh's favour in response to their faithfulness, favour shown especially in security from military threats. If LXX is followed there is a play on / דרש ('seek'), 'Because we have sought Yahweh . . . he has sought us [in favour].' The address is related to the context by the use of / נוח ('to rest'; see also v. 5) and the general theme of 'peace', emphasised by the repetition of / שקט ('to be quiet', 14:1/13:23, 14:5/4).

Contents

The Deuteronomistic History had already passed a favourable verdict, albeit a qualified one, on Asa (I Kgs. 15:9–24). We are told he removed the male cult prostitutes and the idols Abijam had made. He removed Ma'acah, his mother, from her position as Queen Mother because of her compromise with other cults. He supported the cult of Yahweh, but did not initiate the policy of centralisation of worship, later to be associated with Hezekiah and Josiah. It recounts the continuing conflict between Judah and Israel in his days, in which he strengthened his position against the North by invoking the alliance with Syria which his father had instituted. He was thus able to make Ramah a defensive stronghold against further Israelite incursions. The Deutero-nomistic Historian's account ends with a typically vague reference to the 'Book of the Chronicles of the kings of Judah' which, it is said, gives details of 'all his might and the cities which he [re?]built'. A concluding note explains that he had diseased feet in his old age.

On this mixed set of notices the Chronicler gives an expanded account, whether drawing, even partially, on alternative and supplementary historical sources need not concern us here.[53] This opens with an account of his reforming and rebuilding activities which includes this brief address.

These words of Asa clearly belong to the 'addresses' in Chronicles, since they echo themes prominent in many of the others. The theme of 'retribution' is expressed by the play on the word 'seek'. The people who 'seek' Yahweh in true worship will find that he 'seeks' them in blessing and prosperity. The theme of the 'rest' given by God in the reign of obedient kings has been heard in the addresses of David (I 22:8, 9, 18; 28:2, see pp. 19–30 above). 'Prosperity' (/צלח) in return for obedience is another theme[54] (see pp. 70f. below), while building as one sign of such prosperity is shown, above all in the building of the temple by Solomon, but also in the reigns of such faithful kings as Jehoshaphat (II 17:12), Uzziah (II 26:2, 6, 9, 10), Jotham (II 27:3f.) and Hezekiah (II 32:5). Indeed, Asa parallels the achievements of David in some respects, not only in his concern for correct worship, but in showing that obedient trust in God which results in the conditions of 'peace' in which building could take place and so the nation live and worship as the true people of God. That is almost certainly how we should understand what appears as something of a contradiction, between energetic defensive preparation and yet complete reliance on God for military success. The same tension is reflected in the reign of Hezekiah (II 32:1–8, see p. 111 below). Yet it was already apparent in the life of David, who 'fought fierce battles' (I 22:8). In each instance, however, it is stressed that victory, and so the resulting 'peace', is God's gift in response to complete trust. It is not achieved by skilful human strategy or the might of national armies. Perhaps, also, the defensive building has an overtone of separation from the nations such as Nehemiah's building of the walls achieved.[55]

The reminder that 'the land is still ours' stresses the need to take the opportunity of faithfulness to Yahweh while it is there. It clearly extends the scope and reference of this address to the post-exilic situation. The Chronicler's contemporaries are here urged to be obedient in worship and dependent in faith so that they too may experience the prosperity of rebuilding and the peace which comes from divine deliverance.

[12] II 15:1–7 *Azariah (the prophet?) to Asa and all Judah and Benjamin*

[1] *Then the spirit of God came upon Azariah, the son of Oded.* [2] *And he went out to confront Asa and said to him, 'Listen to me, Asa and all Judah and Benjamin. Yahweh is with you all the while you are with him. If you seek him he will be found by you. But if you abandon him he will abandon you.* [3] *For a long time[a] Israel had[b] no true God, no priest to instruct them and no Torah.[c]* [4] *Then, in their distress, they came back to Yahweh, the God of Israel, and sought him, and he let himself be found by them.* [5] *In those days there was no security[d] as they went about their business[e] but only times of growing confusion for the citizens of all lands.* [6] *Nations and cities destroyed each other, for God plunged them into confusion with every kind of disaster.* [7] *Now, be strong! Do not weaken. There will be a reward for all your effort.'*

Text

[a] Lit. 'for many days'.

[b] The tense of Azariah's address is uncertain. JB, for example, interprets the whole of it as prophecy of the future. The Hebrew construction of v. 3 could refer either to past or future. The verb which opens v. 6, by the strict rules of classical Hebrew grammar (the *waw* consecutive construction) should be rendered as a future in English. We have seen already, however, signs which suggest that these strict rules were breaking down in the Chronicler's time. Since the other verbs do relate to the past it still seems best to take the address

as referring to some time in Israel's history. See the discussion below.

c The Hebrew *Torah* can mean either 'law' or, more generally 'instruction'. The likelihood is, however, that the Chronicler is already using it in the technical sense of the written law, and hence I have kept the technical term. See discussion below.

d The Hebrew word is שָׁלוֹם (*shālôm*).

e The Hebrew idiom reads literally, 'There was no security for him who went out or came in.'

General description

The address opens (v. 2b) and closes (v. 7) with prophetic exhortation, while vv. 3–6 offer an historical retrospect to reinforce the imperative of that exhortation. The whole lacks any opening or closing messenger formula but is introduced by a 'prophetic-type' phrase in v. 1, 'Then the spirit of God came upon Azariah.' Rhetorical devices include inversion (v. 2a), play on words (v. 2b), illustration (from past history, vv. 3–6) and, appeal to 'Scripture' (vv. 5–7), while the address closes with a type of 'Encouragement for a Task' formula. It opens with a call for attention which marks many, but by no means all, of the addresses.

Contents

Having given some details of the mention of Asa's rebuilding in the Deuteronomistic History, the Chronicler proceeds to give a specific instance of what was there described as 'all his might' (I Kgs. 15:23), namely the defeat of Zerah, the Ethiopian. Whether behind the grossly exaggerated numbers of the Ethiopian army of a million men and 300 chariots and the characteristic 'holy war' motifs in the Chronicler's narration there lies an historical incident is again hardly relevant for our purposes.[56] The Chronicler's use of it is to show Asa as (here) the ideal king who responds to the threat of overwhelming human might by faith expressed in a prayer entrusting the matter to God (II 14:11). In traditional formulae of the Chronicler we read, 'So Yahweh defeated the Ethiopians before Asa and before Judah and the Ethiopians fled' (v. 12). As usual, all that is left for the Judaeans to do is to chase and 'mop up'.

It is at this point in the story that Azariah comes to meet him and delivers the address recorded in vv. 2–7. Several commentators have said that the address does not really fit its context. Rudolph, for example, sees the connection between cc. 14 and 15 as secondary. Asa acts on his own initiative in 14:2–4, but here needs to be urged by a prophet.[57] Certainly, the two accounts of Asa's reforms (II 14:3–5, 15:8–15) seem superfluous, while 15:19 appears to contradict 14:9–15. Nevertheless we shall see in the Chronicler's treatment of various kings that faithfulness is never secure. The same kings can show obedience and failure and so need the words of prophets and others to warn them against complacency. The themes of Azariah's address are two. It seeks to drive home the lesson of trust which it illustrates, not from the event just narrated, but from some unspecified and rather vaguely generalised period in Israel's history. Further, it urges Asa to show courage and energy in work which will be rewarded. The nature of the work is again unspecified, but it is interpreted by the Chronicler in what follows as relating to a new burst of reforming zeal by Asa. This takes up in part the description of the reform in Kings, but adds much more (vv. 8–19).

The address is introduced by the description of the spirit of God coming upon Asa, which sets it firmly in the line of prophetic pronouncement. It has often been noticed that while, in the early stage of prophecy, inspiration by the spirit plays an important role, mention of the spirit as a means of inspiration tends to be replaced by other formulae in the eighth- and seventh-century canonical prophets.[58] With Ezekiel the concept is brought back into prominence. In the Zechariah tradition the same connection between prophecy and spirit is made (Zech. 7:12), and it is also emphasised elsewhere in the Chronicler's writing.[59] Further, the words of Azariah are probably described in v. 8 as 'prophecy'.[60] It has to be said, however, that there is no very clear reason why sometimes addresses are said to be inspired by the coming of the spirit, while at other times some other formula such as 'The word of Yahweh came to . . .' is used. Yet, whatever the reason and whatever the formula, the effect is to place them firmly in the prophetic tradition and vest them with prophetic authority while, at the same time, the variety may indicate that, by the time of the Chronicler, the old forms are breaking down.[61] Williamson (p. 267) says that the Chronicler usually attributes this kind of prophetic, spirit-inspired address to historically attested prophets and so, perhaps, is here using an older, genuine source. However, the Chronicler is equally capable of using such language to describe utterances as 'prophetic', so lending authority and verisimilitude to a composition of his own.

It is not only in form but in rhetorical style, vocabulary and content that the address closely resembles many of the others in Chronicles. We find the same emphasis on the presence of God which we have seen elsewhere (v. 2) together with the familiar device of play on words: 'Yahweh is *with* you all the while you are *with* him.' We have the formula which is repeated elsewhere, 'If you seek him he will be found by you' (see I Chr. 28:9). The fulfilment of this promise is narrated in v. 15. There is, possibly, an echo of Jer. 29:13f. here from the letter to the exiles, which may itself be an example of Deuteronomistic 'preaching' to those in exile.[62]

There follows an appeal to their history, but a most enigmatic reference. 'For a long time Israel had no true God, no priest to instruct them and no Torah' (v. 3). The vagueness of the reference is heightened by the fact that the Hebrew has no verb, so that the tense is not certain. Does it refer to the time before Moses? Does it refer, as some commentators argue, to the period of Judg. cc. 17–21? Yet there the disorder has been attributed, at least by editorial comment, to the absence of a king (19:1, 21:25).[63] While I have shown (in the textual notes above) that it is unlikely to be specifically a prediction of the future, the very vagueness of the time reference may well be intentional. Indeed, this and a number of points make it likely that we have here another instance in these addresses of a deliberate 'extension' to a more general reference of what is purportedly set in a particular context in the past. The Hebrew reads literally, 'For many days, no true God for Israel, no teaching priest and no Torah'. This is a state of affairs which has characterised Israel's life in bad times at all periods of her history.

Weingreen has argued that the participial form of the verb 'no *teaching* (מוֹרֶה) prophet' means that the real sense is, 'For a long time Israel was without the true God and without any priest *giving authoritative direction* and without any authoritative direction' (i.e. Torah).[64] This may be a further indication of a more general application of the words of this address. Willi has argued that 'Torah' for the Chronicler does not have a specific connotation of that which was given in a past revelation and cites S. Japhet with approval when she says that, for the Chronicler, terms like 'Torah', 'Mizvah' etc. do not serve as clear definitions but as living ideas or concepts. Speaking of this passage Willi says that what is in mind is not so much past legislation of Moses as the living institution of the prophets in the Chronicler's own time.[65] I have suggested (see textual notes above) that by this time 'Torah' has come to have its later 'technical' sense, but this also would mean that it has acquired a much more general sense.

Further, it cannot be without significance that a number of prophecies are recalled, even if only in a general way. For example, Hos. 3:4 warned of a judgement to come by way of exile when the children of Israel would have to dwell 'for many days' without ephod or teraphim. Amos had predicted a famine 'of hearing the word of Yahweh' (8:11), and something of the same thought is expressed in the lament for the loss of prophets in Ps. 74:9. Again, the return to the 'confusion' among the nations predicted in vv. 5f. seems to echo a number of earlier references in both the Deuteronomistic History, Deuteronomy and the prophets (e.g. Isa. 3:5, 19:2, 22:5, Zech. 8:10, Judg. 5:6, Deut. 7:23, I Sam. 14:20). Indeed, the theme seems to become one of the traditional signs of God's judgement and, as such, is here no merely local or even national affair. It affects 'nations', 'cities' and 'lands' (vv. 5f.). Perhaps the very wording of these verses, then, extends the force of this address to those who, later, had known the uncertainty and insecurity of the exilic period which is seen in prophetic terms of God's judgement. The post-exilic community have to learn from that which has characterised their history so repeatedly. They must show a spirit of penitence similar to that shown by Asa and his contemporaries and, indeed, by others in their history. Then they will know such judgements no more. In the present, if they are obedient, they will experience the presence of the true God and hear his 'teaching' through those he has ordained to preach it.

The parallels with the form in which Zechariah's preaching was remembered in the tradition and is expressed in Zech. 8:9f., 13 are particularly close and instructive. This can be demonstrated by setting out the two passages in synoptic parallel and emphasising words and phrases which in the Hebrew occur in both, and ideas which both have in common (the Hebrew is rendered literally):

Zech. 8:9f., 13
Thus says the LORD of Hosts, '*Let your hands be strong*, you who hear in these days these words from the mouth of the prophets. For before *those days* there was no *reward* for man or beast. There was no *peace* for *him who went out and came in*. There was no *peace* from the

II Chr. 15:5–7
In those times there was no *peace for him who went out and came in*, but there was a time of growing confusion for the citizens of all lands. *And nation was shattered by nation and city by city*, for God plunged them into confusion with every

distress, for I *set each against his fellow . . . Do not be afraid. Let your hands be strong.'*

kind of *distress*. You now, *be strong, do not let your hands be weak*, for there will be a *reward* for all your effort.

The Zechariah passage is one which we shall be considering later, and we shall examine its resemblances to the addresses in Chronicles (see pp. 228ff. below). We shall see that it is based to some extent on the preaching of Haggai as well as that of Zechariah. It recalls the allusions, especially of Haggi, to the time of the Babylonian exile and the immediate return as the time when God visited them with 'confuson' in judgement. The call of Haggai for strength and energetic work had been specifically a call to rebuild the temple after the exile. We shall see that there are indications in Zech. 8:9ff. that this word has there become the basis for a more general call to later hearers for a religious zeal and loyalty akin to that shown by the returned exiles who literally built the temple. Haggai had promised that their effort would all be worth while because the time of distress and confusion when there was no 'reward' was to be reversed in a period of blessing in the future. That is echoed in the words of Zech. 8:11–13a, but is only hinted at in Azariah's address by the simple and terse assurance that there will be a 'reward' (v. 7b). The very vague reference in Chronicles to the task about which they should be busy and 'not let their hands be weak' suggests that the process of 'generalisation' of Haggai's original words has gone further than it had even in Zech. 8:9ff. Both the hint at the fuller and more detailed words of the Zechariah passage by the one word 'reward' and the much blunter and more general nature of the call in Azariah's address suggest that it is this which is exegesis of the Zechariah passage rather than the other way round. So, by citation of Scripture this address also has been extended to a much more general level. Specific oracles have become general exhortation of religious truths to a later congregation.

We appear to have here, then, an address to the people after the exile which, by being set in the form of a prophecy (v. 1), is credited with prophetic authority. We know from the Zechariah material that the prophets were held to have continuing authority and relevance for the post-exilic community (Zech. 1:4, 8:9). This is driven home by apparent reference to, and exposition of, particular prophetic passages. If this is what has happened it must have something to say about date for, as we shall see, Zech. 8:9–13 is almost certainly one of the passages in Zech. 1:1–8 and cc. 8f. which represent expansions of the prophet's original message within the tradition. While this need not make the Chronicler, or this passage within the work, a great deal later, it must put us on our guard against recent tendencies to date the Chronicler about the time of Haggai and Zechariah and the completion of the temple in 515 BCE.[66] As we have seen, this early date is based on the shared interest in and concern for the temple and its cult in both Chronicler and the prophets of the restoration. But if we are right in seeing dependence on the Zechariah tradition in such a passage as Azariah's address, then Zechariah's own prophecy must have had time to have achieved some definitive form, to become regarded as authoritative and to have been reflected in the circles which passed it on. Azariah's address, anyway, like others in Chronicles, shows us how easily words and ideas that grew out of some specific historical context could take on a more general and enduring reference. Concern for the temple and its cult must have continued in preaching and pastoral circles long after the building's completion, although the actual work of rebuilding in the face of all obstacles could be seen as paradigmatic and held up as an example to later generations.

Once again, there can be no question that we are dealing with a genuine 'ancient' prophecy, for this is too much of a pattern with the Chronicler's own ideas and style, and too much of a piece with the other addresses, to represent a genuine 'source' which he took over from the past. Some features need to be noted. It follows no recognisable prophetic genre or form. It is, to a considerable extent, derivative from earlier scriptural material. It displays a number of rhetorical devices such as appeal to history by way of illustration and play on words. It delivers warning to the community and calls for immediate response. These are some of the hallmarks of what, in the broadest sense, can be termed 'preaching'.

[13] II 16:7–9 *Hanani, the seer, to Asa*

[7] *At that time Hanani the seer came to Asa, king of Judah, and said to him, 'It is because you depended[a] on the king of Syria and did not depend on Yahweh your God that the army of the king of Israel[b] has eluded your grasp.* [8] *Were not the Ethiopians and the Libyans a great force with chariots[c] and a vast number of horsemen? Yet then you depended on Yahweh and he gave them into your power.*

⁹*For Yahweh's eyes rove through all the earth so that he can come to the help of those whose hearts are sound before him. You have acted foolishly in this. From now on war will dog your steps.ᵈ'*

Text

a The Hebrew verb means literally 'to lean on', but in modern, idiomatic English this has acquired a rather different meaning.

b The MT and LXX read 'the army of the king of Syria'. It seems strange, however, that the army of the king of Syria should escape because of an alliance with the king of Syria, and therefore the text is often emended to read 'the army of the king of Israel'.

c In place of 'with chariots' LXX reads here 'a great force *in courage* and in vast numbers of horsemen'. This strengthens the impression of the formidable nature of the army only to show that no human might or bravado can prevail against Yahweh.

d Lit. 'wars will be *with* you'.

General description

Hanani is described as a 'seer', and in some ways his address resembles a prophetic reproach and announcement of judgement. It contains the grounds of accusation (vv. 7bα, 9bα) and anouncement of judgement (9bβ). However, it lacks opening and concluding prophetic messenger formulae and breaks into an historical retrospect (7b–8) which might be described as an 'Explanation of Judgement' as well as functioning to strengthen the note of reproach. It also affirms the omniscience and power of Yahweh. Stylistic features include the use of rhetorical question (8a), 'citation of Scripture' (9a; see also Zech. 4:10b and perhaps Isa. 10:20 – see discussion below) and appeal to (recent) history by way of illustration of theological truth.

Contents

We have already seen that a certain ambivalence towards Asa is apparent in the Deuteronomistic History. The Chronicler picks on the negative notes there, and by elaborating them and divining theological reasons for certain aspects of the reign, he is able to develop the theme of the faithful king who could, however, turn unfaithful. Unfaithfulness must account for his diseased feet in old age, which become an occasion for sinning in that he sought help from physicians rather than from Yahweh (v. 12).[67] The note in I Kgs. 15:16 about continuing warfare is seen by the Chronicler as judgement for his lack of trust (v. 9). But, above all, his appeal to Ben-hadad of Syria for help against Israel is seen as the cardinal sin, the supreme example of his failure to trust Yahweh.

Rudolph has dealt in detail with the structure of the Chronicler's account of the reign of Asa.[68] He recognises that the Chronicler's motives are 'theological' and that this, rather than some supposed alternative system of dating to that of Kings, is the explanation for the difference of chronology to be found here (p. 368). Strangely, he then insists that the two accounts of religious reform in 14:2–4 and 15:8ff. must be doublets, interrupted by the account of the Ethiopian war, and that all this must be due to the Chronicler's 'extra-canonical source'. This is possible, but the Chronicler is quite capable of shaping things in this way in order to construct a theological theme of faithfulness and disobedience. He is not one to let a little logical or chronological inconsistency stand in his way! P. Welten shows a surer appreciation of the Chronicler's method and purpose here.[69] He argues that the Chronicler wanted to show the first Judaean kings to be substantially 'faithful' kings in contrast to the apostate rulers of the North. However, the subsequent narrative shows that he could not ignore the Deuteronomistic Historian's estimate of Asa and, indeed, found in this the grounds which could account for the negative characteristics of the reign. Ackroyd, rightly, sees a more deliberate and calculated interweaving of the theme of judgement and grace, belief and unbelief, in the Chronicler's account.[70]

Hanani, described as a 'seer', and apparently identified with the father of Jehu (I Kgs. 16:1) – it is not clear why – comes to Asa to deliver a reproach leading to an announcement of imminent judgement, two elements which often belong together in the oracles of the classical prophets.[71] Hanani is presented as a prophetic figure and, even although the structure of his address breaks with the forms of earlier prophecy (see n. 71), he takes up a major theme of classical prophecy in denouncing Asa for his lack of reliance on God. This is what has accounted for his failure to repeat the military success he had known earlier against the Ethiopians and Libyans. The use of the verbal root /שׁען, to 'lean' or 'depend', links the motif of the address closely to the teaching of Isaiah of Jerusalem (e.g. 30:12ff., 31:1). In particular, in Isa. 10:20 (probably vv. 20–3 represent a later expansion of Isaiah's basic thought on both the themes of 'trust' and 'remnant') such reliance on God is seen as a sign of the ideal 'remnant'. There can be no surer betrayal of their calling than for God's people to lack trust in him and seek for substitute forms of help. The word is also a favourite of the Chronicler's as, for example, in II 13:18, where it occurs in the Chronicler's own narrative expressing his theological conviction that the reason for Judah's victory over Israel was just their reliance on God. He uses the word again in II 14:11 (10) in Asa's prayer before battle. There can be little doubt, therefore, that Hanani is the spokesman for the Chronicler's own teaching and that he is presented as one who expounds prophetic teaching.

This is developed further by another unmistakable parallel with the prophecy of Zechariah. Zech. 4:10b is quoted verbatim: 'The eyes of Yahweh rove through the whole earth.' The reference is not quite clear in Zechariah. It could be to the seven facets of the stone in Joshua's turban (3:9) or to the seven lamps (4:2). Either would speak of the ever watchful and powerful presence of God in his temple, whence he exercises sovereign power everywhere. Hanani's address takes up the theme of the watchful presence of God, but emphasises that his strength is available to those whose hearts are 'whole' or, as we might say, 'sound' towards him (v. 9). The Hithpa'el of the Hebrew /חזק is used here. Of the twenty-seven occurrences of this in the Old Testament, fifteen are to be found in the Books of Chronicles. Again, then, vocabulary suggests a close link between this address, many of the other addresses and the Chronicler's own narrative.

Asa, who did act so well and faithfully, now earns from Hanani the very rebuke the faithless Saul earned from Samuel, he 'acted foolishly' (I Sam. 13:13). Inevitably judgement must follow, in this case in the continuation of warfare with the northern kingdom. Asa now slips further into sin by rejecting the word of God through the 'seer' and showing this rejection by submitting him to the same fate that was meted out to Jeremiah (Jer. 20:2). Perhaps the reference is intended to recall the whole issue of 'true' and 'false' prophecy, so prominent a theme in the Book of Jeremiah, and to remind the Chronicler's contemporaries of the great disaster that can follow persistent rejection of God's word spoken through 'his servants the prophets'.

It is interesting that one and the same king, Asa, has two different prophetic addresses directed to him, and two so different. Together they give warning that obedience to God has to be constant. Past faithfulness will not excuse later betrayal. By citing again the post-exilic prophet, Zechariah, the address widens the whole issue of trust and faithlessness beyond the 'historical' context of Asa's campaigns. Later Israel, called to be the 'true Israel', the 'remnant', must continue to show that essential mark of Israel, namely faith. They also have still the presence of God in the temple, as Zechariah assured the returned exiles. He is ever watchful on their behalf and all-powerful throughout all the earth. He can still give the 'strength' for which these addresses call again and again. What is really needful is to have a heart that is 'sound' before God. Rejection of God's word will always bring judgement.

[14] II 19:1–3 *Jehu (the prophet?) to king Jehoshaphat*

[1] *And Jehoshaphat, king of Judah, returned home to Jerusalem in safety.* [2] *And Jehu, son of Hanani, the seer, came out to confront him and said to king Jehoshaphat, 'Do you enjoy[a] helping the wicked and those who hate Yahweh? This is why Yahweh's wrath will fall on you.* [3] *However, some good is to be found in you. You have wiped out the Asheroth[b] throughout the land and you have determined[c] to seek God.'*

Text

[a] Lit. 'Do you *love* helping . . .?'
[b] Some kind of wooden cultic symbols (perhaps poles or images of the deity) dedicated to Asherah, an Amorite or Canaanite goddess.[72]
[c] The Hebrew idiom reads literally, 'You have set your heart to seek God.'

General description

Jehu, again described as a seer like his father Hanani (16:7), delivers a prophetic-like address bringing to Jehoshaphat the grounds of accusation which takes the form of a prophetic reproach concerning his alliance with foreigners, and is cast in the form of a rhetorical question (v. 2bα). It is followed by an announcement of judgement (unspecified) (2bβ). Again there are no opening or concluding prophetic formulae. The address concludes (v. 3) with a qualification of Jehoshaphat's guilt which does not, however, explicitly affect the judgement just announced.

Contents

There are a number of striking parallels between the address of Hanani to Asa and that of Jehu to Jehoshaphat. Here, Hanani's son, Jehu, addresses Asa's son, Jehoshaphat. Both father and son are met by prophets on their return from a battle. The Chronicler's account of the battle at Ramoth-Gilead has significant variations from that presented in I Kgs. c. 22. The effect of these is to reduce the Deuteronomistic History's impression of Jehoshaphat as, possibly, rather an unwilling junior partner in the enterprise. His wealth and reputation are stressed (18:1); the reason for his alliance with Israel is seen as due to his marriage into Ahab's family (18:1; see also II Kgs 8:18); and the final phrase of v. 3, 'I will go with you to the war', suggests a rather more measured and freely offered co-operation. The reason for the Aramaeans sparing Jehoshaphat is not, as suggested in I Kgs. 22:33, that he was not the significant target, but that God providentially saved him (v. 31). Yet the impression given in Kings that Jehoshaphat rather weakly and foolishly allowed himself to be drawn into a venture that was not only ill-advised, but contrary to the word of God spoken through a true prophet, Micaiah, has given grounds for the Chronicler to show judgement by another prophet. So a further parallel between the addresses of Hanani and his son Jehu is that both denounce the respective kings for foreign alliances. But where Asa turned to Syria for help against Israel, his son Jehoshaphat went to give help to Israel against the Syrians. No kind of foreign alliance, for whatever reason, is suitable for the true people of God. In recent discussion on the supposed difference of authorship between Chronicles and Ezra/Nehemiah, much has been made of the Chronicler's alleged 'openness' to peoples of other nations, an attitude to which the separatist policies of Ezra and Nehemiah are seen to be strongly opposed.[73] Whatever the right in the matter of authorship, this particular point needs some qualification. The Chronicler is 'open' to people of other nations who come, individually, to submit to God's law in his true sanctuary. There is no hint anywhere that he is less conscious than were Ezra and Nehemiah of the need for a separation of the people of God from other nations in order to preserve their purity. One final parallel between the addresses of Hanani and Jehu should be noted. Both combine reproach with threat of judgement. While the threat appears to be qualified by the measure of goodness found in Jehoshaphat, it is not made explicit how this might affect the judgement. Nevertheless, the Chronicler clearly sees Jehoshaphat in some ways as an ideal king, and he has to account for the successes of the reign.

The address opens with a rhetorical question. The vocabulary of this, contrasting 'hate' (Heb. שנא/) and 'love' (Heb. אהב/), is not typical of the Chronicler himself. The verb 'hate' hardly occurs in Chronicles, apart from II Chr. 18:7, where it is parallel to Kings. Strangely, in view of this, the word is introduced into the account of God's response to Solomon's prayer for wisdom in II 1:11, 'You have not asked for the lives of those who hate you' (see also I Kgs. 3:11, 'enemies'). However, this verb does appear in the Psalms a great deal, and one is reminded in particular of Ps. 139:21f.:

> Do I not hate them that hate thee, O Lord?
> And do I not loathe them that rise against thee?
> I hate them with perfect hatred,
> I count them thy enemies.

The verb 'love' again occurs infrequently in Chronicles. It is found in the Deuteronomistic literature, both of God's love to men and the love they are called upon to show him in response. It can function as a 'covenant' term.[74] But, again, it occurs frequently in the language of Israel's cult as, for example, in Ps. 97:10, where the Massoretic Text gives the following rendering:

> You who love Yahweh, hate evil.[75]

This address, therefore, may reflect exposition of familiar words and themes from the temple worship. In this case the Chronicler may have been drawing on familiar material rather than composing in his own words. The exposition may be entirely his, but one suspects that such familiar words of the Psalms must often have provided a basis for the preacher and teacher of the second temple, and so he may have been following current homiletical practice here. On the other hand, the Chronicler's touch can be sensed in the use of the theme of 'help' and in the concept of 'wrath' going forth from Yahweh. This theme of God's help (Heb. עזר/) is a dominant one throughout the Chronicler's writings, not least in the addresses we are considering (e.g. II Chr. 14:10ff., 18:31 etc.). We have seen how strong an emphasis it is in I Chr. c. 12 (see pp. 15f. above). To offer help to those of God's choice is to offer help which must be effective because it will be based on God's own 'help'.[76] But Jehoshaphat has offered it to one outside the Davidic line of God's choice. When we read that, for this, 'wrath' will go out from God, we find another characteristic term in the Chronicler's vocabulary occurring equally in the addresses (e.g. II Chr. 19:10, 29:8) and elsewhere (e.g. II Chr. 24:18, 32:25f.). We shall note that it also occurs in the Zechariah tradition (Zech. 1:15, 8:14).[77]

Finally we may note that 'love' of God is equated with faithfulness in cultic matters (v. 3). As McCarthy has shown, in the Chronicler's writings cult attracts to itself the language of the Deuteronomistic (Mosaic) convenant.[78] Yet he is also surely right to stress that, at least in Chronicles, cult and law have not become entities — one is almost tempted to say 'ends' — in themselves. They stand for, and effect, a relationship with God (McCarthy, p. 41).

So, once more, one of these addresses sounds a dual note. No amount of past faithfulness renders the people of God immune from the need for constant watchfulness and ever-renewed obedience. Yet judgement is not the only movement from God to man. There is also grace, as the mitigation of the good king Hezekiah's judgement will later show (32:26). The lesson is that it is never too late to 'seek Yahweh' and turn back to him, and no one who ever does so seeks him in vain. Not only is this the theme of more than one of the addresses, it is the lesson of the 'immediacy' of retribution which is so prominent a feature in the Chronicler's history.[79] While, then, there are some special features of this address, notably in some of the vocabulary used, it is, once more, in its general terminology and teaching firmly anchored in its context and in the Chronicler's own theology.

[15] II 19:6f., 9–11 *Jehoshaphat, the king, to the judges, Levites, priests and heads of Judaea*

[6] *Then Jehoshaphat said to the judges, 'Take care how you act. You judge, not for man, but for Yahweh, and he will be with you[a] in the sentence of judgement.* [7] *So now, let the fear of Yahweh rule you. Take care how you act, for there is no injustice, no partiality, no openness to bribery with Yahweh our God.'*

[9] *And he charged them, saying, 'So you are to act in the fear of Yahweh, in integrity and in soundness of heart.* [10] *And in every dispute which is brought to you from your kinsmen who live in the cities over matters of bloodshed, and over matters relating to Torah, the commandments, the statutes and the ordinances, you shall give them instruction[b] so that they shall not incur guilt before Yahweh and so bring wrath on you and your kinsmen. If you act in this way you will not incur guilt.* [11] *See, Amariah, the high priest, will be over you in all matters pertaining to Yahweh, and Zebediah,[c] the son of Ishmael, the leader[d] of the House of Judah, in all matters pertaining to the king. Be strong! Be zealous![e] May Yahweh be on the side of the good.'*

Text

[a] The word 'he' does not appear in MT, but since the divine name immediately preceding ends with the Hebrew letter 'h' and the pronoun 'he' begins with the same letter, the pronoun could easily have dropped out by haplography.

b Or, 'you shall give light [i.e. by your well-versed judgements]'. See discussion below.

c Some Versions read the name 'Zechariah' here. The two names would then have some theological aptness in this charge to judge faithfully: Amariah, 'Yahweh speaks', and Zechariah, 'Yahweh remembers [take note].'

d Heb. *nāgîd*, which can also mean 'prince'.

e The Heb. reads simply, 'Be strong *and* act.'

General description

Both these short addresses belong to the type we have characterised as 'The Assignment of a Task' (vv. 6aβ, bα, 7, 9–11). Each contains an 'encouragement formula' (6bβ, 11bβ). They are characterised by none of the rhetorical devices found in many of the other addresses except for possible relation to (dependence on?) other biblical material (see discussion below).

Contents

The brief address of vv. 6f. is one which von Rad included among his 'Levitical Sermons', and was held by him to support his case that such sermons are all similar whether on the lips of prophet, Levite or king, although he argues that it is simpler in form than the prophetic addresses, lacking parallelism.[80] However, my examination below questions the similarity to the other addresses in some respects.[81] Further, it is interesting to note that whenever, as here, an address is put on the lips of a king, he is giving, or arranging for, legislation and direction about some aspects of the cultic life of the theocracy. In appointing judges from among the priests, Levites and heads of the tribes, Jehoshaphat is acting in line with his ancestor, David (I Chr. 23:4; see also 26:29ff.). To be concerned with the sound administration of justice is to be a true descendant of the Chronicler's David. Thus, against von Rad, there is some appropriateness at least about the addresses assigned to kings.

Whether there is any historical worth in this notice, or whether the whole episode has been suggested by the king's name (Jehoshaphat = 'Yahweh judges'), is a complex issue which need not be decided here.[82] As we shall see, it is the Chronicler's exposition and application of the legal reform, whether historical or not, by means of the addresses, which is germane for this study.

The address to the officials appointed in 'all the fortified cities of Judah' reminds the judges of the presence of God, a frequent theme of the addresses.[83] Here it serves to remind them of their responsibility, just as elsewhere it is to encourage those, such as Solomon, who are taking particular office, or, more generally, the people of God as a whole. Yet again in this address we encounter some vocabulary which is not characteristic of the Chronicler. He seldom uses the imperative 'see' (Heb. רְאֵה) in the sense of 'take care' (but cf. I 28:10). He does not use the word rendered in RSV as 'perversion of justice' (עַוְלָה). Nor elsewhere does he use the idiom of 'lifting up the face' for 'showing partiality', or the phrase for 'taking a bribe' (מִקַּח שֹׁחַד). Yet we find such language in Deuteronomy, as in Deut. 1:16f. and 15:18–21. We find it also in some Psalms, particularly, for example, in Ps. 82:2, where the (false) gods are asked:

> How long will you judge unjustly (תִּשְׁפְּטוּ עָוֶל)
> and show partiality to the wicked? (וּפְנֵי רְשָׁעִים תִּשְׂאוּ)

The description of the maladministration of justice by Samuel's sons suggests that these were almost stereotyped phrases. We read that 'they perverted justice' and that 'they took bribes' (וַיִּקְחוּ שֹׁחַד I Sam. 8:3). When one reflects how vital a factor integrity of the legal administration is in stable community life, it is small wonder that such phrases became stereotypes, and perhaps in this process we may suspect that the cult played a regulative part.

In this brief address, then, we have a vital concern of the Chronicler, namely that the Davidic pattern for the life of the theocracy shall be maintained and, indeed, constantly renewed by his faithful descendants. It may be, however, that we have here less free composition of the Chronicler than echo of the kind of words and phrases that were embedded in Israel's legal tradition and perpetuated in the cult. Jehoshaphat's address therefore may allow us to catch echoes of words that would often have been heard in the worship of the second temple. It should not then surprise us if such words frequently echo earlier writings and draw their inspiration from the liturgy.

In the second charge of vv. 9–11, addressed to the officials appointed to oversee judicial matters in Jerusalem, we find that the general 'sermonic' characteristics are couched in phraseology more typical of the Chronicler. They must act in 'the fear of Yahweh' and in 'integrity' (בֶּאֱמוּנָה): a term the Chronicler uses to designate loyal, capable and willing service in the theocracy (e.g. I Chr. 9:26, 31, II 31:12, 15, 34:12). They were to show 'soundness of heart' (לֵבָב שָׁלֵם), one of the Chronicler's favourite ways of describing a right relationship to God. Its force is seen in that it describes the relationship of the men of war who came to Hebron in support of David as king. They came (בלבב שָׁלֵם), that is, with 'a single-minded devotion' to him (I 12:38/39). So David calls Solomon to serve Yahweh (I 28:9; see also 29:19). Such an attitude is shown by the people in their proper support of the temple (I 29:9), and it is the condition which must be shown by every true Davidide king (II 15:17, Asa, contrast Amaziah, 25:2). We have already seen how, in citing from Zech. 4:10, Hanani takes the words 'the eyes of the LORD run to and fro throughout the whole earth', which Zechariah saw as evidence of the protective power of God, but applies them, in characteristic Chronicler fashion, to those whose heart is 'sound before' God (II 16:9).

What follows is instructive. The range of cases includes bloodshed, Torah, commandments, statutes and ordinances, thus placing 'legal' and 'cultic' affairs on an equal footing.[84] It is perhaps of interest to observe that this 'court of appeal' brings together the 'chief priest', who is over them in all matters pertaining to Yahweh, and the 'governor' of the house of Judah (or his son – the Hebrew could give either sense), in all matters of the 'king' (v. 11). Just what the Hebrew *nāgîd* means in this context is far from clear. It usually means 'prince' or 'leader'. Perhaps it can carry the sense 'governor', but to whom would this refer in the period of the monarchy (the definite article in Hebrew makes it clear that one, distinctive office is intended)? Is it an indication that we are not really in the period of the monarchy at all but that it reflects the kind of diarchy we see in the post-exilic period, as illustrated in the joint roles of Joshua and Zerubbabel and, later, Ezra with the governor and Nehemiah with the high priest?

The verb used of these leaders, that they are to 'give light' (the Hebrew verb is /זהר), could indicate either a chiefly teaching role, or that they are to give 'enlightened' verdicts which truly reveal God's will in all difficult cases of behaviour. The same verb occurs in Exod. 18:20ff. There it is used in the context of the advice given to Moses by his father-in-law to appoint 'rulers' who shall 'judge' the people at all times. They are to be men who 'fear God' (see II Chr. 19:9) and who are 'trustworthy' and who 'hate a bribe' (cf. II Chr. 19:9). The role of Moses is to represent the people before God by bringing their disputes to him (Exod. 18:19) and by 'teaching' them (Heb. /זהר) the statutes and decisions, thus making known to them the way they should walk. The judges then appointed appear from Exod. 18:22, 26 to exercise judgement in civil matters. Indeed, this is often represented as a division between the religious and civil spheres of law.[85] However, this is not completely clear, and Rylaarsdam[86] is right to insert a question mark at this point. Moses (and so *sacral* means of deciding verdicts?) is still the final court of appeal. Since the Exodus passage is usually assigned to the Elohistic source of the Pentateuch it most probably represents, or seeks to justify, conditions at some stage in the pre-exilic period. So not only may some differentiation between the role of 'priest' and 'civil judge' have been known before the exile, but already the 'teaching' role of the priests may have received some recognition.[87]

It is possible, then, that the two sections of Jehoshaphat's address (vv. 5–7, 8–11) represent an attempt to see such a distinction as that envisaged in Exod. c. 18 between local administrative judges in the towns and cities (vv. 5–7) and the role of an 'ecclesiastical' court of Moses (vv. 9–11). However, we always have to bear in mind that our knowledge of the administration of justice before the exile is sketchy. The king appears to have been the ultimate court of appeal, embodying as he did both 'sacral' and 'civil' realms under his authority. The passages in Chronicles may reflect one attempt to secure the situation after the exile when the original role of the monarch had to be exercised through different channels.

The important thing for our consideration here, however, is that, whatever the background, the addresses give admonitory application of the historical incidents of Jehoshaphat's reign to the Chronicler's contemporaries and appear to make use of other biblical material to do so, especially that which related to correct legal procedures. So these 'judges' are admonished in Chronicler-type language. Only a faithful discharge of their duties will enable them to avoid 'guilt' and the divine 'wrath' which would otherwise come upon them. Also typical of such charges, as we have seen, is the call to 'be strong'. Finally, they are also reminded of the promise of the 'presence' of God with them in their office.

The total impression of II Chr. 19:4–11 is not altogether clear. Some of the vocabulary is not typical of the Chronicler but does echo Exod. 18:17–26 as well as Deut. 16:18–20. This suggests that there may have been a tradition of the terms by which judges were appointed and that this is reflected in the language of the two addresses. Further, it may be that behind the double appointment and charge to the judges there is an attempt to establish a legal practice based on Exod. 18 by which 'religious' and 'civil' matters and procedure were demarcated. It is possible that, with the actual names used (unknown to us as individuals) the Chronicler had some testimony to an attempt at legal reform in the reign of Jehoshaphat. However, it is just likely that the names are seen as 'symbolic' (see textual notes above), just as Jehoshaphat's own name is suspiciously useful ('Yahweh judges') for him to be introduced as a king who reformed the legal procedures of the kingdom. Whatever the case, some very characteristic Chronicler words and phraseology, and the interesting bringing together of high priest and governor in what might be termed the ecclesiastical court, may well reflect efforts in the post-exilic period to translate pre-exilic procedures of the monarchical period into the new situation of a later time.

One should not miss the very close parallel in the words attributed to Haggai which are addressed to the leaders Zerubbabel and Joshua in Hag. 2:4f., a passage which Beuken rightly assigns to the editorial framework of the book.[88] Note the parallel 'Be strong!' (Heb.חֲזַק) (Hag. 2:4f.; see also II Chr. 19:6, 11). It might be argued that both fit the 'Installation genre' McCarthy describes.[89] He sees this as extending to a call to those who bear any office, namely a call to show 'fidelity'. In this case the Chronicler may have used material that comes from an earlier level of tradition and made it the basis of a sermon to all who have any role of significance, especially those which affect the administration of justice. It is, therefore, interesting that the admonition of the second charge in vv. 9–11 is more general and consistent with the exhortations of other addresses.

Another feature which would suggest an extension of reference beyond the immediate circle of judicial officials is the close parallel in form, not only to the 'installation' charges to Zerubbabel and Joshua in Hag. c. 2, but also to the charges to Solomon. We have already seen how these were extended in application to address leaders and people of the theocracy of a later time. The Chronicler also finds it natural to emphasise the teaching and admonitory role of the priests, Levites and 'heads of families' (v. 8).

Clearly this is a more specific address than the others we have examined and lacks some of their distinctive rhetorical features, but it contains a good deal of the same message. The pre-condition of God's blessing upon, and presence with, the judges in their work would apply equally to all in the theocratic community who had any part in its activities. All need the counsel to 'Take care' (lit. 'Be watchful' (v. 7)), to act 'in the fear of Yahweh', in 'integrity' and 'in soundness of heart' (v. 9). All need the injunction 'Be strong!' and the assurance of God's 'presence' (v. 11).

[16] II 20:14–17 *Jahaziel, the Levite, to Jehoshaphat and all Judah*

¹⁴*Then the spirit of Yahweh came upon Jahaziel, the son of Zechariah, the son of Benaiah, the son of Je'iel, son of Mattaniah, a Levite of the guild of Asaphites, in the midst of the assembly,* ¹⁵*and he said, 'Pay attention, all Judah, citizens of Jerusalem and king Jehoshaphat! This is what Yahweh is saying to you. You are not to be afraid or dismayed when confronted by this great army, for the battle is not yours, but God's.* ¹⁶*Fall upon them tomorrow. They are climbing the ascent of Ziz. You will find them at the end of the wadi to the east of the desert of Jeruel.* ¹⁷*You will have no need even to fight in this battle. Take your stations. Stand firm and you will witness Yahweh's victory for you. Do not be afraid. Do not be dismayed. Tomorrow, go out against them, and Yahweh will be with you.'*

General description

The address is introduced by a narrative, setting it in the category of a prophetic utterance, 'Then the spirit of Yahweh came upon Jahaziel . . .' (v. 14). It includes the messenger formula, 'This is what Yahweh is saying . . .' (15bα). However, the form is mixed, since this is preceded by the call for attention which characterises some of the royal proclamations (15aβ). The address might generally be termed 'An Assignment of a Task', in this case the summons to the holy war (16, 17aβ). It includes formulae of encouragement to undertake the task (15bβ, 17a, bβ), assuring the hearers of a divine victory. It belongs firmly within the 'holy war' tradition and echoes other instances of such calls, expounding earlier biblical material (see discussion below).[90]

Contents

Jahaziel's address comes in the course of a narration by the Chronicler of an attack by the Ammonites, Moabites and some Meunites[91] against the Judaeans, in which they camped at Engedi on the western side of the Dead Sea. King Jehoshaphat reacts to the news as a model Davidic king should. He 'seeks Yahweh' and proclaims a fast throughout Judah, from all parts of which the people come to join him in 'seeking Yahweh' (vv. 3f.). The king leads them in a prayer which emphasises God's sovereign power and recalls how mercifully he has shown that power in his people's history. Confessing their helplessness, he throws himself upon God's grace (vv. 5–12). It is at this point that Jahaziel, an Asaphite Levite (v. 14), is inspired by the spirit to deliver this 'oracle' assuring king and people of victory and calling on them not to be afraid (vv. 14–17). To this they respond with worship (vv. 18f.). Jehoshaphat then addresses the assembly (v. 20) and there follows a highly stylised account of a battle in which the people's part is only to pray and praise while God gives victory over the enemy (vv. 21, 27). Finally, an act of praise and thanksgiving is recorded (v. 28), and we are told that thereafter Jehoshaphat's kingdom was quiet, for God gave them 'rest' round about (v. 30).

There is nothing of all this in Kings.[92] Whether there is any historical kernel to it all is a question hardly worth pursuing.[93] Many characteristics argue against any kind of historical nature to this material. The site of the enemy's encampment, 'Hozazon-tamar', i.e. Engedi, is the place where David had been delivered from the threat of Saul (I Sam. 24:1ff.). Does this suggest that when Jehoshaphat shows David-like trust in God he knows the kind of deliverance God gave David? Further, de Vries in his study of temporal terms as structural elements in the holy war tradition[94] has shown how the temporal terms in II Chr. 20, 'tomorrow' (vv. 16f.) and 'early morning' (v. 20) have lost all their original force and the whole represents 'the extremest example of holy war time ideology within the Canon of the Old Testament' (p. 103). He argues that the narrative has been completely 'stylised' so that it represents a 'complete sacramentalisation of Heilsgeschichte' (p. 105). De Vries, in fact, goes so far as to depict the whole account as 'ritualised drama', while Ackroyd speaks of it in general terms as a 'liturgical account' presenting important reinterpretation of themes belonging to the holy war ideology.[95] With slightly different emphasis from de Vries, B. S. Childs has argued that 'to this day' is a 'formula of personal testimony added to, and confirming, a received tradition'.[96]

To all this we must add the overt theological overtones of the place name of 'The Valley of Berachah' (v. 26), which means 'The Valley of Blessing'.[97] The theological themes of 'trust', 'deliverance' and 'rest' are also prominent. The use of / שקט ('rest') and / נוח ('to be quiet') has been discussed above (see pp. 16, 20f., 26f.). It is not surprising that this 'rest' could be seen in something of an eschatological sense when one considers its use by the prophets, particularly Isaiah (30:15, 32:17). It is a theme taken up also in Zech. 6:8.

This is the context, then, in which the address of Jahaziel is delivered. Again, it is impossible to say why Jahaziel is named and why he is given the long and circumstantial genealogy which in fact tells us nothing. We might apply to the genealogy what Ackroyd says of the details of the topography of the battle: 'Such precision is as much the mark of legend as of history.'[98]

Further, in a passage where the names seem to have theological and symbolic significance, we should not miss the fact that the name Jahaziel means 'God sees' or even 'God gives vision.' What is of interest is that he belongs to one of the guilds of temple singers, Asaph, which seem to have come into prominence in the period of the second temple, and he delivers his message in the context of a religious assembly.[99] While we need not assume that such a role was limited to the Levites (a wider reference is suggested by the descriptions of those who deliver other addresses in Chronicles), the function of current temple preaching may well be genuinely reflected here. Though cast in the form of a prophetic oracle by the introduction and messenger formula, the introductory 'Pay attention!' used by itself and not in parallelism shows that we have moved away from the true forms of earlier prophecy. It is akin to the call 'Hear me!' which we have already seen to be a feature of a number of these addresses. Form critical considerations therefore suggest a late prose form of instructive address rather than a classical prophetic oracle, which is not to deny to this, as to many of the addresses, a strong prophetic influence. It would be strange if later preaching and teaching in the second temple owed nothing to the example and influence of earlier prophecy.

In a detailed examination of this address of Jahaziel, A. Schmitt rejects von Rad's inclusion of it in his general classification of 'Levitical preaching', and also his contention that it 'borrows' from such passages as Exod. 14:13f.[100] He criticises von Rad for insufficient attention in his study to detailed linguistic and structural aspects of the passages he chose (a criticism which must be allowed to have force, if it is at the same time remembered that all was compressed into the space of an article). From a detailed study of form and language Schmitt says that this address shows peculiar and individual characteristics. There is a relationship to such passages as Exod. 14:13f., but it is not that of direct 'borrowing'. Both show similar structure, including (1) an address to the group; (2) a warning against fear; (3) an imperative as strict command, and (4) a word of salvation. Schmitt finds an exactly similar structure in the Mari letters (Archives Royales de Mari × 7, × 50) and in other scriptural passages such as Jos. 8:1f., Judg. 4:6–9, II Kgs. 19:1–7 = Isa. 37:1–7, Isa. 7:7–9. From such passages five elements recur: (1) a divine word arising from a time of acute need, particularly that posed by threat from enemies; (2) the divine word made more precise by details of time, place, name of messenger and the way in which the message is conveyed; (3) a personal address and message formula; (4) a series of imperatives and, later, also prohibitions, and (5) a promise of salvation. From all this Schmitt deduces that the Chronicler is here being influenced by ancient Near Eastern and biblical traditions and that this separates such an address as Jahaziel's from Levitical preaching. He concludes, 'Perhaps the current use of theological formulae betrays a weakening of spontaneous, religious speech' (p. 279).

Schmitt's argument is open to a criticism different from, but not unrelated to, that which he directed towards von Rad. His whole treatment of II Chr. 20:14–17 suffers from being taken in isolation from the other addresses in Chronicles. We have seen already that these 'formulae' occur frequently in varied ways in the other addresses, particularly in those of David to Solomon, but elsewhere also. It is true that in view of de Vries's analysis of the extreme 'stylising' of time in this example of the holy war theme, direct dependence upon passages such as Exod. 14:13f. might appear less likely.[101] That there is a 'holy war' background to much of the Chronicler's terminology and ideology need not be doubted. But all the indications are that these are now mediated through earlier scriptural examples which are being expounded and applied in a much more general hortatory and admonitory way. It is similar to Williamson's argument, which we have supported, that an older and more precise 'Installation to Office' genre is mediated in the Chronicler's work through a conscious echo and reinterpretation of earlier biblical material. We are dealing more with inner-biblical exegesis than conscious and deliberate use of a particular genre.[102]

This conclusion is strengthened by the striking and almost exact verbal parallels between Jahaziel's address and Exod. 14:13f., parallels which a table helps to make clearer.

Exod. 14:13f	*II Chr. 20:14–17*
Do not be afraid (v. 13)	Do not be afraid (vv. 15, 17)
(אַל־תִּירָאוּ)	(אַל־תִּירְאוּ)
	Do not be dismayed (15, 17)
	(אַל־תֵּחַתּוּ)
Station yourselves (13)	Station yourselves (17)
(הִתְיַצְּבוּ)	(הִתְיַצְּבוּ)
and see (13)	and see (17)
(וּרְאוּ)	(וּרְאוּ)
the victory of Yahweh (13)	the victory of Yahweh (17)
(יְשׁוּעַת יְהוָה)	(יְשׁוּעַת יְהוָה)

Yahweh will fight for you (14)   it is not for you to fight (17)

(יְהוָה יִלָּחֵם לָכֶם)   (לֹא לָכֶם לְהִלָּחֵם)

The addition (twice) of the formula 'Do not be dismayed' in Jahaziel's address is surely due to the Chronicler's employing his own often-repeated phrase in such contexts. The other passages cited by Schmitt do not have these strong verbal similarities in addition to the general similarities of structure of which he speaks, and this strengthens the impression that it is earlier *scriptural* motifs which the Chronicler is taking and relating to his own day. This seems to be the method of teaching and exhortation with which he and his hearers are familiar. That is why the term 'preaching' is not inappropriate, however generally and guardedly we must use it. Further, we have seen that a feature of such exposition is the 'generalising' of what was once specific and local to its given context. This has characterised the application to Solomon of such themes derived from the holy war and the way they have then been broadened to apply to the whole community in their task of building the temple. The same is true of the charges given to those with special judicial tasks and other responsibilities of leadership. This 'broadening' takes place here in the prayer attributed to Jehoshaphat (vv. 6–12) with its strong echo of Solomon's prayer (I Kgs 8:33, 37; cf. II Chr. 6:20, 28–30), the universal phrase 'God of heaven' (v. 6) and its appeal to Israel's history (v. 10). All this serves to generalise and broaden the scope of the incident and the address attached to it.[103] The community of faith of all times need to hear the call of Jahaziel to face the enemies of God who threaten their life and well-being. They need to respond to such a call, however, in a similar spirit of quiet trust and confidence based on a like belief in God's power to act on their behalf. A parallel wider application of these concepts also takes place in the brief, final address of Jehoshaphat himself to the assembly (v. 20), to a consideration of which we now turn.

[17] II 20:20 *Jehoshaphat, the king, to the people of Judah and Jerusalem*

[20] *So in the early morning they marched out to the wilderness of Tekoa. And, as they were leaving, Jehoshaphat stood and said, 'Hear me, Judah and citizens of Jerusalem! Trust in Yahweh your God and you will be supported;[a] trust in his prophets and you will succeed.'*

Text

a It is difficult to reproduce in English the play on the Hebrew word 'trust' (/ אמן). Perhaps the basic idea of the word is 'to support', since the noun 'pillar' stems from it. We might then attempt to render the play on the word here and in Isa. 7:9, 'Lean on Yahweh and you will be supported.' However, it would be difficult so to render the second use of the imperative of the verb in relation to the prophets.

General description

The address is introduced by an historical narrative (v. 20aα) and opens with the formula 'Hear me!' It comprises a double exhortation to trust in Yahweh and his prophets, each part of the exhortation containing an assurance of salvation by way of encouragement. Rhetorically the words are marked by poetic parallelism, but lack any opening or concluding messenger formula. It appears to carry an allusion to other biblical material (cf. Isa. 7:9b).

Contents

Having responded to the divine, prophetic word as a good Davidide should, in humble submission (v. 18), praise and obedience (v. 19), and having led his people in just such a response (v. 19), Jehoshaphat, on the verge of battle, himself addresses the people. This royal address opens with the same call for attention, 'Hear me!', that marks the great Davidic address to the leaders and warriors in assembly (I 28:2), King Abijam to Jeroboam and the people of the North (II 13:4), and Hezekiah to the Levites (II 29:5). Only twice is it heard on the mouths of prophets (II 15:2, 28:11).[104] The faithful king always speaks at one with his illustrious ancestor, David. Though not cast in the form of a prophetic oracle, this message coincides exactly with the word of God, which does come through the prophets. We have found cause to believe, anyway, that the Chronicler regarded David as a great 'prophetic' figure.[105]

For one whose message is to call for belief in the divine word mediated through the prophets, Jehoshaphat adopts exemplary technique. He quotes from a prophet, Isaiah of Jerusalem. His message is, 'Trust in Yahweh your God and you will be supported', which echoes the play on the Heb /אמן found in Isa. 7:9, where the prophet addresses the doubting Ahaz, 'If you do not trust, surely you will not be supported.'

If this were an isolated instance of apparent citation from the canonical prophets, we might argue that two people had chanced on the same play on words. But since, as we have seen, such echoes of the prophets are a recurring feature of these addresses, it is difficult to attribute this to verbal chance. Yet what despair for those who insist on looking for 'historicity' in the Chronicler! Jehoshaphat quotes from a prophet who did not appear until a hundred years after his time! And such an historical absurdity should drive us to ask what point is really being made in this address. For the citation of Isaiah's oracle calling for trust in God is paralleled exactly by a call for 'trust in his prophets' (אמן/). They are God's prophets, and their significance is that they are a mouth-piece for the word of God. But more than a call for belief in the words of Jehoshaphat just uttered is being made. It is a call to belief in 'the prophets' in general, now become a 'body', surely well on the way to being regarded as a collection (corpus) of canonical and, by the quotation from Isa. 7:9, 'written' authorities for all matters of faith and conduct.[106] The prophets are shown to be so regarded elsewhere in the Chronicler's writing (e.g. II 36:15, significantly an addition at that point to the Kings material). They are similarly spoken of in Zech. 1:4 and 8:9. This point is made strongly by Seeligman. The citation of, and allusion to, the canonical prophets by the Chronicler and his citation of 'fictional' prophetic sources (e.g. I 29:29f.) show that for him the prophets had become 'a canonical corpus'.[107] Similarly, his reliance on prophetic sources may be said to make the point that he regarded the life of the post-exilic theocracy as a valid fulfilment of the promises of the earlier prophets.

The result of such faith is to be that 'you will succeed' (צלח/). This is a term used by the Chronicler several times to denote the successful completion of a God-given task which results in the well-being of the community (e.g. Solomon, II 7:11, Asa, II 14:7/6, Uzziah, 26:5, for as long as he sought God and followed the instructions of Zechariah; and Hezekiah, 31:21). This had been David's prayer for his son, Solomon (I 22:11). It will be fulfilled in the theocratic community if they observe the conditions for its realisation. Again, a king is shown to be acting as a true descendant of David, promoting the Davidic pattern for people and king. And this leads us to ask what the point of Jehoshaphat's short address may be. Why should the king speak when Jahaziel has already done so? Surely, the purpose of this address is to widen the application of the particular context and thrust of Jahaziel's prophecy? By the citation of Isa. 7:9 and the reference to the prophets as a canonical body through whom the authoritative word of God comes to his people at all times and on all occasions, the lesson is driven home to the Chronicler's contemporaries. The call is not for them to go out to battle against the Persians, or their more immediate antagonists. On the contrary, they need do nothing of an active military nature. It is God alone who gives victory of that kind in his own time. Meanwhile, they can get on with being the people of God, whose word for them is expressed in the (written) prophets. If they do that, God will give them 'success' in all their undertakings, and what content 'success' has may be left to him. A true Davidic king here generalises a particular word of God, showing beyond doubt that Jahaziel was called into being by the Chronicler, not in some spirit of historical quest, but in a spirit of pastoral concern for the well-being of the religious community of his own day, to point forward to that true fulfilment towards which the Davidic line pointed, and for which it paved the way.

[18] II 20:37 *Eliezer, the prophet, to Jehoshaphat*

37 *Then Eliezer, the son of Dodavahu from Moreshah, prophesied against Jehoshaphat and said, 'Because you made a treaty with Ahaziah, Yahweh has shattered[a] your designs.[b] The ships have been destroyed and have not been able to sail for Tarshish.'*

Text

[a] The tense of the verb is perfect, which usually denotes past action. If that is so here, Eliezer's words offer a theological explanation for a disaster which has already happened. If, however, it is an example of 'the prophetic perfect' which a prophet uses to denote a future action of God which is so certain that it can be spoken of as already having happened, then it is a prediction of judgement to come.

[b] Lit. 'your works'. This may refer to the actual ships and their construction and fitting, or, more figuratively, of Jehoshaphat's whole 'design' in this mercantile adventure. See discussion below.

General description

According to our interpretation of the verb פרץ (here 'to break up', 'shatter') as past or future either this is an announcement of judgement which opens in classical prophetic style with the grounds of accusation (37bα) but lacks the actual prediction of judgement (although there follows the narration of the fulfilment of the judgement, 37bβ), or the whole is an explanation of judgement already enacted. It is put in the category of prophecy by the use of the verb נבא / to describe Eliezer's words.

Contents

We have already seen how the Chronicler has depicted the reign of Jehoshaphat as a mixture of faithfulness and disobedience. One such act of disobedience was his military alliance with king Ahab of Israel in the battle against Ramoth-Gilead. He is, nevertheless, depicted in a more favourable light in II Chr. c. 18 than in the parallel I Kgs. c. 22, and the fact that he returned in 'peace' to his home in Jerusalem (19:1) was no doubt attributed to earlier trust in Yahweh, as the address of Jehu had made clear (vv. 2f.). After his dutiful and exemplary appointment of judicial officials and his charges to them (19:4–11), his conduct before the assault of the coalition at Engedi (20:1–30) and continuing, if not total, obedience throughout much of the rest of his reign (20:32ff.), we have a note of yet another alliance with Israel, this time in a mercantile, rather than a military venture, and with Ahaziah, the son of Ahab, his ill-starred former partner. This episode, whose narration (vv. 35–7) occurs as a kind of postscript following what looks like a concluding note to his reign (v. 34), also ends in disaster and also earns him the rebuke of a prophet.

One effect of the Chronicler's account of this incident, in comparison with that of Kings, is to highlight the alliance with Ahaziah, king of Israel. In Kings, it appears that Ahaziah offered help only after the destruction of Jehoshaphat's fleet at Ezion-geber (I Kgs. 22:49). It is true that Williamson, followed by Willi, argues that the Kings text could be interpreted differently by rendering the Hebrew אז as 'at that time' rather than 'then', and taking the perfect of the verb 'to say' as pluperfect, so reading '*At that time* Ahaziah *had said* to Jehoshaphat . . .'.[108] While this is possible, it is not, perhaps, the obvious rendering. Nevertheless, however it is read, the fact remains that the Chronicler has chosen to make the alliance explicit from the first and, by doing so, to highlight it as a theme of lack of trust. The sinking (literally) of the venture before it has even begun is seen as a judgement of God upon such disobedience, and the contrast with Solomon, all of whose ventures God had blessed, could hardly be greater. For, where Kings had narrated how Solomon had built a fleet at this very port of Ezion-geber which brought home great quantities of gold (I Kgs. 9:26–8) and told how he had a fleet of Tarshish ships at sea[109] which brought riches home triennially (I Kgs. 10:22), the Chronicler had expressly said that they had voyaged to Tarshish (II Chr. 9:21) and brought back the great wealth which showed God's blessing on the reign of Solomon. By contrast, Jehoshaphat's attempt to do the same never even started.

It might be held that, once again, the details of the specific name of a prophet, otherwise unknown, and of his father, together with the name of his town, suggest an authentic source for the Chronicler additional to that of Kings. But in this case also, the name of the prophet might be symbolic, for it means 'God is help.' The prophet's name matches his message to a remarkable degree. The town, Mareshah, by another chance, gives a forcible reminder of the contrast with Asa who, when confronted at the same place by the might of the Ethiopian army (19:9ff.), responded with faithful trust in God.

It seems, then, that the Chronicler has used the basic, bald statement found in Kings as the platform for another 'prophetic' address which had a message of wider relevance and appeal. The themes of obedience and disobedience, grace and judgement, show the people of God of all ages that they cannot rest on past right decisions and responses. To any tempted to make alliance, either for military, economic or any other purpose, with those who are not the people of God, the warning of Eliezer to Jehoshaphat remains pertinent.[110] Human activity, 'what you have made' (Heb. מַעֲשֶׂיךָ), is ineffective and doomed to frustration without trust in God's power and blessing. Another post-exilic 'preacher', Haggai, makes exactly the same point when he says, 'So it is with this people, and this nation . . . and so with all the work of their hands' (מַעֲשֵׂה יְדֵיהֶם , Hag. 2:14). We should remember also the overtones this term carries of contemptuous reference to idolatry, to the worship of gods who are 'the work of men's hands'.[111] The Chronicler elsewhere uses the phrase explicitly of idolatry (II 32:19). Alliance with those who are not God's people is no better than a form of idolatry.

[19] II 21:12–15 *Elijah, the prophet, to Jehoram (by letter)*

[12] *And a letter came to Jehoram from Elijah, the prophet. It ran, 'This is what Yahweh, the God of your father David, is saying: "You have not followed the ways of your father Jehoshaphat or Asa, king of Judah,* [13] *but have gone the way of the kings of Israel and seduced Judah and the people of Jerusalem into committing apostasy,ᵃ just like the apostasyᵃ of the house of Ahab. Indeed, you killed your*

brothers of your own father's house, who were more loyal[b] than you. [14]*For this Yahweh is going to afflict your people, your children, your wives, even all your possessions severely with terrible calamities.[c]* [15]*You yourself will know many diseases, especially disease of your bowels until gradually they rot."*[d]

Text

a The Hebrew verb means literally 'to fornicate' and is a symbol of religious apostasy.

b Lit. 'were better than you'.

c Lit. 'plagues' or 'afflictions'.

d The Hebrew is (perhaps deliberately) prosaic and pedantic. It reads, 'You [will have] many diseases with disease of your bowels until your bowels come out from the disease day after day.' Whatever exact details are meant it is neither a cheerful nor pleasant prognosis. In the way of the Chronicler, the prophetic prediction is fulfilled to the letter (vv. 16–19).

General description

This 'address', although in the form of a letter, follows more closely the classical structure of a prophetic announcement of judgement than any of the others. It opens with a messenger formula (12bα) which leads into a statement of the 'ground of accusation' (12bβ, 13), introduced by the Heb. כִּי , 'because' or 'since', following which the announcement of judgement (14f.) is introduced by הִנֵּה, 'Behold.' Westermann says that although in this 'oracle' earlier and later elements are mixed, 'one can presume that behind the Chronicler's work is an older, very short, and pregnant prophetic speech'.[112]

Contents

At first sight it may seem inconsistent to include what purports to be a 'letter' (Heb. מִכְתָּב, 'a writing') in a survey of the 'addresses' in Chronicles. However, even a brief examination of the letter shows that we are dealing here with the same genre as the 'prophetic' addresses.

We need not delay over the issue of whether Elijah could, or would, have sent a letter to Jehoram. The attempt to defend the historicity of the letter has led to such desperate shifts as to suggest a letter written and sent by supernatural means 'from the other side', or that Elijah wrote it before his death. Rudolph suggests that the phrase 'A letter came to him from Elijah', rather than 'Elijah wrote, or sent him a letter', may have fed such speculations (p. 267). While the chronology is just uncertain enough to forbid our dismissing it as an historical impossibility,[113] it remains extremely unlikely as an historical incident. But, as we shall see, it is the appearance in the letter of features which are characteristically those of the Chronicler that really shows much of it, at least, to be as much an 'invention' as the other addresses. What might seem to place this letter in a category of its own is not its fictional epistolary character, but its very direct and immediate relation to Jehoram and the circumstances of his reign. Yet we shall see that it does not lack features we have met elsewhere which give the apparently local and contextually determined address a wider and more universal reference and appeal, and to this the very 'written' form of the prophecy contributes in no small measure.

Again, there are some significant leads in the account of Jehoram's reign in the Deuteronomistic History for the Chronicler to develop. The unfavourable verdict recorded there is worded, 'And he walked in all the ways of the kings of Israel, as the house of Ahab had done, for the daughter of Ahab was his wife' (II Kgs. 8:18). It ascribes the fact that this did not lead to the same judgement as befell Israel to the grace of God 'for the sake of David his servant', to whom he had promised to give a 'lamp', both to him and to his sons for ever (v. 19). It further describes the revolt of Edom, giving an explanation for the puzzling apparent contradiction in the Chronicler's account (II 21:8–10) between the report that Jehoram 'smote' the surrounding Edomites and the statement that the Edomite revolt proved lastingly effective. By telling us that Jehoram's army 'fled home', the Deuteronomistic Historian shows that it was a case of the king's breaking out of the ring of Edomite forces so as to effect an escape but in no way to administer a military defeat. Kittel thinks the Chronicler omitted this information because it showed a Judaean army behaving in a cowardly manner.[114] This, while possible, is unlikely, since the Chronicler is aiming to show that Jehoram acted no better than a northern, Israelite king. Just as God miraculously gives victory in battle when a king trusts him, so he allows confusion and defeat to come to those who do not. It is more probable that this is an instance where the Chronicler assumes knowledge of earlier texts relating to the incident. He also ascribes to the grace of God the fact that the disaster was not total, but with a significant change of wording. Where Kings says that Yahweh would not destroy *Judah* 'for the sake of David his servant' (II Kgs. 8:19), Chronicles says that Yahweh would not destroy *the house of David*, 'because of the covenant he had made with David' (v. 7). The theocratic community, which we have seen to be the true manifestation of the Davidic line, is more important than the political, national entity of Judah.

It is impossible, for lack of evidence, to say whether the elaboration on the 'sins' of Jehoram and the resulting judgement of God in his illness recorded by the Chronicler have any historical foundation. The murder of his brothers and some leaders in Judah (v. 4, where 'Israel' must surely mean 'Judah' rather than referring literally to northern leaders resident and active in Judah) either because they opposed his religious policies[115] or, more likely, for political motives,[116] is not inherently improbable. Additional incursions from Philistines and Arabs (vv. 16f.) might be historical, but could be theological elaboration by the Chronicler on the theme of the totality of divine judgement. He did give similarly elaborated descriptions of invasions on other occasions, as when he adds to the account of the Syro/Ephraimite invasion against Ahaz in II Kgs. 16:5 (cf. Isa. 7:1) an invasion by the Philistines (II Chr. 28:18f.). He thus illustrated the theological motif indicated in the following verse, 'For the LORD brought Judah low because of Ahaz, king of Israel.' It may be recalled that, for the Chronicler, one sign of blessing on faithful kings was subjugation of the Philistines (David, I 11:14, Solomon, II 9:26, Jehoshaphat, 17:11, Uzziah, 26:7). Similarly, faithful kings exercised control over the Arabs (Solomon, II 9:14, Jehoshaphat, 17:11, Uzziah, 26:7). This leads one to expect elaboration on the hints provided by the Deuteronomistic History aimed at bringing out the doctrine of divine retribution and judgement for sin, rather than some additional historical source not used in Kings. Such a source is posited by Rudolph on grounds of a mixture of 'historical' and 'unhistorical' elements in vv. 12ff.[117] Similarly, a theologically motivated theme may lie behind the account of the illness by which Jehoram was struck and from which he died (vv. 18ff.). For, again, we have to note that some form of the / חלה, meaning 'illness' or 'wounding', befalls kings who come under the judgement of God. Asa's diseased feet were referred to in the Deuteronomistic History (I Kgs. 15:23), but it can be seen how the Chronicler draws a theological lesson from this. It came because he sought help from physicians rather than from God (II 16:12). By contrast, the curing of Hezekiah's illness, an illness also mentioned in the Deuteronomistic History (II Kgs. c. 20, where his humble prayer to God is seen as the *occasion* of God's healing him) is shown by the Chronicler in a quite explicit statement to have been *caused* by this very response of faith and trust: 'But Hezekiah humbled himself for the pride of his heart . . . *so that* the wrath of the LORD did not come upon them in the days of

Hezekiah' (II 32:24, 26). Unfaithful kings, however, can die of 'injuries', as did Saul (I 10:3), Joash (II 24:25) and Josiah (35:23).

Perhaps such a theological theme of judgement would also help to explain the difficulties raised by the carrying away by the Philistines and Arabs of 'all the possessions (הָרְכוּשׁ) they found that belonged to the king's house, and also his sons and wives' (v. 17). Did they capture these and, if so, where? Rudolph rightly says it is strange that, if Jerusalem was stormed at this time, there is no trace of it in Kings.[118] Did Jehoram offer them as tribute (cf. I Kgs. 20:5)? Again, how is it that Athaliah was left to make such a mark on subsequent history? And is not 22:1 a bit of patent harmonising?[119] Further, it is necessary to remember that 'sons' and 'possessions' are seen by the Chronicler as evidence of God's blessing on faithful kings. David ascribes his sons to God as a gift (I 28:5).[120] Solomon was famed for his 'possessions'. Similarly, God gave the faithful Hezekiah 'very great possessions' (רְכוּשׁ רַב מְאֹד, II 32:27). Jehoshaphat gained them after a victorious battle (II 20:25). It is certainly possible, then, that this daring and successful raid by the Philistines and Arabs represents the use of this blessing and judgement theme in reverse by the Chronicler rather than its being 'history' based on another source.

This is the place to notice another theological theme running through II Chr. c. 21. While some very specific charges are brought against Jehoram, the whole theme is made general, not only by the retention of the Deuteronomistic Historian's 'he did what was evil in the sight of the LORD' (v. 6), but because to a reference to the almost coventional 'high places' in Judah (v. 11) there is added the phrase 'and he seduced the inhabitants of Jerusalem into committing apostasy', using the Hiph'il of the verb/זנה, 'he caused them to commit fornication', and 'he led them astray' (Hiph'il of / נדה). Such a statement that the kings sinned themselves and thereby caused the people to sin is made often in the Deuteronomistic History. But there the characteristic verb is / כעס, the / זנה appearing only in Judges. In Judg. 2:17 it is used of religious apostasy in a general survey passage, 'they played the harlot after other gods'. In Judg. 8:27 it is used of Gideon and his ephod, and in v. 33 of the worship of the Ba'alim in general. But its chief use in the sense of 'apostasy' is in the book of the northern prophet, Hosea (e.g. 9:1). From there it passes into the vocabulary of Jeremiah and Ezekiel and, presumably, into the language of the Deuteronomists who make the editorial comments in Judges just cited. It is interesting, then, that elsewhere the Chronicler uses it of the *northern* tribe of Manasseh (I 5:25) while, in his account of that arch northern apostate, Jeroboam, he picks up the

Deuteronomistic Historian's use of the verb / נדה (II 13:9). The use of this term in II 21:11 and again in this letter (v. 13) suggests strongly that he saw Jehoram, a Judaean king of the Davidic line but related by marriage to the hated, apostate northern kingdom (v. 6), to be acting in a thoroughly 'northern' manner.

This provides a very strong reason for choosing Elijah, that scourge of the northern house of Omri, to deliver the rebuke from Yahweh that Jehoram was seen to deserve because of his treachery.[121] The letter picks up all the themes from the context in which it is set. Yahweh is especially bound to David (v. 12, cf. v. 7); Jehoram has acted in the way of the kings of Israel and, in particular, that wicked representative of the house of Omri, Ahab (v. 13, cf. v. 11). As a result judgement will come upon him by the reversal of all the traditional signs of God's blessing on faithful kings, 'children', 'wives', 'possessions' (v. 14, cf. v. 17) and he himself will die of disease (v. 15, cf. vv. 18f.). It is of course theoretically possible that the Chronicler picks these themes out of an historical document that had come to him. But since they recur so often in the addresses and elsewhere it is far more likely that the 'letter' has been invented to draw out the lessons of the whole episode.

Thus, for all its apparent specific references relating to the particular case of Jehoram, the letter is couched in such a way as to draw out theological lessons of a far more general and cautionary kind. Jehoram's particular acts represent a fearful warning against 'Israel-like' behaviour.[122] If ever the chosen kingdom of Judah falls into similar sins it too will know God's judgement in the removal of such signs of God's blessing as have characterised it, even if God's grace is such that it will not ultimately be swept away as Israel was.

Indeed, the very form of a 'letter', written by Elijah, fits such a generalising oracle of warning for all time. It is possible that the Chronicler wanted, for reasons stated above, to introduce Elijah as the messenger of God who had challenged the house of Omri in the North, as messenger now to Jehoram. A Judaean Jehoram may have been, but he was related by marriage to that house of Omri and was perpetrator of its ways in the South. Even he realised that it was very unlikely that Elijah would have confronted Jehoram directly, and so he introduced the convention of a letter. But Ackroyd takes us deeper here. By the Chronicler's time, much of the prophetic 'corpus' must have existed already in writing. We have seen how 'the prophets' could be appealed to virtually as a canonical 'corpus', belief in whom was equated with belief in God (II 20:20). Here is the Chronicler's recognition that the words of prophecy, once spoken in particular situations and historical contexts, had received validity and continuing life for all times and for all peoples by their committal to writing. Ackroyd draws attention to Zech. 1:4–6 at this point.[123] This means that the very 'written' form of this prophetic word to Jehoram is part of the means by which it is given reference on a much wider scale and becomes the word of God to the Chronicler's own contemporaries. It is now 'preached' to them with all the urgency and call for response in the light of a particular historical illustration from their past as the people of God. 'Northernness' is a constant temptation to God's people. Let them take the warning and remain faithful to God and obedient to his word, which is binding for all time.

[20] II 24:20–2 *Zechariah, son of Jehoida the priest (a priest?), to Joash and the people*

[20] *And the spirit of God took possession[a] of Zechariah, the son of Jehoida, the priest, and he stood above the people and said to them, 'This is what God is saying: "Why do you keep transgressing the commandments of Yahweh? You will not prosper. When you forsake Yahweh he forsakes you."'* [21] *And they conspired against him and stoned him to death in the temple courtyard by command of the king.* [22] *And Joash the king did not remember the kindness Jehoida, Zechariah's father, had shown him, but killed the son. And as Zechariah died he cried out, 'May Yahweh see and exact justice!'*

Text

[a] Heb. lit. 'the spirit of God clothed itself with Zechariah'.

General description

This address consists of a prophetic denunciation and announcement of judgement. It is introduced by a prophetic narrative formula (20a) and the messenger formula (20bα). The ground of accusation takes the form of a rhetorical question which itself 'cites' Scripture (20bβ), and this is followed by an announcement of future, or declaration of present, judgement (20bγ, c). This is characterised by a play on the word 'forsake' which shows how God's judgement corresponds exactly to their sin. The final words of Zechariah are an imprecation (22bβ).

Contents

This is one of the shortest addresses of its kind in Chronicles but, in its context in the account of the reign of Joash, it illustrates with great clarity both the Chronicler's methods and some of the main themes of his theology. There are several significant features in the account of Joash's reign in this chapter. The statement in Kings that 'Joash did what was right in the eyes of the LORD all his days because Jehoida the priest instructed him' (II Kgs 12:2) becomes 'And Joash did what was right in the eyes of the LORD all the days of Jehoida the priest' (II 24:2). The account of the reign which follows divides sharply into two phases: the first is one of faithfulness to Yahweh while Jehoida was alive (vv. 1–14); the second is one of apostasy (vv. 17–27) following the death of Jehoida (vv. 15f.). The reasons for such a schematised version of the reign are not difficult to detect. Once more he has a mixed account of a king in the Deuteronomistic History which gives Joash a favourable verdict yet records that 'the high places were not taken away: the people continued to sacrifice and burn incense on the high places' (II Kgs. 12:3). Further, a defeat, or at best an incomplete victory, is recorded. Hazael of Syria had to be bought off with a tribute comprising treasures from the temple when he marched against Jerusalem (II Kgs. 12:17f.). Again, Joash was murdered in a conspiracy involving his servants (vv. 19–21). Thus the Chronicler, who sees such events as judgements from God, must show reasons why such divine retribution took place. In doing so, he can offer yet another illustration of his theme of mixed piety and apostasy, blessing and judgement in the reign of individual kings.[124]

Such mixed fortunes demonstrate the Chronicler's theology of the *immediacy* of divine judgement both for good and ill, a theology which is both admonitory and helpful, since penitence, even when shown by the evil, always encounters grace. There is a word here for his contemporaries. Finally, he seizes on the hint in the Deuteronomistic History of the important role played by Jehoida the priest in this reign, no doubt because of the circumstances in which Joash as a baby had been snatched from Athaliah's purge. It is clear that Jehoida played a significant part because the boy became king at his direction at the age of seven. By highlighting and magnifying this role the Chronicler can show the importance of the priesthood from a time as early as that of the monarchy. Jehoida, even after his death, has the last word, for Zechariah, who brings God's word to the, by then, apostate Joash, is Jehoida's son (II Chr. 24:20, 22).

The chapter is full of interesting inversions and other points of literary structure. While the king 'listens' to Jehoida, all is well. Indeed, the gift of wives, sons and daughters is a traditional sign of God's blessing (see pp. 76f. above).[125] But later he 'listens' to the princes of Judah (v. 17) and, in death, is robbed of all his kingdom. His concern for the well-being of the house of God in the earlier phase is followed later by his 'forsaking the house of the LORD' (v. 18). Indeed, the play on the word 'forsake' in vv. 18, 24, is matched by the play on the same word in Zechariah's address (v. 20), thus strongly suggesting that the address is the Chronicler's own composition with the needs of the context in mind. Again, the contrast between the honoured death and burial of Jehoida (vv. 15f.) and the ignominious death and burial of Joash (vv. 24f.) cannot be missed. The 'conspiracy' against Zechariah by the people, but especially by the king (v. 21), is matched exactly by the 'conspiracy' of the king's servants against him (vv. 25f.), while there is irony in the charge by Zechariah that the people are 'transgressing the commandments of Yahweh' (מִצְוֹת) while acting on the king's 'command' (מִצְוַת) in killing the priest.

The address of Zechariah is prefaced by a very general statement on the place of prophecy in the history of the nation: 'And he sent prophets among them to restore them to Yahweh, and they bore testimony against them. But they paid no heed' (v. 19). This can hardly refer to the particular historical context of Joash's reign. It is unlikely that the Chronicler intends us to understand that a plethora of prophets suddenly became active at this one juncture of Judah's history. It is, rather, a general comment on the entire history of God's people, somewhat akin to the statement in Zech. 1:4. Its function is to 'generalise' the particular words of Zechariah addressed, purportedly, to this one time and set of historical circumstances. It shows how this is to be seen as but one instance in the continuing ministry of those who can now be referred to as 'prophets' in general. Its effect is to relate the address of Zechariah to later generations who, in their historical circumstances, might also be tempted to yield to pressures to apostasy and faithlessness and feel that the words of individual prophets, spoken long ago, had no particular force for them now. On the contrary, the message of the 'prophets' must be 'heeded' and 'obeyed' at all times. Otherwise the judgement which came on king and people in the time of Joash will come also upon their generation. Past faithfulness will not stand them in credit any more than Joash's did once he abandoned Jehoida's teaching, teaching now passed on by the 'priestly' oracle. For, in the Chronicler's time, the priests are the true descendants and heirs to the prophets.

The address of Zechariah is introduced as authentic prophecy, 'The spirit of God took possession of Zechariah', a phrase echoing the description of Gideon's spirit-possession in Judg. 6:34. The Chronicler has used it elsewhere of Amasai (I 12:18/19). This, together with the messenger formula 'This is what God is saying . . .', puts Zechariah firmly in the (charismatic) prophetic tradition and vests his words with prophetic authority. We are not told whether he himself was a priest or not. As Jehoida's son, however, he is surely fulfilling the dramatic role of being Jehoida's mouth-piece. Thus the priestly line, with its preaching and admonition, is the divinely appointed custodian of the prophetic role and authority. The original promise to Moses (Deut. 18:15ff.) is not broken, and how significant it is that this address expounds a word of Moses, 'Why are you transgressing the commandment of Yahweh? For you cannot prosper' (Hiph'il of / צלח)! In Num. 14:41 Moses asks the people, 'Why are you transgressing the commandment [lit. the 'mouth'] of Yahweh? For that will not succeed' (Hiph'il / צלח). This occurs in a context of disobedience by the people who long to return to Egypt, for which they are doomed to be defeated in battle if they march against the Amalekites and Canaanites. In the defeat which the Chronicler sees to have been implicit in the Deuteronomistic History's account of Joash's tribute to Hazael, he finds a close analogy to the situation outlined in Num. c. 14, and the prophet/priest brings the same word as Moses with renewed relevance. But the generalising of the whole oracle means that the Chronicler sees the real analogy as being to his own day. Possibly, even the gratuitous detail that Joash stood 'above' (מֵעַל) the people while addressing them (v. 20) drives home the divine authority with which his words are vested. For, according to the Priestly Code, God himself speaks 'from above' the 'kapporeth' between the cherubim (Exod. 25:22, Num. 7:89), something recalled in Ezek. 1:25, where God speaks to Ezekiel 'from above' (מֵעַל) the firmament over the heads of the creatures of the throne chariot, the counterpart of 'kapporeth' and cherubim away in exile in Babylon. It is even possible that the description of Zechariah's position as he addressed the people reflects the position of those who spoke to the people in God's name in the second temple from some kind of platform or 'pulpit' (cf. Neh. 8:4).

We note again not only the citation of 'Scripture' in this address, but the effective rhetorical device of play on words in the statement 'When you forsake Yahweh he forsakes you' (v. 20).

The 'stoning' of the prophet Zechariah becomes symbolic in the tradition of the continued rejection of the prophets by successive generations of the people of God in exactly the way the Chronicler intended (II Chr. 36:15f., cf. Matt. 23:35–7). Further, we should note the plural form of address which is directed ostensibly to the 'people' (v. 20), whereas the context demands that it was the king and, at most, the 'princes of Judah' (vv. 17f.) who were guilty. In this way the reference of the address has again been widened to a much larger audience.

Finally we should note the irony of Zechariah's dying words, 'May Yahweh see and exact justice!' The use of the Hebrew / דרש, 'to enquire into', 'to seek out', is striking. For /דרש is the word used so often, especially in the writings of the Chronicler, for 'seeking God'. Often the kings are charged with not 'seeking Yahweh' (e.g. Saul, I 10:14, Asa, II 16:12, Jehoshaphat, in a favourable sense, 17:3f., Amaziah, 25:15). If a king like Joash does not 'seek Yahweh', there will come a time when Yahweh will 'seek' him out in vengeance. The imprecation of the priest/prophet Zechariah proves effective, as the sequel bears out all too clearly. Again, the warning for all later generations is made plain by such 'preaching' in the Chronicler tradition.

[21] II 25:7–9 *A 'man of God' to Amaziah*

⁷And a man of God came to Amaziah and said, 'O king, do not let the Israelite army go with you, for Yahweh is not with Israel, not, indeed, with any of the Ephraimites. ⁸If you do go [even though] you act resolutely in the battle, God will cast you down before the enemy,ᵃ for God is able to help and to cast down.' ⁹And Amaziah said to the man of God, 'But what is to be done about the hundred talents I have paid to the Israelite troops?' And the man of God said, 'Yahweh is able to give you far more than this.'

Text

ᵃ The Hebrew reads literally, 'But if you are going, be strong for war: God will cast you down before the enemy.' Some have suggested reading it as a question, 'Why are you going and making yourself strong, for God will cast you down?'[126] Curtis reads a negative before the verb, 'But go [without them] and be strong for war, for God will not cast you down.'[127] We have suggested that the sense is ironic, especially as the verb rendered 'be strong' or 'act resolutely' is /חזק, a verb we have so often seen in the calls to action for God's service. We could paraphrase, 'If you go [that is, with Israelite help] act as resolutely as you will in what you imagine to be God's service, God will in fact be against you.' Fortunately the sense is clear however we deal with the difficulties of the text.

General description

After a narrative introduction (7a) the address opens with a prophetic admonition against military alliance (7bc). There follows what appears to be, for all the difficulty of the text (see above), a threat of judgement (8ab). Two prophetic announcements of God's power follow, one to assure of his power to fulfil his threat (8c) and the other, in answer to the king's objection, of his power to fulfil his promise (9c). The rhetorical device of play on words occurs by the double use of the preposition 'with' (v. 7).

Contents

With Amaziah we have yet another instance where the Chronicler found a mixed notice of a king in his Deuteronomistic *Vorlage* of good fortune and bad. Of him II Kgs. 14:3f. says, 'And he did what was right in the eyes of the LORD, yet not like David his father: he did in all things as Joash his father had done. But the high places were not removed; the people still sacrificed and burned incense on the high places.' Presumably the Deuteronomistic Historian saw his avenging of his father's death in a favourable light. Perhaps this was because it was tempered by obedience to the Deuteronomic law limiting legal responsibility to the perpetrators of a crime, and not extending it to their descendants (Deut. 24:16). This favourable view is reproduced by the Chronicler. Amaziah's dramatic and bloody victory over Edom is briefly recorded in II Kgs. 14:7. But his persistence in a campaign against the northern kingdom of Israel led to defeat by Jehoash of Israel, a defeat which resulted in a destruction of part of the walls of Jerusalem, the seizure of tribute from the temple and the taking of hostages. Jehoash's fable of the thistle and cedar of Lebanon, charging Amaziah with pride, seems to be cited by the Deuteronomistic editor as though it were a word of God and as the reason for his judgement. Fifteen years later he faces a conspiracy against him which drives him to Lachish where, however, his conspirators catch him and kill him. Finally, he has at least the honour of having been buried in Jerusalem (cf. Josiah, II Kgs. 23:30).

This 'mixed bag' of faithfulness and disobedience is, then, again the basic theme on which the Chronicler elaborates, not least in the two addresses delivered to Amaziah, this one by a 'man of God' and the other by a 'prophet' in vv. 15f. The Chronicler adds considerable detail in his account of the Edomite campaign including, crucially, the fact that Amaziah hired one hundred thousand mercenaries from the northern kingdom of Israel (v. 6). It is difficult to be sure whether the Chronicler is here drawing on any particular historical source not used by the editor of the Books of Kings. The case for this has been strongly urged by Junge.[128] Others have felt there to be some historical fact behind this because of the supposed conflict between Amaziah's obedience to the word spoken through the man of God in vv. 7–9 and yet the judgement which befell him because of the discontent of these very mercenaries. Presumably this was because, although they had been paid their wages, by their dismissal before the battle they had no share in the spoils of war.[129] But against this we must notice the fantastic numbers said to have been involved. Further, the Chronicler, as we have seen, often employs this theme of mixed obedience and disobedience accompanied by blessing and judgement. In this case judgement can be explained, not only by the fact that Amaziah even toyed with the idea of military alliance with Israel, but by the (surely unhistorical) notice that he brought back the gods of the Edomites to Jerusalem (v. 14). Indeed, the two addresses taken together, as we shall see, serve the purpose of illustrating both acceptance and rejection of God's word. It would be possible to argue the other way and maintain that the story of the bringing back of the Edomite gods was itself invented by the Chronicler to explain the awkward fact of the damage inflicted by the disgruntled Israelite mercenaries. But the Chronicler is perfectly capable of just omitting whatever does not suit his theological purposes. It is just as likely that he felt that the mixed blessing and judgement which marked this part of Amaziah's reign marked all of it, so that all his victories were partial yet none of his disgrace was complete.[130] Certainty here is not possible, but, whatever the situation, it is the theology of the passage which is important rather than its 'history'.

That theology is expressed by the man of God whose words denounce any reliance on the help of those who do not know the 'presence' of God (v. 7). We note immediately the rhetorical device of play on words so familiar to these addresses:

O king, do not let the Israelite army go *with* you,
For Yahweh is not *with* Israel.

The importance of the concept of Yahweh's being 'with' people, both in the sense of offering his presence to them and bestowing his help and favour on them, has already been discussed, especially in the comments on II 13:4–11, where it is also the main theme of Abijah's address. Clearly it is a favourite theme of the Chronicler's, for whom this 'man of God' must be the mouth-piece at this point. Perhaps we should note the irony of the fact that, in his writing, the preposition 'with' can also indicate being 'against' someone. To fight 'with' someone can mean fighting against them.[131]

The general principle stated in the address that it is God who by his power (כֹּחַ) 'casts down' (Hiph. /כשל) and 'helps' (עזר) is itself an echo of other Scriptures. One is reminded of Lam. 1:14, where the fall of Jerusalem and the consequent exile are described thus:

> He caused my strength to fail
> (הִכְשִׁיל כֹּחִי);
> The LORD gave me into the hands
> of those whom I cannot withstand.

The same verb is used in this address, 'God will cast you down before the enemy' (יַכְשִׁילְךָ). The theme is echoed also in the Chronicler's denunciation of Ahaz, who turned to the gods of Syria because, he said, 'they will help me' (עזר/). But 'they proved his downfall' and that of all Israel (וְהֵם הָיוּ לוֹ לְהַכְשִׁילוֹ , II 28:23). So, whether this is exposition of known Scriptures such as Lam. 1:14 or not, it is a general theme of the Chronicler's that God helps or casts down his people according to their trust in him alone, whereas other gods do exactly the reverse for those who trust them. Again we see what appears to be a specific word in a concrete situation made into a general truth for all times.

Amaziah's somewhat pragmatic objection that it seems a pity to waste the good money which he has already paid to the Israelite mercenaries gets short shrift from the man of God. 'Yahweh is able (lit. it is God's property (יֵשׁ לַיהוה)) to give you far more than this.' This strange construction may evoke earlier passages. In Gen. 33:11 Jacob urges Esau to accept his gift because he has 'everything' (יֶשׁ לִי כֹל). This is so because God has dealt graciously with him. The one through whom God's line of promise runs can give to one who is not in this line because of God's generosity. Possibly there is also some echo of the theme of the prophetic narrative of Elijah in I Kgs. 17:12, perhaps repeated in an alternative form of Elisha (II Kgs. 4:1–7). In I Kgs. 17:12 the widow complains to Elijah in response to his request for food that she has very little left (אִם־יֶשׁ לִי מָעוֹג). Elijah assures her, however, that she can spare it in obedience to a word of God spoken through a prophet, for she will find that all her needs continue to be met. Always there are those who urge practical difficulties and expediency as arguments against following what seems an idealistic line of obedience to God's call for non-reliance on human resources. In answer to such doubts the man of God assures Amaziah, and through him the Chronicler assures his contemporaries, that they can look to

God to supply all their needs as his faithful people have done at all times. It is an echo of Haggai's words of assurance to those who doubted the possibility of rebuilding the temple:

'"The silver is mine and the gold is mine" says the LORD of Hosts.' *(Hag. 2:8, cf. Zech. 8:9–13)*.

It appears that this was a theme familiar to the 'preaching' of the second temple.

[22] II 25:15f. *A 'prophet' to Amaziah*

¹⁵ *And Yahweh was angry with Amaziah and he sent a prophet to him who said, 'Why have you prayed to the gods of the nations who have not delivered their own people from your power?'* ¹⁶ *But while he was speaking the king said to him, 'Who made you an adviser to the king? Be quiet. Do you want to get hurt?' So the prophet stopped prophesying, but he added, 'I know God has determined to destroy you because you have acted in this way and have not listened to my counsel.'*

General description

A prophetic narrative of dialogue with a hearer, somewhat akin to such passages as Amos 7:10–17, the whole forming a threat of judgement. After introductory narrative (15a) the ground of accusation occurs as a question (15b). The announcement of judgement in 16b follows the account of the king's repudiation of the prophet and his message and his threat of bodily harm to him (16a). There is play on the word 'counsel'. The kings asks in scorn who made the prophet a royal 'counsellor' ('adviser') (16a). Irony marks the response which announces judgement because the king had not listened to what was, in fact, God's 'counsel' (16b).

Contents

The address of the unnamed 'prophet' to Amaziah after he had 'sought' (/דרש) the Edomite gods recalls another prophetic narrative, that recorded in II Kgs. c. 1, of Elijah's reproach to king Ahaziah when he sent for an oracle to Baal-zebub, god of Ekron, concerning his chances of recovery following an accident. Elijah said, 'Is it because there is no God in Israel that you are sending to enquire (/דרש) of Baal-zebub?' The fate of Ahaziah would probably have been well known in the Chronicler's time, and the implication here is that it illustrates the timelessness of such warnings against flirtation with the cults of gods other than Yahweh. The irony of it is driven home here (and the close connection between the two addresses to Amaziah is also underlined) by the fact that these gods failed to 'deliver' their own people from Amaziah himself, whereas the true God had demonstrated that it was he alone who had power to 'help' or 'cast down'. Beyond the ironic play on the word 'counsel' within the address noted above, there is irony in the king's rejecting what was in fact God's 'counsel' but taking instead the 'counsel' of those who gave false counsel (v. 17). It is a case, as Rudolph has said, of whom the gods wish to destroy they first make mad.[132] But the lesson of the whole incident is the folly of turning to any source of help other then Yahweh, whether it is to apparently powerful nations for practical help, or for the counsel of those who are shown not to be true prophets of Yahweh. The corollary of this is the attempt to stop the witness of a true prophet (v. 16) by threats. Yet this is impossible also, for the 'silenced' prophet still brings the effective word of God's judgement. That word cannot be avoided by attempts to muzzle the messenger. By this means the Chronicler welds the whole reign of Amaziah, the Edomite wars, the defeat by Israel, and the outbreak of rebellion at home (protracted for all the remaining fifteen years of his life, according to the Chronicler, vv. 27f.), into a single whole, illustrating a unified theological concept of prophecy accepted and prophecy rejected.

P. R. Ackroyd has seen in this passage a very interesting thematic link with two other accounts of an altercation between a king (or a king's priest, another Amaziah) and a prophet. These occur in Amos 7:10–17 and in I Kgs. 13:1–10 (a passage which has certain parallels with the Amos tradition). The Amos and Kings traditions have the name Jeroboam in common, and the Amos and Chronicles passages the name Amaziah. Each relates an attempt to silence a prophet which recoiled on the head of the king who attempted it. Ackroyd says,

The natural inference is that the Chronicler was making use of a form of the same tradition which we have seen in the other two passages: this tradition preserved the name of Amaziah, and so the Chronicler attached it in a suitable position to his account of the king of that name. It provides a good example of the Chronicler's exegetical method.[133]

So perhaps all three passages share the larger theme of apostasy in the northern kingdom and the assurance of doom on all who try to deflect the true will of God and the mediator of his word.

All this suggests that the purpose of these addresses in II Chr. c. 25, so closely bound in theme, in theology and in their function in the Chronicler's shaping of the reign of Amaziah, is yet again to take the particular and relate its general truths to the Chronicler's later situation. How often in the era of post-exilic theocracy must there have been temptation to be open to the cults of apparently powerful and successful nations, and how often must the temptation to take some short-cut method to political independence by the expedient military alliance have proved attractive! It must have been a real task of the preaching in the second temple to warn against just such dangers and to show that the blessing or judgement which followed acceptance or rejection of God's word at various stages of the people's earlier history had relevance and force still. Such warning appears, for example, in Zech. 4:6b–10a, while another theme of these addresses, God's ability to provide the economic and material needs of those who are faithful, is heard again in Hag. 2:8, Zech. 8:9–13 and Mal. 3:6–13.

[23] II 26:17f. *Azariah, the priest, to Uzziah*

[17] *And Azariah, the priest, accompanied by eighty courageous priests, went in after him,* [18] *and they stood out against Uzziah the king, and said to him, 'It is not for you, Uzziah, to offer sacrifice to Yahweh but for the Aaronite priests who have been consecrated for this office. Leave the sanctuary, for you have acted treacherously. This will bring you no honour from the* LORD *God.'*

General description

A disputation saying in which Azariah challenges the right of the king to usurp the priestly prerogative of offering sacrifice.

Contents

Just as the Chronicler had shown that the reign of Uzziah's father, Amaziah, divided into two parts, of faithfulness and disobedience, blessing and judgement, the turning-point being marked by a warning from a 'prophet', so he patterns Uzziah's reign in the same way. Again, the Deuteronomistic History supplies him with a mixed report to justify his schema. Uzziah was said there to have reigned for fifty-two years, such a long reign being a sure sign of God's blessing, yet 'the LORD smote the king, so that he was a leper to the day of his

death' (II Kgs. 15:5). Once more, therefore, the Chronicler is able to introduce his teaching that only constant faithfulness brings continued blessing
and prosperity. No one can take God for granted. His people need constant
vigilance against apostasy.

The Chronicler's vocabulary is seen here in his twice-repeated use of the
verb 'to act treacherously' (Heb. /מעל, v. 16), the word thus firmly setting the
'address' of Azariah in its context. His theology is heard because Uzziah's
hubris (lit. 'his heart became tall', v. 16) brings judgement. He failed to show
the humble trust and obedience of the ideal Davidic king.

The actual nature of his 'sin' is surprising only if we try to look for some
'historical' fact behind this episode, or for some earlier historical record on
which the Chronicler was drawing.[134] In pre-exilic times it it clear that kings
did officiate in the cult, including the making of sacrifices.[135] This claim to the
exclusive right of the priesthood in the cult is post-exilic and is made only in
late texts.[136] The 'address' of Azariah, in its way, strengthens the impression
that, for the Chronicler, the post-exilic temple community, with its properly
ordained leaders, was the true and legitimate heir to the Davidic line.

[24] II 28:9–11 *Oded, the prophet, to the army of Israel*

[9] *Now there was a prophet of Yahweh there called Oded, and he came out to meet
the army as they were marching to Samaria and said to them, 'It was because of the
anger of Yahweh, the God of your fathers, against Judah, that he delivered them
into your power. But you have slaughtered them with a savagery which has
reached to heaven.* [10] *Even now, you are planning to submit the Judaeans, both men
and women, to slavery to you. Have you not sins of your own against Yahweh, your
God?* [11] *Now, hear me! Set free the captives you have taken from your own
kinsmen, for Yahweh's anger burns against you.'*

General description

A prophetic call for repentance with a threat of judgement or, possibly, an
explanation of judgement already experienced. After a narrative introduction
(9a) there follows the ground of accusation denouncing the Israelite army for
the savagery of their treatment of the Judaeans (9b) and their intention to
enslave those who are their brothers (10a). All this only adds to sins already
committed (10b), sins unspecified but presumably referring to the North's
secession from the house of David and the Jerusalem temple. The announce-

ment of judgement in 11b (or explanation of judgement already falling on the Israelites) is the basis of the call for repentance (11a). The address utilises the rhetorical question (10b). There is interplay between the concept of God's righteous 'anger' against both Judah and Israel and Israel's unnatural anger against their kinsmen, the Judaeans.

Contents

There are several interesting variants in the Chronicler's account of the reign of king Ahaz from that given in II Kgs. 16 and, indeed, the glimpses given in Isa. 7.[137] The Deuteronomistic Historian's totally unfavourable view of him is here intensified in a number of ways. To the general statement of II Kgs. 16:3 that 'Ahaz walked in the way of the kings of Israel', which becomes in Chronicles a plural, 'the ways of the kings of Israel', he adds the specific charge that 'he made molten images for the Ba'alim' (28:2). The Kings statement that 'he burned his son as an offering' the Chronicler again makes plural, 'he burned his sons', thus suggesting that this was a regular practice, as Coggins remarks.[138] A different account of historical events is also found. Where Kings and Isa. 7 imply a combined campaign against Judah by both Israel and Syria, the Chronicler suggests they were distinct and sequential and their results together more devastating. The Syrians took a great number of captives back with them, while Israel slew 120,000 Judahites, including the king's son (an ironic touch concerning a king who was in the habit of sacrificing his own sons), the commanders of the palace and the king's own deputy. The Kings account says that, while the invaders put Ahaz under siege, 'they could not conquer him', although Isa. 7 suggests the extreme gravity of his situation (a gravity perhaps implied by Kings by the necessity of Ahaz's appeal to Tiglath-Pileser, the king of Assyria). Where Kings speaks simply of a successful Edomite rebellion against some Judaean cities (II Kgs. 16:6), the Chronicler tells us more positively that they invaded and defeated Judah (v. 17) and adds an account of serious and successful raids by the Philistines against Judaean settlements in the Shephelah and the Negeb (v. 18).

Further, where Kings tells us that Ahaz appealed to the king of Assyria for help, help which had to be bought certainly, but which was forthcoming in a campaign against Syria (II Kgs. 16:7–9), the Chronicler tells us that Tiglath-Pileser came *against* Ahaz, and not even the payment of (forced) tribute helped his cause (vv. 20f.). Finally, there are significant differences in the two accounts of Ahaz's cultic measures. At II Kgs. 16:10–18 they are recounted with sufficient neutrality to leave modern commentators in doubt how they are intended to be understood. Some see them as apostasy, followed by political subversion,[139] while others see them only as a kind of aesthetically motivated attempt to emulate Near Eastern cultic patterns, the cult of Yahweh already having been strongly influenced by ancient Near Eastern influences of all kinds.[140] There can, however, be no possible doubt left by the Chronicler's account (vv. 22–5), where Ahaz's foreign importation and his alterations to the temple and its precincts are seen as downright apostasy.

There has been the usual scholarly discussion as to whether these variants in the Chronicler's narrative are his own invention or are based on (reliable) alternative historical sources. It is impossible to be certain, but two observations may be made. The effect of the changes is to make Ahaz's sin and its consequences more total (leaving aside vv. 8–15 for the present). That this is the Chronicler's aim is supported by his two explicit theological statements. Pekah attacks 'because they had forsaken the LORD, the God of their fathers' (v. 6). Again, 'For the LORD brought Judah low because of Ahaz king of Israel, for he had dealt wantonly in Judah and had been faithless to the LORD' (v. 19). The success of the Syrian attack leads Ahaz to sacrifice to the gods of Syria, for they 'helped him' (v. 23, an ironic contrast to his own tribute to the king of Assyria – 'it did not help him', v. 21). In fact 'they were the ruin of him and all Israel' (v. 23). Thus, as Ackroyd suggests, the two separate attacks of the Syrians and Israelites may well be a device to underline the judgement theme.[141] Such an approach seems to fit the nature of the material much better than attempts such as Williamson's to establish alleged historical sources behind all this because, according to him, the present shape is 'not demanded by the Chronicler's message'.[142]

Another point needs to be made, however. Vv. 8–15, the prophecy of Oded, the call by certain leaders of Israel and the response of the people of the North, occupy a central place (literally and thematically) in the Chronicler's account of the reign of Ahaz. Since, by its very nature, it concerns Israel as the (apostate) 'brethren' of Judah, it would have lost much of its force if it had been related of the people of Syria as well as Israel as in other accounts of the Syro-Ephraimite invasion. This may offer another reason why their invasions are recounted as separate events.

The section comprising vv. 8–15 is marked out clearly as a separate unit in this chapter, partly by its nature as a narrative, offering a framework for the address of Oded, itself reinforced by the words of the Israelite leaders repudiating the excessive actions of their military compatriots, but partly also, as Rudolph points out,[143] because it relieves the picture of total disaster for Judah which is otherwise found throughout c. 28. Rudolph, with Williamson, thinks that this episode must rest on some historical source because it reflects what is otherwise an uncharacteristically favourable attitude to the people of the North, and because of the circumstantial nature of the list of the names of the leaders in v. 12. However, it is not clear that the source is 'pro-northern'. Israel also is shown to be under God's rightful judgement apart from this their present action (vv. 10, 11b). Further, she may have been chosen by God as his instrument for judgement on this occasion, but has overstepped her divinely set limits, acting in the heat of her own vengeance. There have been precedents for God's judgement against nations who have acted in this way. One has only to recall the attack which Isaiah made on Assyria (10:7, 12ff.). Nations which act like this will bring God's 'wrath' upon them. Nor can we assume that a list of names guarantees some authentic source. Such a list in descriptions of the response of people to the word of God in the framework of a prophetic oracle is a phenomenon we encounter elsewhere in these addresses and in other passages in Chronicles (e.g. II 15:8ff., 19:11, 29:12ff.) as well as in Haggai and Zechariah (e.g. Hag. 1:12f., Zech. 6:9ff.).[144]

It is not clear that Oded was a northerner. It is simply said, 'There was a prophet of Yahweh . . .' (v. 9). We have noted that the northerners do not act in mercy without a stern word of warning from this prophet of Yahweh. It is the Chronicler who speaks of the Judaeans as the 'kinsmen' of the Israelites (vv. 8, 15), and Oded stresses the point (v. 11). This seems to be in accord with the law in the Code of Holiness (Lev. 17–26) which forbids the enslaving of fellow-Israelites, while allowing for the purchase of *male* and *female* slaves from surrounding nations, and even of foreign sojourners in Israel (Lev. 25:44ff.), but not from 'your brethren the people of Israel' (v. 46). There is an interesting echo of this law in Oded's statement concerning the subjugation of the people of Judah and Jerusalem as *male* and *female* slaves (v. 10). This same law in 'H', in different terminology, forbids them to rule over fellow-Israelites with 'harshness' (Heb. בְּפֶרֶךְ) – terminology peculiar to the Code of Holiness and the Priestly Code. Oded uses the Heb. כבש/ of their intended suppression of the Judaeans to slavery. The same word is used by Nehemiah of the enslavement of fellow-Israelites (Neh. 5:5, where, again, 'sons' and 'daughters' are specifically mentioned). It also occurs in the very interesting passage in Jer. 34:8–22. According to this (probably Deuteronomistic) passage,

Zedekiah had entered into a covenant with the people of Jerusalem that each should set free his male and female Hebrew slaves, so that 'no one should enslave a Jew, his brother'. The passage narrates their subsequent failure to keep this promise and how this brings an oracle from Jeremiah of strong condemnation (vv. 12–22).

Oded, then, is an exponent both of law and of the prophetic word. In this, his words here fit exactly with the addresses we have already considered. Through him the earlier prophets speak again. His words bring to the congregation of the Chronicler's day the same charge not to repeat the sins of their fathers by repudiating that word for, if they do, they will bring the same judgement on their heads.

[25] II 28:12f. *Some Israelite leaders to the army of Israel*

[12] *And some men from the leaders of the Israelites, Azariah the son of Johanan, Berechiah the son of Meshillemoth, Jehizkiah the son of Shallum and Amasa the son of Hadlai, stood up against those who were returning from the war.* [13] *They said to them, 'You are not to bring the captives here. To our present guilt before Yahweh you intend to add further guilt. But our guilt is already great and Yahweh's[a] wrath burns against us.'*

Text

[a] Adding the word 'Yahweh' with some Greek and Latin MSS.

General description

The address, following narrative introduction (v. 12), comprises a prohibition against the proposal to bring the Judaean captives into Samaria (13a). The ground of this prohibition is that it would add to the Israelites' already existing guilt, against which Yahweh is justly kindled to anger.

Contents

The function of these speakers seems to be to endorse the words of Oded, for they echo extremely closely not only his sentiments but also the vocabulary of the address assigned to him. It is not clear whether the opening *waw* consecutive construction with which the narrative opens – 'and there arose men from the leaders of the Israelites' (v. 12) – is to be construed consecutively or consequentially. It is possible that, by introducing them and their words immediately after Oded's prophecy, the Chronicler intends it to be understood that they responded to the word of God spoken by him and acted as responsible leaders in calling on the people to obey. On the other hand it is specifically stated that Oded went out to meet the army as it was coming back to Samaria (v. 12), in which case it is more likely that the leaders who 'stood up against' those who were returning acted on their own initiative. It is even possible that some contrast of an anti-military nature may be intended between these (civil?) leaders and the army. While the Chronicler has a place for armies all the while they are mere tools, almost the passive tools of God's action, he may well have felt that this army had taken far too much into its own hands. In any event, they dissociate themselves from the actions of the army, seeing it as bringing 'guiltiness' in addition to the nation's present 'sins and guilt'. These are acknowledged as being already great enough, as Oded had said (v. 10b). So there is no diminishing of the Chronicler's concept of the North's guilt before God in this passage. The really remarkable thing is that the army abandons both captives and plunder, and the leaders act in a still more remarkable way, anticipating the 'Good Samaritan' of the parable of Jesus in the generosity of their treatment of 'their brethren', so fulfilling the spirit as well as the letter of the law.

We can say, then, that this passage continues and makes explicit a theme which is implicit in Oded's address. It is not nationality which matters, but obedient response to God's law and God's words through his prophets. This is acceptable wherever it is found (there is a similar generosity of outlook to be found in 30:18f.). The thrust of this passage is not so much pro-northern, as a warning to those who claim to be God's people that they must show this in their lives, a thrust which takes up the theme of Ezek. 18. As such, it fits very closely indeed with the other addresses in Chronicles.

Finally, we should note another theme running through the passage. This also is one we have encountered before. It is that of the interplay of judgement and grace. Even in judgement God in his grace does not wholly abandon his people. This is true even for Judah here who, in the midst of Ahaz's evil reign and all the suffering of judgement this brings, get some good news and signs of grace to cheer them. This brings some comfort to the Chronicler's contemporaries, still languishing under the foreign yoke. Arrogant rulers will be judged.

God will protect even his sinful people. But this is true also of the apostate North, who are not left unaddressed by God's word, here through a prophet and later through Hezekiah, a Judaean king.

[26] II 29:5–11, 31 *Hezekiah to the (priests and) Levites*

⁵ *Then Hezekiah said to them, 'Hear me, Levites! Sanctify yourselves now and sanctify the temple of Yahweh, the God of your fathers, and bring out what is unclean from the holy place.* ⁶ *For our fathers acted treacherously and did evil in the sight of Yahweh our God. They abandoned him and turned their attention[a] away from the dwelling of Yahweh, turning their backs on him.* ⁷ *Indeed, they shut up the doors of the vestibule, extinguished the lamps and neither burned incense nor offered whole burnt offerings in the holy place of the God of Israel.* ⁸ *So Yahweh's wrath came on Judah and Jerusalem and he abandoned them to horror, scorn and derision as you have seen with your own eyes.* ⁹ *And mark how our fathers have fallen by the sword and our sons, daughters and wives are in captivity on account of this.* ¹⁰ *Now it is my intention to make a covenant with Yahweh, the God of Israel, in order that the heat of his anger may turn away from us.* ¹¹ *My children, do not be negligent now, for God has chosen you to stand in his presence, to lead worship to him and offer him worship and sacrifice.'*

³¹ *Then Hezekiah answered and said, 'Now, dedicate yourselves[b] to Yahweh. Approach him. Bring sacrifices and thankofferings to the temple of Yahweh.'*

Text

a Heb. lit. 'turned their faces from . . .'.
b The Heb. idiom is 'to fill the hand', which is a phrase indicating consecration as a priest. The MT reads an indicative, 'You have consecrated yourselves.' A very slight change of pointing and redistribution of the consonantal text would give the pi'el imperative, which is read here.

General description

Both addresses form calls to faithfulness in office. They differ from earlier examples of the 'Encouragement Formulae' or 'Assignation of a Task' in that their appeal is based, not on the encouragement of God's strength and call, but on the warning of the bad examples of the 'fathers' and the judgement of God which has followed both for their fathers and for them. Thus illustration from history appears again as a rhetorical device, together with allusion to Scripture (v. 8). The first address takes the form of a 'royal proclamation' with the opening call 'Hear me!' It involves some play on ideas rather than on exact vocabulary. The fathers 'abandoned' (/עזב, 6bα) Yahweh and, lit., 'gave him / נתן their back' (6bβ), so Yahweh 'abandoned them' (/נתן, 8b) to become objects of horror. They 'turned their faces' from Yahweh's dwelling place (6bβ), so now Hezekiah intends to make a covenant with Yahweh in order that the heat of his anger may 'turn away' (/שוב, 10b) from them.

Contents

It might well be said that if, after David, Josiah is the hero of the Deuteronomistic History, Hezekiah is the hero of the Chronicler. Four chapters are devoted to him, three of which describe his religious reforms, while one presents the military and political events of his reign in a much more favourable light than II Kgs. 18–20.[145] After using the Deuteronomistic Historian's introduction to his reign without the synchronistic reference to Hoshea, king of Israel (II Chr. 29:1f. = II Kgs. 18:1f.), the Chronicler expands the brief statement of Hezekiah's reforms in II Kgs. 18:4 by describing his assembling of the priests and Levites and calling on them to sanctify themselves; it tells of his cleansing of the temple; his restoration of the offering of sacrifice and praise by a purified personnel in the purified sanctuary; his invitation to all, both North and South, to a central Passover; and his establishment of the divisions of the priests and Levites. Interestingly, in all this expansion of II Kgs. 18:4, there is no reference to the removal of Nehushtan from the temple. Perhaps the strange association of it with Moses, with the implication that Solomon had countenanced it, was too much for the Chronicler. C. 22 makes reference to his building of the famous water conduit and then offers a harmonised account of Sennacherib's campaign, with no mention of tribute paid by Hezekiah, the whole episode being presented as a divinely wrought deliverance.[146] There is a brief reference to Hezekiah's illness which is said to have been a result of his 'pride', but, upon his humbling himself, 'the wrath of the LORD did not come upon them in the days of Hezekiah', a somewhat Targumic paraphrase of Isaiah's prophecy in II Kgs. 20:16–18, with the Deuteronomistic Historian's interesting note on Hezekiah's response (v. 19). The brief concluding note in II Kgs. 20:20f. is expanded and highlighted (II Chr. 32:27–33), a passage which contains in v. 31 yet another glossed allusion to what was categorically denounced as sin by Isaiah, according to II Kgs. 20:12–19.

The three concluding major addresses in Chronicles are all attributed to Hezekiah, the central one taking the form of a letter. This, the first, is his call to the priests and Levites, the assembling of both groups being recorded in v. 4. As has often been recognised, it clearly belongs in style, theme and structure to the other addresses. The opening 'Hear me!' has been met before (I 28:2, II 13:4, 15:2, 20:20, 28:11). There are apparent allusions to earlier Scripture, especially in v. 8, while vocabulary characteristic of the Chronicler himself suggests we are not dealing with a verbatim report of an address by the historical Hezekiah. It is strange that only the Levites are specified in v. 5, for v. 4 speaks of the assembling of both groups, while v. 16 tells of the priests carrying out the work of cleansing. This led some older commentators to suggest that vv. 4 and 16 betrayed the hand of a later, pro-priestly editor,[147] but this is usually now discounted.[148] What should be noted is that Hezekiah is here showing himself a true descendant of David who called on the priests and Levites, 'Sanctify yourselves, you and your brethren, so that you may bring up the ark of the LORD, the God of Israel, to the place I have prepared for it' (I Chr. 15:12). Indeed, it is just possible that it is the parallel to this incident which is responsible for the use of 'Levites' in the address here in Hezekiah's call. There it had been shown that David's assessment of the earlier disaster with the ark was that the Levites had not carried it (I 15:2). Further, the words of v. 12 just quoted are addressed, 'You are the heads of the fathers' houses of the Levites', yet in v. 14 it could be said, 'So the priests and the Levites sanctified themselves to bring up the ark of the LORD . . .' So we see that such alternation of the two titles is a practice of the Chronicler's elsewhere and, in this instance, in a place very much related to the present address.

There now follow several features which broaden the scope of this address from the historical situation in which it was purportedly set. The first is the use of the term נִדָּה for what I have rendered as 'what is unclean' ('filth', RSV, 'pollution', NEB, 'what is impure', JB), which is to be removed from the sanctuary. This is used in the Code of Holiness (H) of sexual impurity (Lev. 20:21) and in the Priestly Code (P) of ritual impurity (Num. 19:9, 13, 20, 21, 31:23, etc.). Interestingly it denotes menstrual impurity (Ezek. 18:6), but in the time of the exile it could be used to symbolise the sin of Israel generally (e.g. Ezek. 36:17. Lam. 1:17). Its use here, therefore, may indicate not only actual ritual defilement, but more generally, that sin of the people which brought the judgement of the exile upon them. The Chronicler is actually addressing his own contemporaries. This impression is strengthened by the reference to 'our fathers' (v. 6). Strictly, the immediate reference must be to Ahaz, and in some respects Hezekiah is shown as reversing Ahaz's specific abuses. This is supposed to be happening 'in the first year of Hezekiah's reign' (v. 3). However, as we shall see, here too the allusions are wider and more general.[149] The immediate abuses of Ahaz, therefore, would have been of much more relevance to those Hezekiah was supposed to have been addressing, some of whom must have acquiesced in them or resigned themselves to them, than the general phrase 'our fathers acted treacherously' would suggest. We meet such language, however, elsewhere in the addresses, as in II 30:7, and we catch it yet again in Zech. 1:4. This much more general kind of warning against the faithlessness of earlier generations must have been a feature of post-exilic preaching.

Further, we note both characteristic Chronicler-type vocabulary and phraseology in the description of the fathers' sins, yet also clear echoes in it of the stock phraseology of the Deuteronomistic tradition as well as that of the prophets. So the use of מעל /, 'to act unfaithfully' or 'treacherously', has been used already by the Chronicler of 'Rehoboam and all Israel with him' (II 12:2), of Uzziah (16:6) and of Ahaz (28:19, 22).[150] The phrase (עָשׂוּ הָרַע) 'to do the evil' occurs frequently in the Deuteronomistic History and is often faithfully reproduced in the Chronicler's history. The verb 'to abandon' (Heb. עזב /) is a feature of the Chronicler's own writing (e.g. II 12:1, of Rehoboam, 13:11, of the North, 24:24, of Joash, 28:6, of Pekah). Furthermore, we have already seen how this word is used in some of the addresses to express a judgement theme, as in 12:5, where Shemaiah says to Rehoboam, 'You abandoned me. Now I, for my part, have abandoned you . . .' (cf. 24:20). The phrase 'they have turned their attention away from the dwelling of Yahweh' is peculiar to this address, but again it closely echoes the Chronicler's thought that faithfulness to the sanctuary and its worship is 'to seek Yahweh', whereas any kind of neglect of it is 'to forsake him'. This is made explicit in 30:8, where Hezekiah's letter equates 'giving' Yahweh his due honour (interestingly paralleled to the injunction 'Do not be stiff-necked' (cf. 29:6, where the phrase 'turned their backs' is literally 'gave the neck')) with 'coming to his temple'. Jehoshaphat's prayer, 'and we will stand before this house, and before thee, for thy name is in this house . . .' (20:9) shows exactly the same equation of the temple with the presence of God. This address, then, contains much of the Chronicler's theology and expression of that theology.

The charges which follow and which serve to give the address at least the appearance of being specific do so in fact only in part. The reference to the 'shutting' of the doors of the porch (v. 7) takes up the statement in 28:24 that Ahaz 'shut the doors of the house of the LORD'. The other charges, however, offer a very interesting reversal of the claims made by Abijah in 13:10ff. to show the faithfulness of Judah and why they can be sure of God's help against the apostate North. They have, he claims, 'Aaronites and Levites ministering to Yahweh as priests in his service' (13:10). Since this is seen as a hallmark of the true people of God it explains why, for the Chronicler, Hezekiah begins his task of leading them back to their true calling by a charge to the priests and Levites to be active and zealous. No doubt, by recording it, the address presents a similar challenge to the priests of the Chronicler's own day. Abijah goes on to say that such duly ordained priests show their faithfulness by offering to God every morning and evening burnt offerings and sweet incense offerings (13:11, cf. 29:7, 11), and by caring for the golden Minorah 'with its lamps for burning at evening' (13:11, cf. 29:7). All this could be summarised by saying, 'We keep the commandment of Yahweh our God' (13:11), and such faithfulness to the temple and its worship could be contrasted with the Israelites for 'You have abandoned him.' The same verse (v. 10) makes the positive assertion of the Judaeans, 'But as for us, Yahweh is our God. We have not abandoned him.' Hezekiah's address makes the same link between 'abandoning Yahweh' and neglect of the temple and its worship (v. 6). Now that the northern kingdom of Israel has fallen, Hezekiah is recalling the Judaeans to their true vocation and status as Yahweh's people. One has only to think of the teaching of Haggai and Malachi, with their urgent calls to the community to concern itself with the upkeep of the temple and with due regard for its cult, to realise that this must have been a prominent feature of the post-exilic preaching. Incidentally, this parallel with the address of Abijah showing that victory is certain because the Judaeans have been faithful to Yahweh demonstrates why the Chronicler needs to present the political and military events of Hezekiah's reign in such a favourable light, and that both addresses enshrine, not accurate reports of actual addresses by the historical persons named in the narrative, but Chronicler-type theology of the kind which must have found frequent expression among teachers in the temple.

The generalising extensions of the address to speak to the post-exilic community can be seen in the summary of the judgements which came on 'our fathers' (vv. 8ff.). The use of the noun קֶצֶף to signify Yahweh's reaction to his people's sins is featured elsewhere in the addresses (see II 19:2, 10), with which may be compared the 'sermon-like' statements of the Chronicler in

24:18, 32:25, cf. Zech. 1:2. In most cases the noun is introduced by the verb היה/, as here, but sometimes also (e.g. 32:26) by the Hebrew root בוא. The result of this 'wrath' breaking out is that Yahweh 'has abandoned them to horror' or 'trembling' (צַוְעָה/זַוְעָה). This appears to be a Deuteronomistic phrase (cf. Deut. 28:25) which is taken up in the Book of Jeremiah, chiefly in the prose (Deuteronomistic) passages (see 15:4, 24:9, 29:18, 34:17), but its use in Isa. 28:19 and Ezek. 23:46 suggests that it also passed over into the prophetic language of judgement. Again, the fact that they had become an object of 'scorn' (שַׁמָּה) and of 'derision', שְׁרֵקָה apparently indicating the whistle of derision, echoes Deuteronomistic language which is also found in the prophetic books, especially in Jeremiah (e.g. Deut. 28:37, Jer. 19:8, 25:9, 29:18, 49:17, 50:13, 51:37).[151] One must be cautious here, for we note that it is always used with שַׁמָּה, so that it may be safer to say that it is the more general Deuteronomistic/prophetic language of judgement which is being employed. But its use must have recalled to its hearers the continuing sins which had brought those threats of judgement down on them, especially in the time of the Babylonian exile. The same may be said for the allusion in v. 9 to some of the 'covenant' curses found in Deut. 28, especially in vv. 26 and 32. Ackroyd has well said, 'Prophetic judgement themes underlie this sermonic address. The point is made still clearer in the emphasis on the people actually *seeing with their own eyes* (v. 8) the present conditions of the land and city, explained in terms of slaughter in battle and captivity (v. 9). The terms are so explicit as to make it clear that the Chronicler is here commenting on the exilic situation . . .'[152]

The king announces his intention in v. 10. Williamson and Japhet have rightly argued here that this is not a reference to 'covenant theology',[153] which anyway is not prominent in the Chronicler's writings. It is, rather, a solemn undertaking to make and fulfil a vow, as in II 15:12 where, after hearing the prophecy of Azariah, the people and king 'entered into a covenant to seek the LORD, the God of their fathers, with all their heart and with all their soul'. The same meaning attaches to the covenant made by Jehoida between himself, the king and all the people, 'that they should be the LORD's people' (23:16).

His charge to the priests and Levites not to be negligent (or 'easy-going') rests on God's 'choice' of them for the high privilege of standing before him, to minister to him, to be his ministers and to offer sacrifice. V. 31 shows how it is only after 'consecration' that leaders and people are fitted to perform their sacred calling. Such a reminder of the privileges and responsibilities of being 'chosen' people would sound an urgent call to all generations.

[27] II 30:6–9 *Hezekiah, the king, to all Israel and Judah (by letter)*

⁶*And messengers with letters^a from Hezekiah and his princes went throughout all Israel and Judah as the king had ordered. These read, 'O Israelites, return to Yahweh, the God of Abraham, Isaac and Israel, that he may turn back to those of you who are left as survivors from the rule of the kings of Assyria. ⁷Do not be like your fathers and your kinsmen who were faithless to Yahweh, the God of your fathers. So he gave them up to be objects of horror even as you have seen for yourselves. ⁸Do not be hard-hearted^b now as your fathers were. Give Yahweh his due honour^c and come to his sanctuary which he consecrated for all time. Serve Yahweh, your God, so that the fierceness of his anger may turn from you. ⁹For if you return to Yahweh, your kinsmen and your descendants will find compassion from their captors and return to this land because of the grace and compassion of Yahweh, your God. He will not turn away from you if you return to him.'*

Text

^a The Heb. plural probably indicates a number of copies of one original.
^b Lit. 'Do not harden your neck.'
^c The Heb. phrase is curious, although its meaning is clear. It reads literally 'Give hand to Yahweh', which must indicate giving way to Yahweh's power or giving him the response which is his due. The LXX rendering 'glory' is probably an attempt to paraphrase in this way.[154]

General description

The letter constitutes an address with a number of parallels to that just considered in 29:5–11. It forms a call to the apostate northerners to repent by returning to make the Jerusalem temple what it always should have been, the one legitimate shrine (6b–8, 9a). In this instance the call is based not only on God's judgement of them and their fathers for their disobedience (7bβ) but on God's mercy and grace (8bβ, 9b). Rhetorical devices include play on words ('turn'/'return'), inversion (v. 9) and illustration by appeal to history.

Contents

It is not surprising that there should be a number of parallel features between Hezekiah's address to the priests and Levites in 29:5–11 and his message,

delivered in writing by couriers, to the people of 'all Israel'. Now that there is
no apostate, schismatic sanctuary in the North and the Jerusalem temple and
its personnel have been duly purified and reconsecrated, a central Passover
can be instituted for all the nation, the people of the old northern kingdom
being addressed in generous and 'brotherly' terms.[155] The two addresses thus
both express the central importance of Hezekiah's reform for the Chronicler,
and there can be no coincidence in the number of parallels, both in the
addresses and the surrounding narratives, to the actions and words of both
David and Solomon. This great pivotal point in the life of the people of God
represents for the Chronicler a continuation and a fulfilment of the golden
Davidic/Solomonic era.

The narrative raises wide-ranging and difficult questions of an historical
nature which are not our concern here, for it is the Chronicler's theological
interpretation of events rather than his historical reconstruction of them
which is our primary interest.[156] All that need be said here is that the idea that
Hezekiah took advantage of the historical and political situation to extend the
influence of the Jerusalem cult into the old northern territory is wholly likely
when one reflects how much that Jerusalem temple and its worship were the
sacral foundation and buttress of the claims of the Davidic dynasty to
power.[157] It has been urged several times that such ambitions are hinted at in
the Rabshakeh's reference to Hezekiah's activity (II Kgs. 18:22, although that
speech with all the narratives from II Kgs. 18:17–19:37 must also be seen as
theological interpretation of history rather than plain narration of fact). Again,
Hezekiah's naming of his son, Manasseh, by the name of a northern tribe, may
also be significant. However, that theology rather than mere history is to the
fore here is indicated firmly by 30:6–9 which, for all its alleged historical form
as a royal proclamation, closely resembles 29:5–11 and other addresses in
Chronicles.

The form of the address is instructive, 'O Israelites . . .' (v. 6). Both those in
Judah and in 'Israel, from Beersheba to Dan' (v. 5) are addressed in this way,
according to the ideal boundaries of the united kingdom under the single
monarchy (I 21:2, cf. II Sam. 3:10, I Kgs. 4:25/5:5 etc.). The Chronicler,
interestingly, reverses the more normal order of the two names, perhaps
because to him the southern reference was the more important. But it is clear
that, for him, the light of a united kingdom under a Davidic monarch, so long
eclipsed, is now shining brightly again in this new day of Hezekiah's reign.
Another interesting feature of the address is the reference to God as 'the LORD
[Yahweh], the God of Abraham, Isaac and Israel'. Not only is this the single

occurrence of this title in the addresses, but it is most atypical of the Chronicler's usage generally. Almost always the designation is, 'The LORD, the God of our/your/their fathers' or 'The LORD, the God of Israel . . .'. The title used here occurs elsewhere only in I 29:18, in the prayer of David after he has gathered all the materials for building the temple, and charged Solomon with its construction and the people with his support. The echo of this in Hezekiah's address may again emphasise that the divine purpose for the united monarchy in establishing the temple at the heart of the life of the whole nation is being fulfilled in the reforming programme of Hezekiah. As with David, the Chronicler gives greatest weight to Hezekiah's cultic reforms. Perhaps the Chronicler's first interest is not so much in showing Hezekiah as a second Solomon, as several commentators have rightly shown that he does,[158] but rather that the David/Solomon golden age, seen by the Chronicler as a unified whole, is finding its expression and fulfilment in the life of a purified temple again functioning at the centre of a unified Israel.

A number of features of this address show it as a close parallel to that of Hezekiah to the priests and Levites in 29:5–11. There is a reference to the unfaithfulness of the 'fathers' (vv. 7f., cf. 29:6–9); in both the verb / מעל is used to describe this faithlessness (v. 8, cf. 29:6); there is in both the idiomatic use of עֹרֶף, 'neck', to indicate rebellion. There is, incidentally, an interesting contrast in the idiom used. In 29:6 we read that they 'gave their neck/back to Yahweh'. Now, by contrast, Hezekiah's hearers are urged to 'give hand to Yahweh' (v. 8, see notes on text above). In both addresses faithfulness to the temple and its worship is equated with faithfulness to Yahweh himself (v. 8, cf. 29:6).

One of the most striking features of this address, as has often been noted, is the recurring interplay of the various senses of the Hebrew verb 'to turn, return, repent' (/ שוב). It opens with its use in the imperative sense of 'turn back', 'repent', 'O Israel, Return to Yahweh.' This is followed by the jussive with simple *waw* to express purpose or consequence, 'so that he may turn back to those of you who are left as survivors' (v. 6). This is taken up again in v. 8. They are to 'serve Yahweh' (the reference being to worship offered in the temple) and, again the jussive with simple *waw*, 'so that the fierceness of his anger may turn from you', another parallel with Hezekiah's first address (29:10). V. 9 opens with the use of the infinitive construct plus pronominal suffix, 'For if [or 'when'] you return to Yahweh . . .'. This in turn is followed again by the infinitive construct to express purpose, '[then] your kinsmen . . .

will find compassion from their captors and return to this land . . .'. It appears again, finally, in v. 9 as an inverted conditional sentence, 'Yahweh will not turn (סור) his face from you [apodosis] if you return (שוב) to him [protasis].'

We have seen that such play on words has been a feature of some of these addresses, and this particular root recurs in Zech. 1:3, cf. Mal. 3:7. Such memory-evoking devices may clearly be a feature of homiletical style. More importantly, however, according to W. L. Holladay,[159] this particular complex of the verbal root stands in a particular tradition, that of Jeremiah. This tradition was passed on by the Deuteronomists who, in this instance, were imitators rather than innovators. Holladay concludes his study of the evidence:

It was Jeremiah who made the first generalization . . . He saw apostasy and repentance as correlative . . . he saw them as aspects of the same act: a changeable people must change . . . that the heart may change in both directions is a tremendous discovery . . . *(p. 157)*

He sees little development beyond this in the post-exilic period, although, dealing with the usage in Kings and Chronicles, he does comment on 'the greater freedom and frequency with which the latter work employs covenantal *sûbh* . . .' (p. 154). Another innovation in the Chronistic literature is the development of the use of the causative Hiph'il, of which the most interesting example, for our purpose, occurs in II 24:19 which, immediately before the prophecy of Zechariah, says, 'Yet he sent prophets among them to bring them back (Hiph. שוב) to the LORD.' But Holladay remains firmly of the opinion that

There are no new patterns to emerge in the subsequent period; the field has been laid out by Jeremiah, and subsequent writings followed his usages as their particular outlook bade them. *(p. 154)*

We might interject here that such a use of the verb שוב/, as we have seen, prominently featured in the 'preaching-type' material from the post-exilic period. This may be another indication that post-exilic preaching gave considerable place to the exegesis of prophetic and other biblical material. More immediately, we see here too another parallel with the address in 29:5–11. There, as we saw in v. 8, there is also dependence on the Jeremianic/Deuteronomistic tradition and application of it to a later situation.

That these ostensible words of the eighth-century Hezekiah really address the post-exilic community is further underlined by the description of those addressed as 'those of you who are left (פְּלֵיטָה), as survivors (הַנִּשְׁאֶרֶת (the remnant)) from the hand of the kings of Assyria'. The Chronicler has recorded a royal address before, that of David in I 13:2, ordering that the 'remnant' should be summoned to engage in the cultic activity of bringing up the ark to Jerusalem, that ark which had been neglected in the days of the preceding monarch, Saul. So, again, the activity of the ideal Davidide monarchy in a united kingdom is being reenacted in the days of Hezekiah. The survival of a 'remnant' has always been a sign of God's mercy in response to penitence. In II 12:7 it is recorded how, following Shemaiah's address to the apostate Rehoboam and Judaean community, they repented. To this God responded, 'Since they have shown themselves contrite, I will not destroy them, but I will grant them some respite' (כִּמְעַט לִפְלֵיטָה). On the other hand, total judgement means there is no 'remnant' left at all. In II 20:24 it is recorded how, when Judah came to survey the scene after the battle against the coalition of Ammonites, Moabites and Edomites, all were slain. The words of Jahaziel (vv. 15–17) had been fulfilled. 'None had escaped' (וְאֵין פְּלֵיטָה). It is interesting that the reforms of a later king, Josiah, are recorded by the Chronicler as being supported by the people of Ephraim and Manasseh, 'from all the *remnant* of Israel' as well as by those of all Judah, Benjamin and Jerusalem (II 34:9). This expands the Deuteronomistic Historian's briefer reference to 'the money . . . which the keepers of the threshold have collected from the people' (II Kgs. 22:4). Of course the references to the 'remnant' in the accounts of the reforms both of Hezekiah and Josiah are to those of the former northern kingdom who had been spared the exile. These, further, had shown their penitence by their response to the call of God uttered by a true Davidide to come to the true temple to worship truly. But in 36:20 we see an extension of the concept to those of Judah who were exiled when we read, '[Nebuchadnezzar] took into exile in Babylon the *remnant* from the sword to Babylon.' In this case it is those who were miraculously spared the slaughter and destruction. Those exiles were the objects of God's mercy which determined to leave a 'remnant' and make it the nucleus of the fulfilment of all his earlier promises to David, promises renewed through the prophets. In this description of those being addressed by the faithful Hezekiah, there must have been an overtone to be picked up by the Chronicler's post-exilic hearers, a hint driven home by the phrase 'as you have seen' or, perhaps, to catch the significance of the participle, 'as you are [now] seeing' (v. 7). Again we catch an echo of the words of Hezekiah in 29:8, 'as you have seen with your own eyes', the same verses both describing the disasters with the same term, (לְשַׁמָּה), a 'desolation'.

This address, therefore, suggests something for which we get plenty of clues elsewhere, that behind it lay a post-exilic preaching which stressed that those who had been miraculously spared during the horrors of 597 and 586 BCE and other such occasions had been preserved by God in Babylon. It was from there that the nucleus of the new 'Israel' had returned to the land. These were the true remnant, the objects of God's mercy. This mercy is splendidly affirmed in v. 9. For just as the address in 29:5–8 had shown that the disasters which had befallen the 'fathers' were fulfilment of the Deuteronomic covenant threats, disasters also hinted at in Solomon's dedicatory prayer (I Kgs. 8/ II Chr. 6), so those who repent can be sure of the Deuteronomic covenant promises (Exod. 34:6, cf. Deut. 28:1–6). These promises are also hinted at in Solomon's prayer, especially in II Chr. 6:36ff., and, even more, in I Kgs. 8:50f. (a strange omission by the Chronicler). After all, God had promised to Solomon that he had chosen and consecrated the sanctuary 'for ever' (II Chr. 7:16), a promise recapitulated here in II 30:8. Such divine grace and compassion are not only stressed in v. 9, but finely illustrated in vv. 17–19, which show that God responds to the attitude of the worshipping and penitent heart rather than to the niceties of ceremonial law, and also to the vicarious prayer of faith uttered by the good king Hezekiah.

Such a vicarious value in faith and prayer is not exclusively a royal prerogative, however. Those who stayed behind in the former northern kingdom are assured that their 'return' to Yahweh will bring blessing upon their exiled brethren (v. 9) and ensure their ultimate return to the land (and, no doubt, also to Yahweh). If we do see reference here to the Chronicler's own contemporaries and their situation, it might appear to give force to those who argue for an early date for the Chronicler after the exile, and even suggest that his message was addressed precisely to those who had stayed in the land. This is unlikely on other grounds, however, and by no means a necessary inference. We know that concern for the growing 'Diaspora' after the exile was felt ever more keenly. Was their exile permanent? How would they share in the final victory of Yahweh in Jerusalem? Such concerns figure prominently among those who passed on and expanded the preaching of Zechariah (see especially Zech. 6:15, 8:7f., 20–3) and also in those chapters often assigned to 'Trito-Isaiah' (e.g. Isa. 56:8, 66:20). It may well have been part of the message of the preachers in the post-exilic period to urge their hearers to that faithfulness which would bring blessing, not only on them, but on all their exiled 'brethren' who were yet to return to share in the final glory of the new age.

[28] II 31:10 *Azariah, the chief priest, to Hezekiah*

[10] *Then Azariah, the chief priest, the Zadokite, said to him, 'Since they began to bring their offering into Yahweh's sanctuary, there has been food in plenty with much to spare. Yahweh has blessed his people so that there is all this surplus.'*

General description

A simple and direct statement of fact to the king by the high priest. The piling up of vocabulary stresses the amazing amount of the produce surplus to requirements, with two forms of the verbal root meaning 'to remain, or be left over' (/יתר), the infinitive absolute of the verb 'to be sated' (/שבע) and two nouns meaning 'abundance' (רוֹב, הָמוֹן).

Contents

Sandwiched between the two final addresses of Hezekiah, this short word of Azariah is recorded. It may seem too brief to belong to the 'addresses', and yet it is significant for two reasons. In its context it continues a logical sequence of actions by Hezekiah and the faithful community of 'Israel'. First the priests and Levites have been reconsecrated and challenged to zealous service (c. 29). Then a central cult for all Yahweh's faithful people, in North and South, has been constituted, with a 'national' Passover as its focal point. All have been urged to 'give Yahweh his due honour', which means coming to his sanctuary (c. 30). Now, as Hezekiah follows David's instruction and Solomon's example by appointing the divisions of the priests and Levites for the regular worship of the sanctuary (31:2) he himself sets the example of support in kind for its worship (v. 3). He then summons the community to give the tithes for the support of the sanctuary and its personnel to which, like the Israelites in the time of Moses, they respond with exemplary zeal and generosity (cf. Exod. 25:1ff., 35:21ff., 36:2ff.)[160] and like those who responded to the call of that second Moses, David (I Chr. 29:1ff., esp. v. 9). We may note that David also provided for the temple out of his own resources (I 29:3ff.). In every way Hezekiah is shown as embodying the ideal Davidic ruler and, as with Moses, David and Solomon, a faithful leader inspires faithfulness in his people. This 'address' of Azariah rubs in the lesson that the general call to 'give Yahweh his due honour' and 'come to his sanctuary' has to be earthed in a specific obedience in the matter of giving. Rudolph has expressed this point well:

The barometer of the religious zeal of any community consists of their willingness and promptness in paying the necessary financial dues.[161]

Preachers in all generations have reiterated the point!

That leads us to the second reason for the significance of this address of Azariah's. Not only does it relate Hezekiah's addresses in cc. 29 and 30 by developing the action for which they call in a logical sequence, but this word affords one of the clear links between such addresses in Chronicles and the tenor and burden of a good deal of post-exilic prophecy, thus suggesting some link between the addresses and the work of the preachers of the temple. Azariah's 'address' makes a very strong link between obedience to Yahweh and material prosperity. The Chronicler tends to use the word 'bless' (ברך/) most often in a material context, and in this follows the kind of emphasis to be found in Deuteronomy and Deuteronomistic literature. Such verses as Deut. 7:12f. set a constant theme:

And because you hearken to these ordinances, and keep and do them, the LORD your God will keep with you the covenant and the steadfast love which he swore to your fathers to keep; he will love you, bless you and multiply you; he will also bless the fruit of your body and the fruit of your ground, your grain, your wine and your oil, the increase of your cattle and the young of your flock . . .

In fact, they will get more of the very things they give to Yahweh (cf. II Chr. 31:5). With Deut. 7:12f. one may compare Deut. 12:7, 28:8, etc. Neither should it be overlooked that the Jerusalem cult saw a close link between faithfulness to Yahweh, especially that shown by the Davidic king, and material blessing (e.g. Pss. 21, 72). Most often, the Chronicler uses the term 'bless' in a similar material context (e.g. I 4:10; 16:2f.; 29:10ff.), and when men 'bless' Yahweh it is often in response to his material gifts (as in the context of this address in II 31:8). That this seems to have been a theme of much preaching and 'prophecy' in the post-exilic period is suggested by the very close relationship between this address and the whole burden of Haggai's message, especially Hag. 2:18ff., which, for all the problems of exegesis of vv. 15–19, is clearly enunciating the same principle as Azariah. Lack of concern for the temple and its worship has led, according to Haggai, to their present material distress. Obedience and zeal in the service of the temple will reverse that. 'From this day, I will bless . . .' (2:19). The same theme is repeated in Zech. 8:10–13 in a passage which, as we shall see, looks remarkably like exegesis of Haggai's message. The people will know fertility, and those who had been a 'curse' among the nations will become a 'blessing' (בְּרָכָה). Nor can one miss the same theme in Malachi where faithfulness and obedience over the payment of tithes will result in the gift of rain and fertility (3:10). Again, it is said, all nations will call you 'blessed' (3:12). The strong similarity in these passages suggests that we are hearing a recurrent theme in the preaching of the post-exilic temple. If preachers keep returning to a theme, one can be sure there is some neglect among the community, and we have the evidence of Neh. 13:10ff. to show that this could happen (see Neh. 10:32ff.). It would be very surprising if that were the only time such encouragement in the matter of financial giving were needed.

[29] II 32:7f. *Hezekiah to the commanders and people*

[7]*'Be brave! Be resolute! Do not fear or be dismayed by the king of Assyria or by all his army with him. For greater is he who is with us than the force[a] with him.* [8]*On his side is human might,[b] but on ours is Yahweh, our God, to help us and fight our battles.'*

Text

[a] Lit. 'with us greater than with him'.
[b] Lit. 'with him is the arm of flesh'.

General description

This address, following a narrative introduction (6b), takes the by now familiar form of what we have termed an 'Encouragement for a Task' formula, in this case, to courage and faith before a battle. It uses play on the word 'with' in both vv. 7 and 8 and also contains allusion to Scripture.

Contents

The final words given to Hezekiah deal with another major theme of the addresses and, indeed, of the Chronicler's theology generally. That in 30:6–9 dealt with the sanctuary and its service; this one calls for quiet trust in Yahweh before the threat of human might. It was either the main theme, or a prominent one, in the addresses recorded in II 13:4–12, 16:7–9, 20:14–17, 20, 37, 25:7–10 and 28:8–15. That there is a close connection between obedience to God in cultic matters and deliverance by God in battle is shown by the use of the formula 'Be strong!' (or, as it might more fittingly be rendered in this context, 'Be brave!'), 'Be resolute!' in both kinds of address (e.g. II 15:7). Also, as has often been pointed out, the vague chronological note in v. 1 which introduces these great political events in Hezekiah's reign serves to link the two themes. In place of the Deuteronomistic History's 'In the fourteenth year of Hezekiah Sennacherib king of Assyria came up . . .' (II Kgs. 18:13), we have 'After these things and *these acts of faithfulness* Sennacherib king of Assyria came . . .' The changes which the Chronicler makes to the account of Sennacherib's invasion in Kings, already alluded to briefly, have been made the subject of a study by B. S. Childs,[162] who sees this as true 'Midrash'. This he defines as a method of scriptural exegesis guided by a two-way interaction between the given, 'canonical' Scripture and the exegetical purpose of the interpreter.[163] Here, it must suffice to show that the narration is presented so as to depict Hezekiah as the faithful king who secured for the nation the same kind of deliverance and military success as did David and Solomon. Indeed, the reference to the 'Millo' (v. 5) in the city of David (see also II Sam. 5:9, I Kgs. 9:15, 24) shows him to continue their work. Perhaps this explains a rather strange feature of this passage, often commented on: the apparent contradiction between the elaborate defensive precautions Hezekiah is described as taking over the defensive walls and water supplies together with the arming of the militia, and the spirit of quiet confidence in God's power expressed in this address. This inconsistency is exacerbated when one recalls that Isaiah himself was most critical of Hezekiah over this (Isa. 22:8b–11), and yet the address and narrative contain a number of Isaianic overtones, as we shall see. The most likely explanation remains that the Chronicler uses the factual information because it shows Hezekiah as continuing the policies of David and Solomon, both of whom combined energetic building programmes, and even military preparedness, with what the Chronicler regarded as exemplary trust in God (see the discussion on Asa's address, II 14:7/6, pp. 43ff. above).

A further link with David is shown by the opening call of the address, 'Be brave! Be resolute! Do not fear or be dismayed . . .', for we have seen how this was part of David's charges to Solomon over the building of the temple (I 22:13, cf. 28:10, 20). In our discussion of the phrase there it was suggested that a formula which had its origin in the context of battle, perhaps especially that of the so-called 'holy war', could be applied by extension to the sacral and cultic realms.[164] The Chronicler can use some form of the charge in military context (e.g. I 19:13), but also in a cultic context (se Azariah's address in II 15:2–7 and, perhaps, 19:11, in addition to David's charges). This should surprise us less now that we see that the structure of the Chronicler's narratives reveals how closely inter-related he saw cultic zeal and military success to be. It is always just possible, as well, that the imperative of the verb 'be strong' (חִזְקוּ) is used in this address as a kind of word-play on Hezekiah's name (יְחִזְקִיָּהוּ = 'Yahweh strengthens').

In the short address which follows we find a number of scriptural themes and allusions. It is difficult to avoid the impression that the phrase 'with us greater than with him' is meant to recall the words of Elisha to his servant in II Kgs. 6:16. That narrative, with its interesting counter-play of 'opening the eyes' of vision and faith at a time of great military fear and danger, with the 'blinding of the eyes' of the pagan hordes in panic and confusion, would have seemed appropriate, not only at the time of Sennacherib's invasion, but at all times of apparent military helplessness in the history of the people of God. Yet the phrase 'with us', with its Hebrew overtones (עִמָּנוּ), also recalls Isa. c. 7 and Isaiah's assurance to Ahaz at just such a time that 'God is with us' (Heb. עִמָּנוּ אֵל). Indeed, earlier in Isa. c. 7, there has been a similar scornful comparison between the apparent might of the leaders of the nations and the might of Israel's God to that suggested in Hezekiah's address:

The head of Syria is Damascus,
and the head of Damascus is Rezin . . .
and the head of Ephraim is Samaria,
and the head of Samaria is the son of Remeliah. *(vv. 8f.)*

A similar call for 'trust' follows (v. 9). Such confidence that 'God is with us' has already been shown earlier in Chronicles, e.g. in the address of Abijah (II 13:12).

Also interesting is the contrast of the presence of God 'to help us and to fight our battles' with 'the arm of flesh'. The 'arm' as a symbol of strength is a familiar Old Testament concept.[165] It occurs prominently in the Deuteronomic literature, especially in the phrase 'a mighty hand and an outstretched arm' (e.g. Deut. 7:19 etc.). Second Isaiah makes considerable use of it (e.g. Isa. 40:10ff., 44:12, 48:14, 51:5, 9, 52:10, 53:1), and it occurs again in so-called 'Trito-Isaiah' (Isa. 59:16, 62:8, 63:12). The occurrences in Jeremiah and Ezekiel with reference to God seem to be mainly imitative of Deuteronomic language, although Ezekiel uses the term a great deal of human power (e.g. 30:21f., 24f.). One Jeremianic passage often thought to have inspired the Chronicler here is Jer. 17:5:

Cursed is the man who trusts in man
and makes flesh his arm,
whose heart turns away from the LORD.

Perhaps it is safer to say that we have here the echo of a general prophetic theme. Certainly, however, the contrasting of 'flesh' as a symbol of human power with God, who is 'spirit', is very clearly expressed in Isa. 31:1, 3.

Also interesting is the use of the Niph'al of the Hebrew verb 'to lean' (/סמך), in the description which follows the address of the people's response, lit. 'they supported themselves with the words of Hezekiah' (v. 8). This word occurs in the Deuteronomistic Historian's account of the Rabshakeh's speech, 'Behold, you are relying now on Egypt, that broken reed of a staff, which will pierce the hand of any man who *leans* on it' (Niph./סמך , II Kgs. 18:21). The first extended account of the invasion of Judah and the siege of Jerusalem by Sennacherib (II Kgs. 18:17–19:9a, 37, Childs's 'BI' account) is full of associations with the teaching of Isaiah. It calls for trust in Yahweh rather than in Egypt with its chariots and horses. It asserts that the Rabshakeh has come at Yahweh's bidding (cf. Isa. 10:6). The location of the encounter is the same as that between Ahaz and Isaiah (cf. 7:3). The taunt uttered by the Rabshakeh is reminiscent of Isa. 10:7ff. Further, it pictures Isaiah as intercessor for king and people. It is striking that the Chronicler seems to evoke all this by his description of the people's response. They rightly trust God by trusting his faithful king, Hezekiah (v. 8), the very thing with which the Rabshakeh taunted them (32:15, cf. II Kgs. 18:32).

This address, then, ascribed to Hezekiah at a time of grave national threat, becomes a word which relates the teaching of the prophets, especially that of Isaiah, to the people of God of all times. A specific historical incident becomes the occasion by which general scriptural truths are made relevant to those in other like times of stress and apparent military impotence.

[30] II 35:3–6 *Josiah to the (priests and?) Levites*

³ *And he said to the Levites who were instructing all Israel and who were dedicated to Yahweh, 'Place the holy ark in the sanctuary which Solomon, David's son, king of Israel, built. It shall no longer be carriedª on your shoulders. Now serve Yahweh, your God, and his people Israel.* ⁴*Prepare yourselves in your family divisions in accordance with the written instructions of David, king of Israel, and his son, Solomon.* ⁵*Serveᵇ in the sanctuary for the sake of the groups of the family households, your brethren the lay people according to the divisions of the household of the Levites.ᶜ* ⁶*Sacrifice the Passover: sanctify yourselves and prepare your brethren to act according to the word of Yahweh given by Moses.'*

Text

a Lit. 'It shall not be a burden for your shoulders.'

b Lit. 'stand', but the verb often has the connotation of serving, as when used of the elders who 'stood before' Solomon (I Kgs. 12:6).

c The Hebrew is so obscure that it is difficult to be sure of the exact meaning.

General description

The address is a commission to the Levites for particular sacral duties in Hezekiah's central Passover. It takes from them responsibility for carrying the ark and calls them to teaching and sacral office for the sake of the whole community. It lacks any of the 'encouragement' formulae which characterise other similar addresses.

Contents

This last address of a Davidide king recalls those of David to Solomon and the leaders of the community in which he charged them with the proper building, maintenance and service of the temple. This address of Josiah charges the Levites (it might be inferred from v. 2 that the priests were included) also with proper maintenance of the temple and its community. Nothing could more fittingly illustrate that the centre of all the Chronicler's interest is not the Davidic line *per se*, but the temple for which that line had been chosen and for whose building and service it had been made responsible. This connection with David and Solomon is made clear in the Chronicler's narrative of the reign of Josiah. To the Deuteronomistic History's opening of the account of his reign in II Kgs. 22:1f., he adds, 'For in the eighth year of his reign, while he was yet a boy, he began to seek the God *of David his father* . . .' The reference to the temple in the address of 35:3–6 is to 'the sanctuary which *Solomon, David's son*, king of Israel, built'. They are to 'prepare themselves', or to 'take their places', by divisions according to the written instructions of 'David, king of Israel and his son, Solomon' (v. 4). This has all the force of a decree of Torah, for instructions about the proper observance of the Passover are 'according to the word of Yahweh given by Moses' (v. 6). It is true that Josiah does not receive the importance in Chronicles which the Deuteronomistic History gives him. Hezekiah is much more central, and this is indicated in part by the three very important addresses attributed to Hezekiah, while Josiah has only this rather brief one. Further, Josiah merely reflects and renews Hezekiah's much more creative work. Rudolph speaks of Hezekiah's Passover as 'pioneering' (*bahnbrechend*, p. 324). The rather contradictory assertion of 35:18 is either an echo of his *Vorlage* in II Kgs. 23:22, or has some special reference to something seen as notable in Josiah's Passover which was not a feature of Hezekiah's (cf. 30:26), possibly the role of the Levites. Both stress the renewal of conditions which obtained in the time of the united kingdom. So, like Hezekiah, Josiah calls on the religious leaders to sanctify themselves before the Festival. Like Hezekiah he institutes a central Passover in Jerusalem (v. 1) and, like Hezekiah, he makes generous provisions himself for its observance (v.7). The only difference is that Josiah is able to keep it at the proper time in the *first* month (cf. 30:2f.). Yet the real emphasis is not on the priority of Hezekiah or Josiah, but rather on the continuity with, and the fulfilment of, the purposes of God achieved through the united monarchy. The reason Hezekiah figures so prominently is, as we have seen, that it is in his reign that the conditions of the period of the united monarchy are reborn for the first time since the division of the kingdoms. Josiah faithfully perpetuates the hallmarks of such an ideal kingdom.

First he appointed the priests to their stations and 'encouraged' them (Heb. יְחַזְּקֵם, v. 2). This is often taken to be a further indication that the priests needed such exhortation.[166] It is true that the Levites receive all the limelight, but the use of the חזק / may mean no more than that Josiah addressed them with the customary call to 'strength' and 'determination' familiar to us from other examples of the 'Encouragement for a Task': Hezekiah to the commanders (חִזְקוּ 32:7) and David to Solomon (I 22:13, 28:20). It is better, therefore, to assume the 'convention' form of such calls rather than some intended slight on the priests. Nevertheless, it is the Levites who are the recorded objects of the address, and the address stresses two things. The first is their role in the instruction of the people. They are described, editorially, as those 'who give understanding to, or 'were instructing (Hiph. / בין) all Israel' (v. 3). This seems to be elevated specifically over their role as 'bearers of the ark'. It is not clear why they are told to 'place the holy ark in the sanctuary . . .' (v. 3). It is not even clear if that is the only possible rendering of the Heb. תְּנוּ (/נתן). It might be rendered 'leave the holy ark in the sanctuary' or 'give up [your role of carrying] the holy ark . . .' without emendation of the text. Some commentators have argued that the ark was taken away in Manasseh's reign and so now had to be replaced, but it is strange if that is the case that the reference is so oblique. What does seem clear is that what at least the Chronicler understood to have been the former role of the Levites was giving way to a new one. That would be perfectly understandable if one remembers that the Chronicler had recorded the charge of none less than David to the Levites in very absolute terms:

Only the Levites shall carry the ark of God, for Yahweh has chosen them to carry the ark of Yahweh and to serve him for ever. *(I 15:2)*

Again, the bringing of the ark into the temple by the Levites in Josiah's reign may be a further echo of David, who did the same by having the Levites bring it into the tabernacle (I 13:2f., 15:1ff., 16:1). Thus it would require a very special word to suggest that they were now no longer to carry it. Josiah's call to them, 'Now serve Yahweh your God and his people Israel' (v. 3) represents just such an authoritative word. It stresses that their cultic and, above all, their teaching role, in the service of the people *is* service of Yahweh. It is thus a legitimate extension of that role which David had assigned to them 'for ever'. Their role of ministry is receiving an interesting and significant reinterpretation. It is naturally of relevance to this enquiry that it is a *teaching* role which is seen to be gaining importance for those who have recorded these 'addresses'. It certainly does not mean that we can leap to the conclusion that the Levites were the *sole* 'preachers',[167] but it does suggest that expository teaching, or preaching, was seen as of growing importance.

The second thing the address stresses is that the Levites are also assigned a role of some importance in the Passover, but, as some have pointed out, the language used in the description of the Passover in vv. 10–17 suggests a wider sacral activity than that envisaged by the Passover alone.[168] This may be just an echo of the description of Hezekiah's Passover, but the part of the Levites there was assigned to unusual circumstances (30:17), whereas here it seems to be regarded as normal practice. Williamson rightly points out that this did not become enduring practice and so we are probably faced here with a special interest, if not special pleading, of the Chronicler himself. If so, it is not without importance for our purpose that one of the addresses can be the vehicle for the Chronicler's own point of view.

This should not obscure the fact, however, that in assigning the (priests and) Levites to their divisions and courses and sacral roles in the temple, Josiah is putting into effect what David arranged for from the beginning (I 23–7, cf. 35:4). And, finally, we should notice another theme which has been prominent throughout. The proper dedication and zeal of the leaders, be they military commanders (as in 32:7f.) or priests and Levites, is of immediate relevance to the community as a whole, just as the Deuteronomistic History had shown the response of the king to God to be. V. 5 is not altogether clear, but it may mean that each group of lay people had its representative Levitical order. Certainly, the cultic role of the Levites had as its aim 'to prepare your brethren to act according to the word of Yahweh given by Moses' (v. 6). This is another emphasis that we shall meet elsewhere in the post-exilic literature.

[31] II 35:21 *Neco, king of Egypt, to Josiah*

²¹*And he sent messengers to him, saying, 'What have we to do with each other,ᵃ king of Judah? It is not against you that I have comeᵇ today, but against the kingdomᶜ which is at war with me.ᵈ God commanded me to speed on my way. Stop resisting God, who is with me, so that he may not slaughter you.'*

Text

ᵃ The Hebrew idiom is literally, 'What to me, to you?'
ᵇ Reading with VSS 'to come' in place of the 2nd m.s. pronoun of the MT. This involves changing only the vocalic pointing of אַתָּה to אֲתֶה.
ᶜ Lit. 'house'.
ᵈ Lit. 'of my warfare'.

General description

An injunction of the Egyptian king to Josiah not to oppose him militarily in his campaign against Babylon. It is based on the certainty of the divine presence with him which would render Josiah's opposition hopeless. It makes use of the rhetorical question.

Contents

The address must be seen as a dramatic device by the Chronicler to give a theological reason for the sudden death in defeat of so worthy a king as Josiah. Of course, the reason given, that Josiah died because he disobeyed a word of God given through however unlikely a messenger, might just provide a further reason for the lesser attention given to Josiah in contrast to the prominence Hezekiah enjoys in Chronicles. The foreign king does not use the name 'Yahweh', but the Chronicler's comment in the following verse, 'He did not listen to the words of Neco from the mouth of God . . .', shows that he believes that word to have been an authentic one from Yahweh.

The 'address' does echo a theme from earlier ones, namely the importance of having God 'with' one (see Abijah, II 13:4–12) and the futility of attempting to fight when he is not 'with' the army. It further illustrates the theme of obedience and disobedience. Even a faithful king like Josiah is by no means exempt from judgement if he fails to keep faith and remain obedient. The account of his death back in Jerusalem, however, may show awareness of the difficulties raised by Huldah's prophecy that he would come to his fathers' tomb 'in peace' (II 34:28, cf. II Kgs. 22:20).

It is, perhaps, surprising that the last two addresses are put in the mouths of foreign kings. However, this one from Neco shows that the Davidic line was not necessarily permanent, while that of Cyrus shows that the real goal of God's purpose was the temple.

[32] II 36:23 *Cyrus, king of Persia, to the exiles (by written decree)*

²³ *Thus says Cyrus, king of Persia, 'All the kingdoms of the world Yahweh, the God of heaven, has given to me, and it is he who has appointed me to build him a sanctuary in Jerusalem of Judah. Any of you, among all his people, may Yahweh his God be with him and may he go back[a]!'*

Text

a Lit. 'may he go up' – i.e. to Jerusalem.

General description

The message is cast in the form of a (written) royal decree, announcing Cyrus' intention to rebuild the temple in Jerusalem. For this he claims divine authority from the God of heaven, whom he explicitly identifies with Yahweh. It calls for support by those who return from the exile and assures them of the divine power with those who go. It may be termed 'Encouragement for a Task' and makes use of the messenger formula.

Contents

It is difficult to say whether these words formed part of the original Books of Chronicles, even if we could ever speak confidently of the 'original' form of any biblical book before it became subject to the interpretative process of the tradents who passed it on. Williamson has argued strongly that the words make sense only in the continuation of them in their Ezra context and that therefore they have been placed here secondarily.[169] Japhet apparently found no real grounds for denying them to the Chronicler's work.[170] Others have pointed out that, since Chronicles ends the Hebrew canon, it would have been found necessary to finish on a positive note and these words have been added for that reason.[171] More traditionally, the overlap of these verses with the first verses of Ezra c. 1 has been seen to establish a link between the two works and to argue for identity of authorship.[172]

Here, we will deal only with that aspect of the issues which is relevant to the investigation we have been undertaking. For it is noteworthy that the words do display some of the characteristics of the earlier addresses. It is seen as fulfilment of the word of an earlier prophet, Jeremiah (v. 22, cf. Jer. 25:12, 29:10). Other 'addresses' have taken written form (those of Elijah and Hezekiah). It again stresses the importance of the 'presence' of Yahweh without which, it is implied, the return of the exiles would be ineffective. It is implicitly a call for support of the rebuilding of the temple from all the people who return, something which is made explicit in Ezra. 1:2–4. But, above all, it suggests that it is the temple which, rising like a phoenix from the ashes, will mark the real continuity between the pre-exilic and post-exilic eras. Hope for the future is founded not on a renascent Davidic line but in the temple the Davidic line was chosen to found and foster.[173] Finally, it demonstrates the power of Yahweh, Israel's God, over all the earth. It is he who gives even to a pagan emperor 'all the kingdoms of the world'. The little band who return will face strong enemies. But the one who is 'with' them will, they will find, be stronger than any these adversaries claim to be acting on their behalf.

Thus the decree continues and even completes many of the themes of the addresses and expresses the theological purpose they have served. Its 'historicity' (certainly not in the present wording) is irrelevant. Theologically it makes a fitting climax to the book and to those concerns which have found expression in the addresses given to protagonists in the sacred drama.

Note on II Chron. 36:15f.

15 And Yahweh, the God of their fathers, kept sending^a to them by means of those who were his messengers because he had concern for his people and the place where he dwelt.^{b} 16 But they kept treating these messengers of God with jesting, scorning their words and making fun of his prophets till God's anger against his people grew until it was beyond appeasement.^{c}

Text

^{a} Lit. 'sent to them persistently early and late'.
^{b} I.e. the temple.
^{c} Lit. 'until there was no healing'.

Contents

We have now completed our examination of the addresses in the Books of Chronicles, but before attempting a summary of conclusions, it would be well to consider the kind of postscript provided by these two verses. Nothing like them appears at the same stage of the Deuteronomistic History, but they might be seen as an extension of II Kgs. 24:20 where, following a brief statement that Zedekiah followed Jehoiakim in doing 'what was evil in the sight of the LORD', the editor comments, 'For because of the anger of the LORD it came to the point in Jerusalem and Judah that he cast them out of his presence.' But the Chronicler's wider description of God's 'messengers' sent to them over and over again because of his 'concern [compassion]' for people and temple, followed by a vivid account of their scornful rejection of these messengers, echoes more closely the Deuteronomistic Historian's assessment of the reason for the fall of the northern kingdom in 721 BCE recorded in II Kgs. c. 17:

Yet the LORD warned Israel and Judah by every prophet and every seer, saying, 'Turn from your evil ways and keep my commandments and my statutes, in accordance with all the law which I commanded you and your fathers, and which I sent to you by my servants the prophets.' But they would not listen . . . They despised his statutes . . . and the warnings which he gave them. *(vv. 13–15)*.

Such a Deuteronomistic explanation of the disaster is found also in the prophets, particularly in Jeremiah: 'they did not heed my words, says the LORD, which I persistently sent to you [the same Hebrew construction as in II

Chr. 36:15] by my servants the prophets, but you would not listen . . .' (Jer. 29:19, a 'Deuteronomistic' passage of the book). In fact, the Chronicler seems to see a fulfilment of Jeremiah's words both in the disaster and the hope of deliverance beyond it. Not only is explicit reference made to 'the word of the LORD by the mouth of Jeremiah' (v. 22), but v. 17, which follows the short extract we have quoted, appears to be almost a direct application of Jer. 21:7:

I will give Zedekiah king of Judah, and his servants, and the people in this city . . . into the hand of Nebuchadnezzar, king of Babylon . . . He shall smite them with the edge of the sword: he shall not pity them, or spare them, or have compassion.

With which we can compare II Chr. 36:17:

Therefore he brought up against them the king of the Chaldeans, who slew their young men with the sword in the house of their sanctuary, and had no compassion on young man or virgin . . .

Indeed, it is Jer. 21:7 which may help us to reconstruct the odd Hebrew of II Chr. 36:14, which has 'princes' in the plural construct, dependent on 'priests', reading literally, 'all the princes [chiefs] of the priests', rendered by RSV as 'all the leading priests'. To avoid this unlikely phrase it is usual to suppose that some such noun as 'Judah' followed, giving 'the princes of Judah and the priests'. This both corresponds to what the Jeremiah verse tells us and fits other occasions when the Chronicler clearly sees three groups (king, civil leaders and priests) as representatives of, and those responsible for, the whole community.

Such reliance on Jeremiah makes all the more striking the use of the general term 'messengers' by the Chronicler to describe those whom God has sent. In the Deuteronomistic History and in Jeremiah it is always 'his servants the prophets' and, elsewhere, the Chronicler also speaks of 'prophets' in a similar context (e.g. II 24:19). Prophets are mentioned here but in a kind of parallelism with the broader term 'messengers', 'they kept treating these messengers of God with jesting . . . and they made fun of his prophets . . .'. The two Hebrew verbs used occur only here. In each case the use of the auxiliary verb with the participle suggests a continuing state of affairs, and this makes an ironic contrast between them and God. God 'kept sending his messengers', but they 'kept rejecting them'. Perhaps the use of these two verbs not found elsewhere suggests we are really hearing the Chronicler's own verdict at this point. He does not appear to be using coventional formulae. Therefore his mention of 'messengers' (twice) and 'prophets' suggests that he is using the term 'messengers' in his own way, more widely in sense. It may be a generic term to refer back to all those who have been given addresses throughout his work. The speakers have included kings, prophets, priests and a Levite, and, on at least one occasion, civil leaders. Taken together they have shown how leadership is a divine gift to the community. God has never left his people without a witness. Through them his words have come again and again.

Thus II Chr. 36:15f. can indeed be seen as a kind of postscript, the point where all these diverse 'addresses' are brought together, apart from all their common features of style, tone and content. The rejection of them by the people affords the Chronicler a theological reason for the judgement of the exile. Yet, these messengers have been recorded as bringing words, not only of threat, warning and judgement, but also of assurance of God's mercy. They therefore also open the door to the hope that God would not abandon his people for ever. When Cyrus proclaims his edict that the temple in Jerusalem is to be rebuilt (v. 23) and all who wish may go back, this is brought about because God 'stirred up the spirit of Cyrus'. But there is also a real sense in which it comes about in order 'that the word of the LORD by the mouth of Jeremiah the prophet might be accomplished' (v. 22). The Hebrew verb used here is כלה / , an interesting word for the fulfilment of prophecy. The Deuteronomistic History tends to use the verb מלא / , meaning 'to fill', or else the Hiph'il of the verb to stand (קום/), meaning 'to cause to stand' in such contexts. For the Chronicler, does the use of the Hebrew כלה/, which means to 'complete' or even 'to finish' at this critical stage of the people's fortunes, recall the promise David gave to Solomon? In I 28:20 we read, 'He will not let you down or desert you until all the work in the service of Yahweh's sanctuary is *complete*' (כלה/). The fulfilment of this promise was recorded in II 7:16, using the same verb: 'Thus was accomplished all the work of Solomon from the day of the foundation of the house of the LORD until it was *finished*.' Now, a rebuilding of that house, another 'completion', is being promised, itself a 'fulfilment' of a word of grace and hope spoken by God through a prophet as well as of the divine purpose through the Davidic line.

It is in this way that II Chr. 36:15f. brings these addresses together. It shows that they testify to God's presence and activity among, and on behalf of, his people. They explain the present disaster, but they testify also to a continuing purpose of grace, so that the hearers may respond in penitence, trust and hope. In the end, the last word is not with the bragging representative of the heathen superpowers, or even with the frailty and sin of the people, but with God, the God who is so often described as 'the God of your fathers', who persistently addresses his people still, as he addressed their fathers, through his various 'messengers'.

3 Summary of the addresses

The themes of the addresses

There are a few general themes which recur throughout these addresses, giving them a homogeneity in spite of their relatedness to their specific contexts and the varying speakers who utter them. Central is their declaration about *the nature of God*. He is the God who *chooses* whom he will in sovereign grace. David tells the leaders and people of Jerusalem:

Nevertheless, Yahweh, the God of Israel, chose me among all my father's family to be king over Israel for ever. He chose Judah as leader and, from the tribe of Judah, my father's family, and among my father's sons it was I he was pleased to make king over all Israel. *(I 28:4)*

It is the election of David and the Davidic dynasty which is central. There is none of the attention paid to the election of all Israel in the Sinaitic covenant that is found in the Deuteronomistic History, for all that the Sinaitic covenant has there been fused with the Davidic tradition, notably in three crucial passages (I Kgs. 2:1–4, 8:15–21, 9:1–9).

This 'choice' extends also to Solomon. As David continues in addressing the elders:

And from all my sons (for Yahweh has given me many sons) he chose my son Solomon to sit on the throne of Yahweh's kingdom over Israel. *(v. 5)*

It extends also to the continuing Davidic line. Abijah says to Jeroboam and the people of Israel:

Should you not know that Yahweh, the God of Israel, has given the kingdom over Israel to David and his successors for ever by an immutable covenant? *(II 13:5)*

It is important to stress, however, against those who see a form of messianism in the Chronicler's emphasis on the choice of David and the Davidic line, that the purpose in this choice is the building of the temple. The opening address of Amasai to David includes the poetic blessing:

> Rich prosperity be yours [Heb. *shalôm*]
> and prosperity to those who help you;
> for your God helps you. *(I 12:18/19)*

Shalôm means more than 'peace' as a greeting. It is the characteristic of the reign of Solomon (*Sh^elômoh*) and is the necessary pre-condition for the building of the temple. David could not build it because his hands were stained with blood, but

A son shall be born to you. He will be a man of rest and I will give him rest from all the enemies who surround him. His name shall be Solomon and I will give Israel *shalôm* and quiet in his time. It is he who will build a sanctuary to my name. *(I 22:9f.)*

Indeed, David makes clear that the choice of Solomon is for this very purpose:

And from all my sons . . . he chose my son Solomon . . . And to me he said, 'It is your son, Solomon, who shall build my sanctuary and my courts . . .' *(I 28:5f.)*

And David can assure Solomon, not just of God's presence in general, but for this particular task:

Yahweh my God is with you. He will not let you down or desert you until all the work in the service of Yahweh's sanctuary is complete. *(I 28:20)*

And, as we have seen, any king of the Davidic line who is given an address is usually showing concern for the temple or its worship – he is, in fact, acting in a David-like way. It is perhaps no wonder that the last free composition of the Chronicler, the decree attributed to Cyrus, concerns the temple. The whole object of the choice of David and his line is the temple, its personnel and its worship. The post-exilic theocracy is the legitimate heir of the pre-exilic monarchy.

This divine choice extends to other leaders in the theocracy beside David and his line, and places its recipients under solemn obligation to zeal and fidelity in their office. So Hezekiah addresses the Levites and priests:

My children, do not be negligent now, for God has chosen you to stand in his presence, to lead worship to him and offer him worship and sacrifice. *(II 29:11)*

Such a call can be made in the confidence that God offers his people all they need for the task for which they have been chosen. Above all, he offers them his *presence*, one of the most frequently heard themes in the addresses. As David charges the leaders of Israel to help Solomon he does so with the reassuring question, 'Is not Yahweh your God with you?' (I 22:18), an assurance repeated to Solomon himself (I 28:20). Abijah is not only confident of victory when confronting the army of Jeroboam and Israel because of this ('Know, then, that God is with us at our head', II 13:12) but is equally sure that without the 'presence' of God, Israel is doomed to failure. The same address shows how intimately the presence of God is bound up with the temple, its duly called and ordained personnel and its sacred vessels.

We have Aaronites and Levites ministering to Yahweh as priests in his service. Morning and evening they offer to Yahweh whole burnt offerings and sweet incense offerings; they arrange the pure showbread on the pure table and the golden Minorah with its lamps for burning at evening. So we keep the commandment of Yahweh our God. But you have abandoned him. Know, then, that God is with us at our head.' *(II 13:10b–12b)*

So much is the presence of God bound up with his presence in the temple that Hezekiah can equate forsaking God with 'turning their attention away from the dwelling of Yahweh' and the consequent neglect of all that care for temple, sacred vessels, institutions and worship which Abijah boasts for Judah (II 29:6). Equally, it is God's presence with armies that makes victory certain. So Jahaziel assures king Jehoshaphat and all the inhabitants of Judah and Jerusalem as they face the Edomite army, 'Do not be afraid. Do not be dismayed. Tomorrow go out against them, and Yahweh will be with you' (II 20:17). Equally, human enterprise, without the presence of God, can lead only to frustration and defeat. Jehoshaphat's proud fleet is ignominiously sunk before it even leaves harbour. It is contemptuously referred to by Eliezer as 'your works' (II 20:37).

God's presence is so effective because *he is all-powerful*, far above human might or resource, however apparently great and fearful. The people of God always face armies of immense size, like the 'million' men of the Ethiopian army (II 14:9). Yet, as Hanani is later to say to Asa, 'Were not the Ethiopians and Libyans a great force with chariots and a vast number of horsemen? Yet then you depended on Yahweh and he gave them into your power' (II 16:8).

The fact is that 'God is able to help and to cast down', as a man of God says to Amaziah (II 25:8b). Even the mighty king of Assyria has only 'human might' to rely on, as Hezekiah tells the army leaders, but 'on our [side] is Yahweh, our God, to help us and fight our battles' (II 32:8). This theme is not new. It featured in the Deuteronomistic History, especially in such passages as Judges cc. 6–8 in the story of Gideon's victory over the Midianites or in I Sam. c. 14, the story of Jonathan's assault on the Philistines, where a concluding editorial statement runs, 'So the LORD delivered Israel that day' (v. 23). It characterises a story like that of David's fight against Goliath when he tells the Philistine, 'You come to me with a sword and with a spear and with a javelin; but I come to you in the name of the LORD of Hosts' (I Sam. 17:45). The addresses in Chronicles evoke such passages, heighten them and might even be seen as exegesis of them.

Not only has God, in his omnipotence, power to help in battle or in the effective discharge of sacred office, but he has all the resources to give his people everything they need. So to Amaziah, worrying about his lost deposit of a hundred talents spent in hiring Israelite mercenaries, the man of God says, 'Yahweh is able to give you far more than this' (II 25:9). Indeed, there is a very close link between the presence of God and material prosperity for his people, which is why they can be generous in providing from their resources for the upkeep of the temple and its personnel. So Azariah says to Hezekiah:

Since they began to bring their offering into Yahweh's sanctuary, there has been food in plenty with much to spare. Yahweh has blessed his people so that there is all this surplus. *(II 31:10)*

Nor must we overlook the 'presence' of God which has been *mediated through his 'word'*, spoken to the people at all stages of their history. This very anthology of addresses, scattered throughout the Chronicler's work, illustrates the fact that God speaks through his 'messengers' whom he has sent to them persistently because 'he had concern for his people and for his dwelling place' (II 36:15). Even in the days of Joash's disobedience, God came to warn the realm of this king who had earlier been faithful, in a gracious attempt to win them back:

Yet he sent prophets among them to bring them back to the LORD; these testified against them, but they would not give heed. *(II 24:19)*

The very frequent citation of earlier 'Scripture' shows how this is seen as an authoritative and still relevant word to his people of all later generations. This is made explicit in the words of Jehoshaphat as he and the people go out to battle against the Moabites and Ammonites, in which belief in God is paralleled with belief in his prophets:

Trust in Yahweh your God and you will be supported; trust in his prophets and you will succeed. *(II 20:20)*

We showed reason to believe as well[1] that the written form of Elijah's address in the guise of a letter to Jehoshaphat (II 21:12–15) was also an allusion to the concept of a written corpus of authoritative prophetic literature.

God also shows himself *sovereign in his mercy and judgement*. He is a God of mercy, and it is never too late to 'seek' him. So Hezekiah announces in a message sent not only through Judah but through the territory of the former northern kingdom of Israel as well:

For if you return to Yahweh, your kinsmen and your descendants will find compassion from their captors and return to this land because of the grace and compassion of Yahweh, your God. He will not turn away from you if you return to him *(II 30:9)*

Nevertheless, he is also the God who judges inexorably those who do not return to him or, having once been loyal, have turned away. So Elijah assures Jehoram:

You have not followed the ways of your father Jehoshaphat . . . but have gone the way of the kings of Israel . . . For this Yahweh is going to afflict your people, your children, your wives, even all your possessions severely with terrible calamities. You yourself will know many diseases . . .' *(II 21:12–15)*

We cannot miss the instances of kings who knew both blessing and judgement because they apostasised even after earlier loyalty to Yahweh or, following apostasy, repented and came back to him. Rehoboam responds to the word that comes through Shemaiah, so Yahweh tempers his judgement, leaving him subject to Shishak but escaping total destruction (II 12:6–8). Asa acted as a model Davidide in his trust in God and so knew victory over the Ethiopians; but later reliance upon the Syrians brings him a rebuke from Hanani and the judgement of continuing warfare (II 16:7–10, 12). Jehoshaphat is one who also obeys Yahweh's laws early in his reign, yet later contracts marriage with the royal family of the northern kingdom, embarking on a military adventure in alliance with them. Jehu tells him of judgement to come for this, and yet, again, it is judgement tempered with mercy because 'some good is found in you' (II 19:2f.) and Jehoshaphat can even utter an address as the mouth-piece of God to the judges of Judah and Jerusalem (19:6–11). The reign of Joash was divided exactly between faithfulness in its first part when the priest Jehoida was alive, and disobedience in its later years for which he suffered defeat at the hand of Syria and final conspiracy against him by his servants, as Zechariah had warned (24:20). Amaziah is another king of mixed fortunes who first acted according to God's law and listened when a 'man of God' warned him against using Israelite mercenaries. But flirtation with Edomite gods led to a rebuke from a 'prophet' and, when he refused to listen to that word, there came judgement by defeat at the hands of Israel and conspiracy against him while on the throne (25:14-25). The double word of God in all this is to warn against complacency. No one can rest on past obedience to God. Very much in the spirit of Ezekiel c. 18, each generation stands on its own feet before God and is answerable to him. But, equally, none need despair. None who seeks God's grace seeks in vain. Even the people of the North can respond to God's word, as they did when Oded called on the army of the North not to be vindictive against their kinsmen from Judah, a call reinforced by some of their own leaders (II 28:8-15). There need be no 'outsiders' to God's grace, as the response of some northerners to Hezekiah's call later also demonstrated (30:18-22). Indeed one wonders whether in these two passages there might be intended some reference to the later situation of those in the Diaspora or to those who considered themselves, or were considered by some others, to be outside the circle of normative Judaism.

To this God *a proper and worthy human response* is called for, and the addresses sound such an hortatory note repeatedly. In the first place, those summoned to particular tasks are to be brave and zealous, in spite of all external difficulties or what they may feel to be their own inadequacy. So David, summoning Solomon to his divinely appointed task of temple building, says, 'Be strong! Be resolute! Do not be afraid! Do not be discouraged! . . . Rise to the task, and may Yahweh be with you' (I 22:13, 16). We have seen that such calls occur in the Deuteronomistic literature, but are not frequent in prophetic preaching. Later, David commands Solomon, 'know the God of your father and serve him with your whole mind and with an enthusiastic heart' (I 28:9). Such a call is addressed by Azariah to Asa and the people, even when it fits the context only obliquely: 'Now, be strong! Do not weaken! There will be a reward for all your effort' (II 15:7). Jehoshaphat calls on the judges and sacral leaders in similar terms: 'Be strong! Be zealous! May Yahweh be on the side of the good!' (II 19:11). Soldiers, about to do battle, hear the same kind of exhortation. 'Do not be afraid! Do not be dismayed! Tomorrow, go out against them, and Yahweh will be with you' (II 20:17). Such lively response is especially to be shown in the service of the temple. Hezekiah calls on the priests and Levites to 'bring out what is unclean from the holy place' to cleanse the temple and purify its worship, and he charges them: 'My children, do not be negligent . . .' (II 29:11). In his message to the people of the North and South he says, 'Give Yahweh his due honour and come to his sanctuary . . . Serve Yahweh your God . . .' (II 30:8).

We have discussed above[2] the nature of such calls as an 'Encouragement for a Task' form. Apart altogether from the exact definition of the form, its frequent recurrence suggests that it was a recognised and familiar one, and its appearance elsewhere in the post-exilic prophets (e.g. Hag. 2:4, Zech. 8:9, 13) may indicate that it was familiar to post-exilic preaching and exhortation. No doubt, in the mind of the speaker it implies potential, if not actual, weakness among the members of the community, a weakness suggested by Haggai's use of it and made explicit in the specific charges brought by Malachi.

In particular, absolute trust in Yahweh is called for, very much in the spirit of Isaiah of Jerusalem calling for a like attitude and, as with Isaiah, such trust means turning away from all other (human) resources, even one's own. Hanani rebuked Asa and announced judgement:

It is because you depended on the king of Syria and did not depend on Yahweh your God that the army of the king of Israel has eluded your grasp. Were not the Ethiopians and the Libyans a great force with chariots and a vast number of horsemen? Yet then you depended on Yahweh and he gave them into your power . . . *(II 16:7f.)*

Hanani's son, Jehu, similarly rebukes Asa's son, Jehoshaphat, after his joint escapade against the Syrians with Israel (II 19:2). So strong is the 'quietist' stance of these addresses when it comes to battle, that Jahaziel can say, 'You will have no need even to fight in this battle. Take your stations. Stand firm and you will witness Yahweh's victory for you' (II 20:17).

It is clear that much of this is development of earlier prophetic teaching, and the form of much of the appeal for response is in line with Deuteronomistic preaching motifs. Yet there is an immediacy and urgency in the calls, related usually to specific acts of obedience and, further, there is an hortatory element about the addresses which, it might be argued, places them in the category of 'preaching' rather than of prophecy. They are not so much the calls (often implicit) of the prophets for a fundamental repentance which will affect the continuance of their status as covenant people of Yahweh, or the annulment of that covenant in a final judgement. The addresses are more often calls to them from within their status as God's people to show those specific attitudes and acts which, as such, they ought to show. To be sure, the response, or lack of it, brings judgement or blessing. But, usually, implicit in the outlook of these addresses is the conviction that the hearers are within the line of the continuing purpose of God and that purpose will not cease. They may lose much of God's blessing if they step out of line. But the grace of God sees to it that judgement is neither total nor final. The temple community, the theocracy, continues. Nevertheless, it has to be said that such differences between the addresses and prophetic preaching are those of nuance and degree, almost of 'atmosphere', and they are extremely hard to objectify or quantify. After all, the prophets also called for specific actions and responses and, apparently, not all prophets saw judgement as total or final.

One more theme of the addresses which must be noted is *the appeal to God's action in their past history*. In one sense, if the approach to the addresses followed here is correct in that they seem to relate particular moments in the people's history to the situation of the Chronicler and his contemporaries, then they all serve as 'sermons with historical illustrations'. More particularly, there are references to the past to illustrate the truth of a point now being made. It is, perhaps, natural that David should tell Solomon of God's past choice of him and dealings with him which have led to the present call to Solomon and the elders to build the temple (I 22:6–10, 28:2–7). But Shemaiah also explains the present judgement of Judah at the hand of Shishak by their own past 'abandoning' of Yahweh (II 12:5). Abijah rehearses the history of the appointment of David and the divisions of the kingdom with the subsequent cultic changes in the North in his call to Jeroboam and his army to desist from attacking the South (II 13:5–9). Azariah makes a much more general and obscure reference to history when he says:

For a long time Israel had no true God, no priests to instruct them and no Torah. Then, in their distress, they came back to Yahweh, the God of Israel, and sought him, and he let himself be found by them. In those days there was no security as they went about their business, but only times of growing confusion for the citizens of all lands. Nations and cities destroyed each other, for God plunged them into confusion with every kind of disaster. *(II 15:3–6)*

In our examination of Azariah's address we suggested that this is left deliberately vague and general (and heavily dependent on earlier biblical material),[3] in order to give it reference to many possible situations, not least to the exile. Its use in Zech. 8:9–13 suggests how such 'generalising' of earlier biblical material was current in the second temple period. Whatever the truth of that, appeal to history is being made to reinforce the point of the address that to be true to God is to know his blessing but to forsake him leads inevitably to his judgement. This is a lesson their past history illustrates. Elijah's letter to Jehoram accuses him of walking in the ways of the kings of Israel and reminds him of the example of 'the house of Ahab' (II 21:13). Hezekiah, in addressing the Levites and priests, points to the unfaithfulness of their fathers in turning away from God, which is paralleled to 'turning their attention away from the dwelling of Yahweh' and refers to their neglect of the temple and its worship (II 29:6). The immediate reference is to the preceding reign of Ahaz, but we saw reason to suppose that, again, the historical reference is more general.[4] The same (negative) example of 'the fathers' as a warning of conduct and attitudes to be avoided is held up in Hezekiah's letter (II 30:7f.). Finally, Josiah reminds the Levites of Solomon's building of the temple (II 35:3). All such 'illustrations' are general except where the context demands some specific (and very recent) occurrence to explain the present situation. With so little material before us it is unwise to argue from omissions. The silence concerning the Exodus or the Sinaitic covenant in the addresses is striking, however, especially if one compares it with Deuteronomic homiletical material or with the 'oracular' element in many of the Psalms. We saw that, in Jahaziel's address (II 20:17), it is possible there may be an evocation of Exod. 14:13f., but even if that is so, we have no explicit reference to the Exodus/Sinai traditions in the addresses. Further, we noted the possibility that David was seen as a successor to Moses. Yet here the parallels are to Moses as transmitter of the instructions concerning the temple, its personnel, sacrifices and worship. It seems as though, for the Chronicler, David and the temple were the climax to all that God had done before and fulfilment of the promise of the Exodus/Sinai traditions. One might almost say David and temple eclipsed these earlier traditions, and that is certainly the impression given by the addresses. The total impression is that the main aim is to justify the post-exilic theocracy in terms of the Davidic covenant promise.[5]

That raises the issue of the period in the history of Israel to which such a theological content most naturally relates. The themes are general enough to fit many periods, but it is clear that they would bear with particular relevance on the post-exilic temple period. It is difficult to exaggerate the profundity and far-reaching consequences of the change from a pre-exilic Yahwism which was the mortar binding the nation-state, so inextricably bound up with the Davidic dynasty and the city of Jerusalem, to a post-exilic religion of a small, non-monarchic and remote province of a foreign world empire. Questions of continuity, identity and authenticity must have been immense. By showing that the real purpose of God with the Davidic dynasty was the temple which, by its proper upkeep and service, functioned as a place of encounter between God and his people, and by thus redefining the promise of the

Davidic covenant so as to show how it had found fulfilment in the temple-centred theocracy, the addresses show how this remarkable translation of Yahwism was expounded to post-exilic congregations. Through the assurance that God had chosen them and that, although the conduct of their fathers had often merited judgement, judgement had never been untempered by mercy, further assurance could be given. By showing how the teaching of the prophets pointed to the present 'fulfilment' of God's promises by exposition of the growing written, authoritative body of the prophetic writings; by extension of earlier prophetic oracles to the present time; and by such contemporary teaching, showing how the temple personnel were legitimate descendants of the prophets, the addresses tackled the searching questions that must often have been asked concerning the apparent non-fulfilment of the great prophetic promises from the past. By assuring them of God's supreme power over all human powers, however apparently strong and victorious, the addresses would have brought hope to those who saw themselves as helpless pawns in the power game of the time. By calling on them to desist from useless military activity and to trust God alone, the addresses gave them solid theological grounds for facing the realities of their situation. They also warn them against turning to any other kind of military help in their weakness and, above all, from compromising alliance of any kind with those who are not the true 'people of God'. The call to be true to God in active support of the temple, its worship and its personnel, and so prove worthy of God's blessing, was a pastoral one which discouraged congregations of many times must always have needed. By assuring them that they now had the 'presence' of God with them in the temple, mediated to them through their divinely appointed leadership and in its worship and preaching, the addresses sought to maintain the faith of the people with a relevant kind of 'realised eschatology'. In other words, the addresses, in addition to reflecting so closely the theology of the Chronicler, seem to let us hear something of the process by which the 'preachers' of the second temple must have offered theodicy and called for the response of fidelity. Such teaching was illustrated and reinforced by reference to their past history as the people of God and also to earlier prophecy. Of those 'fathers' they are now the true and legitimate descendants. Let them emulate their faithfulness and avoid their failures. Let them know that the God of their fathers is with them yet. Such general themes certainly do not of themselves permit any precise attempt at dating. But perhaps they suggest a long enough period of time into the post-exilic, second temple period for the difficulties and questions to have arisen which they attempt to meet.

For all the weight of scholarly opinion now wishing to date the Chronicler in the immediate time of the rebuilding of the temple (c. 520–515 BCE), it does seem as if at least the stage of the work which included the bulk of the addresses is more suitably to be dated later than that.

The speakers

The following diagram shows the distribution of the thirty-two addresses which have been discussed.

Among the fifteen addresses given to 'Israelite' kings (after the division of the kingdoms only Judaean kings are assigned addresses) seven are spoken by David, one by Abijah, one by Asa, two by Jehoshaphat, three by Hezekiah and one by Josiah. Pharaoh Neco and Cyrus also speak or issue a decree but, for the purpose of our classification here, they have been included among 'others'.

Nine of the addresses are spoken by prophetic figures, of whom four are described as 'prophets' (Shemaiah, Elijah, an unnamed prophet who addresses Amaziah and Oded). Azariah is not given a title, but his words are referred to as 'the prophecy' and the address is introduced by a description of the spirit coming upon him in a typical prophetic-type formula (II 15:1, 8). The unnamed speaker who addresses Amaziah is described as 'a man of God' (II 16:7, 10), while of Jehu it is said that he was 'the son of Hanani the seer' (II 19:2). Eliezer is said to have 'prophesied' (II 20:37). Three addresses may probably be ascribed to priests: Azariah (II 26:17f.), Azariah the 'chief' or 'high' priest (II 31:10), while Zechariah speaks for his dead father, Jehoida. Nevertheless, his address is introduced by the interesting and more 'prophetic' sounding sentence, 'The spirit of God clothed itself with Zechariah.' One address is assigned to a Levite, Jahaziel (included in the 'priestly-type' group of speakers in our classification). But his words are introduced by the prophetic-type description, 'the spirit of Yahweh came upon Jahaziel' (II 20:14), and he uses the prophetic messenger formula, 'This is what Yahweh is saying to you.' Those classified as 'others' include Amasai, the first of the speakers and an army officer, whose words are, however, introduced by a prophetic formula, 'Then the spirit came upon Amasai' (I 12:18/19). Another is the address spoken by certain leaders of the Ephraimites who respond to and underline the words of Oded the prophet (II 28:12f.). There are also the words of the Egyptian king, Neco, to Josiah (II 35:21) and the decree of Cyrus (II 36:23), which brings the wheel full circle with the promise of a rebuilt temple in Jerusalem. His words are seen as a fulfilment of a prophecy of Jeremiah (v. 22).

One observation which comes immediately to mind is that the adjective, at least, in von Rad's phrase 'the *Levitical* sermon' is misleading where only one of the thirty-two addresses is assigned specifically to a Levite. It seems that von Rad has been too much influenced by his belief that the Deuteronomic 'preachers' were Levites.[6] Further, as we said above,[7] too much weight has been put on such passages as II 19:8 and Neh. 8:7f. This is not to deny the Levites *any* instructive role (e.g. II 35:3), but it is difficult to maintain that such a role was exclusive to them or that they alone were the preachers of the 'sermons'.[8] Petersen[9] probably generalises too much on the role of the Levites in the post-exilic temple on the basis of the one episode of Jahaziel, recorded in II Chr. 20:1–30.

We have sought to show that the faithful kings (faithful, at least, at the time of speaking) who utter addresses do so when they are acting in the true interests of the temple, its worship and its personnel, and so in accordance with David's actions and instructions. In this respect they are mouth-pieces for David and represent the continuing fulfilment of the Davidic covenant as it leads to, and issues in, the life of the theocracy.[10] Throntveit has argued that the royal speeches in Chronicles fulfil the same role as that assigned by Noth to certain speeches and prayers in the Deuteronomistic History, that is, they mark off significant moments in the Chronicler's structure of history. While this is true to some degree, the argument appears at times to be forced. Of Asa's speech (II 14:7/6) it is said, 'As the speech both culminates the peaceful years and provides the backdrop for the holy war of vv. 9–14, it may be seen as occurring at a turning point in the narrative' (*When Kings Speak*, pp. 38f.). On such reading *any* point in history may be held to be significant because it comes between one event, or set of events, and another. In our view the role of the addresses of faithful Davidide kings is to show the continuation of David's concern for the temple and its worship and so the continuity of God's original promises to David. This is certainly not to deny the force of Throntveit's argument that the Chronicler has structured the history along the broad lines of periods of united monarchy, divided monarchy and united monarchy again from the time of Hezekiah onwards.

The two 'priestly' addresses might also be said to be appropriately assigned, since Zechariah charges king and people with transgressing 'the commandments' of Yahweh (II 24:20). If anyone should be concerned with the proper observance of 'commandments' it should surely be the priest. Azariah (II 31:10) speaks of the contributions of tithes for the temple, another clearly demarcated area of priestly concern. Nevertheless, this is only a superficial classification of the themes of the addresses, for Zechariah accuses the people of 'forsaking Yahweh', and that is exactly the charge of Shemaiah, the prophet (II 12:5). In the former case the forsaking of Yahweh has shown itself in cultic neglect and abuses, in the latter with 'forsaking the Torah' of Yahweh (cf. II 12:1) – in which way is not specified. Both make the point that forsaking Yahweh leads to being forsaken by Yahweh, also the theme of Azariah's 'prophecy' (II 15:3). Other themes in the prophetic addresses include the need to rely wholly on Yahweh in battle and to avoid any kind of alliance with those who are not his (Hanani, II 16:7–9; Jehu, 19:2; the 'man of God', 25:7–9); the duty to worship Yahweh exclusively (Elijah, II 21:12f.; the 'prophet', 26:15); and the call for ethical behaviour in line with Yahweh's direction (Elijah, 21:12ff., against Jehoram for the murder of his brothers; Oded, 28:8ff., against the victorious Israelite army for its vindictive treatment of its Judaean captives). Such ethical preoccupation found in the addresses should not be missed in their apparently rather greater attention to cultic matters. All of these themes are, broadly, those of the canonical prophets of the Old Testament, and each can be matched by words attributed to Hosea, Isaiah of Jerusalem and others.[11]

Jahaziel, the one Levitical representative, encourages Jehoshaphat and the army of Judah with an assurance of victory in their battle against the Moabites and Ammonites (II 20:14-17). Yet this address includes a call for whole-hearted trust in Yahweh's power alone in line with similar such calls from the prophets. Further, it immediately follows the account of Jehoshaphat's prayer of complete trust in Yahweh, so that we should be wary of classifying Jahaziel, the Levite, as among the superficial professional prophets of weal. He is really stating the same theological principle as do Hanani, Jehu and the 'man of God'.

It is extremely difficult to discern any rationale in the difference of terminology between 'seer', 'prophet' or 'man of God' used by the Chronicler. D. L. Petersen attempted to classify the use of the terms in the more classical period of prophecy,[12] and concluded that 'man of God' indicated a peripheral prophet, while 'seer' (Heb. חֹזֶה) and 'prophet' indicated more central roles, the former belonging to Judah and the latter to the North. 'Seer' (Heb. רֹאֶה) indicated a residential urban figure who functioned in the public sacrificial cultus. Even if these results are accepted, it is interesting that he does not cite one reference from Chronicles. Almost certainly this must be because, by the Chronicler's day, the exact nature of prophecy and the precise roles of various kinds of prophets must have been becoming blurred just, as it seems, the 'forms' of prophetic oracles were (see below). R. R. Wilson is cautious about making any attempt to reconstruct an 'historical' view of pre- or post-exilic prophecy from the Chronicler's writings.[13] Further, it is difficult to say why, in some instances, one of the figures is left unnamed or with no descriptive title, while, in others, full and detailed genealogies are given. It is possible that this is because of different received traditions which came to the Chronicler. We have seen, however, that such details, whether in the description of a place or in a genealogy, may be as much the mark of legend as of history.[14] If, however, all the characters who utter addresses are part of the Chronicler's own invention, it is difficult to see why he did not achieve consistency in this matter. On the other hand, inconsistency may suggest various levels of the handling of the text and be its own witness to the issue of the 'unity' of the Chronicler's work.

All we can do is to observe that Elijah is the only certainly northern prophet given an 'address' (in his case in the form of a letter) by the Chronicler. Possibly the process had already begun by which Elijah came to be viewed as a 'type-prophet', a process seen in Mal. 4:5f., and later in Ecclus. 48:10 and the New Testament (e.g. Mark 9:11f.). Oded may, or may not, have been from the North. We are not told. The titles given make no distinction that can be clearly observed. Shemaiah is described as 'the prophet' and addresses king Rehoboam and his princes. Azariah is not described, but he also addresses 'Asa and all Judah and Benjamin' and his words are described as 'the prophecy'. Elijah is called 'the prophet' and delivers an oracle of judgement to Jehoram. The unnamed prophet of II 25:15 issues a similar rebuke to Amaziah. Yet Hanani is called 'the seer' (הָרֹאֶה), but he equally brings a rebuke and threat of judgement to a king, to Asa. Jehu, his son, not given a descriptive title, issues a similar rebuke to Asa's son, Jehoshaphat, though the threat of judgement in his case is less total.

Whether or not, then, the speakers are named or given genealogies, and however they are described, they all seem to be doing and saying very similar things. It would certainly be hazardous to use the pictures given of those who utter the prophetic addresses in Chronicles in any attempted reconstruction of prophecy in Israel.[15] We have seen that we must even be careful how we use the material for evidence of post-exilic developments.

All we can say is that there is a certain broad fitness in the themes of the addresses given to kings, priests, or the prophetic figures. Beyond that we can say only that the Chronicler sees them all as 'messengers' (II 36:15f.). They are those through whom God has spoken to his people at every stage of their history. And, through those who expound the truths they spoke to the people of the post-exilic temple age, these great figures of the past are believed to speak still, and God to speak through them. Perhaps we are already seeing the influences and processes that led towards the greater use of pseudepigraphy in the post-exilic period.

Form and characteristics of the addresses

Consideration of the speakers to whom the addresses were assigned led us to question the suitability of the adjective in von Rad's description of them as 'Levitical Sermons'. A decision about the correctness of the nominal element in the phrase, 'Sermon', requires some attention to their form and structure. In this, for convenience, we will keep to our broad classification of the addresses into those spoken by, first royal, then priestly, and finally prophetic-type figures.

In the royal utterances the actual form of address is interesting. Probably we should not make too much of the fact that in two addresses of David to Solomon he uses the term 'my son' (I 22:7, 28:9), since this would be natural usage. It does occur again, in the plural, in Hezekiah's address to the priests and Levites (II 29:11). This may be used, however, to afford yet another example of the parallels between David and Hezekiah. It does give a certain 'wisdom' ring to the addresses, interesting in view of the 'royal' associations of some Wisdom literature, but it is not a frequent enough feature in the material in Chronicles to provide a basis for any generalisation. What is much more common to several of the royal addresses to a larger number of people is the call for attention, 'Hear me!' (David, I 28:2; Abijah, II 13:4; Jehoshaphat, 20:20; Hezekiah, 29:5). Such an often-repeated phrase gives the addresses the appearance of a 'royal proclamation'. Yet the phrase, or some equivalent like 'Give heed!' can be used also by other speakers to secure attention. Another frequently repeated formula is some version of the so-called 'Installation to Office' genre, to which we have given the broader and more general title of 'Encouragement for a Task'.[16] Typical of this form are the words used by David to Solomon, 'Be strong! (Heb. חֲזַק) Be resolute! (Heb. אֱמָץ) Do not be afraid! (Heb. אַל־תִּירָא) Do not be discouraged!' (Heb. אַל־תֵּחָת). To this can be added a call for action, 'Rise to the task' (Heb. קוּם), and, often, some assurance of God's presence (I 22:13–16). For other royal examples compare Jehoshaphat to the judges and other leaders, II 19:6f., 11; Hezekiah to the priests and Levites, 29:5, 11, and Hezekiah to the commanders and people, 32:7f. The recurrence of the formula thus gives a certain cohesion to the royal addresses, although its use by later kings may serve the purpose of showing them to be acting in a David-like way. Again, it is not limited to use by kings.

Another feature of some of the royal addresses is the repeated use of inverted sayings, sometimes involving play on words, an apparent rhetorical device for making speech memorable. So David says to Solomon,

If you seek him he will be found by you.
But if you forsake him he will reject you for ever. *(I 28:9)*

Asa's words in II 14:7/6 play on different aspects of the word 'to seek', while one of Jehoshaphat's addresses employs straight parallelism:

Trust in Yahweh your God
and you will be supported;

trust in his prophets
and you will succeed. *(II 20:20)*

Hezekiah's proclamation says:

O Israelites, return to Yahweh . . .
that he may turn to back those of you who are left
as survivors from the rule of the kings
of Assyria. *(II 30:6)*

Such passages, incidentally, raise the interesting question of how far von Rad
was correct in saying that sermons are in prose. The distinction in Hebrew
between prose and poetry is not always clear, and the border-line is obscured
when von Rad allows that they show a preference for high-sounding, elevated
vocabulary and solemn, formal phraseology and even, at times, a style akin to
poetic parallelism.[17] What does not seem to be in doubt, however, is the strong
rhetorical style and form of the addresses. This is shown by other features as
well. The use of the rhetorical question appears only twice in the royal
addresses. So, for example, Abijah, speaking to Jeroboam and the Israelites,
says,

Should you not know that Yahweh . . . has given the kingdom over Israel to David and
his successors for ever by an immutable covenant? *(II 13:5)*

The appeal to past history by way of illustration of a truth occurs three times,
in the same address of Abijah (II 13:6ff.), in Hezekiah's proclamation (II 30:7)
and Josiah's charge to the Levites (II 35:3). More of the royal addresses
contain citation of, or clear allusion to, earlier Scripture. Jehoshaphat echoes
Isa. 7:9 when he says, 'Trust in Yahweh your God and you will be supported'
(II 20:20); the repeated call 'Be strong! Be brave!' recalls Moses' charge to
Joshua and other such passages. Hezekiah's assurance of God's mercy and
grace (II 30:9) evokes the appearance of Yahweh to Moses, recorded in Exod.
34:6f. Hezekiah reinterprets the words of Isaiah (Isa. 31:3) in his call for faith
before a mighty army, 'With him is the arm of flesh but with us is Yahweh . . .'
(II 32:7f.).

Of the four addresses attributed to 'priestly-type' figures, those of Azariah,
the priests (II 26: 17f., 31:10) are too short to evince any clearly recognisable
formal structure. The other two are striking, if we concentrate on formal and
not just thematic characteristics. Both are strongly *prophetic* in form. Of
Jahaziel we read, 'the spirit of Yahweh came upon him' (II 20:14). His address
opens with the kind of call for attention that marked the royal proclamation,
'Give heed!' (הַקְשִׁיבוּ, rather than שְׁמָעוּנִי). It includes the prophetic messenger

formula, 'This is what Yahweh is saying to you' (v. 15). The oracle which
follows could be described as an 'assurance of salvation', but it includes the
formula we have termed an 'Encouragement for a Task', which also marks
some of the royal addresses (vv. 15, 17). Of Zechariah we read, 'And the spirit
of God clothed itself with Zechariah' (II 24:20). He also begins with the
messenger formula, 'This is what God is saying.' The 'oracle' begins with a
rhetorical question which might be termed 'the ground of accusation', 'Why
do you keep transgressing the commandments of Yahweh?' Yet the 'announcement of judgement' takes the form of just such an inversion as we have
seen characterises some royal addresses:

When you forsake Yahweh
he forsakes you. *(v. 20)*

The greater number of oracles by 'prophetic-type' figures betray a still
more bewildering variety of forms. Of the nine we have so described, only two
have the messenger formula, those of Shemaiah (II 12:5) and Elijah (II 21:12).
Indeed, Elijah's 'letter' contains the purest form of classical prophetic threat
of judgement with (1) messenger formula (v. 12); (2) ground of accusation (vv.
12f.); and (3) announcement of future, total judgement (vv. 14f.). Of only one
prophet, Azariah (II 15:1), is it said, 'The spirit of God came upon' him.
Others use similar inversions or parallelisms to those found in the royal and
priestly addresses. So Shemaiah says:

You abandoned me.
Now I . . . have abandoned you. *(II 12:5)*

Azariah says,

Yahweh is with you
all the while you are with him.
If you seek him
he will be found by you.
But if you abandon him
he will abandon you. *(II 15:2)*

Others employ the device of rhetorical question, as, for example, Jehu:

Do you enjoy helping the wicked
and those who hate Yahweh? *(II 19:2)*

Oded asks the question,

Have you not sins of your own against Yahweh? *(II 28:10)*

We find illustration by way of appeal to history in Azariah's address (II 15:3–

Table 2.1 *Distribution of formal characteristics in the addresses*

Formal characteristics	Royal	Priestly	Prophetic	Others	TOTAL
A. Specific address: (e.g. 'my son⟨s⟩', or those addressed named)	7 (47%)	3 (75%)	3 (33%)	2 (50%)	15 (47%)
B. Call for attention: ('Hear me!'/'Give heed!')	4 (27%)	1 (25%)	2 (22%)	—	7 (22%)
C. A prophetic formula: ('The spirit came upon . . .' messenger formula, etc.)	—	2 (50%)	3 (33%)	2 (50%)	7 (22%)
D. Appeal to or citation of 'Scripture'	4 (27%)	1 (25%)	4 (44%)	—	9 (28%)
E. Illustration from history	3 (20%)	—	4 (44%)	—	7 (22%)
F. 'Encouragement formula'	4 (27%)	1 (25%)	1 (11%)	2 (50%)	8 (25%)
G. Inversion/play on words	7 (47%)	1 (25%)	5 (55%)	1 (25%)	14 (44%)
H. Rhetorical question	2 (13%)	1 (25%)	4 (44%)	1 (25%)	8 (25%)

6); Hanani (16:8); Elijah (21:13) and Oded (28:9). Further, we have seen that several of these prophetic addresses are also marked by allusion to earlier Scripture: Azariah's (II 15:2–7); Hanani's (16:7–9); Jehu's (19:2f.) and the unnamed prophet's (25:15) are particularly clear examples.

At this point it may be useful to attempt a statistical analysis of the occurrence of some of the major formal features in each type of the addresses. They are set out in Table 2.1, with the number of times they appear in each of our main classifications of the addresses. In the final column the numbers are given for the addresses taken as a whole.

What can be deduced from this brief survey of the form and characteristics of the addresses? Of course, the categories are too small to draw sweeping inferences from our attempted statistical analysis. Nevertheless, we can say that the 'pure' forms of classical prophecy are breaking down. We are clearly in the post-classical age of prophecy. The recurring formal and rhetorical elements, as well as those of theme, cut across the boundaries of categories of those who speak, surely suggesting that the addresses all come from the same milieu. Only minor indications of the appropriateness of the address to the speaker appear. For example, the royal speeches have the largest number of calls for attention, giving the appearance of royal proclamations. Royal addresses avoid the use of any prophetic formulae. Yet the closest parallels of form and structure are shared by the royal and prophetic addresses, suggesting that the Davidic dynasty is seen as standing to some degree in the prophetic line, perhaps as inheritor of the Mosaic traditions, although there are also parallels between the 'priestly' and prophetic addresses. In general, however, apart from such slight variations, it may be said that all the addresses reflect certain broadly shared patterns, patterns which appear strongly rhetorical and admonitory.

Can we go further and claim for them the genre of 'sermon'? I have discussed this in some detail elsewhere.[18] The great difficulty is to establish precise and objective criteria by which such a genre can be defined.[19] It might be argued that an essential characteristic of the 'sermon' is agreement by preacher and hearers alike on the authority of some written word of Scripture, an authoritative corpus, which is the basis of exegesis and application to the hearers. Both expositor and hearers must recognise the authority of that which is being expounded, or the 'sermon' cannot function. It might further be claimed that there should be an objective note of affirmation of theological truth in preaching. It is not preaching if it is merely 'ad hominem' exhortation. But it should be marked also by urgent call for immediate response on the part of the hearers.

Even if it be agreed that these are essential marks of the 'sermon', however (and even the forming of a list of 'essential characteristics' of the genre has a subjective element to it, so that a different list might be supplied by each critic), how can they provide criteria by which to distinguish the sermon from the prophetic oracle? The prophets, it is often said, expounded received traditions. They proclaimed theological truths. They called for response. And even if we feel there to be a different balance, intensity and quality about these characteristics as they mark the oracles of the classical prophets and distinguish them from the addresses we have been considering, it is virtually impossible to objectify, classify and quantify such differences so that they become useful and reliable criteria. The addresses in Chronicles, for all their remarkable similarity of theme and formal characteristics, are too varied in setting, length, style and method, all to be grouped as one 'genre', that of the 'sermon'. To say the least, congregations in the second temple must have been remarkably fortunate if some of these represent the average length of the sermons which were preached to them.

It seems that the most we might possibly be able to claim is that they echo some of the themes and rhetorical methods of the preaching which was delivered and heard in the temple. And, as has been indicated earlier,[20] we have to understand the term 'preaching', in so far as it is appropriate at all, in a broad sense so as to include all oral methods of instruction in the 'tradition'. This raises, finally, the interesting question of the function of these addresses. It is noticeable that the résumé of their themes and their theological contents reads remarkably like a précis of the theology of the Chronicler, i.e. of the Books of Chronicles more or less in the form in which we now have them. This must suggest that the 'addresses', and their attribution to those who, the Chronicler tells us, uttered them, serve primarily as mouth-piece for the Chronicler himself. To the extent that they serve such a purpose they belong to the category of literary fiction. Yet it is the aim of this study to show in the second part that many of the stylistic features, and sometimes the themes and vocabulary, of the addresses in Chronicles are to be found elsewhere in the post-exilic literature. This may suggest that such addresses are not entirely *ad hoc* free inventions of the Chronicler. Even where there is 'free composition' by him, is there not likely to be in the mind of the composer some idea of the forms and content such oral communications were known to assume? It may well be the practice of what Michael Fishbane has termed the 'rhetors' of the exegetical traditions[21] which has left its influences on the methods the Chronicler assigns to the 'messengers' he has called into being for his purpose. We do not have any explicit evidence for these 'rhetors', although J. Blenkinsopp has argued a strong and, perhaps, too exclusive a case for evidence which suggests the teaching role of the Levites.[22] Yet it is quite possible that we catch here some echo of the voices of the rhetors and some insight into their exegetical and homiletical practices. The position may not be altogether different from that which some New Testament scholars find in The Acts of the Apostles. Undeniably, the speeches in Acts express Lucan ideas and theology and serve what might be called his 'dramatic' interests as he traces the course of the Christian mission. Yet their contents may well also reflect a 'given' element of at least some versions of the early Christian kerugma and didache, and their form reflect the preaching which was familiar in the tradition of at least some sectors of the Christian church.[23] The function of these addresses in Chronicles may well be to express the Chronicler's interpretation of his people's history in a vivid and memorable way. Parallels elsewhere may suggest that, in this attempt, his was not entirely a lone or idiosyncratic voice. He may have been reflecting and expressing exegetical methods and homiletical practices which were common to others in the post-exilic period. It is at least with this possibility in mind that we shall turn to an examination of other post-exilic biblical material to see if these have left their traces elsewhere.

Part II

.•◦"◦"◦"◦"◦"◦"◦"◦"◦"◦"◦"◦"◦"◦•.

A comparison of the themes and characteristics of the addresses in the Books of Chronicles with some other post-exilic biblical material

4 The 'speeches' in the Books of Ezra and Nehemiah

1 Ezra 1:2–4 *The decree of Cyrus*

²Thus says Cyrus, king of Persia, 'All the kingdoms of the world Yahweh, the God of heaven, has given to me, and it is he who has appointed me to build him a sanctuary in Jerusalem of Judah. ³Any of you, among all his people, may Yahweh his God be with him and may he go up to Jerusalem which is in Judah and rebuild the sanctuary of Yahweh, the God of Israel. He is the God who is in Jerusalem. ⁴And anyone who is left from among the regions where he sojourns, may he be assisted[a] by the people of his region with silver, gold, possessions, animals and with free-will offerings for the sanctuary of the God who is in Jerusalem.'

Text

[a] Lit. 'let them [i.e. the people of the returning sojourner's region] bear him up with . . .'.

General description

A written 'royal decree' making use of the messenger formula. It calls for support of those who return and virtually amounts to 'An Encouragement for a Task' formula.

Contents

The decree of Cyrus, with which Chronicles ends and the Book of Ezra begins, has been discussed above (see pp. 118f.). It is verbally identical here with the form in which it occurs in Chronicles except that to the motif of rebuilding the temple is added that of the support in kind of those among the exiles in each region who return to undertake the task. The two themes are joined in that, just as it is Yahweh who 'stirs up the spirit' of Cyrus to allow exiled Jews to return (v. 1), so it is Yahweh who 'stirs up the spirit', not only of all the heads of the households, the priests and the Levites who return to help in the building (v. 5), but of 'those round about them' who 'strengthen their hands' with their gifts (v. 6).

The passage faces us with a problem in interpretation. Who are those who are called upon to help with gifts in kind? It is often argued that, since the Jewish exiles are allowed to return, the support by 'the men of his region' must be from their Babylonian neighbours.[1] This unlikely historical event is usually attributed to the Chronicler's theological interpretation of the return from exile as a 'Second Exodus' in which 'the spoiling of the Egyptians' theme is repeated (cf. Exod. 11:2, 12:35f.).[2] However, it is more likely that this is a recognition that not all exiled Jews returned, but that *all* had a part in this ideal response to God's call to them through Cyrus to concern themselves with the temple. This is the view of J. M. Myers.[3]

If that is so we have here an echo of the description of those who willingly and freely contributed to the construction of the tabernacle in the time of Moses (Exod. 35:29, 36:2f.). We have seen this theme expressed in the Chronicler's account of David's assembling of the materials for the Jerusalem temple, both those which he himself provided (I Chr. 22:3f., 14ff., 29:2–5) and that which was provided by the leaders of the community (I 29:6–9). It was a theme also expressed in Hezekiah's own gifts for the temple (II 31:3) and in the contribution of the whole community at his direction (vv. 4–9). Azariah's 'address' showed how it was just this spirit of generosity to the temple which had led to God's blessing (v. 10).

We find also a strong parallel to Ezr. 1:5 in the account in the Book of Haggai of how the returned 'remnant' of the people, together with their leaders, everyone in fact whose spirit 'the LORD stirred up', came and worked on the temple in obedient response to the words of the prophet (Hag. 1:12–14). Haggai clearly demonstrated the truth of Azariah's words, that disobedience and slackness over the affairs of the temple brought judgement and deprivation, while obedience and zeal would result in the age of blessing and plenty (2:15–19).

So in both the extension of Cyrus' decree and the narrative in which it is set, Ezra sounds a theme familiar from the addresses and narratives in Chronicles. The temple is of God's ordaining, but that ordaining makes use of human zeal and devotion, which he himself inspires. A call for practical support for the temple, support in kind being an acceptable alternative to actual physical presence for those living out of reach of Jerusalem, is a relevant and familiar theme for the post-exilic era.

2 Ezra 4:3 *Zerubbabel and the leaders to the 'adversaries'*

[3] *But Zerubbabel, Jeshua and the rest of the heads of the households in Israel said to them, 'You have nothing to do with us in building a sanctuary for our God. United with each other,[a] we will build for Yahweh, the God of Israel, as Cyrus, king of Persia, sanctioned us to do.'*

Text

[a] Heb. 'together' (יַחַד). This is often emended in accordance with some Versions to read, 'We will build alone' (לְבַד). However, it may well suggest that the people of Judah and Benjamin are sufficiently united with each other to need no outside help.

General description

A repudiation of foreign involvement in the building of the temple. The announcement of intention amounts almost to an exhortation to the people of Judah.

Contents

The true community of faith is described in v. 1 as 'Judah and Benjamin'. These, the returned exiles, as they are depicted, are the ones chosen and commissioned by God, through Cyrus, to build the temple. However, the temple was not completed for twenty years, a delay which the post-exilic prophet Haggai attributed to the lethargy and self-seeking interests of the community (Hag. 1:2–11). Here, the delay is attributed to continuing opposition from others, of which examples are given (out of historical sequence) throughout c. 4.[4] The offer of help from those labelled as 'adversaries' of the people of God is rejected by governor, chief priest and leaders of the community. The reason given, and the real theme of the reply, is that the true people of God must never make alliance of any kind in the pursuit of any venture with others. To do so would be a denial both of their unique status and of the power of God.

The theme of these words, then, is closely parallel to a prevalent theme in the addresses in Chronicles. Hanani rebuked Asa for making alliance with the king of Syria (II 16:7f.) and Jehu rebuked Jehoshaphat for alliance with the king of Israel (II 19:2). Jehoshaphat was slow to learn the lesson, however, for Eliezer told him that the reason his fleet was sunk before it even left harbour was that the proposed mercantile adventure had been planned in alliance with the Israelite king, Ahaziah (II 20:35–7). It is interesting that God can make use of foreign kings, such as Cyrus or Artaxerxes, but his people must rely on no one but him. God, of course, does not make alliances with foreign kings, but uses them in a display of his universal sovereignty. For his people to have truck with them is a denial of that sovereignty. So, at this point, the words of the leaders recorded in Ezra coincide exactly with the burden of addresses assigned to prophetic-type figures in Chronicles.

3 Ezra 5:11–16 *The reply of the Jews to the Persian officials*

[11] *And this is the answer they returned to the question: 'We are servants of the God of heaven and earth and we are rebuilding the sanctuary which was built earlier, these many years ago [the sanctuary] which a great king of Jerusalem built and completed.* [12] *But because our fathers angered the God of heaven he gave them into the power of Nebuchadnezzar of the Chaldeans, king of Babylon, and he destroyed this sanctuary and exiled the people to Babylon.* [13] *However, in the first year of Cyrus, king of Babylon, Cyrus the king decreed that this sanctuary should be rebuilt.* [14] *Furthermore, the golden and silver vessels which Nebuchadnezzar had taken from the temple in Jerusalem and had carried to the temple in Babylon, Cyrus the king had taken from the temple in Babylon and turned them over to one, Sheshbazzar by name, whom he made governor.* [15] *And he said to him, "Take these vessels. Go, put them in the temple in Jerusalem and let God's sanctuary be rebuilt on its site."* [16] *So Sheshbazzar came and laid the foundations of the sanctuary of*

God in Jerusalem and, from that time to the present, building has been going on, but it is not yet complete.'

General description

A written defence by the Jewish community claiming that their action in rebuilding the Jerusalem temple had Persian royal sanction. It forms part of the correspondence in Aramaic between the Persian court and officials in the Province Beyond the River. Appeal to past history, both to Solomon's role in building the original temple and the disaster of the exile when it was destroyed, fits naturally into the context.

Contents

In one respect this passage can hardly be classed as a 'speech' or an 'address', although we have seen that, on occasions, these can be expressed in written form. Nevertheless, as an expression of Jewish defence of their actions, quoted and passed on by local officials to the Persian court, it bears certain features which are relevant to the present enquiry.

A number of historical issues are raised which cannot be dealt with here, for they are not immediately relevant to the thought and theology of what might almost be termed this Jewish 'apologia'. These questions include the historical authenticity of the Aramaic 'correspondence' section of the Book of Ezra; the relation of the work undertaken by Sheshbazzar (vv. 14–16) to the rebuilding of the temple carried out under Zerubbabel with the inspiration of the prophets Haggai and Zechariah; and the historicity and nature of the 'opposition' to the rebuilding programme raised by the provincial officials, and whether this opposition was hostile in intent or not.[5]

The content of the apologia attributed to the Jews is of interest for several reasons. It is to be noted that the whole sad episode of the destruction of Jerusalem and the consequent exile is attributed to the 'anger' of God with the 'fathers' (v. 12). This theme was found also in the proclamation of Hezekiah (II Chr. 30:6–9) and is pronounced in the Zechariah tradition (Zech. 1:4, 7:10–14). Furthermore, both the disaster and, by implication, the restoration, are seen as the work of Yahweh, tactfully and appropriately referred to in an address to Persian officials as 'The God of heaven and earth'. The temple period is seen as a new era of God's favour in contrast to the previous age of judgement. Yet the continuity between the two is also stressed in the reference to the return of the sacred temple vessels which Chronicles had recorded as being taken by Nebuchadnezzar to Babylon (II Chr. 36:7, 18). It was stressed earlier (Ezra 1:7–11) that Cyrus had arranged their restoration. These vessels thus formed a link of the greatest theological significance between first and second temples. The theme argued for the continuity of the validity of the first temple in the second and the establishment of a vital link between the two.[6] Nor should we miss the historical reference to the building of the first temple by Solomon who, as the instrument chosen by God for that very purpose, was so prominent a figure in the record of the Chronicler and in the 'addresses' he assigned, particularly to David.

Solomon is here recalled, not as a great military or political figure, but as temple builder. Perhaps the context demanded this, but it indicates another significant element in this passage. For, while it ascribes these great events of history to divine ordering, it frankly acknowledges the part played in them by the representatives of the great world powers, by Nebuchadnezzar, Cyrus and Darius himself, to whom appeal is being made here. The political reality for the post-exilic Jewish community is that their life and place in the divine purpose have now to be played out on a stage in which other actors appear to have the leading roles. They do not doubt that God is the creative and all-powerful 'playwright', but his power is exercised, at least for the time being, through foreign and heathen potentates. This, surely, provides the context for the religious 'quietism' which we found to be such a feature of the addresses in Chronicles and in the theology of the Chronicler himself. While groups from time to time could, and, especially later, would arise with increasing frequency who were impatient with the state of affairs and sought more violent methods to short-circuit its frustrations, that is not the theology of what we might call 'the temple tradition'. That is the tradition which finds expression in the preaching represented by the addresses in Chronicles and in the outlook expressed in this passage, whether that be an authentic historical document or has been assigned to these Jewish apologists much as the Chronicler assigned the addresses to significant actors in his story.

4 Ezra 6:2–12 *The decree of Cyrus and the reply of Darius*

[2] *And there was found in Ecbatana, the fortress of the province of Media, a scroll, and this is what was written on it: 'A Memorandum:* [3] *In the first year of Cyrus, king Cyrus issued a decree concerning the sanctuary of God in Jerusalem: 'Let the*

sanctuary be rebuilt at the place where sacrifices are offered, and let its foundation support a height of sixty cubits and a breadth of sixty cubits [4]*with three courses of hewn stone and one course of timber. Let the cost be donated from the royal treasury.* [5]*In addition, the golden and silver vessels which belonged to the sanctuary of God and which Nebuchadnezzar had taken away from the temple in Jerusalem and carried to Babylon shall be taken back to the temple in Jerusalem, each to its rightful place, and put in the sanctuary of God.* [6]*Now, Tattenai, governor of the Province Beyond the River, Shathar-Bozenai and your associates, keep away from the site.* [7]*Let the work on the sanctuary of God alone and let the governor of Judah and the Judaean elders rebuild this sanctuary of God on its site.* [8]*From me comes this decree concerning that which you are to do for these Judaean elders in rebuilding this sanctuary of God. From the royal treasury, that is, the tribute of the Province Beyond the River, the expense in full shall be given to these men in order that they may not be hindered.* [9]*Whatever they need by way of bullocks, rams, any lambs for sacrificing to the God of heaven, wheat, salt, wine or oil, as the priests in Jerusalem stipulate, let these be given to them without fail* [10]*so that they may present pleasant sacrifices to the God of heaven and intercede for the well-being of the king and his sons.* [11]*I make a decree that anyone who frustrates this edict shall have a timber, pulled from his own house, set up and he be impaled upon it. His house shall be made into a dunghill.* [12]*And may God who has caused his name to dwell there overthrow any king or people who reach out a hand to frustrate this or damage the sanctuary of God in Jerusalem. I, Darius, make a decree. Let it be carried out to the letter.'*

General description

A royal decree which includes direct address to named recipients (v. 6). It sanctions the rebuilding of the temple and authorises payment from the royal funds in the provincial exchequer.

Contents

Another version of the decree of Cyrus is incorporated here into what purports to be a decree from Darius. Again it raises what are probably insoluble problems of an historical nature. We know from the 'Cyrus Cylinder' that he did foster the cults of his subject peoples and looked to the favour of their gods acting on his behalf as a result. On the other hand, the overt theological themes of this decree suggest composition for a particular purpose. These motifs seem to go beyond the possibility of a Jewish official in the Persian court advising on the precise wording of such a royal decree, a claim often made by those who wish to defend its historicity.[7] In any event, it is the theological motifs rather than the historical issues which are our concern here.

Here also the note of continuity with the pre-exilic temple is stressed. This occurs in the reference to the restitution of the temple vessels in Cyrus' decree (v. 5). It sounds also in the instructions concerning the dimensions of the rebuilt temple (vv. 5f.). Three courses of stone and one of timber is exactly that provided for in the inner and main courts of Solomon's temple (I Kgs. 6:36, 7:12). It sounds also in the use of the Deuteronomic phrase 'the God who has caused his name to dwell there' (v. 12). That which was used so often of the first temple is, by implication, carried over to the second. By its use the 'presence' of God in the temple is emphasised in a way which we saw to be characteristic of the addresses in Chronicles. Solomon's temple was also sixty cubits long (I Kgs. 6:2) but, in fact, the size specified here for the new temple exceeds the dimensions of Solomon's. We are not told the length, but its height is twice and its breadth three times that of the earlier pattern (cf. I Kgs. 6:2). The words of Haggai to the dispirited builders suggest that, to many of them, the rebuilt temple was not as large or splendid as the first (Hag. 2:3). Yet Haggai does also promise that 'the latter glory of this house shall be greater than the former' (2:8). Perhaps these measurements represent an idealised expression of this theological hope.

A second motif of this decree also parallels words of Haggai. For both Cyrus and Darius stress that provision is to be made from the royal treasury (vv. 4b, 8f.), although the words of Darius suggest that these are to come from provincial taxes. Thus the theme of 'the tribute of the nations' to the temple of Yahweh is spelled out, again echoing Haggai's words, 'and I will shake all nations, so that the treasure of all nations shall come in, and I will fill this house with glory ... the silver is mine and the gold is mine ...' (2:7f.). In fact the royal decree of Ezra c. 6 reads almost like commentary on Haggai's prophecy, although such a theme is found elsewhere in the post-exilic literature (e.g. Isa. 60:6f., which actually mentions animals being brought in the tribute for sacrifice in the temple). This appears to be the tradition which is emphasised here rather than that of the 'spoiling of the Egyptians', for this version of the decree, unlike that in 1:2–4, makes no mention of a permitted 'return' of the exiles, so providing a parallel with the Exodus from Egypt.

Further, the idea that God will make plentiful material provision to a people obedient to a call to honour the temple is found, not only in the preaching of

Haggai, but also in the addresses in Chronicles. Azariah comments on the prosperity of the people once the tithes have been faithfully and generously given (II Chr. 31:10) and the 'man of God' assures Amaziah 'Yahweh is able to give you much more than this' (II 25:9). Darius' decree also rubs in the alternative. Any slackness or attempt to frustrate the proper worship of the temple will lead inevitably to judgement. Failure to build the house of God will bring one's own 'house' to desolation (vv. 11f.). The decree shows, in fact, that the proper worship of God is the whole *raison d'être* of the temple (vv. 9f.).

Again, as we saw in the answer of the Jews in c. 5, the centrality of foreign rulers in God's purpose for temple and post-exilic Jewish community is stressed here. Cyrus and Darius act almost as representatives of the Davidic line in their concern for the temple and for its proper worship. This is interesting in view of the reference in Second Isaiah to Cyrus as Yahweh's 'anointed' (Isa. 45:1). That is the way of things for the present. The proper concern for the Jewish theocracy is the temple and its rightly ordered worship. The Chronicler showed that such was the purpose of the choice of the Davidic line in making this a major theme of the addresses in Chronicles.

5 Ezra 7:11–26 *The decree of Artaxerxes concerning Ezra*

[11] *And this is a copy of the letter which king Artaxerxes gave to Ezra, the priest, the scribe, one versed in the terms of the commandments[a] of Yahweh and of his statutes for Israel.* [12] *Artaxerxes, supreme king, to Ezra, the priest, the scribe of the law of the God of heaven, 'Peace![b]* [13] *From me comes this decree, that everyone of the people of Israel, priest or Levite in my kingdom who freely offers himself to go to Jerusalem, is to go with you.* [14] *For you are sent by the king and his seven counsellors to examine the situation in Jerusalem in the light of the law of your God which you have with you* [15] *and to take the silver and gold which the king and his counsellors have offered to the God of Israel, whose dwelling is in Jerusalem,* [16] *together with all the silver and gold which you find throughout the region of Babylonia and the free-will offerings of the people and the priests which they offer freely for the sanctuary of God in Jerusalem.* [17] *With this money you shall diligently acquire rams and lambs, together with the cereal and drink-offerings, and you shall offer them upon the altar of the sanctuary of your God in Jerusalem.* [18] *And use whatever is left from the silver and gold in whatever way seems most fitting to you and your kinsmen. Act in accordance with the will of your God.* [19] *And the vessels which have been given to you for the worship of the sanctuary of*

your God, present in their entirety before the God of Jerusalem. [20] *And anything else needed for the sanctuary of your God which it falls to you to provide, you may give from the royal treasury.*

[21] *And I, Artaxerxes, make a decree to all the treasurers in the Province Beyond the River, that you shall carry out fully everything which Ezra, the priest, the scribe of the law of the God of heaven, requires of you,* [22] *up to one hundred talents of silver, one hundred kôrs of wheat, one hundred baths of wine, one hundred baths of oil and any amount of salt;* [23] *let everything that is decreed by the God of heaven be done with zeal[c] for the sanctuary of the God of heaven, in case there is anger against the realm of the king and his descendants.* [24] *And be it known to you that it shall not be lawful to impose tax, tribute or toll upon any priest, Levite, singer, gatekeeper, temple attendant or servant of this sanctuary of God.*

[25] *And you, Ezra, according to the wisdom of your God which is in your hand, appoint magistrates[d] and judges who shall judge all the people in the Province Beyond the River, all those who know the laws of your God. And you shall instruct any who do not know them.* [26] *As for anyone who does not observe the law of your God and the law of the king, let judgement be exacted speedily upon him, whether for death, banishment,[e] confiscation of goods or imprisonment.'*

Text

[a] Lit. 'a scribe of the words of the commandments'.

[b] Text dubious. This rendering is based on the Syriac version.

[c] See P. Nober, 'Ezr. 7:23', *Bibl. Zeit.* (1958), 134–8, who takes אָדְרַזְדָּא here to mean, 'with faith', 'faithfully'.

[d] The Greek reads 'scribes' here.

[e] Possibly the term שְׁרֹשִׁי refers to physical chastisement. See F. Rundgren, 'Zur Bedeutung von SRSW – Esr. vii 26', *VT*, 7 (1957), 400–4 and Z. W. Falk, 'Esra vii 26', *VT*, 9 (1959), 89–99.

General description

This written document takes the form of a tripartite royal decree. The first section (vv. 11–20) commissions Ezra to go to Jerusalem with all who will accompany him, to investigate the state of affairs in Judah and Jerusalem in relation to the law and to use royal funds for the provision of proper worship in the temple. The second section (vv. 21–4) orders financial ministers throughout the Province Beyond the River to give Ezra full financial backing within certain very generous limits and to exempt all Jewish cult personnel from state taxes, all this in order to ward off the wrath of the God of heaven. The final section (vv. 25f.) again commissions Ezra but, in this case, to appoint local administrators and with them to instruct in the laws of God either the whole Jewish community or, possibly, all who lived in the region of Judah, and to make these laws a basis for the life of the society.

Contents

Once more complex historical issues are raised by this 'royal decree' of Artaxerxes. Is it likely that a Persian king would have given such a 'blank cheque' to a Jewish leader, and would he have worded it in such terms? Those who argue for its historicity appeal to epigraphical evidence which, it is alleged, show that the Persians did foster the religious cults of their subject peoples, and they argue for the prominent part of a Jewish court 'adviser' in the drafting of the terms of the decree.[8] The endlessly debated question of the date of Ezra's mission, especially in relation to that of Nehemiah, and in the reign of which Artaxerxes he came, continues to baffle solution.[9] Further, the historicity of Ezra and the nature of his 'mission' are uncertain and divide scholars still. However, again we cannot, and should not, miss the theological nature and purpose evident in this 'decree'.

Without attempting to enter into these continuing questions it seems clear to me that the present strange order to the text of Ezra–Nehemiah, especially when compared with the Greek text and Josephus, shows that there has been a deliberate insertion of a block of Nehemiah material (cc. 1–7) into the story of Ezra's work. The aim must be to show that they were contemporaries. If this had a theological rather than an historical purpose it would explain why attempts to use the text for alleged historical reconstructions of the order of events seem doomed to frustration. Such attempts would clearly be a misuse of the material and be based on a misunderstanding of its nature. Further, whatever the historicity of Ezra and the nature and time of his ministry, the text as we have it bears witness to the way he came to be understood and evaluated in the later tradition, and it is for this reason that we should read the text and in this way value its 'historicity'.

Turning, then, to the theological motifs, we find several of the themes of the earlier decrees of Cyrus and Darius again made explicit. In so far as they are renewed here they do not need repeated discussion. We should note, however, the emphasis on the way *the whole community* acted in an ideal way with Ezra.

The decree is addressed to Ezra, but it invites all lay members of the community, the priests and the Levites who wish to do so, to accompany him (vv. 13f.). As with David's address to the whole community, its viewpoint is that the temple and its worship are the focal point for, and the responsibility of, the whole ideal community of the people of God. All, far or near, find the true expression of their life here.

All Jews, whether accompanying Ezra or not, are summoned to make free-will contributions vowed for the temple (v. 16). It is not clear whether the somewhat comprehensive wording of v. 16 ('all the silver and gold which you find throughout the region of Babylonia', which appears in addition to the free-will offerings of laypeople, priests and Levites) refers to gifts from those other than Jews. However, the decree certainly brings together the ideas of loyal and sacrificial support by the community of Israel and the 'tribute of the nations' coming in to the temple. This last becomes explicit in that part of the decree addressed to the finance ministers of the province (vv. 21–4).

Again, the notion that a foreign king is the instrument of God and that it is God who is acting through him to bring his purposes to pass, implicit in the earlier decrees, is spelled out in full here. In v. 23 that which Artaxerxes is decreeing is equated with that which is decreed by the God of heaven. Disobedience in this, even by so powerful a king as Artaxerxes, would be to bring God's judgement on king and realm.

Another point of especial interest is the teaching role assigned to Ezra (v. 25), for which he is to appoint magistrates and judges over the whole region. In this he follows the example of a faithful Davidide king, Jehoshaphat, who appointed and charged judges in Judah and priests, Levites and lay leaders in Jerusalem (II Chr. 19:5–11). They also had an educative role (v. 10). In this, both followed the example of Moses (Exod. 18:19). To that extent, Ezra stands in the Mosaic, Davidide tradition, a point of no small significance when we have seen reason to believe that the function of the Davidic dynasty found its true fulfilment, not in military and nationalistic terms, but in the emergence of the post-exilic theocracy.[10] Nor is this the only echo of the addresses in Chronicles, for v. 23 shows that 'wrath' (Aram. קְצַף) from God is the consequence of breach of the divine laws, a feature we have seen to be prominent in the addresses with their repeated use of the Hebrew equivalent קֶצֶף .

Whatever the historical realities of his mission, Ezra was remembered and venerated in the tradition as a 'scribe', one versed in the commandments of

God (v. 11). The prophet with a direct word from God is giving way to the skilful exegete of written Torah. He was remembered as one who founded the life of the post-exilic community on the basis of Torah and who instituted the instruction of the community in that law by those qualified for the task (vv. 14, 25). Thus concern for temple worship and Torah established the parameters of the identity of this community ('all such as know the laws of your God', v. 25). To step outside Torah was to step outside the community (v. 26). But, as we have seen, the Chronicler presented faithful Davidic kings and others who were 'messengers', whether prophet, priest or Levite, as discharging just such an educative role to God's people. Their words are recorded in what we have suggested were terms familiar from the teaching of the tradents in the second temple period. Here, surely, in the way Ezra's ministry was remembered, is the context in which such post-exilic 'preachers' would have operated. To them, these divinely appointed 'messengers', the community looked for that instruction and exhortation which maintained faith, corrected abuses and kept hope alive.

6 Ezra 8:28f. *Ezra's charge to the twelve leading priests*

[28] *So I said to them, 'You are holy to Yahweh and the vessels are holy, and the silver and gold are a free-will offering to Yahweh, the God of your fathers.* [29] *Be watchful, and guard them until you weigh them in the presence of the chief priests, the Levites and the leading heads of the households of Israel in Jerusalem, in[a] the chambers of the sanctuary of Yahweh.'*

Text

[a] Reading 'in' with the Greek text in place of the impossible definite article of MT.

General description

A commission and admonition to twelve leading priests to guard the vast treasures coming from Babylon to the temple in Jerusalem. The holiness of both vessels and their bearers is the ground for an admonition for ceaseless vigilance.

Contents

The context for these words of Ezra to the twelve leading priests is the narrative of the execution of the terms of the decree of Artaxerxes. The stressing of the holiness of those who bear the vessels and the vessels themselves is clearly the ground for the admonition to vigilance. But it stresses also the theme of continuity between the two temple eras, since the new temple will contain the vessels of the old, miraculously preserved and spared by God, and its worship will be led by true successors of those who ministered in the temple before the exile.

These words have none of the rhetorical devices of the addresses in Chronicles, but in context and tone they strikingly recall Hezekiah's address to the leaders. He called on priests and Levites to sanctify themselves and then the polluted temple, and charged them not to be 'negligent' since Yahweh had chosen them to stand in his presence and minister to him (II Chr. 29:5–11). The same sense of the responsibility imposed by status and call is laid before these leaders by Ezra. Faithful and dedicated ministry by the leadership must have been seen as a very essential ingredient in the life and health of the post-exilic community.

7 Ezra 10:10f. *Ezra to the people*

[10] *And Ezra the priest stood up and said to them, 'You have acted treacherously by marrying foreign women, so adding to Israel's guilt.* [11] *Now, give praise[a] to Yahweh, the God of your fathers, and do what pleases him. Separate yourselves from the peoples of the land and from foreign wives.'*

Text

[a] The Hebrew verb from which the noun תּוֹדָה comes usually means 'to praise' or 'give thanks'. In some contexts it clearly has the overtone of 'confessing sin' (e.g. Prov. 28:13) and is usually so rendered here. However, the two ideas are closely related. Acknowledging sin springs from acknowledgement of the goodness and rightness of God's will, and praise of his grace in accepting confession and forgiving sin.

General description

An indictment of the community for the sin of intermarriage with alien women and a summons to repentance both in word and deed.

Contents

Ezra's indictment of the community (all are apparently seen as tainted by the sin of the few) charges them with 'acting treacherously' (Heb./מעל). This is a favourite term of the Chronicler, who uses some form of the verb eleven times and its related noun six times. In the addresses it is used by Hezekiah when he charges the priests to cleanse the temple: 'Our fathers acted treacherously' (II Chr. 29:6). It occurs also in Hezekiah's letter, where he says, 'Do not be like your fathers who were faithless' (the same Hebrew verb) (II Chr. 30:7). The enormity of the people's action is that they have reenacted the errors of their predecessors from before the exile. It may be a different sin, but it is a symptom of the same disease of the heart and mind. No wonder Ezra calls on them to confess and acknowledge 'the God of your fathers'. His grace persevered with them and his grace is their only hope now. That is why the word used in the call contains elements of 'praise' and 'thanksgiving' in the confession of sin.

The challenge is for the people of God to be a separated community, inclusive of all those who live in obedience to God's law (i.e. 'that which is pleasing to him') but exclusive of all others. 'Peoples of the land' is a phrase which seems to mean different things in different contexts[11] but here clearly represents those of different, or mixed, nationality who live around, or even among, the little Judaean community. The call for 'separation' is one which, as we have seen, is familiar both to addresses in Chronicles (where, however, intermarriage is not an issue),[12] and an earlier speech in the Book of Ezra (Ezr. 4:3).

8 Neh. 2:3, 5, 7f. *Nehemiah to Artaxerxes*

[3] *And I said to the king, 'May the king live for ever!*[a] *Why should my face not be overcast since the city containing the graves of my ancestors is in ruins with its defences*[b] *destroyed by fire?'* [4] *And the king said to me, 'What is it you are asking?' So I prayed to the God of heaven.* [5] *And I said to the king, 'If it pleases the king and if your servant has found favour with you, that you would send me to the city, the*

city of the graves of my ancestors, so that I might rebuild it.' [6] *And the king, with the queen sitting beside him, said to me, 'How long will your journey take and when will you return?' So it pleased the king to send me, and I set a time-limit with him.* [7] *And I said to the king, 'If it pleases the king, give me letters to the governors of the Province Beyond the River, so that they will expedite my passage when I get to Judah.* [8] *Also a letter to Asaph, who keeps the king's estates, that he may give me wood to provide the posts for the gates of the temple-fortress, for the city walls and for the house[c] when I come to it.' And this the king granted me because the hand of my God was upon me.*

Text

[a] Strictly, the verb is not a jussive, as P. Juon pointed out in 'Neh. 2:3', *Biblica*, 12 (1931), 85f. He read it as an imperative, 'O king, live for ever!'
[b] Lit. 'the gates'.
[c] All the EVV and most commentators assume that this is a reference to the governor's palace which Nehemiah speaks of occupying. This is certainly possible, but such a house is not mentioned in the following chapter. It is possible, therefore, that the reference to the 'house' is to the temple itself, which Nehemiah speaks of restoring when he gets to Jerusalem.

General description

A dialogue between Nehemiah and the king. In no way can it be likened to an 'address', but it is included for the sake of completeness and for the recurrence of themes we have already encountered in the Ezra narratives and the addresses in Chronicles.

Contents

This dialogue, with its careful, deferential approach by Nehemiah to the Persian king whose all-powerful decisions are cast in his favour (perhaps to some extent influenced by the queen, v. 6), again expresses the political realities of life for the post-exilic Jewish community. Yet, once more, the overriding impression is not of the power of the Persian king but the overruling providence of God (vv. 4b, 8bβ). The 'good hand' of God upon him is a tribute to the generosity as well as the power of God (cf. I Kgs. 10:13). It had been stressed that Ezra's activity was also due to this generous and powerful intervention of God on his behalf (Ezra 7:6, 9, 28; 8:18, 22, 31). So two themes from the addresses in Chronicles recur here, the 'power' of God which is better able to prevail over heathen powers than any army, and the generous provision of material needs which he makes to his people when they are obedient to him.

Nehemiah's reference to Jerusalem as the city of his ancestors' graves may be just a diplomatic allusion, calculated to appeal to a king for its piety.[13] On the other hand it may imply some claim to royal descent since it was, above all, kings whose sepulchres were honoured in a city. It was considered very important for a king to be buried in honour in such sepulchres.[14] So Josiah was brought back to be buried in Jerusalem after his defeat at Megiddo, according to the Deuteronomistic History (II Kgs. 23:30), in fulfilment of Huldah's prophecy (22:20). There is an allusion to David's sepulchre in Neh. 3:16. The prophet Ahijah predicted that only one of the house of Jeroboam would have the honour of a burial since 'something pleasing to Yahweh' was found in him (I Kgs. 14:13, cf. v. 11). The point at issue here is not whether, historically, Nehemiah made such a claim to the Persian king, but whether the writer of the narratives and of this dialogue is anxious to show him as being in some way in the line of the older kings of Jerusalem. At the least he is shown to be acting like David in his concern for the good of Jerusalem and 'building up its walls' (cf. I Chr. 11:4–9). Indeed, Nehemiah is shown not to have lacked trust in Yahweh, any more than David did, in capturing or building up the city's defences, since each acted by God's power and generosity alone. And the accomplishment of each in making Jerusalem secure led to their making provision for a proper and obedient worship of God in the city.

9 Neh. 2:17f. *Nehemiah to the Jews*

[17] *Then I said to them, ' You can see the plight we are in with Jerusalem in ruins and its defences[a] burned down. Come, let us rebuild Jerusalem's wall so that we are no longer an object of shame.'* [18] *And I told them how well my God had directed me[b] and, in addition, the promises which the king had made to me. And they responded,[c] 'We will begin work on the rebuilding.' And they resolved[d] to undertake this good work.*

Text

[a] Lit. 'its gates'.
[b] Lit. 'about the hand of my God which had been good to me'.

c LXX here makes this continued speech of Nehemiah, 'And I said, "Let us arise and rebuild", and they resolved . . .'
d Lit. 'they strengthened their hands'.

General description

This is a call for action which shares some features with the form of those addresses in Chronicles which we termed an 'Encouragement for a Task' (v. 17). However, the grounds of encouragement, namely the overriding power and goodness of God resulting in the full support of the Persian king, are given in reported speech (v. 18a). In the addresses they were always in direct speech. The people's response echoes words used in such earlier forms, however.

Contents

This incident affords a number of parallels between Nehemiah and David, who also encouraged Solomon and the Jewish leaders of his time to a task of building. The verbs 'to arise' and 'to be strong' (חזק) also featured in his exhortations, as they do here (e.g. I Chr. 22:13, 15, 16, 19, 28:20 etc.). The call 'to build' also, naturally, occurred there (I Chr. 22:11, 19, 28:10). Here it is the wall of Jerusalem which is to be built, a symbol, nevertheless, of the safety and separateness of Jerusalem which will enable true worship of God to take place there. Nehemiah, in fact, is to establish, against all opposition, that condition of 'peace' which was the pre-condition for the building of the temple itself (I Chr. 22:9f.). As noted above, while the whole passage bears many of the characteristics of the 'Encouragement for a Task' formula of the addresses in Chronicles and elsewhere, it differs in that the grounds of encouragement are expressed in reported speech. Here, as elsewhere in Ezra and Nehemiah, the form of the words given to the leading characters is influenced more by the narrative context and the 'genre' of that contextual material as alleged 'historical' material (memoirs, court records, etc.) than was the case with the addresses in Chronicles. Theme and function, however, are remarkably similar. The present account affords parallels, not only with the Chronicler's description of David's building activity and his calls for support, but with the role of Haggai and Zechariah at the time of the rebuilding of the temple after the exile. Haggai is also reported as using the verb 'be strong' (חזק) in his

encouragement to the community to build and offers as grounds of encouragement the 'presence' of God, as Nehemiah does here (Hag. 2:4f.). Zechariah
also calls on his hearers, 'Let your hands be strong' (8:9). It seems as though
the tradents of the post-exilic period saw strong lines of continuity from
Moses, through David, to the post-exilic reconstruction of the temple on to
the 'rebuilding' activity of Ezra and Nehemiah.[15] The close parallels of
phraseology and, sometimes, of form in the words attributed to them suggests
that we catch in such words familiar strains of the teaching of these tradents.

10 Neh. 2:20 *Nehemiah to his opponents*

[20] *But I replied to them, 'It is the God of heaven who will give us success, for we are
his servants. We shall be active in building. But you have no part or right or
memorial in Jerusalem.'*

General description

A disputation saying in which Nehemiah replies to the charge of sedition by
Sanballat, Tobiah and Geshem (v. 19).

Contents

These words attributed to Nehemiah again provide a direct line to the
addresses assigned to David by the Chronicler. In saying, 'The God of heaven
will give us success' (Hiph'il of / צלח) he echoes David's charge to Solomon.
David was reported as saying:

Now my son, may Yahweh be with you so that he may give you success. (Hiph'il / צלח)
(I Chr. 22:11)

The Chronicler recorded the fulfilment of that prayer in II 7:11:

all that Solomon had planned to do in the house of the LORD and in his home he
successfully accomplished. (Hiph. / צלח)

It is also a theme of the addresses assigned to others. Abijah, that faithful
Davidide, tells the people of the North whom he accuses of abandoning the
temple, the Davidic line and God,

Israelites, do not fight against Yahweh, the God of your fathers, for you can never
succeed *(II Chr. 13:12)*

Jehoshaphat says,

Trust in Yahweh, your God, and you will be supported;
trust in his prophets and you will succeed. *(II 20:20)*

Zechariah makes the same point when he asks,

Why do you keep transgressing the commandments of Yahweh? You will not succeed.
(II 24:20)

So Nehemiah's words not only repudiate the implicit threats of his accusers, but give the grounds of confidence for the task to which he has summoned his people. By implication, he contrasts the limited powers of the Persian king, whose authority is being invoked by their enemies, with the power of the 'God of heaven' whose might can be thwarted by no human effort – yet another theme of the addresses in Chronicles.

But this short saying contains yet a third theme from the addresses, that of separation from, and repudiation of, those who are not the true people of God. And here it is of interest that the words in which he does this have overtones of a cultic nature. 'You have no *part* or right of memorial in Jerusalem' (Heb. / חֵלֶק). This partly recalls the fateful cry with which the apostate North seceded from loyalty to the Davidic king (I Kgs. 12:16, cf. II Chr. 10:16), 'We have no *part* in David.' The Chronicler has also used this verbal root to describe the 'share' of duties falling to the various divisions of the priestly orders (I 24:4f.). Again, the word used to say 'You have no *right*' in Jerusalem (Heb. צְדָקָה) normally means 'righteousness', although it can be used in a narrower sense (e.g. II Sam. 19:28/29). This same word has been used to characterise the rule of both David (I Chr. 18:14, cf. II Sam. 8:15) and Solomon (II Chr. 9:8, cf. I Kgs. 10:9). Finally, the word 'memorial' (Heb. זִכָּרוֹן), while it has a wide range of uses, is employed often in a broadly 'cultic' sense. The Priestly Writer uses it of the stones on the high priest's ephod (e.g. Exod. 28:12). It is used in a story concerned with the usurpation of priestly privilege relating to the brazen censers whose function was to be a 'reminder' to the people of Israel. No one who was not a priest of the line of Aaron should draw near to burn incense before the LORD, 'lest he become as Korah and as his company' (Num. 16:39f.). Further, the word was associated with the 'book of rememberance' referred to in Exod. 17:14 in which Moses was to inscribe God's intention to blot out the 'remembrance' of Amalek. This idea, in Malachi, has been used more positively of the book in which God records those who are truly his, his 'special possession' (Heb. סְגֻלָּה, Mal. 3:16f.).

Perhaps the words ascribed to Nehemiah are not only a general repudiation of the hostile surrounding nations and their claimed right to influence and government in Jerusalem, but a very specific statement of the religious 'separation' of the true people of God. This short saying encapsulates no fewer than three of the major themes of the addresses in Chronicles, and one may suspect that it has been shaped in similar tradition circles and that it reflects teaching of the same kind of tradents.

11 Neh. 4:14 (8) *Nehemiah to those who were building*

[14] *And I saw . . .[a] and I rose up and said to the nobles, leaders and the rest of the people, 'Do not be afraid of them. Remember Yahweh who is great and terrible, and fight for your kinsmen, your sons and daughters, your wives and your houses.'*

Text

[a] Something seems to have dropped from the text. Perhaps it read, 'I saw *their fear . . .*'

General description

An 'Encouragement for a Task' formula using the familiar words, 'Do not be afraid!' The encouragement is to continue the building and to withstand the enemy, and the ground of the encouragement is the greatness of God.

Contents

These words of Nehemiah are spoken in the context of mounting hostility against the Jews from their neighbours, the vulnerability of the community to surprise attack with only half the wall completed (v. 6), and the breaches only in the initial stages of being stopped up (v. 7). In addition, some of the builders were prey to fear and disillusion, perhaps daunted by alarmist rumours from infiltrators (v. 12). Ackroyd points out that there may well lie behind this narrative the theme of Jerusalem surrounded on all sides by attackers, with God as defender repulsing and confusing their assault.[16] Nehemiah's 'address' to them follows the form of those addresses in Chronicles we have termed 'Encouragement for a Task' passages, with the characteristic phrase

'Do not be afraid!' This marked David's calls to Solomon and the leaders of the community to build the temple (e.g. I Chr. 22:13, 28:20) and recurred in summons to battle which called for complete trust in God (e.g. II Chr. 20:15, 17). The ground of confidence is in God, who is 'great and terrible'. This is a phrase attributed to Nehemiah elsewhere (1:5, 9:32) but has a particular, almost exegetical, force here. It is a Deuteronomic phrase. Its appearance in Deut. c. 7 gives its use special interest here in Neh. c. 4. Deut. c. 7 opens with a promise that God will 'clear away' the nations who inhabited the land he was giving to Israel (vv. 1–5), and continues with an assurance of the divine election of Israel based on God's grace (vv. 6–11). For this reason, providing that they keep the commandments, God will bless them and destroy all their enemies (vv. 12–16). Yet they well might wonder at this, considering the strength and size of these nations in Canaan and their own weakness.

If you say in your heart, 'These nations are greater than I; how can I dispossess them?' you shall not be afraid of them . . .' *(vv. 17, 18a).*

They are, instead, to take heart from the memory of what God had done to the Egyptians at the time of the Exodus. In the light of that, Moses continues,

You shall not be in dread of them; for the LORD your God is in the midst of you, a great and terrible God.' *(v. 21)*

Apparently Nehemiah calls for a more active share in the battle than Jahaziel, for example, who said, 'You will not need to fight in this battle' ((II Chr. 20: 17). Yet it is clear that Nehemiah's emphasis is also on the power of God, both by his use of this Deuteronomic description of God and his later words, recorded in v. 20, 'Our God will fight for us.'

Further, even the call to them to defend 'kinsmen, sons, daughters, wives and houses' is a reminder that they have been objects of God's blessing. The Chronicler has more than once shown that such 'possessions' are a sign of God's favour to those who are true to him. This is so of David, who is given sons, wives and a 'house' by God (I Chr. 14:1–4), a fact he himself also acknowledges (I 28:5). Rehoboam, who also built up defences for Jerusalem, was similarly favoured (II 18:25), as is Abijah (II 13:21). So the very possessions the community is being called on to defend are themselves signs that they are objects of God's favour.

In this instance, then, the words of Nehemiah compare closely with the addresses in Chronicles, in form, theme and in exegetical, even homiletical, use of earlier Scripture.

12 Neh. 4:19f., 22 (13f., 16) *Nehemiah to the builders*

[19] And I said to the nobles and to the rest of the people, 'The work is extensive and widely spaced and we are separated each from his neighbour along the wall. [20] Rally to us in the place where you hear the trumpet. Our God will fight for us!' . . .[22] And, in addition, I said to the people, 'Let each man, with his servant, spend the night in Jerusalem. So, by night, they will be a guard for us and, by day, a workforce.'

General description

Nehemiah gives instruction to those who are working on the wall to combine their work with military vigilance and preparedness. It continues the theme of encouraging the anxious workers in the task and gives as the basis of that encouragement the assurance of God's care and power active on their behalf.

Contents

This passage offers little to provide comment additional to that given on the previous section. It stresses the combination of military preparedness and of trust in God's power to fight on Israel's behalf which has characterised the work and words attributed already to Nehemiah and which stands so firmly in the tradition also expressed in the addresses in Chronicles. It recalls the words of Moses spoken at the time of the Exodus, 'The LORD will fight for you, and you have only to be still' (Exod. 14:14), a promise renewed before the entry into Canaan (Deut. 1:30). In this way the epoch of the rebuilding of the walls of Jerusalem is linked with the great moments in Israel's salvation history. It is further to be noted that in recording no assault by the swaggering enemies who launch only verbal missiles, the author is showing God's power to be effective still in staying his enemies. Mention of the workforce spending the night in Jerusalem may be just a detail to counter the sparseness of the inhabitants which was such a problem for Nehemiah (7:4), but it may hint at the beginning of the fulfilment of the promises that, in the new age, Jerusalem would again be full of people (e.g. Isa. 49:18–21). Indeed, the whole Nehemiah enterprise may be seen as fulfilment of Second Isaiah's promises concerning the rebuilding of Jerusalem:

> Behold, I have graven you on the palms of my hands;
> your walls are continually before me.

> Your builders outstrip your destroyers,
> and those who laid you waste go forth from you. *(Isa. 49:16f.)*

Further, the Chronicler has shown how faithful Davidide kings have 'rebuilt' walls, and the fact that they were able to do so was a sign of God's presence and favour (Asa, II 14:7/6, Jotham, II 27:3f., Hezekiah, II 32:5, Manasseh, after his 'conversion', II 33:14). So, once again, Nehemiah is shown as standing in the tradition of the Davidic kings.

13 Neh. 5:6–13 *Nehemiah to the leaders and officials*

⁶I was very angry when I heard their cry and their complaints.ᵃ ⁷My feelings got the better of meᵇ and I brought a charge against the chief citizens and officials and declared to them, 'You are placing a burden on your kinsmen.'ᶜ Then I convened a great assembly before which to charge them.ᵈ ⁸And I said, 'As far as lay within our power we have been freeingᵉ our Judaean kinsmen who were sold to the Gentiles. You, however, have been selling your own kinsmen whom we have had to buy back.' They were silent. They could find no answer. ⁹Then I said to them, 'What you are doing is not good. Should you not live in the fear of God to avoid the reproach of our enemies, the Gentiles? ¹⁰Indeed, I, my family and my servants are lending them money and grain. Let us stop imposing this burden. ¹¹Return to them this very day their fields, vineyards, olive orchards, houses, and the percentage of money, grain, wine and oil which you have been exacting from them.' ¹²And they replied, 'We will restore all this and will seek no more money from them. We will do as you say.' So I called the priests [as witnesses] and made them swear to act accordingly. ¹³I shook out my cloak and said, 'So let God shake out anyone who does not keep this promise. He shall be shaken out from his house and his work and made empty.' And the whole assembly said, 'Amen', and they praised Yahweh. So the people kept their oath.

Text

ᵃ Lit. 'these words'.

ᵇ The Hebrew idiom reads literally, 'My heart was made king over me.'

ᶜ According to the way we read the text we get either 'You have imposed a burden on them' or 'You have exacted interest from them.' It is clear that the 'burden' includes prohibited interest, but this was symptomatic of a more general 'oppression'.

ᵈ Lit. 'a great assembly against them'.

e Heb. /קנה often means 'to buy', and this is probably what Nehemiah means. They have had to 'buy back' their fellow-Jews sold into foreign ownership by their own Jewish kinsmen. However, the verb can also have the wider connotation of 'freeing from bondage' (e.g. Deut. 32:6).

General description

Nehemiah brings a legal charge (Heb. רִיב) against the influential and wealthy leaders of the Jewish community concerning their exploitation of the weak and poor for their own financial gain. Apparently, some of these were driven to the straits of selling themselves into slavery (vv. 6–11). To this they respond with an acknowledgement of guilt (v. 12), and Nehemiah replies with a conditional threat of judgement backed by a symbolic act (v. 13).

Contents

The account of the building of the wall (cc. 4, 6f.) is interrupted by this narrative in c. 5 reflecting social abuses within the community. The old pre-exilic wrongs done to the poor by the powerful and wealthy, so criticised by the earlier prophets, are being repeated (vv. 1–5). The heavy interest charged by those who were lending money to hard-pressed householders and smallholders was crippling them and forcing them into debt, dispossession of land and house, and to selling their children into slavery. Nevertheless, Nehemiah's response to all this in this chapter still shows him as active in 'building up the walls of Jerusalem' in a metaphorical as well as a literal sense (cf. Ps. 51:18f./20f.). If such practices were allowed to persist, the community would be as fatally weakened by internal dissension as it would be by external enemies (who can more easily be kept at bay by a defensive wall).

It has been rightly pointed out that Nehemiah is here presented as one who acts in the great prophetic tradition of the past. He defends the rights of the weak and oppressed against the wealthy and oppressive leaders of society in exactly the manner of the pre-exilic prophets. He performs an act of prophetic symbolism (v. 13). He predicts God's judgement (v. 13).[17] Yet, in seeking to establish justice in society and calling on the leaders to administer it rightly, he is also presented as acting as a true Davidide. David enjoined Solomon that, when he was given charge over Israel, he should 'follow the teaching of Yahweh' and be careful to observe 'the statutes and the decrees which Yahweh imposed on Moses for Israel' (I Chr. 22:12f., cf. 28:7). Again, Jehoshaphat appointed judges in the cities to see 'that there is no injustice' on earth as there is none with God (II Chr. 19:7).

In seeking to establish *mishpat* (justice) in the community, Nehemiah thus fulfils the true function of both prophet and Davidic king as this has been expressed in the narratives of the Chronicler and in the addresses he assigned to both David and Jehoshaphat.[18] The parallels between Nehemiah and the practices of Mesopotamian kings who instituted a set of temporary reforms at the beginning of their reign to alleviate acute social distress has been noted by Fishbane.[19] This stengthens the 'royal' image given to Nehemiah.

14 Neh. 6:3, 8, 11 *Nehemiah to his detractors and opponents*

[3] *And I sent messengers to them, saying, 'I am engaged in a great work and I cannot come down. Why should the work stop because I leave it and come down to you?'* ... [8] *And I sent to him, saying, 'It is not as you say. It is an invention of your own mind.'* [a] ... [11] *But I said, 'Shall such a man as I run away? And should such a man as I enter the temple and live? I will not come.'*

Text

[a] Lit. 'From your own heart you are devising.'

General description

Three more disputation sayings in Nehemiah's verbal conflict with his detractors and opponents.

Contents

The function of these short sayings assigned to Nehemiah is to show him still as the faithful, zealous, uncompromising and humble servant of God who will make no alliance with God's enemies. Nor will he arrogantly assume power and position for himself but, as ideal servant, he trusts alone in God's power to deliver him and his people from the threats of force of those who oppose him. Also, he has the insight to detect the false prophet and refuses to be led astray by him (vv. 10, 12f.). Presumably his refusal to enter the holy court in the

temple was because only a priest had such a right.[20] The refusal to be led astray
by 'northern' advisers shows him avoiding the sin Jeroboam was charged with
by Abijah (II Chr. 13:6f.). His zeal for the work, which refuses to be deflected,
is such as was called for by Azariah (II Chr. 15:7). His courage in the face of
threats answers to the call of Jahaziel to Jehoshaphat and the people of Judah
(II Chr. 20:15, 17) and of Jehoshaphat to the people (II 20:20). His refusal to
let arrogance sweep him into grandiose claims of royal powers (vv. 6–8) or to
priestly prerogative (vv. 10f.) shows him as refusing to repeat the sins of
Jeroboam (II Chr. 13:8–12) and, more especially, of Uzziah, who was rebuked
by Azariah for just such 'hubris' (II Chr. 26:16–21). In fact, these words
appear to serve more to show the traits of ideal leadership in Nehemiah than to
inform us in detail of historical fact.

15 Neh. 8:9f., 11 *Ezra (and Nehemiah?) and Levites to the people*

[9] *And Nehemiah, the governor,[a] and Ezra, the priest and scribe, with the Levites
who were instructing the people, said to all the people, 'Today is holy to Yahweh,
your God. Do not mourn and weep', for all the people had been weeping as they
heard the words of the law.* [10] *And he said to them, 'Come, eat fat and drink wine.
Send portions to those for whom nothing is prepared, for today is holy to our Lord.
Do not be sorrowful. The joy of Yahweh is your strength.'* [11] *And the Levites
calmed all the people, saying, 'Be quiet! For today is holy. Do not be sorrowful.'*

Text

[a] The reference to Nehemiah does not appear in Esdras, while some LXX
texts have only the term 'governor' and others only the name 'Nehemiah'. The
word for 'governor' (תִּרְשָׁתָה) is not given to Nehemiah elsewhere. Always
another word is used (פֶּחָד). All this suggests that this phrase is a secondary
insertion and forms part of that redaction of the material which sought to show
that Ezra and Nehemiah were contemporaries.

General description

A summons to the people to renounce their mourning and celebrate joyfully
the giving of the law in feasting, reinforced by a parallel call from the Levites
(v. 11).

Contents

The reading of the law reduced the people to consternation, penitence and grief. This was a 'model' response, as we know from the accounts of Josiah's reaction when he tore his clothes in penitence on hearing the scroll of the law read to him (II Kgs. 22:11, cf. II Chr. 34:19). However, to those who do respond in obedience, the law is a source of joy, for it is the means by which Yahweh is present in the community, directing their life and assuring them of 'blessing'. Indeed, it is a 'sign' of the kingdom, for the instruction of Ezra and the Levites to 'eat the fat' and 'drink wine' is reminiscent of the picture of the 'banquet of God's kingdom' on Mount Zion, predicted in Isa. 25:6:

On this mountain the LORD of hosts will make for all peoples a feast of fat things, a feast of wine on the lees, of fat things full of marrow, of wine on the lees well refined.

Further, the incident strongly recalls the narrative of the visit of the delegates from Bethel to Jerusalem, recorded in Zech. 7:2f. They asked if they were to continue mourning and fasting as they had been doing during the judgement period of the exile. Zechariah assures them that the new era has dawned and that all mourning will give way to joyful feasting (8:18f.: see discussion below, pp. 212f.). It is another instance of one stress of the Chronicler. When he depicts the inauguration of great new eras in the story of God's dealing with his people, he describes them as occasions of great joy and of feasting. So the completion of the temple preparations by David led to a similar command to feasting and joy (I Chr. 29:20–2), and the same happend at the completion and dedication of the building (II Chr. 7:3–10).

16 Neh. 10:28–39/29–40 *The people's oath of continued allegiance to the law*

[28] *The rest of the people, the priests, Levites, gate-keepers, singers, temple servants, and all who have separated themselves from the nations of the lands to the law of God, their wives, sons and daughters, everyone of knowledge and discernment,* [29] *resolve with their brethren, the leaders,* [a] *and enter into a solemn vow* [b] *to live by the law of God which he gave by Moses, God's servant, and to keep and perform all the commandments, statutes and decrees of Yahweh our Lord.* [30] *We will not let our daughters be given in marriage to the nations of the earth, nor shall their daughters marry our sons.* [31] *And if the nations of the earth bring in their wares or any grain to sell on the sabbath, we will not buy from them on the sabbath or any holy day. We*

will leave [the produce of the land] every seventh year and the payment of any loan. [32] *And we lay upon ourselves the obligation to give from our own income a third of a shekel yearly for the service of the temple of our God,* [33] *for the showbread, the perpetual cereal offering, burnt offerings, sabbaths, new moons, for the festivals, the sacred vessels and for the sin offering to make expiation for Israel, and all the work involved in the temple of God.* [34] *Further, we, the priests, Levites and people by our family divisions, cast lots for the bringing of the wood-offering to the temple of our God at the appointed times, year by year, for burning on the altar of Yahweh our God as it is written in the law.* [35] *Also to present the first-fruit of our land, of all the fruit of every tree year by year, for the temple of Yahweh.* [36] *And the first-born of our sons, and our cattle, as it is written in the law, and the first-born of our herds and flocks, to present at the temple of God for the priests who minister in the temple of our God;* [37] *the first-fruits of our meal, our offerings, the fruit of every tree, new wine and oil to present for the priests, to the store-rooms of the temple of our God, and a tenth of the produce of our land for the Levites, for the Levites are they who collect the tithes in our country districts.*[c] [38] *And the Aaronite priest shall be with the Levites when the Levites collect the tithes, and the Levites shall bring up a tenth of the tithes to the temple of our God, to the store-rooms of the treasure-house.* [39] *The Israelites and the Levites shall bring the offering of corn, new wine and oil to the store-rooms because the sacred vessels are there, and the priests who minister, the gate-keepers and the singers. We shall not neglect the temple of our God.'*

Text

[a] LXX adds, 'and coming with an oath' (Heb. אֹרְרֵיהֶם) rather than 'their leaders' (Heb. אַדִּירְהֶם).

[b] Lit. 'into a curse and an oath'.

[c] Lit. 'the cities of our labour'.

General description

A pledge to keep the law relating to the temple, its worship and its upkeep, taken by the whole community.

Contents

This detached account of an oath, or pledge, taken by the whole community, raises a number of questions concerning the exact context in which it is supposed to have occurred and the relationship between the details of what is prescribed and some other law-codes.[21] Such issues are not our concern here. Perhaps it might be said that, in the light of the continuing tradition themes we find here which occur also in the addresses in Chronicles, the view of D. J. Clines that Neh. c. 10 represents an early example of Jewish biblical exegesis on the Torah is of especial interest.[22]

For our purpose it is significant that the community are described here in ideal terms. They are the 'remnant' of the people (Heb. שְׁאָר), with all the sacral orders who officiated in the temple (v. 28). These are all described as 'those who have separated themselves from the nations of the lands'. This theme of the separateness of the people of God is by now too familiar from our study of the addresses in Chronicles and the Ezra/Nehemiah material to need further elaboration.

They are also described as those who had 'knowledge and discernment' (Heb. יֹדֵעַ מֵבִין, v. 28). This recalls the Chronicler's description of the words of Hiram, the king of Tyre, about Solomon, who built the temple. In a passage peculiar to the Chronicler, Hiram says, 'Blessed be the LORD, the God of Israel, who made heaven and earth, who has given king David a wise son, endued with "discretion and understanding"' (II Chr. 2:12/11, Heb. יוֹדֵעַ שֵׂכֶל וּבִינָה). This community emulates Solomon in 'resolving' to fulfil to the letter the law of God, especially as it relates to separation from the Gentiles, sabbath, tithe and sacrifical laws. All can be summed up in their promise, 'We will not neglect (Heb. /עזב) the temple of our God' (v. 39/40). We have seen the play on this word in Chronicles. In particular, this community show the very concern with the temple which Abijah called for from the apostate North (II Chr. 13:4–12) and that faithfulness in bringing material possessions to the temple which Azariah saw to be the pre-condition of God's blessing (II Chr. 31:10).

17 Neh. 13:17f. *Nehemiah to the leaders*

[17] *Then I remonstrated with the chief citizens of Judah and said to them, 'What is this wicked thing you are doing in profaning the sabbath?* [18] *Was not this how your fathers acted and brought all this calamity on us[a] and on this city? Yet you are heaping wrath on Israel by profaning the sabbath.'*

Text

a In the MT there is an unnecessary reduplication of the first-person plural pronoun. The LXX suggests that it may have read originally, 'upon *them* and upon us . . .'.

General description

A 'disputation saying' in which Nehemiah chides the leading citizens (the Heb. literally means 'nobles') with work and trading on the sabbath. Note the literary device of rhetorical question, twice, (vv. 17b, 18a) and appeal to past history by way of illustration of the point being made.

Contents

It is not surprising that sabbath observance seems to have gained added prominence during and after the exile, at least in some circles. Together with the practice of circumcision, it would be an observance which would emphasise the distinctiveness of the Jews and be an expression of faithfulness when cultic worship was denied them. We hear calls for strict sabbath observance in much late prophetic literature, as in Ezek. 20:12–24 and in Jer. 17:19–24. The passage in Jeremiah is Deuteronomistic and there are some linguistic parallels between that and the words of Nehemiah, particularly the phrase about 'bringing in a burden to Jerusalem on the sabbath day'. Its essential nature for any who wanted to adhere to the Jewish faith is heard also in Isa. 56:8, and 66:23. It is not prominent in the prophecies of Haggai, Zechariah and Malachi, or in the addresses in Chronicles. Nevertheless, it is important to see from the context of this chapter that the real purpose of enforcing sabbath legislation was to preserve Jewish separateness from the nations. It was partly, at least, because it brought them into contact with Tyrian traders that breaking of the sabbath was seen as particularly grave (v. 16). 'Separateness', as we have seen, is an important theme of the addresses in Chronicles.

Indeed, in these words attributed to Nehemiah, we see more plainly than elsewhere links with the formal structure and the themes of the addresses in Chronicles. We note the double use of the device of rhetorical question and also the appeal to avoid the bad example of the 'fathers' and to learn from the judgement which befell them. The term 'wrath' also features in the addresses, either the Hebrew word הָמוֹן being used or, as here, קֶצֶף . This word is used by Oded in his appeal to the northern armies (II Chr. 28:11, 13) and, even more interestingly, by Hezekiah. He also uses it in a context of appeal to the example of the 'fathers' (II Chr. 29:9f.) and again in the letter he sent out to all Israel:

Do not be hard-hearted now as your fathers were . . . that the fierceness of his anger may turn from you. *(II Chr. 30:8)*

We shall meet similar examples in the tradition material in Zech. cc. 1–8. The specific charge may be unique to the Nehemiah material here, but the form and content of his words are those which we meet frequently elsewhere in the post-exilic literature. Clearly it belongs to 'the tradition'.

18 Neh. 13:21f. *Nehemiah to the merchants and levites*

[21] *And I warned them and said to them, 'Why are you lodging in front of the wall? If you do it again I shall take action against you.'[a] And from that time on they did not come on the sabbath.* [22] *And I commanded the Levites to cleanse themselves and come and guard the gates and keep the sabbath day sacred. Remember me for this, O my God, and have mercy on me according to the greatness of your grace.*

Text

[a] Lit. 'I shall put forth a hand against you.'

General description

An accusation against foreigners and Jewish merchants for trading on the sabbath. The accusation takes the form of a question (v. 21a) and is followed by a conditional threat of punishment (v. 21b). There follows an exhortation to the Levites, given in reported speech, charging them with execution of Nehemiah's orders about the sabbath (v. 22a). The saying concludes with one of Nehemiah's repeated 'remembrance' requests addressed to God (v. 22b).

Contents

These two short sayings of Nehemiah add little to that in vv. 17f. just considered, except to report that Nehemiah supported his words of accusation about trading on the sabbath with effective action. So he not only speaks prophetic words but establishes compliance with Torah by the same kind of faithful and effective action which had characterised good Davidic kings in the Chronicler's account. In setting the Levites to faithful discharge of their responsibilities, in particular, he emulates David (I Chr. 15:16–24, 23:2–32), Jehoshaphat (II 19:8–11), Jehoida (II 23:18) and Hezekiah (II 29:25–30). The aim of the whole enterprise is the separation of the people of God from the ways of the nations by faithfulness to Torah.

19 Neh. 13:25–7 *Nehemiah to the Jews who had married foreigners*

25 *And I contended with them and cursed them and beat some of the men, pulled out their hair and made them swear by God, 'You shall not give your daughters to their sons and you shall not take their daughters for your sons or for yourselves.* 26 *Was it not because of such women that Solomon, king of Israel, sinned? Among the many nations there was no king like him, and he was loved by God. God appointed him king over all Israel. Yet foreign wives led even him into sin.* 27 *Shall we take you as an example[a] in committing the same great evil and betraying God by co-habiting with foreign women?'[b]*

Text

[a] Lit. 'listen to you'.

[b] The verb means, literally, 'to cause foreign women to dwell'. It is used in this way in Ezekiel (10:2, 10, 14, 17, 18) and here in Nehemiah. It is normally translated 'to marry' and, no doubt, implies this. I have sought, however, to retain the flavour of the original, since part of the abhorrence of foreign marriages to some was that the actual physical presence of foreigners living in the community impaired Israel's 'separation'.

General description

A disputation between Nehemiah and those who had married foreign wives, changing from reported (v. 25a) to direct speech (vv. 25b–27). Supported by public humiliation of wrongdoers, he imposes an oath on them to repudiate such practice. This is strengthened by an appeal to the example of Solomon, expressed in a rhetorical question (v. 26). A further rhetorical question repudiates those who have sinned in this way as any kind of example for the community as a whole (v. 27).

Contents

'Separateness' is also the theme of these final words of Nehemiah, for the real objection to intermarriage is that it fatally compromises the distinctiveness of the temple/Torah community. Even the fact that some children could not speak the language of the Hebrews was symbolic of that lack of distinctiveness (vv. 23f.).

In this instance, also, Nehemiah matches stern words with stern deeds. We may note two features of his words which also marked the addresses in Chronicles, the rhetorical question and the appeal to past history. It is strange that Solomon is singled out in this way. The memory of him appears to be based on the Deuteronomistic History with its account of his foreign marriages in I Kgs. c. 11. The disapproval of these foreign marriages by the editors is clear from the way they structure their history of the life of Solomon. Before I Kgs. c. 11 all is blessing and prosperity. After the report of his foreign marriages there follows judgement. Possibly, even the description of Solomon as 'loved by God' shows dependence on the Deuteronomistic History, for there it was recorded that he was named 'Jedidah', which means 'beloved of the LORD' (II Sam. 12:24f.), although in Neh. 13:26 a different Hebrew word is used.

This explicit disapproval of Solomon's foreign marriages has been used to argue that these must be the exact words of Nehemiah himself, since the Chronicler nowhere mentions Solomon's foreign marriages.[23] Or, for the same reason, that Ezra and Nehemiah must be from a hand other than the Chronicler's since the Chronicler nowhere shows the harsh disapproval of Solomon's foreign marriages which appears in the Books of Ezra and Nehemiah.[24] Either of these arguments might be true, but it could equally be said that the Chronicler shows his disapproval of Solomon's marriages by his silence over them. They would spoil his picture of Solomon as the ideal successor of David. Further, Mal. 2:11f. shows that disapproval of foreign marriages was a theme of at least part of the post-exilic tradition. Nehemiah, therefore, might be just as much a mouth-piece for that tradition on this issue as we have reason to suspect that he is on other issues.

Certainly the theme of intermarriage is not one that featured in the addresses in Chronicles but, as we have seen, that of the 'separateness' of the people of God does. This is the real issue behind all the deeds and words attributed to Nehemiah in the tradition which tells both of the rebuilding of

Table 4.1   *Division of speeches according to types of speakers (%)*

'Royal' speeches	73	(47)
Prophetic speeches	0	(28)
Priestly speeches (i.e. Ezra)	21	(13)
Others	5	(13)

the wall and the building of a 'fence' around the Torah of sabbath observance and intermarriage.

Summary

The main aim of this examination of the 'speeches' (which seemed a more fitting description of the varied material here) in the Books of Ezra and Nehemiah has been to compare them with the 'addresses' in Chronicles. It may be best to make one or two objective observations as a basis for any more general conclusions.

The speakers

Of the nineteen speeches (including written documents) considered, three are attributed to royal speakers (Cyrus, one; Cyrus/Darius, one; Artaxerxes, one); one is attributed to Zerubbabel and his fellow-leaders, one to the people as a whole, four to Ezra and ten to Nehemiah.

If, however, it were taken that Zerubbabel is presented as in some way of the 'Davidic' line (cf. Ezr. 3:8, cf. I Chr. 3:17), that increases the number of 'royal' speeches. Further, we have had cause to see that Nehemiah is shown as acting in the way of faithful Davidide kings. This would make the proportion of 'royal' addresses increase dramatically. Table 4.1 gives the division of speeches on this understanding. Comparable percentages for the address in Chronicles are given in parentheses.

The absence of any prophetic speakers in Ezra/Nehemiah can be slightly off-set by the fact that Nehemiah also, on at least one occasion, exhibits 'prophetic' characteristics in his words and deeds.

Table 4.2   *Distribution of formal characteristics in the speeches*

Characteristic	Ezra/Nehemiah	Chronicles
Specific address	—	47%
Call for attention	—	22%
Prophetic formula	—	22%
Appeal to/citation of 'Scripture'	2(10%)	28%
Illustration from history	3(16%)	22%
'Encouragement formula'	5(26%)	25%
Play on words	—	44%
Rhetorical question	8(42%)	25%

Formal characteristics

It will be useful to list the tabulated characteristics of the addresses in Chronicles and compare them with the speeches in Ezra/Nehemiah (see Table 4.2).

Themes

Some of the major themes of the speeches in Ezra/Nehemiah are listed below with the number of times each occurs. These may be compared with the discussion of the themes of the addresses in Chronicles above (p. 123ff.).

1. The 'separateness' of God's people:
   (a) shown in refusing foreign help — 3⎫
   (b) in obedience to some aspect of Torah — 2⎬Total 7
   (c) in rejecting intermarriage with foreigners — 2⎭
2. Concern for the temple, its building or its worship — 7
3. The 'tribute' of the nations — 3
4. The 'wrath' of God in judgement on his people — 2
5. God's use of foreign powers — 5
6. God's 'material' blessings for his faithful people — 4
7. The centrality of 'Torah' — 5
8. The importance of Jerusalem — 4
9. Trust in God's power — 6
10. The 'presence' of God — 1

Do such statistics enable us to draw any conclusions? It has to be said that the 'speeches' in Ezra/Nehemiah do not parallel the addresses in Chronicles in formal structure. They appear to be much more bedded in their context and influenced by their supposed 'historical' setting than those in Chronicles. This gives the comparison of the division among categories of speakers little significance except that both show the 'royal' calling of the Davidic line as finding expression and continuity in the leaders of the post-exilic community. This in itself is a point of no small importance, however.

On the other hand, the prominence of themes common both to the speeches in Ezra/Nehemiah and the addresses in Chronicles does give ground to question how far the alleged 'literary source material' found in Ezra/Nehemiah (royal decrees, memoirs of Ezra and Nehemiah, reports of disputations between Nehemiah and his opponents, oaths taken by the community) really is 'historical'. May these not be just as much the product of the post-exilic temple tradition as we have seen the addresses in Chronicles to be? If so, it would have to be argued that the books of Ezra and Nehemiah as we have them emanate from circles similar to those which we call 'the Chronicler'. Whatever the exact arguments about 'authorship', there is strong continuity of tradition-outlook.

Finally, while the speeches in Ezra/Nehemiah lack the formal structure of the addresses in Chronicles, the recurrence of a number of rhetorical features such as the rhetorical question, appeal to past history, apparent allusion to 'Scripture', encouragement formulae, and calls for trust in God's power alone (although the absence of the device of play on words is striking) suggests that this material may also owe something of its shaping and expression to the tradents and rhetors of the post-exilic temple community.

5   The Book of Haggai

As we turn to our survey of the post-exilic prophetic books, it must be stressed that our aim is not to attempt a thorough, detailed exegesis of the message of the prophets or the contents of the books. Our concern is with the extent to which parallels to the kind of material we have been examining in Chronicles and Ezra/Nehemiah occur here, whether they be parallels in theme and matter or in style and form.[1]

The Book of Haggai presents special questions of interpretation since even a casual glance reveals two different types of material. There are the direct oracles of Haggai in which he addresses the people and/or their leader(s). These are found in 1:2, 4–11, 13b, 2:3 (4f.), 6–9, 11–14, 15–19, 21–3. Secondly, there is the editorial 'framework' in which these oracles have been set. This is found in 1:1, 3, 12, 13a, 14, 15, 2:1 (2), (4f.), 10, 20. The reference in brackets cannot be assigned to either category with certainty although, as we shall see, form and contents suggest that they belong more probably to the editorial strand of the book.[2]

We turn first to the direct oracles of Haggai. In 1:2, 4–11, we find a complex series of oracles, whose form, extent and relation to each other have provoked much discussion and disagreement. We find a messenger formula in v. 2a, although it announces a word of accusation against 'this people' for failing to rebuild the temple. This is referred to in the third person as 'the house of the

LORD', strange in an oracle which is announced as direct speech of Yahweh. Beuken sees it functioning as a connecting link between the editorial framework and the prophetic narrative.[3] There follows another introductory formula in v. 3, 'And the word of the LORD came by Haggai the prophet, saying . . .', which introduces the direct address of Haggai to the community. This challenges their priorities by way of a question: 'Is it time for you, *you* to live in panelled houses, while this house [i.e. the temple] is neglected?'[4] This in turn is followed by another 'messenger formula' introducing a direct oracle of Yahweh to the people, inviting them to consider ('lay to heart') their situation of small harvests, inadequate supplies of food and drink, poor clothing and inflation (v. 6). V. 7 sees another introductory messenger formula again calling the people to 'lay to heart' their situation. V. 8, with its call to engage in rebuilding the temple, its conditional promise of Yahweh that he will 'be glorified' in the restored building and its concluding prophetic formula 'says Yahweh', appears to interrupt the sequel to the call in v. 7. In vv. 9–11 direct speech of Yahweh to the people again describes their frustration with their disappointing harvests. Yahweh asks the rhetorical question, 'Why?' and again gives the answer. His 'house' is neglected while each of them 'rushes' (/ רוץ) about looking after his own 'house'. Perhaps this last implies not merely repairing and redecorating the building, but each being preoccupied with the affairs of his own 'household'.[5] The oracle closes (vv. 10f.) with a restatement of the conditions they have been experiencing, in terms similar to, but differently expressed from, vv. 6–9. Now the reference to drought is made explicit with its consequent famine, and this is concluded with a more general note on the frustration of all the endeavours of the community, 'all the toil of their hands'.

The main questions posed by this particular series of oracles are: (1) the unity, or lack of it, of vv. 2b, 4–6; (2) the relation of vv. 7, 9–11 to 2b, 4–6, and (3) the place of v. 8 in vv. 7–11. Fortunately, for our purpose here, we do not need to pass judgement on either the process by which they have arrived at their present form or their exact relation in the original preaching of Haggai. We can take it for granted that they represent various strands of his preaching. Whether he, or others, are responsible for the present order is immaterial.[6]

What elements in Haggai's preaching are revealed here? It must be said first that he shows himself to be standing firmly in the line of the Zion/temple traditions. The temple is Yahweh's 'house', and for this reason plays a central and pivotal part in the life of the community. Whether or not we allow with

Johnson that Haggai (and also Zechariah) was a 'cultic prophet',[7] he calls for priority to be given to the 'service' of the temple. Here, the actual form of words in v. 2 is interesting. The Hebrew reads literally:

This people has said,
'It is not a time of coming (לֹא עֶת־בֹּא),
A time to build the house of Yahweh.'

The text may be corrupt here, and the VSS certainly suggest that we should read לֹא עַתָּ(ה) בָּא, giving the more familiar rendering, 'The time has not come to rebuild the house of Yahweh.'[8] Yet there is an interesting echo of the call in the addresses in Chronicles which stress that truly 'to seek Yahweh' is 'to come' to his house. So Hezekiah calls in his letter to 'all Israel', 'Do not be hard-hearted now as your fathers were. Give Yahweh his due honour and come (בֹּאוּ/) to his sanctuary . . .' (II Chr 30:8). Apart from this verbal parallel, however, the importance of seeking God in the temple and showing zeal in its service recurs in the addresses. It is found in David's first charge to the leaders:

Now, give heart and soul to seeking Yahweh, your God. Stir yourselves to build the sanctuary of Yahweh . . . *(I Chr. 22:19)*

Hezekiah calls on the Levites:

Sanctify yourselves now and sanctify the temple of Yahweh, the God of your fathers, and bring out what is unclean from the holy place. *(II Chr. 29:5)*

Because their 'fathers' had 'turned their attention away from the dwelling of Yahweh' (מִשְׁכַּן יהוה, v. 6) and 'shut up the doors of the vestibule' and generally neglected the worship due in the temple, 'Yahweh's wrath (קֶצֶף) came on Judah and Jerusalem . . .' (vv. 8f.). Thus Haggai's hearers may be charged with an attitude which says, 'There is no time for *coming*' to God's house, and so with showing neglect of God himself.

This introduces another theme of the addresses which is strongly represented in Haggai's preaching, that is, the firm, direct link between faithful care for the house of God and material prosperity. Equally, poverty is connected with neglect of the temple. This had always been an element in the Zion tradition. Pss. 29, 72, 132 and II Sam. 33:1–7 show the link between God's rule in Zion as universal king and his control over the forces of nature. Rudolph cites also Ezek. c. 47, Joel. 3(4):18, Pss. 46:4(5), 65:9ff. (10ff.). That is why Beuken is surely wrong to see two separate strands in the present composition of Hag. 1:2–11, one of call for concern for the temple and the other about the hardness of the time (see n. 6 above). Nowhere is this link expressed more forcefully than in the address of Azariah, the chief priest, in II Chr. 31:10:

Since they began to bring their offering into Yahweh's sanctuary, there has been food in plenty with much to spare. Yahweh has blessed his people so that there is all this surplus.

The Hebrew shows interesting parallels with the words of Haggai. Azariah, using two infinitive absolutes (אָכוֹל וְשָׂבוֹעַ), says literally, '[There has been] eating and satiety.' Haggai, using an infinitive absolute and a noun, says, '[There has been] eating but no satiety' (אָכוֹל וְאֵין־לְשָׂבְעָה). To some extent both reflect the form of the covenant curses found in Deut. 28:36–46 and Hos. 4:10,[9] yet the parallel between Haggai's words and those attributed to Azariah is striking.

Another such coincidence of theme is found in Haggai's promise of God's 'presence'. In v. 13b the words occur, '"I am with you", says the LORD.' This is addressed to the people as a whole (in the editorial framework it is the leaders who are given pride of place). This finds echo in 2:4, but 2:4f. probably belongs to the expansion of Haggai's message in the tradition (see below). However, 2:6–9 gives a distinctive eschatological slant to this theme. It is important for the temple to be rebuilt because it is the place to which Yahweh's 'glory' (vv. 7f.) will return and where his 'presence' will be made effective among them. Such a vision stands in the tradition of Ezekiel (e.g. Ezek. 43:4f.) and Second Isaiah (e.g. Isa. 40:5) but behind that stands the Zion tradition – Zion, the dwelling place of Yahweh to which all nations will come in homage (e.g. Pss. 132:13ff., 46:7/8, 10f./11f., 68:35/36, 96:6–13 etc.). It is the 'presence' of a God to whom belong all resources ('The silver is mine, and the gold is mine', v. 8) and who is thus well able to 'bless' his people (v. 19). Again, vv. 15–19, for all their difficulties of interpretation,[10] clearly show that his presence, which the rebuilt temple will make effective among them, will mark a change in their fortunes. Twice they are summoned to 'lay to heart' (vv. 15, 18), in an act of faith in Yahweh's purpose of grace for the future, just as they were twice summoned to 'lay to heart' (1:5, 7) their present plight following their neglect of Yahweh's house. Yet again Azariah's address in II Chr. 31:10 is paralleled where the faithfulness of the people in bringing their gifts into Yahweh's house has resulted in his 'blessing' for his people. Or, again, the words of the man of God to Amaziah are brought to mind, 'Yahweh is able to give you far more than this' (II Chr. 25:9).

We have seen how prominent a theme the 'presence' of God is in the addresses in Chronicles and how it appears also in the Ezra/Nehemiah material (see especially pp. 125, 182 above), and how closely linked it is to temple and 'blessing'. Of course, in Haggai's oracles it is an anticipated promise still to come. In the addresses the emphasis is on the presence as a reality in the contemporary situation, but this is a difference we should expect given the fact that Haggai was preaching before the temple was completed, while the addresses reflect the situation in the second temple period.

Again, there is an interesting parallel between the direct oracles of Haggai and that of the addresses in Chronicles when we hear his slighting reference to 'the work of their [human] hands'. The ineffectiveness of human effort without God is implicit in all of 1:3–11. In 2:14 it is made explicit: '"So it is with this people, and with this nation before me," says the LORD: "and so with every work of their hands; and what they offer there is unclean."' This is not the place to enter into a full and detailed discussion of 2:10–14, which has caused many problems for commentators and given rise to a number of different interpretations.[11] The belief that the 'this people' of v. 14 refers to the 'adversaries of Judah and Benjamin' and that this oracle was Haggai's instruction to refuse their offer of help is ingenious but implausible. To the many who have linked this whole 'priestly Torah' with the oracles of c. 1 and seen here a continued explanation for the hardships endured by the Judaean community must now be added the names of D. L. Petersen and Meyers and Meyers.[12] But this leaves unexplained the date given in v. 10 which would indicate that work on the rebuilding had been going on for about two or three months (cf. 1:15, 2:1). Petersen argues that it is their sacrifices (Heb. 'that which they were bringing near', v. 14) which are unclean because the temple has not yet been constructed (p. 85). While it is true that the Hiph'il of / קרב is often used in a sacrificial context, the difficulty with this view is that nothing explicit is said about the reconstruction of the temple. All the emphasis in Haggai's preaching is on its rebuilding. Once that is completed Yahweh will come in and fill it with his 'glory' (2:7f.). Further, in the Priestly texts in which the Hiph'il of / קרב is used in a sacrificial sense, the references are to animal sacrifices. It is most unlikely that this would be paralleled with 'the work of their hands' as it is in 2:14 and, indeed, such a parallel is never made in the Old Testament. The very thought would have been seen as almost impious, for the 'life' offered in animal sacrifice, symbolised by the blood, was God's gift, not the product of men's hands. The same phrase, with only a change of personal pronoun, we should note, is used in 2:17, where it clearly refers to the *products* of their work. This near parallel between 2:14 and 17 makes it far more likely that 'the work of their hands' refers to the actual building of the temple (as the date in 2:10 suggests) and that it is a warning to the people that only the 'coming' (presence) of God will make that work fruitful and effective. It is his 'glory' alone which will cleanse the community and 'bless' their work. The people, however hard they toil, have no capacity for self-regeneration. The sacrificial overtone in 'what they offer' is certainly there, but it is ironic. All human work and achievement offered to God is 'unclean' unless it is the offering of that which God has blessed and made vital by his presence. They are not wrong to build the temple. But only God's presence in the future will fill it with power and make it a source of blessing to the community.[13]

However, the details of the interpretation of the passage do not really affect the central point, which is the futility of all human effort which is not directed and blessed by God. This was also a theme we found in the addresses in Chronicles, especially in the words of Eliezer to Jehoshaphat in II 20:37. A fleet which was contemptuously described as 'your work' was destroyed by God because it was used in a wrongful alliance with Ahaziah of Israel.

In addition to some similarities of theme between the direct oracles of Haggai and the addresses in Chronicles we should note a number of parallels in form and rhetorical style. Haggai makes use of the rhetorical question (1:4, 9, 2:15, 19). He also uses play on words. Particularly noticeable is that between the words in 1:9, 'My house . . . is *neglected*' (Heb. חָרֵב), and those in 1:11, 'I summoned a *drought* (Heb. חֹרֶב) upon the land.' We have noted also the repeated phrase 'lay to heart' (Heb. שִׂימוּ לְבַבְכֶם) in 1:5, 7 and 2:15, 18. Striking also is the device of citation of earlier Scripture. The words of Amos (4:9) are recalled in 2:17. Both have the opening phrase, 'I smote you with blight and mildew', word for word in common. Interestingly, Haggai again brings in the phrase, 'the work of your hands', which was frustrated and destroyed by God. Both lament that, in spite of God's judgements, 'you did not return to me', although the literal rendering of the rather difficult text in Haggai is, 'You were not for me.' Amos uses the שׁוּב/('return') in the repeated refrain at this point.[14]

Nevertheless, a false impression would be given if we were to concentrate only on such points of contact between the oracles of Haggai and the addresses in Chronicles. No one could mistake Haggai for one of the 'preachers' of these addresses. His vocabulary is distinctive. At almost no point can the actual words and phrases he used be found also in the addresses. Further, there is a stongly eschatological note in Haggai's preaching, especially in such oracles as 2:6–9 and 20–3, which is quite foreign to the addresses. In particular, the apparent 'messianic' hope which is attached to Zerubbabel in 2:23 (cf. Jer.

22:24) has been completely modified in the Chronicler's writings and finds no kind of echo in the addresses. Nevertheless, the parallels, such as they are, are interesting, and some of the differences may, as we have argued, be due to different circumstances and times. Further, he is calling for a response from his hearers of concern for, and action on behalf of, the temple, in the same kind of way which characterised more generally some of the addresses. Perhaps the preaching of Haggai had its influence on the preaching which took place in the second temple in so far as that may be represented in the addresses in Chronicles just as, in turn, it may itself have been influenced by earlier 'Zion' themes in the liturgy of the pre-exilic temple. We might expect to find closer echoes of the addresses in the 'editorial framework' of the book in which the oracles of Haggai have been passed down, and it is to this which we now turn.

I have dealt elsewhere in detail with the main characteristics of the editorial framework of the Book of Haggai.[15] Earlier, Beuken examined it at length, concluding that it emerged in a 'Chronistic milieu'.[16] Any treatment must remain deeply indebted to him, although most recently D. L. Petersen has expressed some agreement with my view that the framework is not necessarily tied quite as closely to the Chronicler as Beuken argued.[17] He sees the book as primarily an historical narrative in which Haggai's oracles have been set, forming a genre similar to that found in Jer. cc. 26 and 36. Our treatment here can be fairly brief since, clearly, the editorial framework does not consist of 'addresses' in any shape or form. Only its main characteristics need be noted to see if they afford any parallels to the outlook which finds expression in the addresses in Chronicles.

It is interesting that it describes Haggai as 'the messenger of the LORD' (1:13), especially in view of our discussion of II Chr. 36:15f. (pp. 120 ff.). This is not in accordance with earlier usage. Apart from the many instances where the phrase *mal'ak Yahweh* means 'an angelic messenger', rarely, and then only in later literature, is it used to denote a prophet. The noun can mean a human being who acts as a messenger, but outside the Books of Haggai, Zechariah and Malachi it implies a prophet only in Second Isaiah (42:19, 44:26) and the first of those references is more probably an allusion to 'Israel' rather than to an individual prophet. In Zech. 12:8 it probably refers to the divinely appointed role of military guardianship by a reconstituted Davidic king, not to a prophet. But it is used in Mal. 1:1 clearly to indicate the prophet's role, whether the word meaning 'my messenger' is a proper name or a title. It appears again in Mal. 3:1 and, interestingly, is used of the priest in 2:7. A number of commentators have argued that all these are additions by the same later hand.[18] It is just as likely, however, that they all betray the fact that the circles which preserved the oracles of these prophets saw them as II Chr. 36:15f. saw all the leaders and special people to whom addresses had been assigned, as spokesmen for God to the people of the second temple community. Here, Haggai is regarded as authentic a 'messenger' to that community as earlier kings, priests and prophets had been in their time.

The use of the formula 'the word of the LORD came *by the hand* of Haggai, the prophet' (בְּיַד חַגַּי, 1:1, 3, 2:1) is interesting. Perhaps too much should not be made of it, since an alternative formula, 'the word of the LORD came *to* the prophet Haggai' (אֶל־חַגַּי) is also used (2:10, 20), and, while the latter occurred in one of the addresses we have considered in Chronicles (that of Shemaiah, II 12:7), nothing can be built on this, since it is widely used as a prophetic formula in Kings, in passages often paralleled in Chronicles. Beuken says of the first formula that it is characteristic both of the Chronicler and the Deuteronomistic History (p. 28) but, in fact, while it occurs as a prophetic formula eleven times in the Deuteronomistic History,[19] it occurs rarely in Chronicles. It is used of prophets generally in II 29:25. Otherwise, when not a parallel to a Kings passage, it is used mainly of Moses as mediator of the law.[20] It is used much more often in the Priestly Writing, not only of Moses as transmitter of the law, but more especially as transmitter of the instructions concerning the building of the tabernacle, its personnel and ritual.[21] We have seen already how, in Chronicles, David is presented as a second Moses to whom God reveals the 'plan' (תַּבְנִית) of the temple and everything connected with it. Possibly, Haggai is seen as standing in this line as the instrument of God's instruction to the returned exiles concerning the building of the second temple. The parallel between this and Moses is certainly suggested by the description of the ready response of the people to the word of God which came through him (1:12–14). They are described as 'the remnant' (כָּל־שְׁאֵרִית הָעָם, 1:12, 14, 2:2), the term which, in the prophetic literature, had become synonymous with those God would deliver, purified, beyond the judgement of the exile.[22] Perhaps the reason the people are not so described in 1:1 is that it was only by their obedience to God's word through his 'messenger', described in 1:12–14, that they proved themselves to be truly the 'remnant' of prophetic promise. That response it described in terms strikingly reminiscent of the response of the people to Moses' call to bring gifts for the construction and ornamentation of the tabernacle, recorded in Exod. 35:29, 36:2. In Haggai, this is seen as God's work with his people:

And the LORD stirred up (וַיָּעַר יהוה) the spirit of Zerubbabel . . . and the spirit of Joshua . . . and the spirit of all the remnant of the people: and they came and worked on the house of the LORD . . . (וַיַּעֲשׂוּ מְלָאכָה בְּבֵית יהוה).

In Exod. 35:29 we read:

All the men and women, the people of Israel, whose hearts moved them (נָדַב לִבָּם אֹתָם) to bring anything for the work (הַמְּלָאכָה)which the LORD had commanded by the hand of Moses (בְּיַד מֹשֶׁה) to be done (לַעֲשׂוֹת), brought it as their free-will offering to the LORD.

Exod. 36:2 reads:

every one whose heart stirred him up to come to the work (הַמְּלָאכָה) to do it (לַעֲשׂוֹת אֹתָהּ).

We have seen already how the account of the response to David's call for diligence and generosity in helping Solomon in the building of the temple also takes up and echoes this theme.[23]

Yet another echo of this is to be found in the framework, however, for in 2:4 we find a clear example of the kind of charge to the leaders and people which we hear from the lips of David to Solomon and the leaders of Israel when he charged them with zeal and courage in the building of the temple.[24] We find the same call to 'Be strong' (חֲזַק), the same command to engage in the work and the same call (v. 5), 'Do not be afraid.' This formula, often described as an 'Installation to Office' genre, is one to which we have given the more general name of an 'Encouragement for a Task'. There follows the same assurance of God's 'presence' as the ground for confidence, a promise extended in this instance by an allusion to past history. The reference is to the Exodus from Egypt, and the 'presence' of God with their fathers in the wilderness is alluded to by the use of the phrase 'My spirit *is standing* (עֹמֶדֶת) in your midst.' The use of the participle 'standing', related as it is to the noun for 'pillar' (עַמּוּד), evokes Exod. 33:10, where it is said that 'all the people saw the pillar of cloud *standing* (Heb. עֹמֵד) at the door of the tent.'[25] Beuken is surely right to see 2:4f. as belonging to the editorial framework.[26] As he says, the real answer to the misgivings felt by the people concerning the second temple is to be found in vv. 6–9. The temple is worth building, for it is to be the scene of the return of God 's 'glory', of his victorious universal kingship and his continuing 'presence' among his people. Vv. 4f. stand fair and square with the outlook and methods of the addresses in Chronicles.

Another point of resemblance between the framework and those addresses is found in the naming of those who are addressed. In the direct oracles of

Haggai it is always the community as a whole who are addressed. Indeed, assuming that 2:2 and 4 belong to the framework, there is no evidence that Haggai addressed such a person as Joshua at all. His appearance in the framework alongside Zerubbabel may well suggest that the process of elevation of the priesthood which took place after the exile had already begun, a process taken farther in Zech. 1–8. In the framework, however, the address is always said to be to the leaders and, usually, to the people as well. This conforms to the pattern of many of the addresses in Chronicles in which certain recipients are named in the address or described in the context.[27]

What, then, can we deduce from our survey of the Book of Haggai? Haggai himself sounds themes and employs techniques which are very close indeed to those heard in the addresses in Chronicles. There can be no doubt of his originality. He has his own vocabulary and idiom and the peculiarity of his message is, no doubt, in part due to the time when he was active. Forward-looking eschatological expectation is strong with him but does not noticeably characterise the addresses. In his apparent messianic hope for Zerubbabel there is a fundamental divergence from the outlook of the addresses which stress that promises to David have been fulfilled in the temple and its community. Nevertheless, it would be in no way fanciful to suggest that Haggai may have exercised a strong influence on the kind of preaching the addresses represent.

What does appear much more strongly in a study of the editorial framework, and, perhaps, in the further development of his oracles (see the comments on Zech. 8:9ff.), is that his oracles were preserved in circles which claimed him as one of the preachers playing a most important role at a critical stage of the people's history, a stage in every way parallel in significance to the times of Moses and David. For them, Haggai is still to be heard in a later period as one of the legitimate and authoritative preachers. In a real sense he is seen as continuing the role of Moses and David in his call for zeal, courage and faith in the building of the temple and, like them, he secured a ready and obedient response from his contemporaries. We have seen also that Ezra and Nehemiah are depicted in not totally dissimilar terms. These contemporaries of Haggai, by their exemplary zeal for the temple, showed themselves to be the true 'remnant', the authentic continuation of Israel, the people of God in the pre-exilic time. Haggai was also an authentic 'messenger' whose words still had authority for later generations and posed them a challenge. These later generations had in the temple the assurance of the continuing presence of God, so they must show a like zeal and concern for its upkeep and service.

They too have been given divinely consecrated leaders. If not all the hopes about Zerubbabel of which Haggai spoke had yet been realised (yet the retention of such oracles shows that eschatological hope had not been abandoned), governor and priests mediated God's word to them and were given by God to inspire the community and keep them faithful and obedient. They must always realise that there is still a vital link between obedience to God and material welfare. The 'silver and gold' are his. He is already among his people in the temple in 'glory'. Already they are being 'blessed'. Ultimately, all nations will come bringing him the tribute of worship and obedience. So, meanwhile, let the people 'be brave', let them 'be active' in the work of his service, for he is 'with' them as he was with their fathers in the Mosaic tabernacle and the Solomonic temple.

All this is very close to the language and theology we have seen to characterise the addresses in Chronicles. Such similarity may be held to show that the Book of Haggai was edited in a 'Chronistic milieu', as Beuken argued. But may it not suggest that it, with the addresses, may have belonged to a '*temple* milieu'? Is it not likely that we are catching in both something of the style and themes of the preachers of that temple? To them must have fallen just that pastoral concern to assure their hearers of their legitimate descent from the true 'Israel' of old; of God's presence with them, despite all appearances to the contrary; of the continuing validity of the future promises of the prophets; of the need, meanwhile, to continue faithful and show themselves worthy of both past and future while accepting the real fulfilment of those promises they were already experiencing now in the present.

6 Zechariah 1–8

Zechariah cc. 1–8 presents questions of structure quite different from those of the Book of Haggai.[1] The kernel of the book is the series of eight 'night visions' together with the oracles which accompany five of them. Three dates appear to divide the book into three sections. The visions and accompanying oracles are introduced by a date in 1:7, and are apparently presented by the book as being received all in one night (cf. 4:1). A date introduces 1:1–6 and another, cc. 7f. There are major differences between the three sections formed by this means. All the visions are narrated in the first person by Zechariah, although with different descriptive formulae. The accompanying oracles, as Petersen has pointed out, fulfil the function of explaining or developing some aspect of the visions.[2] Yet, in at least three instances, such 'oracular' expansions of the visions appear to be more 'corrective' than others and to exhibit sufficient resemblances to the tradition material which is the subject of this book to deserve attention here. These are 3:6–10, appended to the fourth vision of the cleansing of Joshua; 4:6b–10a, an oracle addressed to Zerubbabel; and 6:9–15, which appears to have little connection with the preceding final vision but to be designed to serve as an 'appendix' to the whole series.

In 1:1–6, however, we have an account of more traditional prophetic preaching by Zechariah, narrated in the third person, calling for repentance. In cc. 7f. we find oracles alternating between first and third person or, in some instances, unattributed. These give a 'Torah-type' reply to questions of a liturgical nature, ethical summaries of the teaching of the earlier prophets and apparent expansions based on the oracles and visions of 1:7–6:15, or even on words of Haggai. There are thus formal differences as well as variations in style and theme between the 'vision' section of the book and the oracular reports of Zechariah's preaching in 1:1–6 and 7f. There is little which approaches the kind of material of the addresses in Chronicles in the visions, for these announce God's future action rather than calling directly on the hearers for some kind of response. For this reason they will not be dealt with here. It is otherwise with the first and last sections of cc. 1–8 and with the passages specified above. Petersen has said of the oracles in the last section, in comparing them with 1:7–6:15:

Here we see Zechariah in a non-visionary mode at the outset, responding to a question with standard prophetic rhetoric and presenting additional oracles as well. *(p. 122)*

Again he says of this material:

this latter collection includes more admonitory rhetoric than do the oracles included among the visions. *(p. 120)*

Here, then, if anywhere, we are likely to be nearer the form, tone and content of the addresses, and it is for this reason that we direct our attention to them, starting with 1:2–6.

Zech. 1:2–6

The date marks this as one of the main sections of the book and shows Zechariah to have been a contemporary of Haggai, beginning his ministry just two months after Haggai's had begun. We have no means of judging its authenticity, but we shall see some evidence in the tradition to suggest that the two came to be seen as equally authoritative spokesmen of God to the post-exilic community (see the treatment of 8:9–13, pp. 228ff. below). The dating reflects this view. It is certainly strange that, if they were contemporaries, neither mentions the other or refers to his teaching. The formula 'The word of the LORD came to . . .' is found frequently in the Book of Ezekiel (thirty times) and in Jeremiah (twenty-one times), although most often in Ezekiel it is followed by the first-person singular pronoun, '. . . came to *me*'. As we have already noted, this opening section is distinguished from the vision reports and oracles by the use of the third person. There is no need, however, to follow Horst, who argued that an editor had changed an original first-person report to the third person.[3] This third-person form, together with the lack of specific description of those to whom the words in the following oracle were addressed,[4] argues for a more general summarisings in this section of what was understood to have been Zechariah's preaching. Perhaps, when we note the one or two points of contact with the visions and their accompanying oracles, we might even say it was intended to be exegesis, rather than merely summary, of Zechariah's preaching.

The opening theme of the section is an allusion to the past history of the nation. The disobedience of their 'fathers' was a theme found in the addresses in Chronicles. Oded refers to this (II 28:9); so does Hezekiah, speaking to the Levites (II 29:6, 9), as well as in his letter to all the people (II 30:7f.). Indeed, it is this note which marks the first very strong parallel with the 'address' recorded in the guise of Hezekiah's letter, found in II Chr. 30:6–9. It is not surprising if the 'disobedience of the fathers' should have become a prominent theme in post-exilic preaching. Appeal to it at one and the same time established the continuity and validity of the line of descent of the returned community from earlier Israel, and gave a theological explanation for the apparent break in the line of that descent and of all the institutions of the 'true Israel' during the exile. This would also explain the more favourable references in such preaching to God as 'the God of your/our fathers'.[5]

The description of God's judgement on those fathers as an example of the divine 'wrath' (קֶצֶף) affords another link with the vocabulary of the addresses in Chronicles and with the Ezra/Nehemiah material. Jehu told Jehoshaphat that, because of his alliance with Ahab and northern Israel, 'Yahweh's wrath (קֶצֶף) will fall on you' (II 19:2). Jehoshaphat apparently digested this lesson, for he admonishes the Levites, priests and leaders to administer justice carefully and in obedience to God, instructing those involved truly so that they will not bring 'wrath on you and your kinsmen' (II 19:10). Hezekiah, as he repairs and opens the doors of the temple, tells the priests and Levites, 'our fathers acted treacherously and did evil in the sight of Yahweh our God . . . So Yahweh's wrath came on Judah and Jerusalem' (II 29:6–8). Beuken argues that 1:2 cannot be from the Chronicler's circle because the Heb. /קצף is never used in Chronicles as a verb.[6] That is true, but Zech. 1:2 contains not only the verb, but the noun, (קֶצֶף), strangely used as an accusative acting as an internal or absolute object to the verb,[7] and this seems strongly to link it with the addresses. The link is found in the vocabulary, the theology and the rhetorical device of illustration by appeal to past history. Yet there is an interesting link also with the first vision of Zechariah himself and its accompanying oracle.

There Yahweh speaks of his great 'wrath', presumably against Judah and Jerusalem. The first vision and its oracle announce that the age of 'wrath' is now past, or rather, that the divine 'wrath' is now turned away from the people of God to their adversaries. We must bear this in mind in seeking to unveil the obscurities of 1:2–6. Meanwhile, we must also be alert to the possibility that the use of the verbal root קצף/ in 1:2 and in 1:15 suggests that behind 1:1–6 lie echoes of actual words of Zechariah himself. Indeed, another link with the visions and oracles of cc. 1–8 is afforded by the use of the phrase 'LORD of hosts'. As well as occurring repeatedly in cc. 7f. (7:9, 8:1, 3, 6, 7, 9, 14, 18, 20, 21, 23) it is found in 1:14, 16, 2:8/12, 3:7, 6:12. Each of these parallels between the vision/oracle material and that of 1:2–6 and 7f. occurs in the oracles accompanying the visions rather than in the visions themselves. If Petersen is right in saying that the oracles offer later explanation and exegesis of the visions, then this suggests that the oracles emerged in circles similar to those in which 1:1–6 and 7f. also developed.

Beuken has characterised vv. 3–6a as a 'Levitical Sermon'.[8] I have already shown reason to doubt whether such a genre can be satisfactorily defined or its existence established, while yet maintaining that these passages, so styled, do evince many of the characteristics of 'preaching' and show remarkable continuity of theme and method. The parallels are strongly marked in these verses with other such material, not least, as has often been noted, with the letter of Hezekiah recorded in II Chr. 30:6–9. We note first, not only the device of play on words which was such a feature of the addresses, but the particular word-play used in Hezekiah's letter based on the word 'turn' (שוב/). Zech 1:3 reads:

Turn to me (שׁוּבוּ אֵלַי)
So that I may turn to you (וְאָשׁוּב אֲלֵיכֶם).

(The use of simple *waw* plus the imperfect indicates purpose here.) Hezekiah's letter runs:

O Israelites, return to Yahweh . . .
(שׁוּבוּ אֶל־יהוה)
that he may turn to the remnant of you . . .
(יָשֹׁב אֶל־הַפְּלֵיטָה) *(v. 6)*

The only difference is that the letter of Hezekiah employs reported third-person speech and uses the jussive form of the verb, where Zech. 1:3 is in the direct speech of a prophetic oracle introduced by one formula, 'Thus says the LORD . . .' and concluded by another, 'Oracle of the LORD of hosts'.

Petersen has done us a service in questioning the very widely accepted assumption that there is a close connection between vv. 3–6a and the letter of Hezekiah, so bringing the issue to the light of re-examination.[9] One of the reasons for this, he maintains, is that the verb /שוב, 'to turn/return' in II Chr. c. 30 has primarily geographical associations, 'Return to Yahweh [who now dwells in Jerusalem].' However, this appears to ignore the many different nuances of the verb in II Chr. 30:6–9 which we discussed above (see pp. 102ff.), and the fact that, in the addresses, faithfulness to Yahweh is seen as finding expression in faithfulness to the temple and its worship. It is clear from the visions and oracles in the main section of Zech. 1:7–6:15 that Yahweh's 'return' to his people and his 'return' to the temple and to Zion are also equated (e.g. 2:10/14).[10] So, while not alien to Zechariah's own thinking, it certainly accords with the view repeatedly expressed in the addresses, where, as in Hezekiah's words, to 'Give Yahweh his due honour' is equated precisely with the call to 'come to his sanctuary' (II Chr. 30:8). Further, the following verse shows that much more than a mere geographical journey to Yahweh is implied. Their return to the LORD will mean that they experience his mercy for themselves ('He will not turn away from you if you return to him', cf. Zech. 1:3b). This mercy, they will find, will extend to their kinsfolk in exile as well (v. 9a).

Having met two rhetorical devices familiar from the addresses, those of appeal to history by way of illustration and of play on words in 1:4, we now meet another, that of citation of, or allusion to, earlier Scripture. It comes, appropriately, in the context of appeal to the warnings of the earlier prophets, just as Jehoshaphat's address which had called for faith in the teaching of God's prophets also appropriately cited words from a prophet (II Chr. 20:20, citing Isa. c. 7). The term 'former prophets' is peculiar to this material in Zechariah (cf. 7:7, 12). Clearly it does not have its later more technical canonical sense, but stands for the pre-exilic prophets in general, for whom Jeremiah seems to figure here as a representative. In Jeremiah the same understanding of the hortatory role of the prophets is seen:

You have neither listened nor inclined your ears to hear, although the LORD persistently sent to you all his servants, the prophets, saying, 'Turn, now (שׁוּבוּ־נָא), every one of you, from his evil way and wrong doings . . .' (מַדַּרְכּוֹ הָרָעָה) *(Jer. 25:4f.)*

With this we may compare Zech. 1:4:

Turn, now (שׁוּבוּ־נָא), from your evil ways and evil deeds (מִדַּרְכֵיכֶם הָרָעִים).

Similar words are found elsewhere in the Jeremiah tradition (e.g. 7:25f., 35:15f.). It is interesting to note that all these are from the prose tradition of the book of Jeremiah which, as we have seen, is often thought to represent the preaching of Jeremiah's oracles by its Deuteronomistic tradents to their contemporaries in exile. Such a note is certainly sounded elsewhere in the Deuteronomistic tradition (e.g. II Kgs. 17:13). This seems, therefore, to stand in a tradition, no doubt given powerful impetus by the Babylonian exile, which served to underscore the authenticity and relevance of the words of those prophets who were understood to have predicted it. This tradition sees in the present, post-exilic situation a time of renewal of God's grace in the offer of a new covenant and so an opportunity to learn from the sins of the previous generations, who were seen to have occasioned the judgement. This certainly marked some of the addresses in Chronicles, as we have observed. Here also, it is possible to find a point of contact with the vision/oracle material of 1:7–6:15, for in 1:12 there is also an appeal to the words of Jeremiah in the reference to the 'seventy years' of exile (cf. Jer. 25:12, 29:10).

Such application of earlier Scripture to the new situation brings in yet another rhetorical device of the addresses, that of rhetorical question. We saw the use of this device in Abijah's address to the people of the North (II Chr. 13:4f.). Hanani asks Asa, 'Were not the Ethiopians and the Libyans a great force with chariots?' (II 16:8). Jehu asks Jehoshaphat, 'Do you enjoy helping the wicked and those who hate Yahweh?' (II 19:2), and Oded asks the people of Israel, 'Have you not sins of your own against Yahweh, your God?' (II 28:10).[11] However, two of the three rhetorical questions posed in Zech. 1:5f. face us with difficulties of interpretation. The first seems straightforward enough: 'Your fathers, where are they?' They had been overtaken by the threatened judgement and swept away into exile. Many of them were now dead in foreign territory far from the land of covenant promise. Petitjean insists that the main burden of these verses is not to labour the fact of exile as judgement, but to assure the hearers that the former age of judgement had now passed and they were entering the new age of salvation.[12] This emphasis is somewhat different from that of van der Woude, who wonders whether this represents the kind of dialogue with the listeners we find in the book of Malachi. Such listeners must have doubted whether the exile had been a divine judgement or whether those old prophecies concerned them any longer now that they had returned to the land.[13] It is difficult to avoid the general note of warning here, however. In all the addresses we have considered, appeal to the history of the 'fathers' has been made with the cautionary aim of warning their descendants against a repetition of their folly, and that note is certainly present here. It is the second question which has raised difficulties. If, in one breath, the disappearance of the fathers is seen as the fulfilment of God's judgement on them, how, in the next, can the disappearance of the prophets be seen in any other way? This has led a number of commentators to assume that it is the false prophets, those who had lulled the people into a false sense of security with their assurances of שָׁלוֹם, 'All is well!', who had shared with their hearers the very judgement they had failed to predict or to warn about.[14] But such a switch, without any further description, is most improbable so shortly after the reference to 'the prophets' as faithful preachers of God's word (v. 4).

We must take seriously the adversative אַךְ with which v. 6 begins. In *contrast* to the transitory generations of those who hear God's word and make their response to it, and of individual spokesmen of that word, *the word of God itself* remains and endures, vital, relevant, commanding.[15] It is interesting that the prophetic word is now becoming regarded as authoritative teaching on a par with Torah, for that is what the paralleling of the legal term 'statutes' (חֻקִּים) with 'my words' must imply. We know that the Deuteronomistic tradents regarded the prophets as supremely expounders of Torah (e.g. Deut. 18:18f.).[16] Such a view continues to find expression here, as it does in the 'prophetic' addresses in Chronicles and, perhaps, in the way Nehemiah is portrayed in prophetic terms. Elliger is surely right to see here an approach to the concept of canon.[17] This is just the kind of theology which would lie behind the practice of the 'preacher', who sees in the recorded words of the past a living and powerful challenge for the present and expounds it accordingly. The power of the enduring word was shown in that it 'overtook (נשג/) your fathers'. That verbal root occurs most prominently in Deuteronomistic passages which expressed the theology of the certainty of the 'blessings' or 'cursings' promised under the terms of the covenant 'overtaking' the people according to their response to the word (e.g. Deut. 28:2, 15). There is no need to follow Wellhausen in emending 'your fathers' (אֶתְכֶם) to 'you' (אֲבוֹתֵיכֶם), giving 'have they not overtaken *you*?' The sure power of the word to bring judgement on the disobedient fathers carries warning enough to the present generation.

It is impossible to dogmatise on the exact force of v. 6b, which RSV renders:

So they repented and said, 'As the LORD of hosts purposed to deal with us for our ways and deeds, so has he dealt with us.'

Is it a continuation of the words of the 'address', and so does it refer to the penitence of the fathers? It is often argued that this is inconsistent with the statement in v. 4 that the fathers 'did *not* hear or heed me'. (The use of the Hiph'il of the קשׁב/ there, rather than the familiar term 'to incline / נטה the ear', interestingly evokes the opening call for attention in a number of the addresses in Chronicles, 'Hear me!', הַקְשִׁיבוּ.) The apparent inconsistency between vv. 4 and 6b can be overcome by taking the response described in v. 6b as a very belated (too late) response by the fathers when the threatened judgements had already begun to come upon them.[18] Taken in this way, such an appeal to history could be a powerful reinforcement of the call for an immediate response now to the same word of God coming to a later generation through a later messenger. Nevertheless, it is strange, if this is so, that no mention is made of the lateness of the repentance, so that it is, perhaps, marginally more likely that this is an editorial description of the response of the hearers of Zechariah's preaching. We have such a third-person account at the opening of c. 7, where the request for a 'Torah' ruling strikingly evokes the incident described in Hag. 2:10ff. It would not be surprising if a parallel to Hag. 1:12–14 were found in Zech. 1:6b, describing the fact that Zechariah's preaching also evoked a willing response. This would have the effect of showing to a later generation that the returned exiles proved a worthy 'remnant', destined to inherit and inaugurate the new age of salvation which was replacing the old age of judgement.[19] As we have argued, such a view does not necessarily require the emendation of 'your fathers' to 'you'. Petitjean takes up the interesting suggestion by Beuken that the words of v. 6b represent a cultic confession showing a conscious sense of solidarity with the fathers by Zechariah's hearers, acknowledging the justice of God's actions in the exile.[20] Possibly that is why no specific indication is given. Both the 'fathers' and the returned exiles were at one in their acknowledgement of the justice of God's actions, the former too late, but the latter in time. There is some community of vocabulary between this section and 8:14, where the same Hebrew root is used (/ זמם) of God's 'determining' to do something both in judgement (on the fathers) and in salvation (for the post-exilic community).

What can be said of Zech. 1:1–6? We have seen that it is difficult to accept Beuken's claim that vv. 3–6a represent a 'Levitical Sermon', since the genre eludes satisfactory definition. Petersen is right to reject this.[21] Nevertheless we cannot miss the striking parallels between this passage and some of the addresses in Chronicles. These parallels include those of theme (the warning to be taken from the bad example of the fathers; the call to hear the continuing word of God; the summons to repentance and faith in God). They include parallels of vocabulary and also of rhetorical style (appeal to 'Scripture', rhetorical questions, play on words, and illustration by allusion to history). Yet, just as the addresses in Chronicles also contain vocabulary peculiar to the Chronicler and showed many of his theological concerns, so some distinctiveness of vocabulary here, including specifically some links to the visions and oracles of 1:7–6:15, suggests that here also some influence of a particular Zechariah tradition has been felt. There are also strong links with the material in cc. 7f. All this would be consistent with a view that saw the tradents of Zechariah making his prophecy the basis of their own continuing preaching in the second temple period, a preaching which did not lose the distinctiveness of their master's emphases, but which conformed to the kind of homiletical methods familiar at the time. The more widespread practice of such lively homiletical methods is further suggested by their obvious influence on the addresses found in the Chronicler tradition.

Zech. 3:6–10

The 'vision' of Joshua, the high priest, being cleansed, described in 3:1–5 raises many complex questions for interpretation, which need not detain us here. It has long been noted that it differs in form from the other visions, with no introductory formula and no enquiry about the meaning of the vision from an interpreting angel. Indeed, the angel here is one of the *dramatis personae* in the events which unfold in heaven independently of the prophet, apart from his one intervention recorded in v. 5a, if the MT is correct here. Elliger argued that the whole episode, with its accompanying oracle in vv. 6–10, must be classed among the oracles rather than the night visions,[22] and Horst agrees that it in no way resembles the other visions.[23] It does seem to show the prophet admitted to the 'council of heaven' as Micaiah and other prophets had been.[24]

The cleansing of Joshua, or rather of his clothing,[25] marks the change in divine favour to the post-exilic community which he represents. This interpretation is strengthened by the idea that God has chosen Jerusalem (v. 2), a fact which elsewhere is seen as the basis of hope for the community as a whole (e.g. 1:14–17, 2:12/16).

Nevertheless, it is interesting that the vision concentrates on the priestly line alone, whereas elsewhere the visions appear to envisage a joint rule of Joshua and Zerubbabel (4:11–14). The exact significance of the 'robe of state' and the 'turban' in which Joshua is clothed (vv. 4f.) is not clear. It is not the usual word for the high priest's turban. Both terms appear in the list of finery satirically denounced by Isaiah (Isa. 3:18ff.) as the luxurious wear of the heedless women of society. All of these will be swept away in judgement. The turban (the Hebrew צָנִיף) is a figure of 'righteousness'. In Isa. 62:3 the returned exiles are promised

> You shall be a crown of beauty in the hand of the LORD,
> and a royal diadem (צָנִיף מְלוּכָה) in the hand of your God.

Thus, whether the items stress the priestly and atoning role of Joshua, or whether he symbolises the change in fortune which God intends to bring to the whole community by which they will know the joy of salvation for the sorrow of judgement and exile, the stress is on the priestly figure alone as their representative, perhaps even already assuming earlier 'royal' characteristics in this respect. Perhaps the representative aspect is made the more likely by the echo of Amos 4:11 in the words about Joshua, 'Is not this a brand plucked from the fire?' (v. 2). In the Amos passage this is a reference to God's intervention on behalf of the whole community in grace, even though they failed to respond.

This emphasis on the priest, even if in a representative capacity, thus means that the oracle(s) in vv. 6–10 expound and expand a theme already present in the vision. Continuity is provided in that the charge to Joshua is delivered by the angel of Yahweh (cf. v. 4). The exact content of the words is not clear since it is not certain where the protasis and apodosis of the conditional sentence begin and end. So we could read:

> If you walk in my ways,
> and if you keep my charge,
> and if you judge my house,
> and keep my courts,
> then I will give you right of access . . .

Alternatively, the promise could begin earlier:

> If you walk in my ways,
> and keep my charge,
> then you shall judge my house . . .

The Hebrew of this last line replaces 'if' with the emphatic personal pronoun, 'then moreover *you* will judge my house'. However we take it, the role of the priest envisaged is little affected. Whether this is a command or a promise, it stresses the high privileges granted to Joshua. The call to 'walk in God's ways' and 'keep his charge' is general enough, but it recalls the conditional nature of the Davidic covenant as recorded in 1 Kgs. 2:3ff. David says to Solomon:

'Keep the charge of the LORD your God (Heb. וְשָׁמַרְתָּ אֶת־מִשְׁמֶרֶת, cf. Zech. 3:7) walking in his ways (אֶת־מִשְׁמַרְתִּי תִּשְׁמֹר) . . .' (cf. 1 Kgs. 8:26, 9:4).

Certainly, the call to 'judge' Yahweh's house (Heb. דִּין /) is reminiscent of the responsibility of the pre-exilic kings as, for example, expressed in Jer. 21:12, 22:16 and in a royal psalm such as Ps. 72:2: 'May he judge (/   ) thy people with righteousness' (cf. Prov. 31:9).

The phrase about the rule of the courts introduces a term which can be used of the royal courts of the palace (I Kgs. 7:8) but more often denotes the courts of the temple. However, since temple and palace had all been earlier part of the royal preserve (cf. Amos 7:13, I Kgs. 8:4f.), it is clear that what was a 'royal' prerogative before the exile is now passing to the priesthood. Even the promise to have the 'right of access among those standing here' (i.e. in the heavenly royal court) is not necessarily a promise of prophetic rights to the post-exilic priesthood in admitting them to the council of heaven.[26] One has only to recall how in the ancient Near East the temple built in a city of divine choice is a counterpart to the temple in heaven to realise that we are still in the realm of pre-exilic royal status and privilege.[27] The purpose of v. 7 must be to show that in the post-exilic era it is the priest who has succeeded to the religious and cultic role the king enjoyed in the pre-exilic period.

Even more remarkable in this exclusive concentration on the priest is the introduction anonymously of the messianic term 'Branch' (Heb צֶמַח, cf. Jer. 23:5, 33:15, where the same word is used explicitly of a future Davidic ruler who will 'execute justice and righteousness in the land'). Not only is he unnamed here, but his coming is cast into an indefinite future. In the mean time Joshua and 'the friends who sit before' him are 'men of sign' (Heb. מוֹפֵת). The term appears in Isa. 8:18 of Isaiah and 'the children whom the LORD has given me' who are signs of the future action of God, presumably in judgement. It is impossible to say who is meant precisely by the 'friends who sit before' Joshua, but it is quite likely to be a reference to the priests who accompanied him or the succession which followed him.

The enigmatic 'stone' of v. 9 eludes precise interpretation. It is not even clear if it belongs here or, as NEB and JB have decided, to the vision in c. 4 (cf. v. 10b).[28] V. 10 appears to add a further description of future peace and bliss in which the conditions of Solomon's reign will again be known (I Kgs. 4:25, cf. Mic. 4:4).

Without probing in depth all such details, however, enough has been said to show that, probably the vision in c. 3, but certainly its accompanying oracle(s), express a view later than that of Zechariah himself or, certainly, later than his own views at the time of the original visions. Now no dyarchy is envisaged. All the attention is on the priesthood which, by divine appointment, has taken over all the old pre-exilic royal privileges and prerogatives. A 'messianic hope' is indeed expressed, but attached in no way to Zerubbabel. On the contrary it is now relegated to a distant and unspecified future. Meanwhile the priestly circles are the custodians of the temple theocracy in Jerusalem and 'signs' of God's intention to fulfil in the future his promises concerning the Davidic royal line.

Well has Ackroyd said of the oracle here that it appears intended 'to obviate any intervention of the secular power in the management of the temple affairs', a viewpoint he sees as echoing that of Ezekiel.[29] Much earlier, Mitchell had said that the passage 'amounts to a charter granting Joshua and his successors a sole and complete control in matters of religion never before enjoyed by the head of the hierarchy at Jerusalem'.[30] Clearly, it expresses in this way the same outlook as that of the addresses in Chronicles. In particular it approaches the outlook expressed in the words of Azariah to king Uzziah rebuking him for usurping priestly prerogatives (II Chr. 26:17f.; see pp. 89ff. above). Like 1:2–6 this element of the Zechariah tradition breathes the same air as that which was native to the tradition which spoke through those addresses.

Zech. 4:6b–10a

It is very widely agreed that 4:6b–10a are intrusive in their present position, interrupting as they do the connection between the introductory formula of v. 6a, 'Then he said to me . . .' and the message thus introduced in v. 10b which explains the reference to the seven lamps of v. 2 and the two olive trees of v. 3.[31] There is less agreement on where it should be placed, but this is hardly surprising if, as seems likely, it represents an expansion very closely in line with 3:6–10. It is not altogether unfitting that whoever was responsible for the expansions should wish to make clear the respective responsibilities of the two 'olive trees', the 'sons of oil' of the fifth vision.

The opening words echo exactly a major theme we found in the addresses in Chronicles, that it is not human might or power, especially military power, which makes any human achievement effective, but only God's strength. Only in 7:12 is the 'spirit' mentioned elsewhere in Zechariah, and that in a 'tradition' piece (see discussion below, pp. 212ff.) which ascribes the effective ministry of earlier prophets to this spirit of Yahweh. This is exactly the way the activity of several 'messengers' is described in Chronicles (e.g. II Chr. 15:1, 20:14, 24:20, 36:22). There is reference to the spirit of God in Hag. 2:5, a passage which we have seen belongs to the tradition in which the records of Haggai's ministry were passed on. Petersen is right to see in the double negative of the opening 'Not by might or by power . . .' a rebuke and a piece of polemic.[32] But it is extraordinary to suggest, as he does, that it is Joshua the high priest who is being warned. There is no hint anywhere else that he was inclined to military means to secure the rebuilding of the temple. We may recall the striking words uttered about Zerubbabel by Haggai (2:23). This was in a context of promise of God's overthrow of the strength of the kingdoms of the nations. It is thus far more probable that this represents a warning to any who were looking for a Davidide governor or ruler to lead the armies of Judah in a military campaign designed to bring this final victory about. On the contrary, like David and Solomon and other faithful Davidic rulers, Zerubbabel is called to be temple builder.

Zerubbabel and the people are assured, however, that by God's power the task will be accomplished. The 'mountain' will be levelled to a plain before Zerubbabel, perhaps the mountain of rubble from the ruined temple, but more probably the 'mountain' of difficulties, including such things as the military situation, financial burdens and the discouragement of the people. So the promise of Second Isaiah will be fulfilled: 'Every mountain and hill shall be made low' (Isa. 40:4, cf. 49:11). Just possibly Jer. 51:24–6 is in mind. There Zion is promised that 'the mountain' of Babylon will be brought down by God and 'no stone shall be taken for you for a cover, and no stone for a foundation'.[33]

Not all the details of what is promised are clear. It may be that the references to the 'chief stone' (v. 7, a 'foundation' or a 'headstone'?) and the reference to the 'stone of separation' (v. 10, an alloy metal plummet?) are based on ancient Near Eastern myths of temple building when a king is commissioned by a god to construct a temple.[34] If such mythological parallels of the divine/royal temple/palace were present here, it would strengthen our suggestion that the circles from which such ideas emanated might be the same as those who believed that Joshua as high priest would have access to the 'divine courts' (3:7). We should not overlook the possibility that the names of the stones have symbolic value. The LXX calls the first 'the stone of possession', and the second might imply that the temple will designate the people who are God's special possession as a 'separated people'.

What is clear is that, by the aid of God's spirit, the temple will be completed and that this will inaugurate the new era of salvation. Indeed the prophet is shown here as seeing this completion to be the sign of the new era and also a divine authentication of his ministry (v. 9). This therefore appears as an answer to the same kind of doubts to which Haggai addressed himself (Hag. 2:3, cf. 6:9). V. 10 therefore seems to function as an assurance that the words of both Haggai and Zechariah will be authenticated.

This reference to Haggai as well as Zechariah; the fact that the 'Branch' is now an unnamed and future figure; the one named reference to Zerubbabel limiting him to the role of 'temple builder' – the same role as that given to the Davidides in the Chronicler tradition; and the assurance of the authenticity of the prophets to those who harboured doubts and disillusionment all suggest the possibility that this section also belongs to the Zechariah tradition. It answers exactly the themes of the addresses. The immediate fulfilment of prophetic hopes is found in the completed temple. By its means the new age has dawned. It constitutes a people separated to God, his 'special possession'. Military independence is not something for which to strive for God can, and will, give that in his own time. Let those who doubt and are disillusioned with the present doubt no more, either the present reality or its completion in the future.

Precise interpretation of 4:6b–10a is difficult. Yet the close parallels of thought to that which we discovered in 3:6–10 suggest that the two passages share a common tradition outlook.

Zech. 6:9–15

It would be a bold commentator who claimed to be able to unravel all the questions raised by Zech. 6:9–15. The allusions are so terse and the connections between the various elements within the pericope so unclear that all attempts at explanation remain, at best, only tentative.

The central action in the passage as it stands is the crowning of Joshua. The contribution of the returned exiles is not for the service of the temple in general, as were the gifts of the people in the Priestly Writer's account of the building of the tabernacle under Moses, and the Chronicler's description of the building of the temple under Solomon. The fact that MT speaks of 'crowns' in the plural is no warrant for assuming that originally the text spoke of a joint crowning of Joshua and Zerubbabel. Elsewhere the plural form is used where clearly only one crown is indicated (e.g. Job 31:36). The passage makes the crowning of Joshua as high priest central as an act of prophetic symbolism. It is not easy to determine why the returned exiles are mentioned at all. The fact that the names are different in the two lists (v. 9; see also v. 14) suggests that they are secondary and symbolic (the suggestion that some are nicknames and that this accounts for the differences represents a desperate shift). It seems to represent a claim for Joshua that he is the true representative of the returned exiles (according to the Chronicler the *true* Israel) and that he is the one who rightly commands their allegiance.

Yet, as has often been noticed, the prophetic word addressed to the priest concerns not him, but the 'Branch' (cf. 3:8). This 'messianic' title (see also Jer. 23:5) goes with a stress on the Branch's role as building the temple and 'bearing royal honour' (v. 13). It is possible that the subject of the verbs in v. 13 alternates between Zerubbabel and Joshua.[35] Nevertheless this involves a forced and unlikely reading of the Hebrew, as Chary has shown.[36] As the text stands the promise attached to these words about the 'Branch' is that a priest shall stand by his throne (or 'at his right hand', LXX). Yet this seems to consort ill with the centrality of the crowning of Joshua.

Several possibilities present themselves. It may be that two separate oracles have been joined. Perhaps vv. 12f. secondarily interrupt the sequence of thought between vv. 11 and 14 where the symbolism of the crown is taken up again. Or it may be that this crowning of Joshua took place, either in Judah or in Babylon, before Zerubbabel returned home.[37] But certain observations need to be made. As in 3:8 the 'Branch' is unnamed. For whatever reason, his coming is in an unspecified future. Again, as in 3:8ff., Joshua is a 'sign' or, in this case, a 'reminder' of the certainty of his coming in the future (v. 14). For, as the passage shows, the 'crown' represents Joshua, and presumably the continuing priestly line, since it is to be deposited in the temple. This latter circumstance makes it unlikely that it is all represented as taking place before Zerubbabel came back, for it was only after his arrival that the temple was built.

A further point is to note the role given to those 'who are far off' to come and help in the building of the temple (v. 15a). Is this a reference to the help of the returned exiles in the literal rebuilding? Did the community have to wait for them to come? Such a wait would have accorded uneasily with Haggai's call for immediacy and speed in the rebuilding. It is, after all, only Ezra cc. 1–6 which speaks of the 'returned exiles' as a body at all. Or is this passage therefore a later assurance to the Jews of the Diaspora that they too will have a part to play in the 'building' of the temple community in the messianic age in the future? The term 'building' could be, and often was, used in a metaphorical as well as a literal sense.[38]

Certainty is beyond us where so much is obscure. But, again, strong parallels with 3:6–10 suggest that, whatever the original core of Zechariah's preaching still to be found here, a similar tradition process has been at work. We are in a time when the priesthood has come to the fore. It does 'rule'. It is Joshua who is crowned as the true representative and leader of the 'true' Israel, returned from exile. His 'crown' is in the temple. That is where the continuing priestly line rules over the theocracy as a constant reminder of God's promise spoken through the prophet, whose words will be vindicated when the 'messianic' age has come. That, however, is now in an indefinite future and the sign of that age, the 'Branch', is a vague figure, not named. In that future 'Branch' and 'priest' will rule together. Those now far from Judah in the Diaspora will return home, and all will play their part in building the temple community.

Such a view of the present role of the priesthood in the theocracy accords perfectly well with the view expressed in the other passages in Zech. 1–8 we have examined and also with the addresses in Chronicles. So does the note of urgent pastoral entreaty added in the postscript of v. 15b. Present faithfulness and obedience by the people of God will ensure the fulfilment of their hopes for the future and the realisation in fact of what they know now only as promise of God.

Zech. 7:4–7, 11–14

Cc. 7f., marked as a new section by the date in 7:1, open with the question posed to the priests and prophets whether mourning and fasting in the fifth month should continue. The actual source, composition and destination of the delegation need not concern us here. The Hebrew is ambiguous.[39] In spite of the testimony of the Versions it seems unlikely that the sanctuary at Bethel was the destination of the enquiry, and the most probable rendering seems to be, 'Bethel-Sharezar, the chief officer of the king, with his men, sent to entreat the favour of the LORD . . .'[40] and that it was the priests and prophets at Jerusalem to whom the question was directed. It is normally taken that the reference is to the fast which commemorated the destruction of the temple, palace and all the notable buildings in Jerusalem (II Kgs. 25:8f.). The force of the question appears to be, 'Does the building of the new temple make mourning for the destruction of the old one unnecessary?' Behind that question appears to lie the deeper one, 'Has the new age, spoken of by the prophets [Haggai and Zechariah], dawned or not?'[41] It is possible that this is the record of an actual incident, although its close similarities to Hag. 2:10–14 might suggest it is a stylised preaching device somewhat akin to those used by the Wisdom writers (e.g. Job 5:3, 'I have seen the fool . . .)'. In Hag. 2:10–14 the priests were asked for a 'Torah'. Here the prophets are included in the question, not unnaturally, in view of what they had been predicting as about to happen when the temple was rebuilt. The occurrence of such similar incidents in the two books may well support A. R. Johnson's view that Haggai and Zechariah functioned as cult, or sanctuary prophets.[42]

It is widely agreed that the real answer which Zechariah gave to the request is to be found in 8:18f., announcing that the new age had indeed dawned and that all fasts associated with the disaster of the siege, capture and destruction of Jerusalem and all which had followed, would be transmuted into joyous feasts celebrating the new age of salvation. The appearance of the answer may have been delayed because the editor saw in the ringing assurance of 8:18f. a fitting and triumphant climax to Zechariah's promises for the future. The arrangement has resulted in the question and answer being separated by some parenetic sermonic material together with some more general eschatological development of notes already heard in Zechariah's (and Haggai's) prophecy.

The more general reference and application of the words introduced in 7:4 is shown both by the description of those addressed and the nature of the material itself. Despite the first-person introduction to the 'oracle' ('Then the word of the LORD of hosts came to me . . .') it is now addressed, not just to the delegation, whoever they were, or merely to the priests and prophets who were among those addressed by the delegation, but also to 'all the people of the land'. It is doubtful if this phrase has any specialised meaning here. Its occurrence in Ezr. 4:4 to denote opponents of the people of Judah who sought to block efforts to rebuild the temple has led some to speculate that this may have been Zechariah's rejection of the so-called 'Samaritan' worship at Bethel and in the territory of the old northern kingdom generally (if they were the ones instigating the enquiry).[43] Others have seen in it a reference to the opposition between those who stayed behind in the land and the returning exiles.[44] However, there is no hint of this in the context, and it is far better to follow those who see the phrase 'people of the land' as having different meanings in different contexts and, here, applying to all the community in Judah.[45] The effect is thus to broaden the scope of the address to the whole community. The relevance of what follows is to be understood more widely and generally than the answer to the specific question from the delegation. That has become the occasion for more general teaching on fasting which directs itself, not to the *occasions* of fasting (the subject of the question), but to the *motives* for engaging in it.

This raises the question of how much this 'address' comprises. A number of commentators see vv. 4–14 as comprising a unit, while some see either v. 8 alone, or vv. 8–10, as intrusive.[46] Certainty is not possible here, but it can be argued that v. 11 comprises the most natural sequence to the question posed in v. 7, in spite of the apparent difficulty that the question seems to suggest that the earlier prophets had given teaching about fasting. It is probable, then, that vv. 8–10 are intrusive, but that they form a very significant addition to the 'address', paralleling, to some extent, similar summarising material in 8:16f. For that reason I defer consideration of vv. 8–10 to my treatment of 8:16f. (pp. 231ff. below).

If we consider first the substance of what is said about fasting in vv. 5f., substance presumably continuing into v. 7, it is not clear exactly what is meant. A literal reading of the Hebrew might run as follows:

> When you fasted and lamented in the fifth and seventh [months],
> And this for seventy years [or, 'Even these seventy years'],
> Were you really fasting for me?
> And when you eat and drink,
> Is it not you who are [the ones] eating and you [the ones] drinking?

There are several peculiarities in the Hebrew here. 'When you fasted' occurs in the perfect tense, which suggests past action or action which has gone on only to the time of the present enquiry. But the verbs 'when you eat and drink', in the imperfect, suggest a continuous action. Possibly some contrast is intended between that which marked the practice of their fasts in the past, about which they are now enquiring, and what always and constantly marks their eating and drinking. On the other hand the variation in tense may be stylistic only, and both may refer to fasts and feasts alike. It is difficult to be sure. There is the slightly unusual use of the infinitive absolute of the verb 'to lament' rather than paralleling the perfect tense of the verb 'fasted'. Yet the infinitive absolute can be used generally for any tense.[47] It can also be used adverbially[48] and mean, 'When you fasted lamentingly.' However, no ambiguity attaches to its use before the finite verb in the second line. Its effect here is to intensify the verb, hence my rendering, 'Were you *really* fasting for me?' The use of personal pronoun 'I' following the pronominal suffix to the verb is also a fairly rare construction, no doubt adding lively, vivid emphasis.[49] The reference to the 'seventh' month is usually taken to refer to the murder of Gedaliah (II Kgs. 25:25). Its addition to the 'fifth' month, which is the only one mentioned in the original question of v. 3, let alone the further additions of fasting in the 'fourth' and 'tenth' months in 8:19, may suggest that the practice of fasting as a regular corporate act of lament and intercession (and penitence? see Jonah 3:5) grew greatly during the exilic period.[50] That these observances marked the exilic period particularly is suggested by the reference to the 'seventy years'. The phrase does not necessarily imply dependence on such passages as Jer. 25:11, 29:10, which were probably intended to indicate a round period of at least two generations, but may have become a general way of referring to the Babylonian exile and period of Jerusalem's destruction.

The meaning of the passage is still ambiguous, however, apart from the peculiarities of the Hebrew. The force of the infinitive absolute might be to query the genuineness of the fasting and lamenting: 'Were you really fasting?'[51] Or the force of the personal pronoun might be to question whose interests really concerned them, 'Were you really fasting for *me*?' Even so, that has been taken to mean 'Was it for my failure that you were fasting or for yours?', meaning that it was judgement for their sins which caused the deprivation which occasioned the fasts and laments, not Yahweh's arbitrary acts.[52] Or it might mean that they were acting only out of pity for themselves rather than from real penitence or fear of Yahweh.[53] There is, however, no such doubt where the emphasis falls in v. 6. The use (twice) of the second-person plural pronoun gives the force, 'When you eat and drink, is it not *you* who are eating and drinking?' But, again, the exact nature of the charge is not clear. Is it being said that God takes no part in their feasts or fasts (see also Amos 5:21–4, Isa. 1:12–17 etc.)? Or is the charge that the same people who fast and lament are those who, on other occasions, eat and drink to their hearts' content? Therefore their fasts and laments are superficial only. Or is the charge, further, that they fast and lament, but then feed and feast themselves only, neglecting the poor and hungry in the land? That would bring the accusation close to the attacks of the former prophets on cultic practices and also to the teaching on fasting in Isa. c. 58.

It is perhaps unexpected that at this stage appeal is made to the teaching of the 'former' prophets, the use of the adjective firmly linking this passage with 1:2–6. For the earlier pre-exilic and exilic prophets are virtually silent on the subject of fasting. Nevertheless, as the passages above show, the prophets had plenty to say on the subject of official cultic acts which neither expressed real penitence nor were matched by obedience to the law, especially those laws which called for compassion to the poor and weaker members of society. It is almost certainly this which has resulted in the editorial insertion of a fine, almost catachetical-like summary of this aspect of the prophets' teaching in vv. 8–10. The addition must be seen as early commentary on the charge made in vv. 5f., and, probably, remarkably accurate exegesis of the intention of 7:5f., for all its obscurity. Indeed, the conditions of the exile and its aftermath which have occasioned the fastings and lamentations are interestingly contrasted with the time before the exile when Jerusalem was 'inhabited', knew quiet security (שְׁלֵוָה) and was the centre of the large prosperous area of the Shephelah and the Negeb with all their cities. The use of the term שְׁלֵוָה may spring from the earlier liturgies of Zion worship, for it occurs in Ps. 122:6:

> Pray for the welfare of Jerusalem.
> May those who love you dwell secure (יִשְׁלָיוּ).[54]

The same root appears in the following verse:

> Security (שַׁלְוָה) [be] to your fortifications.

This motif had already been the subject of prophetic comment, however. A very interesting passage occurs in Jer. 22:20–3 which, sandwiched between oracles addressed to Jehoiachim and Jehoiachin, is clearly intended as a call to Jerusalem to lament. God complains that,

> I spoke to you in your security (בְּשַׁלְוֺתַיִךְ),
> but you said, 'I will not listen.' *(v. 21)*

But twice in the lament it is said that 'those who love you' (מְאַהֲבַיִךְ) will either 'be broken' (v. 20b) or shall 'go into captivity' (v. 22a). This exactly reverses the prayer of Ps. 122 and may well represent the kind of passage of prophetic warning being thought of in Zech. 7:7, which had been spoken in the days when Jerusalem was 'in security', but rejected.

The same theme occurs in a most striking contrast in Ezek. 16:49. Here, the sins of Jerusalem (v. 2) are being compared with those of her 'sister' Samaria. She and her sister had pride, abundance of food, security (שַׁלְוָה) and tranquillity, but still 'they did not feed the poor and needy'. Here, then, is the prophetic context which not only reverses the prayer of Ps. 122, but accuses a city, whose sins were only 'half' (v. 51) those of Jerusalem, of failing to feed the hungry in her prosperity. This may well explain the addition of vv. 8–10 in Zech. c. 7 as well as throwing light on what is meant in vv. 5f.

The appeal to the former prophets, then, seems in part to be to their general warning against cultic activity unmatched by inward penitence and obedience to the law, but it may also pick up a theme of prophetic threat of judgement by way of reversal of the hopes and confidence of the pre-exilic Zion worship. If that is so, we should not miss the point that yet once more, material of this parenetic, even hermeneutic kind is characterised by exegesis of earlier prophetic and scriptural material.

Nor can we miss the seeming close parallel to its teaching in Isa. c. 58, especially in v. 3.[55] Isa. 58 is a prophetic oracle, highly poetic in language and metre, on the subject of fasting. It is extremely difficult to date. To argue that it is post-exilic because the pre-exilic prophets do not mention fasting is to argue in a circle. On the other hand, to argue for a pre-exilic date from its style and form is to miss the possibility that a later speaker may consciously imitate earlier prophetic utterance. Possibly v. 12 suggests a time soon after the exile, but the conditions described of 'ruins' and 'breaches' could fit a number of possible historical contexts. Perhaps the dependence on earlier prophetic material is a more reliable guide to its date.[56]

More interestingly, a number of commentators find the passage composite and see especially vv. 3bf. to be an interpolation, separating the lament of the people in v. 3a (a people who like to ask Yahweh for 'righteous judgements', v. 2b) from the prophetic answer in vv. 5f. on the nature of true fasting. This is to obey the laws calling for compassion on the weak and the oppressed. Whybray goes so far as to describe vv. 3bf. as an 'interpolation which entirely misses the original point'.[57] Westermann points out that the question of fasting which is not genuine is answered in different ways in vv. 3b–4 and v. 5 and concludes, 'Quite obviously the speech has been put together from entirely disparate elements.'[58] This may be to go a little too far, for G. Fohrer and D. R. Jones both manage to treat the passage as a unity. Yet it is interesting to see that the two notes sounded in Zech. 7:5f., self-regarding motives in fasting and true fasting being a sincere regard for the poor, occur also in the present form of the text in Isa. c. 58. Strangely, the exact meaning of 58:3b is also unclear. It could be rendered,

Behold, on the day of your fast
You find your own pleasure (/חפץ)

However, the use of the same root in v. 13, and in such a verse as Isa. 53:10, might suggest not just 'pleasure' in the general sense of enjoyment, but concern for one's own affairs, or even 'profit', since the next line continues,

And you oppress all your workers.

Such a meaning would fit the context well here. We have suggested elsewhere that both elements might be caught if we rendered it:

You have put your own interests first.[59]

This again may cast some light on the force of the accusation in Zech. 7:5f. Such parallelism between the two passages, for all the questions surrounding the issues of exact date and interpretation, which sees each of them blending two apparently distinct ideas about the nature of true fasting as well as employing similar use of earlier prophetic material, may suggest that this was the familiar type of exhortation about fasting which was heard in the second temple period. Perhaps such cultic activity was more relevant then as a subject of the preaching when compared with the charges of the pre-exilic prophets about sacrifice. For the evidence seems to suggest that fasting became a more established practice after the exile while, apart from the sacrifices offered in the temple, the ordinary member of the worshipping community had no direct share in the offering of sacrifice. Fasting, however, was something which all worshippers could share in from time to time.

There is nothing directly about fasting in the addresses we considered in Chronicles. However, we have noted repeatedly that they are deeply concerned with proper care for the temple and its worship and right cultic observance. We must conclude that, whatever the similarities in style and form of the comparative material we have been considering (and we should not miss the use of the rhetorical question in vv. 5, 6 and 7), it certainly does not suggest that all variety and individual emphases were ironed out into a bland amalgam of lifeless repetition of given points in the preaching. Whatever general interests and similarity of style the preachers may have shared, as lively an individuality and variety must have existed among them then as perhaps at any time in the history of the people of God.

There can be no doubt, that in vv. 11–14 we are very much in the world of the addresses in Chronicles as well as that of Zech. 1:2–6. We encounter again the appeal to history illustrated by the disobedience of the fathers to the words God spoke to them through the prophets. We have already suggested that v. 11 is the natural sequence to the rhetorical question of v. 7 and that 'the words which the LORD proclaimed through the former prophets' refers to the general background of their teaching on motives and integrity in cultic practices rather than to the words of vv. 9f. Thus there is reason to think not only that it is v. 8 which is intrusive but that it introduces a section in vv. 8–10 which was early exegesis along lines already familiar in the prophetic material and paralleled in the development of Isa. 58:3bf. We have seen the appeal to the disobedience of the fathers, with the resulting judgement, not only in 1:2–6 but also in Chronicles (II 28:9, Oded; II 29:6, 30:7f., Hezekiah). We find a parallel to those addresses in the use of the Hiph'il of the verb / קשׁב :

'They refused to pay attention.'

This may be compared with the opening injunction of the address of Jehu in II Chr. 20:20 (see the discussion above, pp. 68ff.). The verb was also used in Zech. 1:4, where we saw that it seemed to be echoing Jeremianic material. To some extent what follows here recalls such passages as Jer. 11:10 and 17:23, yet such echo is general only, and the idea of making their hearts like 'adamant' seems peculiar to this passage. Similarly the terms of the punishment in v. 14 may echo, in general terms, earlier prophetic motifs. The use of / סער as a verb to depict judgement as by a driving tempest is rare. It is used in the passive in Second Isaiah in an address to Jerusalem:

O afflicted one, storm tossed . . . *(Isa. 54:11)*

Such a judgement was now about to be reversed, according to the prophet. The active form is used in the context of a threat against Ephraim in Hos. 13:3. The noun is used in Jeremiah as a sign of judgement (Jer. 23:19, 25:32) as well as in Amos (1:14) and Isaiah (29:6). It is thus a fairly general, even obvious picture of judgement. The idea of exile among a strange people in a foreign land expressed in the phrase 'nations which you have not known' occurs in Ezek. 32:9. Possibly it carried an echo of the cause of judgement, for the Deuteronomistic tradition warns strongly against the worship of gods neither the Israelites nor their fathers have known (Deut. 29:25, 32:17; see also Jer. 19:4, 44:3). The idea of Israel as a 'pleasant' land is also found in the Jeremianic tradition (Jer. 3:19), and we have already seen that the concept of this land turned into a 'devastation' is very common in Jeremiah (see p. 101 above), a theme also echoed in the addresses in Chronicles. It occurs in II Chr. 29:8 in Hezekiah's explanation of what happened in the time of their disobedient fathers and in II 30:7 in a similar context in his letter. It seems, then, that a number of prophetic themes and phrases are echoed in these verses, all brought together to show why the judgement fell, why it took the form it did and what lessons it offered for the present and the future. It is not a bad set of prophetic 'proof texts' from which to draw out lessons taught by the 'former prophets'.

However, not only does such an appeal to Scripture afford a general parallel to the addresses in Chronicles, but more specific ones are found here. There is the strong link between God's 'spirit' and prophecy which characterised some of the addresses either explicitly or in the kind of utterance they attributed to some speakers. So 'the spirit of God came upon Azariah' (II 15:1); 'Then the spirit of Yahweh came upon Jahaziel' (II 20:14); 'And the spirit of God took possession of Zechariah' (II 24:20). We find the same explanation of judgement in terms of God's 'wrath' (Heb. קֶצֶף , see pp. 199f. above). We have the same rhetorical device of play on words:

As I[60] called, but they did not listen;
So they call, but I do not listen.

Of this change of person Ackroyd says that it 'emphasises the permanence of the divine word'.[61] This, no doubt, in addition to its memorable rhetorical effect, was the exact purpose of the preachers who used such a device, for they saw themselves relating the divine word of the past to their own present. The change of tense, which I have tried to reproduce in my rendering, between what was completed in the past and what remains continually true as a consequence, does not indicate a gloss as Mitchell argued,[62] but, as Winton Thomas saw rather more penetratingly, it introduces an eschatological note indicating that the present condition must be changed. The preachers, in showing the continuing condition in which they do not yet see Yahweh's final deliverance, are calling for that response which will enable it to come. As Elliger says, 'Eschatological hope is to lead, not to dreams, but to concern for right living in the time of pre-salvation.'[63]

For all the particularity of its theme of fasting, then, this passage generalises it in a way wholly consonant with the addresses in Chronicles and in Zech. 1:2–6. The particular has become the occasion for a general call to obedience to the 'words' of Yahweh, even the 'Torah', for so the teaching of the prophets has come to be regarded (v. 12). All this is in the light of the example of the fathers and the consequent judgement which is seen as fulfilment of the warnings of the earlier prophets. By historical allusion, appeal to Scripture, rhetorical question and play on words, the lessons for the post-exilic generation are driven home. As I have said of this elsewhere:

The oracles and visions of Zechariah giving joyful assurance that fasts belong to the past age of judgement, now to be replaced by the feasting of the Heilszeit, have given way to instruction for the faithful on the right way to fast. As so often in preaching, the indicative has given way to the imperative or, rather, the cohortative. Pastoral concern for the temple community whose faith is sorely tried while they still await the prophet's promises, and thus are tempted to doubt or to slackness, has come to the fore.[64]

Much here, therefore, again argues for a background in the general homiletical practice of the second temple.

Zech. 8:1–23

The structure of c. 8 is extremely complex. No fewer than five introductory prophetic formulae occur in vv. 1–8 alone, while others introduce vv. 9–13, 14–17, 18f., 20–2, 23.[65] There is also a mixture of oracles of eschatological hope and ethical and cultic teaching. While, then, we must deal with each section in turn and be prepared to find diverse tradition elements even within individual pericopae, we must not lose sight of the effect of the final arrangement of the chapter which brings such elements together and holds them in tension.

Vv. 1–8

Since the major English Versions are misleading here, it is important to notice that v. 1 opens with a most unusual prophetic formula, 'The word of the LORD of Hosts came, saying . . .' The more usual introduction is 'the word of the LORD . . . came to me', or 'to X'. It is possible that the words 'to me' dropped out by accident (although there is no textual evidence to suggest they were ever there). But it may indicate that what follows is to be seen as extension of Zechariah's own words, which were addressed by God not only to him, but to those who came after him. Certainly, there occurs citation of at least two of Zechariah's own oracles in what follows.

I have been jealous for Zion with great jealousy *(v. 2a)*

is a word-for-word quotation of 1:14 except that, in the latter, 'for Jerusalem' is added before 'and for Zion'. In addition 1:15 is echoed in 8:2b, but with an interesting variation. In 1:15 Yahweh speaks of the 'great wrath' (קֶצֶף) with which he was 'wrathful', and the verse leaves no doubt that this wrath was directed specifically against the oppressor nations who furthered the disaster while Yahweh was 'angry' against Jerusalem 'only a little'. His 'jealousy' is clearly exercised on behalf of Jerusalem. As we have seen, this term 'wrath' (קֶצֶף) is echoed in some of the addresses in Chronicles as well as in Zech. 1:2. Here, in 8:2b however, the phrase is varied:

I have been jealous with great 'heat' (חֵמָה) towards her.

The Hebrew חֵמָה is often used of anger in the Old Testament, both human and divine. It is difficult to know if there is any specific reason for the variation. Petersen points out that the combination of 'jealousy' and 'wrath' occurs in Ezek. 36:6b[66] and this, together with the very frequent use of חֵמָה in both Jeremiah and Ezekiel, may indicate a broadening out of Zechariah's words in 1:14 to give what is said there a place in a more general prophetic description of God's judgement in the exile. For an interesting note of ambiguity creeps into 8:2b which is explicitly excluded in 1:14f. Does the 'jealousy' here refer to Yahweh's anger against the nations on behalf of Jerusalem,[67] or against Jerusalem itself? In spite of the fact that the preposition קִנֵּא after ל / is usually employed in a favourable sense,[68] it can be used with other verbs in a hostile sense (e.g. Gen. 27:42, II Kgs. 5:7, Exod. 11:7, Jos. 10:21 etc.). In any event, the effect is to turn a straightforward assurance of salvation in 1:14f. to a part explanation of the judgements which have befallen the Zion community. Here, two passages are of special interest. The term is used in Jer. 23:19 in conjunction with Yahweh's judgement by a 'storm-wind', thus forming a link with Zech. 7:14. Another such link is forged by Ezek. 5:15 where חֵמָה is associated with the idea of Yahweh's making Jerusalem a reproach among the nations, a taunt, an object lesson and a 'desolation' (לְשַׁמָּה – cf. מְשַׁמָּה in 7:14) when Yahweh wreaks judgements in 'anger' and in 'wrath' (חֵמָה). We should not, incidentally, miss the fact that חֵמָה forms part of the vocabulary of the addresses in Chronicles. It is used by Oded in II 28:9 to warn the people of Yahweh's past anger with the fathers of Israel, and it is used in II 36:16 in a passage which we have seen reason to believe was intended as a summary of the teaching of the addresses in an attempt to drive their lessons home to the hearers. Thus the use of the term חֵמָה in Zech. 8:2 extends the word of Zechariah in 1:14 on to a wider and more general map of prophetic warning about the exile. In doing so it forms a link with the warnings and threats recalled in 7:11–14 and, in doing this, it modifies the promise of 'jealousy' for Zion on God's part and 'anger' against their oppressor nations in 1:14f. It becomes a reminder of the two-edged nature of this divine 'jealousy'. It backs up the warning of 7:11–14 by echoing the teaching of Zechariah and the prophets generally, showing that continuing deprivations are a sign of continuing disobedience. Yet it points also to God's 'zeal' for this people. Such modification may well indicate the kind of adaptation of a Zechariah 'text' like 1:14f. for more general hortatory and parenetic purposes. It suggests just the kind of exposition and application of a biblical text by a preacher to the needs of his congregation.

That there is the other side to this divine 'zeal', namely God's determination to save and deliver, is shown by the second citation from the oracles of Zechariah in v. 3:

> I have returned (/שוב) to Zion,
> And I will dwell (/שכן) in the midst of Jerusalem.

This echoes 1:16a:

I have returned to Jerusalem in compassion . . .

but also 2:10/14:

I will dwell (/שכן) in your midst.

However, in 1:16 the consequence of Yahweh's returning to Jerusalem was that the temple should be rebuilt and the work of restoring the city undertaken. In 2:10/14 the 'presence' of Yahweh would lead to the pilgrimage of the nations to Jerusalem. Both may be considered as 'reversal of judgement' themes by which the oppressor nations will themselves become the objects of the divine judgement while the fortunes of Jerusalem are restored. Rebuilding will replace ruin, world prestige years of poverty and shame. In 8:3, however, the result of Yahweh's return to the city and dwelling in it will be the purification of the community. Jerusalem will become the 'faithful city' (lit. 'the city of truth', עִיר הָאֱמֶת). Further, the description of the city as 'the mountain of the LORD of hosts', with its recollection of Isa. 2:2–4/Mic. 4:1–4 which foretold the pilgrimage of the nations to Jerusalem, an idea taken up in Zech. 2:11f./15f., is now intensified by saying that this mountain will indeed be the 'holy mountain' (הַר הַקֹּדֶשׁ). So the ideal of the ancient Jerusalem liturgy will be realised (Ps. 48:1/2), and the prophetic vision of Isa. 1:21–6 will be fulfilled that once again Jerusalem would become a 'faithful city' (נֶאֱמָנָה). Thus it is the note of moral and religious renewal of the community which is stressed here in this exegesis of the earlier oracles of Zechariah.

Along with the note of warning against the disobedience of the fathers this suggests the preoccupation of the preachers with the actual moral condition of the community at a time when the rebuilding of the city was an accomplished fact. The actual return from exile and the physical rebuilding of the city are seen as only the first stage in God's whole purpose for his people. Such emphasis meets the objection that must often have been heard, that the consequences which Haggai and Zechariah had predicted as following the completion of the temple had so signally failed to materialise. The outward building is seen here only as sign and symbol of the spiritual 'rebuilding' of the community which alone will mark the realisation of God's ultimate purpose in the restoration. Such a homiletical practice serves at least three purposes. It explains why the promises of the prophets have not yet been fully experienced; it puts the stress on moral regeneration which is where the preachers believe it must be; and it serves to keep hope and faith alive in the face of any temptation to despair and disillusion.[69]

This also explains why, in what follows, older prophetic motifs are used to hold out the hope of an almost mythical picture of God's future purpose, hopes which come near to bursting the bounds of this world's ordinary and normative history. There has been much heard recently of the features which gave rise to the 'supramundane' hopes of Apocalyptic. One factor at least, doubtless among many others, may have been that the mundane fulfilment spoken of by the prophets came and went without the age of God's reign being obvious in quality of life. More and more, hopes must then have become focussed on the 'supramundane', and perhaps we see some such process beginning here. So, earlier prophetic motifs such as the peace and prosperity of the new age, as in Mic. 4:4, are taken up:

> They shall sit, each one beneath his vine
> and under his fig tree,
> and there shall be none to terrify.

This is echoed, albeit in an urban setting, in Zech. 8:4:

> Old men and women shall again sit
> in the squares of Jerusalem:
> Each with his staff in his hand
> because of his length of life.

This takes up the promise of miraculous longevity in the new age in such a passage as Isa. 65:19ff., following as it does the promise of 'a new heaven and a new earth' (v. 17):

> I will rejoice in Jerusalem
> and be glad in my people;
> no more shall be heard in it the sound of weeping
> and the cry of distress.
> No more shall there be in it
> an infant who lives but a few days,
> or an old man who does not fill out his days,

> for the child shall die a hundred years old,
> and the sinner who dies a hundred years old
> shall be accursed.

Whatever the last phrase means (perhaps 'anyone who fails to live to a hundred years of age will be deemed to have been cursed for some sin'[70]), it is clear that longevity is seen to be the mark of the new age. We can have no idea of the date of Isa. 65:17ff. The first part of the chapter, with its mixed oracles of threat for some and promise for others, is likely to be later rather than earlier, and so we cannot speak of 'influence' from this passage to Zech. c. 8. But both may be developing in somewhat mythical terms hints implicit in the Torah that obedience to God brings 'length of days' (e.g. Deut. 4:40, 5:16 etc.), a note which is also present in prophetic passages (e.g. Isa. 52:10). Indeed, the note is sometimes there in reverse. Take, for example, the judgement oracle of Jer. 6:11:

> Therefore I am full of the wrath of the LORD;
> I am weary of holding it in.
> 'Pour it out upon the children in the streets
> and upon the gatherings of young men also;
> both husband and wife shall be taken,
> the old folk and the very aged.
> Their houses shall be turned over to others,
> their fields and vines together;
> for I will stretch out my hand
> against the inhabitants of the land',
> says the LORD.

It is this state of insecurity and terror, of premature death for all ages and groups of the community, which will, however, be reversed in the time of salvation. Similar 'reversal of doom' oracles are found elsewhere, e.g. Jer. 32:36ff. They appear, indeed, in the hymnic tradition of Israel, as in Ps. 107.

This seems to be the kind of background which has inspired the hope and lively imagination of details in such passages as Isa. 65:20 and Zech. 8:4f. In passing, it is worth noting that the Chronicler does not lack such characteristics in describing God's reign in the ideal theocracy. It is said of David that 'he dies in a good old age' (I 29:25) and of Jehoida, that good and faithful priest, that he 'grew old and full of days, and died; he was a hundred and thirty years old at his death' (II 24:15).

To the concept of future security and longevity is added another prophetic theme, that of enlarged population. If this seems a strange longing for the future in our days of urban overcrowding, we should not forget that the emptiness of the streets of a city were a cause of lamentation (e.g. Lam. 1:3, 5; 5:14f.; Isa. 27:10 etc.), and the economic value of more hands to achieve greater security and a higher standard of living is seen behind Nehemiah's efforts to bring more people into the city from the surrounding countryside (Neh. 11:1f.; see also 7:4). It is small wonder that the idea of a larger population of the city features as a theme of prophetic hope for the future, especially with Second Isaiah (Isa. 49:19–21, where it is linked with the hope of the return of the exiles, 54:1–3). Here, in Zech. c. 8, it is also linked with the idea of God bringing back the dispersed Israelites 'from the east country and the west country' (v. 7). In Zechariah's own oracle the exiles were called upon to flee from the 'north country' (2:6/10), and in his last vision the chariots which went to patrol all the earth at God's command and to report that his sovereign control ran everywhere went forth 'to the four winds of heaven', that is, to all quarters of the earth.[71] Presumably, 'east' and 'west' are mentioned here to refer to Babylon and Egypt as symbols of the oppressor nations and to represent all the places where Israelites were dispersed or in captivity.[72] Yet still the emphasis is on the religious renewal of his people. The covenant relationship will be renewed: 'They shall be my people and I will be their God' (Exod. 6:7, Hos. 1:9, 2:23 etc.), and this covenant relationship will be characterised by 'truth' (אֱמֶת) and 'righteousness' (צְדָקָה) so that the character of the restored Jerusalem (v. 3) will be an expression of the character of its inhabitants. In this passage, then, eschatological speculation is anchored firmly to the moral regeneration of the people. It is this, as well as the more mythical aspects of prophetic hopes for reconstruction and repopulation, that forms the 'marvellous' action of God on behalf of the 'remnant' of this people in v. 6. Nowhere in the visions or oracles does Zechariah describe the community as a 'remnant' (שְׁאֵרִית), although, as we have seen, they are so described in the editorial framework of the Book of Haggai. Presumably, therefore, it is from circles similar to those which produced that framework that the doubts of the people are here receiving reassurance. The sort of hopes they have heard from the prophets have not materialised or, at least, have materialised in nothing like the terms in which the prophets expressed them. So they are reminded in traditional language that God is able to do what might seem beyond belief.[73] In that traditional language, it seems 'marvellous' (/ פלא). So with this word, tradition recorded that Yahweh met the incredulity with which Sarah greeted the news that, at her age, she would bear the child of promise: 'Is anything too marvellous for the LORD?' (Gen. 18:4). The word can be used also in a covenant context:

Behold, I make a covenant. Before all your people I will do marvels (נִפְלָאוֹת), such as have not been wrought in all the earth or in any nation. *(Exod. 34:10)*

Such a context receives added force here, where a renewal of the covenant is being promised. The word figures also in the Exodus traditions, depicting the 'wonderful things' Yahweh will do in smiting Egypt to effect the release of his people (e.g. Exod. 3:20, 15:11, Judg. 6:13 etc.). It forms part of the language of worship:

> This is the LORD's doing:
> it is marvellous (/פלא) in our eyes.
> *(Ps. 118:23; see also Pss. 72:18, 139:14 etc.)*

Not surprisingly it passes into the language of the prophetic literature:

Ah, Lord GOD! It is thou who hast made the heavens and the earth by thy great power and by thy outstretched arm! Nothing is too hard (/פלא) for thee. *(Jer. 32:17)*

Or, later in the same chapter:

Behold, I am the LORD, the God of all flesh; is anything too hard (הֲמִמֶּנִּי יִפָּלֵא) for me? *(v. 27)*

Thus, all the weighty tradition of law, liturgy and prophecy is called upon in a comprehensive appeal to Scripture to drive home the encouragement of hope for a bewildered and sceptical people. The wonders of return, reconstruction and enlarged population are not beyond God's power. He has power equally to renew his covenant with his people and to renew his covenant people. That is the burden of this 'preaching' of Zechariah's earlier promises to the continuing generations by those who sought to relate them to their contemporaries. The promises are given a more 'mythical' and future exposition while, at the same time, they are subordinated to an increased emphasis on the moral and spiritual renewal of the community. The people are encouraged and exhorted at one and the same time.

There is nothing of such hope of the future reign of God in the addresses in Chronicles. Clearly this 'preaching' belongs to the particular bearers of the Zechariah tradition who are expounding the prophet's teaching. But we should not miss the emphases in the Chronicler which indicate the presence of the reign of God even by way of anticipation. He too sees old age as one sign of faithfulness and blessing. The addresses leave no doubt that abundance and prosperity follow faithfulness (II Chr. 31:10). They too assure their hearers of God's supreme power to deliver them and bring his purposes about, largely by drawing on the 'holy war' motif. They too stress the centrality of Jerusalem and the presence of God in the temple among his people. Those addresses also appeal to Scripture and assure the hearers of the certainty of the fulfilment of all God's purposes begun in the past. They too stress that God's aim is to produce an obedient, worshipping, holy community centred on his temple. In a sense, both the addresses in Chronicles and this pericope in Zechariah are eschatological, but those in Chronicles stress more the realisation of that future age in the present experience of the temple community, while those who perpetuated Zechariah's message assured that community that the promises were to find a more complete fulfilment than they had as yet experienced. It is impossible to date them by some supposed 'development' of eschatological ideas in the post-exilic community, and we certainly should not naïvely apportion their different emphases to different (and rival) groups. In most religious communities the faithful are encouraged both by appeal to what God has done and is doing among them, and by assurance that he will act decisively in their future. There is room for both elements in faithful preaching and, no doubt, both accents were heard in the preaching in the second temple.

Zech. 8:9–13

If 8:1–8 could be viewed as exegesis of the preaching of Zechariah, then vv. 9–13 can best be understood equally as exegesis of the preaching of Haggai.[74] As Petersen has argued, the section is shown to be a unit by the repetition of the phrase 'Let your hands be strong' at the beginning (v. 9) and at the end (v. 13).[75] It is, further, introduced by a messenger formula, while the next such formula occurs at v. 14. The passage begins with the kind of call to action which Haggai is recorded as having addressed to leaders and people (2:4). The contrast between judgement beforehand and the blessings of salvation to come is reminiscent of Haggai's insistence on the differences between the time preceding and following the beginning of work on the temple, especially in 2:15–19. The claim that there was no 'wage' (שָׂכָר) for man or beast reminds us of Haggai's shrewd observation that those who earned wages (שכר/) earned them only to put them into bags with holes (1:6). The statement that there was no 'peace' (שָׁלוֹם) recalls Haggai's promise that

Yahweh, once returned to his temple, would give 'peace' (שָׁלוֹם, 2:9). We find
in v. 11 the description of the community as the 'remnant of the people', a
phrase which we have seen characterised the editorial framework of the Book
of Haggai. The promises of change of fortune, the fecundity of seed, vine and
ground, the gift of dew and the wealth of the 'remnant' all recall Haggai's
description both negatively of the deprivations suffered by the people because
of God's judgement (1:10f., 2:16) and also of the positive reversal of all this
(2:19). This is driven home by a reminder that 'these are the words of the
prophets since the days that the foundation of the house of the LORD of hosts
was laid, that the temple might be built' (v. 9).

This section, with the one which preceded it, makes it clear that it is Haggai
and Zechariah who are meant. We must be at a stage when they were both
coming to be regarded as of equal authority with their joint ministries, which
spanned that crucial time when the temple was being rebuilt. The teaching of
both now forms equally the 'text' to which the preachers can appeal to
reinforce their hopes for the future and their lessons for the present 'remnant',
heirs to both past and future. Yet we must note a significant change from
Haggai's own recorded teaching. For in 2:15–19 he makes it clear that it is the
actual building of the temple itself which marks the watershed in the fortunes
of the community. They are to look for change 'from this day forward' (2:15,
18). The contrast will be with the very recent days 'Before a stone was placed
upon a stone in the temple of the LORD' (2:15b). That must have caused
precisely the problem for the people who, in a later time, saw the completed
temple. Not all that the prophets had promised would characterise that that
time had come about. So the preacher who is expounding the text of Haggai's
words makes it all more general. The time before these prophets began to
preach is referred to vaguely as 'before those days' (v. 10), or the 'former days'
(v. 11). And the promises are now placed in a quite undefined future. It is true
that all is introduced by the phrase 'but now', which marks the transition from
time of judgement to time of salvation, but there is nothing which associates
this specifically with the completion of the temple. It is therefore more likely
to be an assurance to later generations that the promises spoken by 'the
prophets' are to be fulfilled. They are entering 'the time of salvation'. Indeed,
the promises Haggai made about the time following the rebuilding of the
temple are extended and made more general by an apparent allusion to the
patriarch, Abraham. The unnatural fate predicted by the prophets, especially
Jeremiah, that God would make his faithless people an example of a divine

'curse' among the nations (Jer. 24:9, 25:18, 42:18, 44:12, 22) will be reversed, and the original promise to Abraham that his descendants would be the objects of 'blessing' among the nations will come to pass:

By you all the families of the earth shall bless themselves. *(Gen. 12:3)*

The 'remnant' are assured that they are yet to 'possess all these things' and fulfil their true destiny and calling as God's people.

The impression that this address represents later exposition of the word of Haggai in a temple context is further strengthened by the remarkable parallels with II Chr. 15:2–7, the address of Azariah to Asa and all Judah and Benjamin. In drawing attention to these parallels, Beuken has characterised Zech. 8:9–17 as a 'Levitical Sermon'.[76] Azariah's address was discussed above (pp. 45ff.). He assured Asa and the nation of God's presence if they sought him and remained true. There then followed a somewhat vague and general reference to a past time of distress when they had been without the 'true God' and had possessed no 'priest to instruct them' or 'Torah'. In this judgement period ('In those days', v. 5), there was no 'security' (שָׁלוֹם) as 'they went about their business' (cf. Zech. 8:11), for in many lands 'Nations and cities destroyed each other' (cf. Zech. 8:10, 'for I set every man against his fellow'). Now, however, Asa and his people are summoned with the call, 'be strong!' (חֲזַק), 'Do not weaken' (cf. Zech. 8:9, 13), and they are assured 'There will be a reward for all your effort', where the Hebrew reads literally, 'For there is a reward (שָׂכָר) for your work': cf. Zech. 8:10). Inspired by this address, Asa began a religious reform of land and temple.

It is impossible to be certain which passage has influenced the other, although it seems more likely that Azariah was citing what was recognised as Scripture than that this addition to Zech. cc. 1–8 should be cited from the Chronicler's work. Possibly, both may reflect the kind of preaching which was heard in the second temple. Certainly, the remarkable parallels cannot be dismissed as 'mere chance'. Both have the kind of 'Installation to Office' call which we saw characterised a number of the addresses in Chronicles and some of the Ezra/Nehemiah material as well as the editorial framework of the Book of Haggai, rather like David's commission to Solomon. Yet Azariah's is a more general call to religious fidelity and purity than to a specific task, and this seems to be more the nature of the general call here. In short, what appears to be happening is that the words of the 'prophets' (Haggai and Zechariah) are being reinforced and their fulfilment assured. They are, however, being given a much more general reference. The promises associated with the completion of the temple will be fulfilled, but now they become part of a more general relation of the teaching of the prophetic and other traditions of promise to Israel to a future that is imminent, to be sure, but no longer bound up with one specific event. Meanwhile, let the people of God exert every effort in the service of the temple and prove worthy of both past and future. The preaching here is more closely related to a particular line of prophetic tradition than the addresses in Chronicles, but it makes use of many of the same techniques, shows much in common with them in style, vocabulary and theme, and is directed to very much the same ends.

Zech. 7:8–10, 8:14–17

It seemed advisable to defer examination of 7:8–10, intruding as it does on the address of 7:4–14, until it could be considered in relation to 8:14–17, with which it shares a number of points of contact and purpose. The passage 7:8–10 is inserted where it is because it is seen as an example of the kind of 'words' which 'the LORD proclaimed by the former prophets' (v. 7). It would be tedious to identify exact precedents for each injunction from the books of the pre-exilic prophets. The very fact that one could cull a great number of such 'originals' for each saying (as many commentators most helpfully do)[77] only shows how effective such a passage is as a summary of the ethical teaching of the earlier prophets. The parallels between this passage and 8:16f. suggest that such summaries may well have assumed almost a 'catechetical' nature and have been part of the stock-in-trade of the 'teaching priests', as Azariah's address described them (II Chr. 15:3), or of those to whom we have referred more generally as the 'preachers' of the second temple. Although the ethical note is not prominent in the addresses in Chronicles, we saw how the 'prophets' had come to be regarded as authoritative teachers, to believe and obey whom was to obey God and so to prosper and succeed (II Chr. 20:20). The call to render 'true judgements' certainly figured in the address of Jehoshaphat to the judges (II 19:6f., 9f.). Oded called for compassion to the Israelites, their 'kinsmen' (II 28:10f.) and, as we have seen, Azariah, by implication, sees a situation where members of nation and city are no longer warring against each other. This would be a sign of God's rule over an obedient and worshipping people, properly instructed in Torah (II 15:5f.). All this suggests that call for an ethical response was a prominent part of the preaching of the post-exilic period. By it, preachers found continuity with the past. It was the breach of this prophetic teaching which they saw as the cause for the terrible judgement of the exile, and Zech. 7:8–10, in its context, serves the function of showing this. Another and even more interesting function is suggested by 8:14–17. For this indicates that their ethical response is not the pre-condition of experiencing the blessings of the new age. The summary of the ethical teaching of the prophets in vv. 16f. *follows* the announcement of God's change of heart and purpose towards them. His purpose for salvation (v. 15) is now every bit as determined and sure as was his purpose of judgement against their fathers (v. 14). Those being addressed are the heirs of the promised salvation. So, as the imperatives imply, the call is that they should 'walk worthily of their calling'. Thus, not only does this aspect of the preaching serve the purpose of reminding them of their link with the pre-exilic past and explain why the break in the continuity of that descent occurred, but it picks out the real heart of the promise of the past. That promise was of a purified, renewed people, characterised by obedience to the law as well as zeal for the temple. In an age when the old institutions had not, for the most part, been renewed, when they were no longer an independent nation-state and there was no Davidic king on the throne, the concept of a purified people of God is seen as a true fulfilment of the old. It is the one essential element which needed to be recreated in the age of salvation. They are in truth the 'remnant'. So let them live up to their calling and, by doing so, show that the new age was already dawning on a people who were ready to receive it.

Zech. 8:18–23

A brief concluding reference can be made to these three oracles which, in their interest, range beyond our concerns in this study but which, for all their disparities, show how those who arranged cc. 7f. in their final form saw the significance of what had gone before. For they continue the twin themes we have suggested are found in these chapters, not least in 7:8–10 and 8:14–17, set as they are in a context of hope for the future reign of God. The two themes we have found there are (a) the ethical character of the people who are to inherit the new age because (b) it is this renewed community which is the fulfilment of the age-old purpose of God and the object of his promises from the past. In the same way we saw that the addresses in Chronicles show that the temple community was the true inheritor of the promises to David and the fulfilment of God's choice of him and his dynasty.

The great majority of commentators agree that vv. 18f. form the true answer to the question of the delegates in 7:1–3. The answer is one of unmitigated assurance. *All* fasts which commemorate the events of God's judgement in the past will be turned to festivals celebrating the new age of his salvation. But, again, someone, the prophet or, more probably, a later exegete, has stressed the true sign of this age to be a people who 'love truth and peace'. It takes the form of an imperative, just as the injunctions of 8:16f. do. In a sense, the addition of v. 19 plays a similar role to that of 6:15b, which must be intended as a conclusion to all the visions and oracles of cc. 1–6:

And this shall come to pass if you sincerely obey the voice of the LORD your God.

The character of the new people is both sign of the advent of the new age and call to prepare for it.

The two concluding oracles of vv. 20–3, which originally had nothing to do with the question of the delegates or its answer in vv. 18f., illustrate, in the final arrangement, the function of the people of God in his universal purpose. They give the highest dignity to their destiny and calling as the means by which 'all nations shall bless themselves'. Vv. 20f. show something of the tradition of the pilgrimage of the nations to Jerusalem (Isa. 2:2–4/Mic. 4:1–4), but also take up the theme of v. 10, where it is said that in the time of judgement God set each man against his companion. Now, in the time of salvation, the true unity of mankind will be found in the worship of Yahweh and in submission to him. Thus the 'universalist' note in Zechariah's teaching (2:11/15) is faithfully maintained. This community, themselves based on the temple in Jerusalem, which will mediate the knowledge of God to the 'many peoples' and 'strong nations', have a destiny of universal significance. Perhaps the addition of the oracle of v. 23 was made to assure the growing number of Jews of the Diaspora that their time of 'exile' was to serve a purpose in the divine plan for the 'nations' also. But the true nature and calling of the people of God is that they experience now, already, the fulfilment of the themes of the older temple worship (e.g. Ps. 46:7, 11) and the promises of the prophets (e.g. Isa. 7:14; see also Amos 5:14): 'God is with them.' It is his presence in the temple in Jerusalem which constitutes them as the true remnant and which will enable them to fulfil their divine calling. Although of independent origin, then, the concluding oracles of vv. 20–3 have been skilfully placed to illustrate the truths enunciated in the 'addresses' based on the teaching of Haggai and Zechariah and the 'former prophets' in the earlier part of the chapter.

To conclude our summary of the Zechariah tradition, then, we may say that, while it clearly carries in a special way elements of the teaching and eschatological hope of the prophet, close parallels of theme, style and vocabulary suggest that we are in a world similar to that of the addresses in Chronicles, the Ezra/Nehemiah material and the editorial framework of the Book of Haggai. While it is impossible to characterise the material as 'Levitical Sermon', there are strong indications that we hear in it echoes of the kind of preaching that was current in the second temple in which the 'preachers' related the hopes of the prophets to a people who could easily have become cynical about their lack of fulfilment, assuring them of both the present degree to which they had been and were being fulfilled and the certainty of their ultimate triumph. They did this partly by generalising the promises and casting them into a less specific, although not far distant, future. But they also drove home the ethical teaching of those prophets, now well on the way to being regarded as canonical teachers of the divine 'Torah'. A people who heeded these lessons would not experience again the terrible judgements which had befallen their fathers. Indeed, such a people would already be a 'sign' of the new age of salvation and the means by which its ultimate fulfilment would be experienced both by Israel and by all the 'nations'.

7 The Book of Malachi

The Book of Malachi consists of six main sections[1] which are bound together in form and structure as well as in general theme. The form is distinctive and has often been described as that of the 'Prophetic Disputation'.[2] In each case the prophet makes an opening statement, either in the first-person divine speech (1:2, 6; 3:6, 13) or in his own words (2:10, 13, 17), setting out a word of God by way of proposition, although this may itself take the form of a question (2:10) or be expanded by a question (1:6). This is then followed by a question from the hearers (1:2, 6; 2:14, 17; 3:8, 13, 14), the answer to which forms the main burden of the message, although this also sometimes involves the use of a further question (1:8, 9, 13; 2:15 [2x]' 3:2). It is often pointed out that there are precedents for such a disputation style in the earlier prophets (e.g. Mic. 2:6–11, Jer. 2:23–5, 29–32; 28:1–11, Amos 5:25f. etc.). Appeal is sometimes made to Westermann's suggestion that there was such a form as 'the Disputation'.[3] Nevertheless, Westermann is careful to distinguish various patterns of the form, and the fluidity of its use in the Book of Malachi suggests that we are dealing with a highly individualised style. Yet, as we have seen, the addresses in Chronicles are also marked by the use of rhetorical question, and this was very much a feature of the Book of Haggai as well as the Zechariah tradition material. All this seems to point to a general stylistic feature of the post-exilic preaching, even if we allow that Malachi makes very much more marked and systematic use of it than is found elsewhere in the extant literature. Chary who, strangely, believes that the style shows a move towards a more literary style, can yet say, 'At the time of Malachi prophecy was still sufficiently vital to appear as effective preaching.'[4] It is most unlikely that these are stenographer-type records of actual debates between Malachi and his hearers, a point strongly made by J. A. Fischer.[5] H. J. Boecker, preferring the term 'Discussion Addresses' for the six main sections in Malachi (see n. 2 above), says that the opening proposition is designed to provoke a reaction from the hearers, and this gives proper recognition to the fact that we are here dealing, not just with a literary device, but with the oral techniques of preaching. G. Wallis has rightly seen that we are not dealing with a 'minuted' account of the discussions, for the opponents are never quoted directly. Rather, despite their form, they are addresses giving God's words to the people, not reporting the discussion again, but arising from it.[6] We may conclude that it is a rhetorical device to engage the interest and interaction of the hearers and to address God's word to their particular doubts, fears and failures.

This raises the interesting question of the name of the book, 'Malachi' (Heb. מַלְאָכִי = 'my messenger'). It has long been debated whether this is the personal name of the prophet or a title, perhaps based on 3:1, identifying the prophet with the coming 'messenger'. There can be no final or determinative answer to the question. The LXX takes it as a title by the form 'his messenger' (ἀγγέλου αὐτοῦ). It may be that the reference to 'Elijah' in 4:5 (3:23) represents another such identification of the 'messenger' of 3:1. Others believe it to be the prophet's personal name, countering arguments that it seems an improbable name to give a child or that it would in any case occur in the longer form 'Malachijah' by pointing out that such shorter forms of personal names do occur elsewhere in the Old Testament (e.g. 'Abi', II Kgs. 18:2, cf. 'Abijah', II Chr. 29:1; 'Uri', I Kgs. 4:19 etc.).[7] A. S. van der Woude made the interesting suggestion that the 'angel of the covenant' mentioned in Mal. 3:1c represented Israel's guardian angel, although he recognised 3:1b–4 to be secondary addition, itself offering some kind of 'exegesis' of the 'messenger' of 3:1a.[8] It has not escaped some commentators that the term is frequently used in the Old Testament for an 'angelic' messenger of Yahweh, and Wallis, in particular, finds this significant for the link with the 'Elijah redivivus' idea and sees a connection between 'Malachi' and the role of the 'interpreting angel' in Zechariah.[9]

All this is interesting and relevant, but it should not escape our attention that, in the text of Malachi, the priest is also described as 'the messenger of the

LORD of Hosts' (2:7), the only place in the Old Testament where he is so described. That does not necessarily imply that Malachi was a priest, although he speaks so warmly of the ideal calling of the Levites (2:4, 6, 8) that it is tempting to think that he himself came from their ranks. It does, however, form a very interesting link with our consideration of II Chr. 36:15f. There we noted the tendency to see all the ideal leaders of the community, kings, prophets, priests and Levites, as 'messengers'. Their main role was that of conveying the living and immutable word of God to the community. It is interesting that in the Book of Malachi it is this element in the priests' role which has come to the fore (2:7–9). We still cannot be sure whether Malachi is a proper name or a title or how far it is used to emphasise that the prophet of these last chapters of the prophetic corpus stands worthily within the line of all the 'messengers' God has sent to his people generation after generation (II Chr. 36:15f.). Nevertheless it serves to link his teaching generally with the kind of hortatory and proclamatory role of the addresses in Chronicles, whatever the distinctiveness of his message.

Questions of the date and unity of the book do not concern us greatly here. The usual practice is to set the book between the time of the ministries of Haggai and Zechariah and the coming of Nehemiah in 445 BCE. This may well be right, although none of the arguments advanced is conclusive. It clearly falls into the post-exilic period since reference is made to a 'governor' (1:8) and the temple stands, with its cult in operation. The topics discussed overlap partially with the concerns of Nehemiah, particularly in the matter of the payment of tithes (3:6–12; see also Neh. 13:10–14) and intermarriage with foreigners (2:11f.; see also Neh. 13:23–7). In a more general way, Nehemiah was concerned with proper provision for sacrifice (13:31; see also Mal. 1:6–14) and with purified cultic officials (13:28–30; see also Mal. 1:1–10, 3:3). Yet Malachi has nothing to say about correct sabbath observance, a matter which greatly concerned Nehemiah (13:15–22). All we can say is that Malachi shows the prevailing laxity in the kind of matters cultic which concerned both Nehemiah and Ezra.[10] Yet such laxity could recur often in any community and, probably, the records exaggerate the achievements of both Ezra and Nehemiah. Further, it is impossible to date Malachi by any reference to the requirements called for in that book to the injunctions of such law-codes as Deuteronomy and the Priestly Code. Even if we knew the date by which such codes achieved their final form and were recognised as authoritative, we should have to reckon still with the fact that law-codes bring together and systematise older prescriptions which may long have been held valid.[11] We probably have to be content with saying that the Book of Malachi is later than the time of Haggai and Zechariah yet must have been written in time to be welded into 'The Book of the Twelve' by the addition of the title מַשָּׂא ('Oracle' see also Zech. 9:1, 12:1) at the beginning, and the addition of the two appendices in 4:4–6 (3:22–4). These seem to form a conclusion, not only to Malachi, or even alone to the Book of the Twelve, but to the whole prophetic section of the canon by bringing the prophetic movement, typified by Elijah, into relationship with Torah (4:4/3:22). Certainly its eschatology is not as sharply 'apocalyptic' as some found in Zech. cc. 9–14, but again, we cannot date material by reference to a supposed unilinear, general evolutionary development from the less to the more apocalyptic. Different circles of contemporaries may have held more or less 'apocalyptic' views simultaneously.

The question of date is to a little extent affected by the issue of whether the book is a unity or the result of a long process of growth. Certain additions have to be argued for. The section against mixed marriages (2:11f.) is held by some to interrupt the main teaching against divorce in 2:10–16. The passage on 'the messenger of the covenant' and his coming to refine the Levites in 3:1c–4 appears to interrupt the promise of God's own coming to the temple and its consequence in the punishment of the wicked of the community (3:1ab, 5). There is no doubt that 4:4–6 (3:22–4) are additions and, for that reason, for all their interest and importance, they are not dealt with here.[12] Nevertheless, for the rest, the book is strongly homogeneous in style, theme and interest, and for this reason the views of McKenzie and Wallace that 3:13–4:3 (3:13–21) is secondary because it shows a more apocalyptic-type view of judgement between different sections of the community must be treated with caution.[13] After all, 3:5 shows exactly the same effect of Yahweh's 'coming' and, in both, the promise is given to encourage the doubters who feel that 'Everyone who does evil is good in the sight of the LORD' (3:17) or 'Evil-doers not only prosper, but when they put God to the test, they escape' (3:5). Similar caution must attach to Wallis's argument that the present arrangement of the book has obscured two distinct sets of oracles, those concerning the priests (1:6–2:9; 3:1–4) and those concerning the laity (1:2–5; 2:10–16; 2:17; 3:5; 3:6–12; 3:13–21). He believes that this muddling of the proper order has obscured an original balance between the two of a sequence which ran from denunciation (*Scheltrede*) through threat of judgement (*Drohwort*) to promise of salvation (*Heilswort*).[14] Apart from any other consideration, a rearrangement along the lines he suggests would break the vital link between 2:17, 3:1ab and 5.

Additions there have been, and the additions doubtless reflect matters of equal concern in the post-exilic community. But still the overall impression of the book is of its remarkable unity of style, theme and purpose.

Mal. 1:2–5

At first sight it seems strange that a book which is to bring such accusations of laxity in ethical and cultic matters against the community, both priests and laypeople, should begin with such a ringing, almost nationalistic assurance of God's electing love of them in contrast to the Edomites. Nevertheless, while castigating the carelessness and wickedness within the community, there is no doubt that Malachi's aim is to encourage the disillusioned and the doubting (2:17; 3:14f.). Indeed, with sure pastoral insight, he sees that the springs of sin and doubt rise very close to one another. The charges in 2:17 and 3:13 show that loss of faith is sin because it is failure to trust in God's goodness and power. By corollary, the sins of cultic neglect and moral indifference spring from doubt and disillusion. The work of Malachi ends with a rousing assurance that God is to act finally and decisively in punishing the wicked and vindicating the righteous (3:16–4:3/3:16–21). It is not so strange, therefore, that it should begin with an equally firm assurance of God's love towards them in the past, and their present position as the elect covenant community whose existence is founded on God's grace. Here, McKenzie and Wallace have performed a service by drawing attention to the strongly covenantal nature of Malachi's preaching.[15] The verb 'to love' (Heb. /אהב) is used both in Hosea (11:1) and in Deuteronomy (7:7, 15 etc.) of God's free election of Isra to a covenant relationship.[16] Those to whom Malachi is speaking have grown to doubt whether this covenant relationship has persisted into the post-exilic situation (1:2). In answer, Malachi points back into their history. He refers to the patriarchal traditions concerning Jacob and Esau. Elliger interestingly points to Gen. 25:28, where we are told that Rebekah loved Jacob (rather than Esau),[17] but the allusion must surely be to the whole thrust of the narratives in Gen. cc. 25ff., which show that the line of election and divine purpose ran through Jacob and his descendants rather than through the line of Esau. However, more than remote history would be brought to the minds of his hearers by the allusion. B. C. Cresson has shown how strongly condemnation of Edom figures in exilic and post-exilic literature.[18] No doubt it was occasioned by the fact that Edom took advantage of Israel's weakness before, during and after the exile, but Cresson stresses that Edom came to be seen as a symbol of the hostile world by which Israel felt herself increasingly menaced after her loss of independent statehood (p. 144). 'Thus Edom came to equal the enemy of the Jews' (p. 148). This suggests that we should look for the promise of the overthrow of Edom in these verses, not by reference to some supposed historical event, such as the incursions of the Nabataeans,[19] but as a much more general eschatological promise that God would overthrow all powers opposed to his rule. All their attempts to avert this, all merely human efforts to rebuild (without God), would be destined to destruction. They are epitomised as a 'wicked territory' (גְּבוּל רִשְׁעָה) and a people who will be the object of Yahweh's wrath 'for ever' (עַד־עוֹלָם). So Malachi not only directs his hearers to their own past history with which the present stands in continuity, but assures them of the future victory of God over all their (and his) enemies. This is so sure that 'Your eyes shall see it.' It assures them that Yahweh's power is universal, stretching far beyond the borders of poor, subject, reduced Israel in her position as outpost in the empire of others (v. 5). Indeed, as has been pointed out,[20] the Hebrew preposition used (מֵעַל) means not primarily '*beyond* the borders . . .' but '*above* the borders of Israel'. God is the sovereign Lord of heaven and all the earth.

Is anything of all this remotely to be connected with the tone and themes of the addresses in the Books of Chronicles and with the material we have considered in Ezra and Nehemiah, Haggai and Zechariah? We have already noted the use of the device of rhetorical question, and here we see again the use of illustration by appeal to past history. It might be argued that two characteristics of this passage mark it off distinctively from the material in Chronicles, the appeal to covenant election and the assurance of eschatological hope. It is true that little is made of the covenant in Chronicles, and it is interesting that the Chronicler uses the verb 'love' (/אהב) only twice of God's love for Israel (II 2:11/10; 9:8). Both these relate to his choice of Solomon as king, and both are taken from the Kings *Vorlage*. Yet we did see that the Chronicler made much of God's choice of David and Solomon and their descendants. We also saw cause to believe that, for the Chronicler, the purpose of that election was the formation of the post-exilic theocratic community who were seen as the true heirs to the promises of the Davidic covenant. This, in turn, stressed that the post-exilic community were the true heirs of God's electing love which flowed through Jacob (see also I Chr. 28:4–8).[21] So, in addressing that same community in terms of God's electing love which first acted through Jacob, Malachi is not so far from the theology of the Chronicler. As to the eschatological element, that is not explicit in the work of the Chronicler (although it is in the

Haggai and Zechariah traditions). Nevertheless, we saw how strong an element in the addresses the 'holy war' concept is. Again and again victory is assured for those who accept that their only role is for passive and obedient trust in Yahweh, who can overcome even the apparently strongest human powers. Whether that has implicit eschatological overtones ('God *will* deliver us in his own time') is another matter. But the assurance that God will show his electing, covenant love for Israel by destroying that symbol of all enemies, Edom, who have come to be represented as an almost abstract example of a 'wicked territory', is closely parallel to the message of the addresses in Chronicles. In this, Edom resembles the enemies in Zechariah's vision who oppressed Judah when Yahweh was angry with them 'but a little' (Zech. 1:15; see also 1:18–21). However, according to Malachi, Yahweh's anger with Edom will not be 'for a little' but 'for ever'.

Another parallel suggests itself, however. We cannot read Mal. 1:2–5 in isolation from all which is to follow. As soon as we set it in its context it becomes clear that this reassuring note is not intended as licence for them to do as they like.[22] It is, rather, the basis for a call to responsible action, to 'live worthily of their calling' and so be ready for Yahweh's final action, which will sort out the wicked from the faithful (3:5, 18). The addresses in Chronicles also call for responsible ethical and cultic action in the light of their calling as the people of God. In a way, Edom symbolises all 'wickedness', and the mystery of God's electing grace is a solemn reminder that even those within Israel who typify 'wickedness' will know a fate similar to that promised to Edom (3:5, 18, 4:1/19). Indeed, whoever has inserted the final addition of 4:4–6 (3:22–4) has certainly so understood it for, if the community do not receive Elijah's reconciling ministry, the land (not Edom, but the land of Israel) stands in danger of the *herem*, that ancient covenant curse of judgement. Here, then, we see the role of the good preacher as we saw it in the addresses in Chronicles and in the Haggai and Zechariah traditions. The proclamation stresses God's grace in the past and the promise of victory in the future, but these are stressed in such a way as to bring out the challenge to the hearers to live worthily of their past and their future calling.

Mal. 1:6–2:9[23]

It is significant that the opening indictment is against the priests before those against laypeople follow, for this order shows that the priests are thought of as holding a position of special responsibility. If they fail, the whole community suffer a loss in their cultic and ethical life. This whole section recalls, in general, and sometimes in detail, the charge to Joshua, the high priest, in Zech. 3:7. Just as the vision which preceded that charge saw the priest being cleansed, presumably as a representative of the whole community, so here it is the sin and defilement of the priests which is responsible for the present weak state of the community as a whole. Further, this section reminds us of the addresses of Hezekiah to the priests and Levites (II Chr. 29:5–11) and of Josiah (II 35:3–6). To some extent, Jehoshaphat's words to the judges (II 19:6f., 9–11) are not wholly irrelevant, for all show the high importance given to the zeal and holiness of leaders for the well-being of the community, and Jehoshaphat's words to the judges show that the chief priest exercised control in all 'matters of the LORD', while Levites served them in some kind of juridical capacity (II 19:11).

The opening 'proposition' points to the honour due to a father by a son and to a master by his servant (v. 6). To some extent it recalls the opening oracle of Isaiah (Isa. 1:2f.) but, more particularly, McKenzie and Wallace rightly call our attention to the use of the father/son, master/servant motifs in treaty and covenant language.[24] They point in the Old Testament to such passages as Deut. 14:1 and II Kgs. 16:7. Further, they draw attention to the continuation of such terminology in this section by the use of the term 'cursed' (אָרוּר) in 1:14 (see also 2:2, and Deut. cc. 27f.) and the description of Yahweh as the 'great king' (1:14, a parallel to secular treaty language). It is 'the covenant with Levi' which is the subject of this passage (2:4f., 8). No such covenant is actually recorded in the Old Testament, but it is presupposed in Jer. 33:21. A covenant with the Aaronic priesthood is recorded in Num. 25:11–13. Possibly the reference is to the blessing of Levi by Moses (Deut. 33:8–11). Clearly, the emphasis in Malachi is on the special responsibility of the priests. However, in disobedience to the law that only animals 'without blemish' should be offered to God in sacrifice (Lev. 1:3) they have presented worthless victims (v. 8). They have, by this, 'despised' (בזה/) the name of God in that they have 'despised' the LORD's table (v. 7). This is a word which occurs three times in Ezekiel in the context of a broken covenant (Ezek. 16:59; 27:16, 19) as well as in more general terms (22:8). It was the word the Chronicler used to describe the rejection of the word of the LORD which came by all the 'messengers' (II 36:16). Further, the 'despising' of the table of the LORD contrasts starkly with the Chronicler's picture of the reforms in the sanctuary carried out by the Levites and priests in response to Hezekiah's address. They are able to report to the king that they have cleansed 'all the house of the LORD, the altar . . . and the table for the showbread and all its utensils' (II Chr. 29:18). In that address, Hezekiah referred to the neglect of the sanctuary during Ahaz's reign, and this included the dreadful fact that the fathers had 'shut the doors of the vestibule'. Malachi sees the present neglect of the priests in ironic contrast to the faithful way they pay their taxes to the governor (v. 8). It would be better, he maintains, if the doors of the sanctuary *were* shut, instead of continuing a currupt and compromised cult which despises rather than honours Yahweh, one which Yahweh will not accept anyway (v. 10). By contrast, the deep gratitude to the Creator shown by men in all places is more honouring to him who is the Creator and provider of all, whether he is known by his proper name or not (v. 11).[25] Vv. 12–14 continue the theme and are still addressed to the priests, for they sin in knowingly pronouncing acceptable for sacrifice that which has been wrongfully gained (v. 13). They have therefore pronounced one verdict (a favourable but a wrong one) on animals presented for sacrifice, and so on those who present them, where God himself pronounces a quite different one, a 'curse' and not a 'blessing' (v. 14). Viewed in this way, v. 14 must not be seen as an intrusive word to laypeople, out of place in a charge against the priests, as so many commentators take it. It is all part of the sin of the priests who condone evil action by accepting the sacrifices such people offer. God's judgement, therefore, exactly fits the sin. He will utter a 'curse' over the priests and so make their 'blessings' (i.e. the blessings they pronounce, a very important part of the priestly role) ineffective. It will be a reversal of the wish of Moses for Levi when he said:

> Bless, O LORD, his substance,
> and accept the work of his hand. *(Deut. 33:11)*

He will render them ceremonially unclean for office,[26] a reversal of the vision of Zechariah concerning Joshua when the filthy garments were taken from him (Zech. 3:4) and also of the promise that Joshua would have rights of access to the heavenly court (Zech. 3:7). That, however, was conditional on 'walking in the ways of Yahweh' and 'keeping his charge'. When the priests fail to observe those conditions they will be 'banished from my presence' (following LXX and Peshitta). All this was because they 'did not lay to heart' the words and commandments of God, an interesting echo of the phrase repeated in the Haggai material (Hag. 1:5, 7; 2:15, 18).

This resulting judgement would show the priests the divine origin of the command by proving it effective in its consequences. As a result 'the covenant with Levi would stand', and this is indeed the stated purpose of God's actions.

Sometimes the text is emended here to give the sense 'that my covenant with Levi might be annulled' (so NEB). There are, however, at least three different ways of understanding what is meant. If the reference is to the covenant with the priesthood, then the announcement that judgement would fall on the priests, so making them an object of the divine curse, rendering them unfit for service and banishing them from God's presence, would imply that the terms of the covenant are being invoked. Such judgement is therefore aimed, in fact, at causing the covenant to *stand*. It will 'stand' by ceasing to apply to its unworthy holders.[27] On the other hand, it might be argued that the covenant would be upheld by the 'messenger of the covenant' when he comes to cleanse the Levites. That is undoubtedly the intention of the addition in 3:1c–4, but there is nothing of this in 2:1–9. The judgement there is total and final, or it will be if they do not sincerely entreat God's favour and 'lay to heart' what is being said. The difference affords an additional reason for taking 3:1c–4 as secondary, beyond its breaking the sequence of thought between 3:1ab and v. 5. One other possibility is left, namely that a distinction is intended in the text between the priests and the Levites. The priests who have been addressed only as such in 1:6 and 2:1 are to be judged in order that the covenant with the Levites might stand (Deut. 33:8–11). The very favourable reference to Levi (vv. 5f.) might be a pro-Levitical, anti-priestly piece of polemic, or a general contrast between the harsh realities of the present and the ideal situation which obtained in the past. It is probably not possible to judge from the text as we have it which of these three possible interpretations is the right one. A pro-Levitical bias would afford parallels to at least one strand in the Chronicler's work.[28]

What is not in doubt is that in vv. 6f. it is the preaching/teaching aspect of the priestly office which is emphasised. This is the only instance in the Old Testament where the priest is referred to as a 'messenger' (cf. II Chr. 36:15f.), but we have seen in the addresses in Chronicles how 'Torah' is viewed as a primary task of the priests and judges (see II Chr. 15:3; 19:10). The worst aspect of the failure of the priests for Malachi is that they caused many to stumble by their teaching. In that teaching they have 'shown partiality' (נֹשְׂאִים פָּנִים, lit. 'lifting up faces'). It is the very quality which has no part in God, according to Jehoshaphat in his address to the judges (II Chr. 19:7).

We must be cautious in our assessment of this section. Nothing can detract from its vigorous, pungent individuality. It is far more than an amalgam of various earlier strands of thought. This prophet feels passionately the betrayal of the whole community by those who should have been its mentors and divine spokesmen (was he himself a Levite?). But, for all its colourful individuality, it stands in a context of thought and expression we have learned to recognise. The responsibility of the priests is stressed in the addresses in Chronicles. The charge to Joshua following the fourth vision of Zechariah comes from circles which see the responsibility and high calling of the priesthood in very much the way they are seen here. We catch echoes of the vocabulary of the addresses and of the Haggai and Zechariah tradition. The appeal to Scripture and to history, the rhetorical question and the emphasis on the teaching role of those who are God's messengers all suggest that this is at home in the milieu we have been considering, that of the preaching of the second temple.

Mal. 2:10–16

There can be no doubt about the originality and uniqueness of Mal. 2:10–16, even if there is doubt about every other aspect of it. If the passage does contain an outright rejection of divorce it stands alone in the Old Testament, and if it has a view of marriage as a 'covenant' between two people with God as witness, it promotes a very high view of marriage indeed. The doubt behind the 'ifs' in the previous sentence arises from the obvious textual corruption which has taken place, especially in v. 15, where the Hebrew as it stands is virtually unintelligible. Speaking of that verse, Vuilleumier says, 'The great number of explanations offered by various exegetes invites caution.'[29] This comment might well be extended to the pericope as a whole, for textual and interpretative problems are not limited to v.15. Further, the thrust of the passage has been somewhat obscured by the addition of vv. 11b–12.

It is not our intention here to attempt the kind of detailed examination and exegesis of the text which would be required in a commentary.[30] Rather, we wish to draw attention to the main 'preaching' themes and methods, to concentrate on the broad issues and to ask whether, for all the distinctiveness of the passage, it finds parallels of any kind elsewhere in the literature we have been considering. There may even be some value in standing back from the details in this way in order to observe the 'shape' of the passage. It is, for example, quite possible in all the attention given to the meaning of v. 15 and the questions of marriage and divorce to fail to observe that violence is also one of the ethical issues Malachi uses to illustrate his main theme (v. 16).

That theme is stated in the opening proposition, which itself takes the form of a rhetorical question: 'Have we not all one father?' It is theoretically possible that the reference might be to Abraham, or to Jacob in view of 1:2, but the parallelism with 'Has not one God created us?' makes it certain that the 'one father' is Yahweh. It is further clear from what follows that the 'all' refers to the Israelites and not to 'all' the peoples of the world, for the conclusion drawn in v. 10b concerning the unnaturalness of their treatment of each other speaks of profaning the 'covenant of their fathers', and the examples of their conduct in vv. 13–16 make it clear that it is to the Jewish community that all attention is directed. This also offers an additional reason for seeing vv. 11b–12, with their reference to intermarriage with foreigners, as secondary. The appeal to the 'one father', if he were the one father of all the nations, would argue *for* intermarriage. If, however, as is far more likely, it is to the one father of all Israelites that appeal is being made, then the issue of the intermarriage of Jews with foreigners is a *non sequitur*. It is the question of their attitude to each other as fellow-Israelites which must arise from such an opening text.

R. L. Smith has well emphasised the repetition of the word 'one' in this pericope. We have *one* father, while *one* God has created us (v. 10). Two more instances occur in the enigmatic v. 15: 'Has not *one* created . . .?' and 'What is the *one* seeking . . .?' The second reference can be taken with some confidence as being to God who, perhaps, is said to be seeking a stable line of God-fearing children from stable marriages. The first reference may be to God, but it is difficult to be sure. So the text of this 'address' is the unity of God, for all the diversity of his creation. Possibly the allusion to 'creation' is not only to Gen. cc. 1f., and it is certainly wider than the thought that he created 'male and female'. It is to his 'creation' of Israel as his son[31] in the covenant he established with the patriarchs (if that is what 'covenant of our fathers' means in 2:10). Possibly it refers in a more general sense to Sinai (see also Isa. 43:1, 15). Whatever the precise allusion, it is the theological basis for the unity of the covenant community, and here Smith again rightly draws our attention to the repeated use of the Hebrew verb / בגד , 'to deal treacherously' (with each other). It comes in vv. 10, 11a (note that neither the word for 'one' nor to 'deal treacherously' occurs in vv. 11b, 12, perhaps another indication that they did not belong to the original unit of vv. 10, 11a, 13–16). Whatever the details of the views about marriage and divorce, we have here a sermon based on the text of the unity of God and therefore of the unity of the community in him. It forms a solemn warning against, and attack on, any ethical or cultic conduct which disrupts that unity and denies it in practice. Indeed, it is this denial of their unity by their ethical and social malpractices which is responsible for the ineffectiveness of their cultic activity. The reference to their 'covering (/ כסה) the altar of the LORD with tears' (v. 13 – we should note the play on words with the ironic comment that they are the same people who 'cover' (/ כסה) their garments with violence, v. 16) and weeping and groaning may be a reference to actual penitential liturgies.[32] It certainly arises from their awareness that the cult is proving ineffective (v. 13). Presumably, it is not securing for them that degree of fertility of the land and general community prosperity which they expected and which the cult, in their eyes, was designed to bring about.

At this point we should notice that this theme of the unity of the people of God because of the unity of God, and the cultic and material frustration which befalls those who act treacherously against that unity, is one we have heard before, in the addresses in Chronicles and, indeed, in the Zechariah tradition. Abijah (II Chr. 13:4–12) addressed Jeroboam and the people of the North, charging them with defecting from God by defecting from Judah. For him the unity was expressed in the divinely appointed Davidic kingship, but that itself was really the instrument of God's own kingship over them and was designed to foster the unity of all Israel. The Davidic rule is described as 'the kingdom of the LORD in the hands of the sons of David' (v. 8). In rebelling against that kingdom they had 'forsaken Yahweh' (v. 11). Indeed, they were fighting, not against the Judaean army, but against 'the LORD, the God of your fathers'. They are in practice denying that unity under the kingship of God which their fathers had known. By this, and the abandonment of the true cultic centre with its true worship, they are doomed to failure. It is in the same spirit that Hezekiah addresses the people of Israel, calling them to return to the LORD by yielding to his overlordship in their return to the temple, a return which will have its fruitful consequences for their brethren and their children (II Chr. 30:6–9). Perhaps the clearest expression of this theology, however, occurs in the address of Oded to the Israelite army as it returns with 200,000 captives from Judah (II Chr. 28:9–11). Oded claims that to subjugate them in slavery would be a sin against Yahweh. These captives from Judah are their 'brethren', that is, they are all, North and South, one people under God. To deny this will be to incur still further wrath from God. We have only to remind ourselves, further, of the summaries of prophetic ethical teaching found in Zech. 7:8–10 and 8:16f. to see how the burden of much of this material is to call the people of the community to realise and express their relationship to each other in the light of their common relationship to God. Malachi's application of the principle is unique, but the principle itself is common to much of the post-exilic 'sermon' material, and so is the manner of its presentation by appeal to history (here, to the covenant with the 'fathers'), rhetorical question and play on words. The question of v. 10, spoken in the first-person plural, is the utterance of the *Seelsorger* (the 'pastor' who is charged with the 'cure of souls'), of whom Ezekiel is a prototype, and such an address speaks to the heart. While it soon reverts to the direct address of the disputation, it does not end, as one might expect from the earlier prophets, with a threat oracle. That only rumbles in the background. It remains throughout the appeal of the pastor to his congregation.[33]

The specific application from Malachi himself appears to be two-fold. Men are breaking covenant with the wives they married when young by 'being faithless'. Smith is right to say that marriage could be thought of as a 'covenant' in the Old Testament (Hos. cc. 1f., Ezek. c. 16, Prov. 2:17).[34] In this case the thought is of Yahweh acting as witness to that covenant. For this reason, the views which go back to Torrey[35] which see this as the language of metaphor for the religious relationship between Yahweh and Israel must be rejected. For one thing, this would be the only use of the marriage metaphor where Yahweh appeared as the wife. Further, the very obscurities of v. 15, which can only be the result of repeated attempts to reinterpret, suggest that this verse probably did originally condemn the practice of divorce.[36] However, whatever the precise unravelling of the obscurities of text and language, it is a remarkably good example of sound homiletical practice. The address is rooted in a great theological principle which is illustrated by specific examples drawn from the field of inter-personal ethics. It does this in a spirit of great compassion for the weaker members of society and has the highest view of marriage as rooted in the nature and care of God. That is not the only example. By a fine play on words he condemns also all 'covering of garments with violence'. It is possible that is a reference to the practice of taking a wife by casting a cloak over her,[37] but it seems more likely to be a reference to the blood-stained garment of the oppressor, as in Isa. 9:5. Here, however, the oppression is exercised towards members of one's own people.

The addition of vv. 11b, 12 could have been made by anyone at any time. Even the prophet himself could have inserted it later. Its theme is one more familiar in the post-exilic period, especially in the Books of Ezra and Nehemiah. Marriage with foreign women (there is no suggestion in the text that men were divorcing their Jewish wives to marry younger Gentile women – that is a connection made entirely in the minds of commentators in their search for some link between these two quite disparate passages) is not condemned just because they are 'foreign', but on religious grounds. They are 'daughters of a foreign god' (v. 11b). Presumably a marriage such as that between Boaz and the Moabite Ruth, who had embraced the Jewish faith

(Ruth 1:16), would not be included in this condemnation. The penalty is excommunication from the religious community of Judaism. They are not to bring an offering to Yahweh (v. 12) and, perhaps, they are excluded from civil and judicial rights as well. Both עֹנֶה and עֵר are to be cut off from the man who does this. Possibly עֵר ought to be emended to עֵד giving the sense 'witness and answerer' or 'witness and advocate'. On the other hand they may just form two composite terms meaning 'everyone' as in I Kgs. 14:10, where the terms 'bond and free' (עָצוּר וְעָזוּב) are used to signify 'everyone, without exception'.[38]

There is no explicit denunciation of marriage with foreigners in the address in Chronicles, but there is the often-repeated call to have no alliance of any kind with people of other nationalities, whether in military sortie (e.g. Hanani to Asa, II 16:7–9) or even in mercantile adventure (e.g. Eliezer to Jehoshaphat, II 20:37). It must have been part of the same sense of the need to keep the delineating boundaries of the religious community clear and well defined when their existence as a political entity was threatened and many pressures to engulf their distinctive faith were being felt increasingly. It is small wonder that 'separation' in a religious sense became a dominant theme in the preaching of the second temple.

Mal. 2:17–3:5

The opening charge here is that the people (the whole community are being addressed as in 2:10–16, not the priests only) have 'wearied' God by what they have been saying. The use of the verb יגע / is reminiscent of the charge of Second Isaiah:

> You burdened me with your sins
> and wearied me (יגע) with your iniquities. *(Isa. 43:24)*

In answering the question with which they respond Malachi tells them that God is 'wearied' by their constant questioning of his justice. He appears to them actively to reward those who do evil. Their prosperity seems to imply that they are the objects of the divine 'pleasure' (/ חפץ). They ask constantly, 'Where is the God of justice?' The last question carries with it the implied question, 'When will God establish his rule of law in the land?' It is not hard to see how often the post-exilic community must have been provoked to such bitter questioning of faith as again and again the prophetic hopes failed to materialise.

The answer comes in 3:1ab and 5. Once we have grasped that vv. 1c–4, with their switch from first-person divine speech to the third person, their hopeless confusion over exactly who is coming, the 'messenger', the 'Lord' (not the name Yahweh but the Hebrew הָאָדוֹן) or the 'messenger of the covenant', and their quite different emphasis on the purification of the priesthood rather than judgement of sinners (which was the cause of the complaint in 2:17), the answer is seen to be direct and straightforward. In the imminent future (for that is the force of the Hebrew construction with its use of הִנֵּה with the participle), God is sending his 'messenger'. Perhaps, as some have argued, this is a step towards a greater concept of the transcendence of God who is seen to act only through intermediaries.[39] Perhaps it is an echo of Isa. 40:3, where God is seen, in the manner of an oriental king, to send a forerunner ahead to announce his coming. In this case it seems likely that the prophet is thinking of himself and seeeing his role in this way. If that is so, the 'messenger' is not just a preacher of God's word in general, but the one who is called to initiate the new age by his proclamation, and here the prophet is defined as one of the long line of 'messengers' through whom God spoke to his people in every generation, just as the priests had been called to be (2:7). Perhaps the thought is of an angelic messenger who, however, so often stands for Yahweh himself (see Exod. 3:2). But perhaps all such speculation is marginal, since what the messenger announces and effects is Yahweh's own coming (v. 5). The result of this will be 'for judgement' (the Heb. לְמִשְׁפָּט), the very state of affairs for which the people were longing when they asked, 'Where is the God of justice?' (הַמִּשְׁפָּט 2:17). This will involve swift witness and action against the evildoers in society who seem to be prospering and getting away with their evil. The answer to the question and the doubts, therefore, is directly eschatological.

In this it stands firmly in the tradition of the kind of material we have seen in the Haggai and Zechariah traditions. The method of the preachers is to reassure the hearers of the certain fulfilment of the future hope of the prophets and to call the community to faithful living in the light of that certainty (see also 3:16–4:3/3:16–21).

The clear addition in 3:1c–4 takes a quite different tack. The 'Lord' is spoken of in the third person as the 'messenger of the covenant'. Presumably this is seen to have some relation to the 'covenant with Levi' (2:4, 8) since this takes up the note of the attack on the priesthood in 1:6–2:9.[40] But now the thought is of purifying the priesthood in order that the temple cult may be resumed in a cleansed and renewed form (v. 4). This is quite other than the eschatological note of v. 5. It might stem from a tradition similar to that of Zech. cc. 9–14, with its bitter attacks on the false priests and its promise of renewal by smelting (Zech. 10:1–3a; 11:4–17; 13:7–9), except that this passage in Malachi still seems to hold out some hope that the priests will respond to this purifying process. There is no such hope in Zech. cc. 9–14.[41] It is certainly a note which would not have been alien to the Chronicler where the addresses, as we have seen, put just such emphasis on the purity, zeal and obedience of the priests and Levites for the well-being of the whole theocratic community.

In a passage such as this where the original oracle probably consisted of 2:17, 3:1ab and 5, with its close parallel in 3:13–4:3 (3:13–21), we surely hear the pastoral note of the preacher seeking to meet the doubts and disappointments of his congregation and to encourage them by an assurance of God's purpose for their good and their future salvation. The 'answer' from God is directed exactly to the questions they raised in their doubts. God will be a swift witness against evildoers who appear to enjoy his favour. Further, he himself will come to establish his 'justice' in the sight of those who ask 'Where is the God of justice?' Nor should we miss, in the list of evildoers and their unjust deeds (3:5), the very close relationship to Zech. 7:8–10 and 8:16f., which we saw reason to believe were catechetical-like summaries of the ethical teaching of the pre-exilic prophets and the 'stock-in-trade' of the preachers. The close parallels between these passages and 3:5 suggest that this oracle, also, comes from circles drawing on similar source material.

Mal. 3:6–12

The opening proposition of this pericope is a theological statement introducing an understanding of the nature of God drawn from their worship, 'I, Yahweh, do not change.' Ps. 77:10 (11) says:

> And I say, 'It is my grief,
> that the right hand of the Most High has changed.' (שנה)

The psalm is a lament in which the Psalmist draws comfort from the great deeds of Yahweh in the past, with the implication that the same power ('right hand') and grace will be experienced in the present.

The phrase in Mal. 3:6 is introduced by כִּי, 'for' or 'because', and this presumably links it with what has gone before in 2:17–3:5. While that is eschatological in its emphasis, this is concerned with the present faithfulness of the members of the theocracy, but the purpose is to relate it to the kind of questioning which was expressed in 2:17. Partly the answer to such doubts is to assure them of Yahweh's swift action in the future. But partly it is to call them to the kind of faithfulness in the present which will result in Yahweh's blessing now. Thus the double emphasis on future hope and present faithfulness that we have seen to characterise so much of the Haggai and Zechariah traditions is found here also. The use of the personal pronouns, '*I*, Yahweh, do not change, but *you*, sons of Jacob . . .' is obviously intended as a contrast. However, the exact force of v. 6b is not clear. It may be that / כלה has its usual sense, and we should render it, 'and you, sons of Jacob, are not destroyed' or 'do not come to an end'. It is because Yahweh does not change that the deceitful descendants of their deceitful ancestor, Jacob, do not get their just deserts. Yahweh remains unchangingly faithful even to the unfaithful. Or it might mean, 'you do not come to an end [of your faithlessness]', i.e. 'You do not change either.' The former offers the more obvious sense of the Hebrew root כלה, and it would carry with it an important assurance for those who preach the past traditions. Yahweh does not change. Although all the circumstances of their lives have changed since the exile, he continues to be faithful to his people, to spare and to preserve them. They are united with the great past of their ancestor by the fact that they, like him, know the presence and care of the same unchanging Yahweh.

Interestingly, this opening assertion of continuity with the past by virtue of Yahweh's constancy is followed by an appeal to the faithlessness of the fathers (v. 7), a feature we have seen to characterise the addresses in Chronicles and the Haggai/Zechariah traditions. The whole history shows how they have constantly turned aside from Yahweh's statutes. This illustration by way of appeal to their history is followed by the familiar device of play on words and, here, on the very word we have heard in Zech. 1:3 and the addresses in Chronicles (e.g. II 30:6), '"Return to me, and I will return to you", says the LORD of Hosts.'

Further, just as in Hezekiah's letter, here also cultic faithfulness is equated with 'returning to Yahweh'. The one is the expression of the other. When the hearers ask, 'How shall we return?', the answer is that they have been 'cheating' God. The / קבע is often rendered as 'to rob'. Yet this meaning is far from certain. BDB pronounces it 'dubious'. KB renders it 'to deceive' on the basis of the LXX πτέρνιξω, 'to strike with the heel'. It is difficult to avoid the impression that LXX is offering exegesis of this verb in the light of the allusion to Jacob in v. 6. The name יַעֲקֹב, by popular etymology, was related to the word for 'heel' (Gen. 25:26) and also to that for 'to cheat' by the extended sense of 'following at heel'.[42] NEB renders it 'defraud' and, in this, the post-exilic community have shown themselves all too clearly to be 'sons of Jacob'. Only a metathesis of consonants separates /קבע, the verb used in 3:8 from /עקב, from which the name of Jacob is held to have derived. It is hard, therefore, to escape the impression that there is play on words here also. This would carry with it an especial irony in view of the opening statement of 1:2f. of God's 'love' for Jacob, that is, of his choice of him for a covenant relationship.

The 'defrauding' of God by denying him of what is righfully his due, just as Jacob supplanted Esau of his birthright by a trick (Gen. 25:26), is seen in their failure to pay tithes for the upkeep of the temple and its personnel. Here we are very manifestly in the world of the addresses in Chronicles, especially that of Azariah in II Chr. 31:10. Following the account of the faithfulness of the people in bringing in the tithes of 'everything' (II 31:5ff.), Azariah says, 'Since they began to bring in the "contributions" [Heb. תְּרוּמָה as in Mal. 3:8] into the house of the LORD, we have eaten and had enough.' This was exactly the thought of Haggai, who urged the people to give the gifts needed to build the temple. Malachi, now that the temple is built, is more concerned with its upkeep and that of its personnel. But the message is the same, and echoes that of the addresses in Chronicles, that faithfulness to God is shown in faithful support of the temple cult. God responds to such faithfulness with 'blessing' by giving fertility. Once more, the hearers are assured, the 'windows' in the firmament will be opened, but unlike that opening remembered from the flood story which released the waters of chaos in judgement (Gen. 7:11), this opening will be to release the 'waters' of salvation, virtually a concept of *Heilsregen*. The congregation are invited to 'put God to the test'. Practical obedience to the law is the only way to prove the unchanging fidelity and mercy of the God who commands. In bringing the tithes into the 'storehouse' they will emulate the faithfulness of the people who responded to David's call for generous response (I Chr. 29:8f.). God would 'rebuke' the pests which destroyed their crops (see also 2:3, where it is said that he would 'rebuke' the descendants of the priests in judgement). As Haggai and Azariah had promised, obedience in matters cultic would bring fertility and wealth in material realms. The people of God would be deemed 'blessed' by the nations of the earth and so would fulfil their destiny as God's people (see Gen. 12:3; Zech. 8:13). In place of their complaint that God appeared to 'delight' (/חפץ) in evildoers (2:17), they themselves would be seen to live in a land of 'delight' (/חפץ).

Mal. 3:13–4:3 (3:13–21)

The opening propositions in Malachi's rhetorical discussions alternate between being propositions about human nature and propositions about God's character. God's love for his people is the theme of 1:2; 'A son honours his father, and a servant his master' (1:6) is an observation about human relationships with, of course, a theological implication about God's relationship as father and master to his people; this is followed by the statement (in the form of a question) that God is father and creator of all his people (2:10); the next proposition is that the people have wearied God (2:17); the unchanging nature of God is the theme of the section we have just considered (3:6); and now, finally, we have another statement about the people, '"Your words have been stout against me", says the LORD' (3:13).[43] It is ironic that the root /חזק, so often encountered in the imperative, 'Be strong!', appears as a repeated call in the addresses in Chronicles and in the Haggai/Zechariah tradition material (although not in this way in Malachi). According to Malachi the irony is that the only way the people have been 'strong' is in their complaints against God. The substance of the charge is virtually equivalent to that recorded in 2:17, and the fact that such doubts are addressed twice within the short compass of this book illustrates forcefully how prevalent such attitudes must have been. It is not clear whether the text originally suggested that those who spoke in this way and 'those who feared Yahweh' (v. 16) were the same people. The introductory אָז in v. 16, 'Then . . .', suggests a different group in the light of the doubts they had been hearing from others. However, the LXX has ταῦτα (Heb. זה/זאת), 'These things spoke those who feared Yahweh with one another', the reference being to the complaints which had just been narrated. This seems more likely in that there is nothing to suggest in the opening proposition of 3:13 that any different audience is in mind than in all the other sections of the book, where it has always been clearly the community at large who are addressed (except where the priests are explicitly named). In fact, God does with their words that which they have so often failed to do with his: he 'paid attention' (Hiph'il /קשב) to them and 'heard' them (v. 16). It is encouraging that this preacher with a pastoral heart believes that God notes their 'fear' of him in his book rather than their doubts. The 'book of remembrance' is not mentioned explicitly as such elsewhere in the Old Testament, but it may echo such ideas as those expressed in Exod. 32:32f., where Moses tells God he would rather his name were blotted 'out of thy book which thou hast written' if he is unwilling to forgive the sins of the people.

Perhaps this is tantamount to a request to die, that is, to be erased from the register of those who live. The Psalmist speaks of it as such when, in a spirit somewhat different from that attributed to Moses in Exod. c. 32, he prays concerning his enemies:

> Let them be blotted out of the book of the living . . . *(Ps. 69:28/29)*

In Isa. 4:3 the thought is rather more eschatological and refers to those destined to share in the life of the restored Jerusalem. Such a thought parallels Mal. 3:16 very well. The faithful (for all their doubts and disillusion) are destined in God's purpose and unchanging grace to share in the glorious future of the restored Jerusalem from which all evil has been burned out (vv. 4:1ff./3:19ff.; see also Isa. 4:4; Zech. 5:1–11). Such people are described not only as 'those who feared Yahweh' but as those who 'think [the Heb. root is חשׁב/] on his name'. This RSV rendering, however, is too weak. חשׁב/ not only means to 'esteem' or to 'value' (e.g. Isa. 13:17) but to 'reckon' (e.g. Gen. 15:6, where Abraham's faith was 'reckoned' or 'accounted' to him as righteousness, and II Sam. 19:19/20, where Shimei implores king David, 'Do not reckon iniquity to me'). So here the thought is of those who 'reckon' on God, that is, who take his power and will to act into account (cf. NEB, 'kept his name in mind'). The addresses in Chronicles contain repeated calls to do this when confronted by enemies and, indeed, in all situations of danger. If those who are the objects of this promise are the same as those who expressed their doubts so forcefully, we are on the way to a concept of justification by faith. They are to know deliverance because they take God's qualities into account, not by reason of their own heroic qualities or their own virtues.

For them, the covenant promises are renewed: '"They shall be mine", says the LORD' (v. 17:cf. Exod. 6:7 and, indeed, Mal. 1:2, where the 'I have loved you' refers to the divine covenant election), and 'my special possession' (Heb. סְגֻלָּה, with its special covenant connotations: cf. Exod. 19:5). Yahweh will act as the 'father' he is and whose rights he has already claimed (1:6). Earlier, the call was for Israelites to show their filial duties. Here it is on the graciousness and love of the father for his son.[44]

As in 3:5, this action of God will lead to the clear differentiation between the righteous and the wicked, between those who serve God and those who do not in the sharp division of fate which awaits them on the day 'when he acts' (cf. 'draws near' in 3:5). The 'Day of Yahweh' concept is a familiar prophetic motif from the time of Amos onwards and here, as elsewhere, it is seen as a day of judgement, although the thought of 'fire' rather than 'darkness' is to the fore. Has it been influenced by the picture of 'fire' as characterising the theophany (e.g. Exod. 3:2ff.; see also Ps. 97:1–3)? Or does it retain a memory of the destruction of Jerusalem by fire in 586 BCE? In any event, as in Isa. 65:8–16, judgement is discriminatory. The fire of judgement and destruction will consume some. For those who fear the name of Yahweh, however, 'the sun of righteousness shall arise with healing in its wings'. God is not often likened to the sun in the Old Testament. However, a great deal of 'light' imagery is to be found in the background to the cultic celebration behind some Psalms (e.g. Pss. 46:5/6; 84:11/12, etc.).[45] It is probably to such influences we should look here rather than to Zoroastrianism with its emphasis on the conflict between the forces of 'light' and 'darkness'. The graphic picture of calves released from the darkness and constraints of the stall gambolling in the open pasture for sheer joy speaks for itself. It could easily be the kind of metaphor used by Second Isaiah but, in fact, the only other occurrence of this verbal root comes in Jer. 50:11, where it is used in a pejorative sense of evildoers. The idea of 'treading underfoot the wicked', for all that /עסס is used only here, to some extent parallels in very general terms the promise of Zech. 9:15 (see also Isa. 49:26). If it seems somewhat repugnant to us, it must be seen as an expression of confidence in the divine victory.

It is fitting that Malachi, who began his message with an assurance of the divine love and grace, in spite of all that he finds to challenge, rebuke and warn against, also ends on a similar note of encouragement. He shows throughout a lively, individual style. Yet the manner and themes of his message suggest that he stands firmly in the circles of the second temple 'rhetors', circles which have left their mark so clearly on the records of the preaching of the second temple period. Perhaps Malachi especially reminds us that the greatest service a preacher can render his congregations is not only to warn and rebuke them, but to direct their faith and hope towards God. Even amid their disappointments and doubts, linked as these are to their own evident shortcomings, they should 'reckon' on the love and power of God which he has amply demonstrated in the past and which will be triumphant at the end. The eschatological note is stronger here, but the assurances and call are the same as we have met elsewhere in the material surveyed in this book. Yahweh is able to conquer all enemies. Malachi is a fitting representative with whom to complete our survey of those who 'preached the tradition' after the exile.

8 Conclusion

The starting point of this study was von Rad's theory that the addresses in the Books of Chronicles represented a recognisable literary genre which he called the 'Levitical Sermon'. The study has suggested that this term cannot stand. It is difficult, if not impossible, to find satisfactory, objective criteria by which to determine a literary type 'sermon' so as to distinguish it clearly from prophetic oracles in general. Further, the connection with the Levites, in particular, is so tenuous as to make the term inappropriate. Nevertheless, we did observe that the addresses are marked by many of the characteristics of preaching. They often quote, or refer to, a text of 'Scripture' which is presumably regarded as authoritative by speakers and hearers alike. They expound some theological truth about God and they call for immediate and lively response to this truth, either by way of encouragement, rebuke or exhortation. We find characteristic rhetorical devices in them such as play on words, the use of illustration, often by way of appeal to past history, the rhetorical question and the formal call for attention on the part of the hearers. This led us to suggest that, in the addresses which the Chronicler gives to some of his principal characters, generally described by him as 'messengers', we might see reflected some of the homiletical practice with which he and his hearers were familiar from the second temple. While, then, we cannot describe the addresses as 'sermons', we may nevertheless catch in them something of the style, themes and interests of those who preached the 'sermons' in the worship of the post-exilic community.

In order to test this inference we then turned to examine other post-exilic literature, similar passages in the books of Ezra and Nehemiah and the books ascribed to the post-exilic prophets, Haggai, Zechariah (cc. 1–8) and Malachi or, at least, especially in the case of Zechariah, to those parts of those books where it seemed likely that the words of the prophet had been subject to reflective and interpretative tradition. Here we found, in some instances, striking echoes of the material and form of the addresses in Chronicles and, in others, enough evocation of their style, theme, interests and use of rhetorical devices to suggest that the same influences which left their marks in the addresses in Chronicles had pervaded the tradition process here also, and all represented what might appropriately be termed a 'temple tradition'. That is, it seemed to provide strong evidence to support the hypothesis that the influence common to them all was a general pattern of preaching and teaching which was familiar from the practice of the second temple.

During the course of the study we have tried to deal with at least three questions which may well be asked of such a conclusion. The first is obvious enough. The only form in which we have the evidence is that of literary texts. Clearly, then, we are dealing with material which has been the subject of literary processes of composition, editing and transmission. Is it reasonable to use such material as evidence of oral and rhetorical practice? The second question is that, for all the points of overlap and matters of theme and style in common, clear differences are to be found in each of the texts examined in relation to each other and, even more, in relation to the Books of Chronicles. This was true of the material in Ezra and Nehemiah as well as in the prophetic literature. Do not such variations deny as much of a common tradition as has been claimed? A third question must also be asked. If it can be argued successfully that these texts reflect current homiletical practice, has this any relevance or importance? In short, does it matter? How would it help us in any way to know, even if we could be sure, that the final texts owe something to preachers of the tradition, rather than to the work of purely literary figures such as editors?

The first question need not detain us long. Obviously the whole process behind the emergence of the final form of the text is known to us only by inference from the written evidence we have in our hands. However much the spoken word has been involved throughout, what we have now is the result of a literary process. Exactly the same holds true for all prophecy in the Old

Testament, yet we do not doubt that behind the literary body of material lies the oral activity of the prophet and his associates. To be sure, we cannot always claim to know which were the *verba ipsissima* of the prophet whose name the book bears and which are the words of later 'preachers' or literary editors. Nevertheless, it has been the contribution of Form Criticism to awaken us to the living, oral stages which lie behind the written documents of our bibles. It has released us from those exclusively literary preoccupations which we often now feel too much dominated the work of some nineteenth-century literary critics. Form Criticism has provided us with criteria by which to detect living, oral 'forms'. While we have argued that von Rad and others failed to establish sufficiently objective criteria by which to identify the 'form' of the 'Levitical Sermon', this study has sought to discover criteria by which we may detect the evidence of homiletical style and preaching behind the final written form of the text. The repetition of these criteria across so much diverse material certainly merits our taking them seriously as evidence for the part 'preaching' played in the emergence of the texts as we have them. I have used the term 'preaching', but have attempted to make clear that we have to allow for a broad understanding of the process it denotes. We do not know if 'sermons' in any way akin to the form in which they are now delivered were preached in the second temple. But there does seem to have been an identifiable process of oral exposition of the 'received tradition'.

It is, however, the very diversity of this material which posits the second question. If the preaching of the second temple played a significant role in the shaping of this material, how is it that such clear differences of outlook remain? The addresses in Chronicles reflect in general the theology of the Chronicler. The 'speeches' in Ezra and Nehemiah, for all the continuity of some themes found in Chronicles, express different motifs and vary in some ways in style. Haggai and Malachi have much in common, but their styles are recognisably different and so, to a considerable extent, are the matters with which they deal, while the Zechariah material has further preoccupations of its own. In particular, the material in the various prophetic traditions we have examined evinces a marked degree of eschatological expectation, albeit tempered with a concern for the proper upkeep of the theocracy in the present and a call to its members for present faithfulness. Such an eschatological note is not at all conspicuous in the work of the Chronicler or in the addresses which he records. This fact has been recognised as the discussion has progressed. Two different, although, it is hoped, complementary observations need to be made. A lively and effective preaching tradition does not mean that the individual preachers are mere processors of a body of received and agreed 'truths', mere pale and lifeless ciphers. While, no doubt, there have always been preachers in every age who merit the accusation against the false prophets of the Jeremiah tradition, that they 'steal my oracles from one another' (Jer. 23:30), preaching is effective to the degree to which it attracts men and women of original thought and powers of expression who can make the traditions their own and present them distinctively. Furthermore, preachers themselves clearly come from different traditions and inherit different understanding of those traditions. Yet, at the same time, there is a remarkable degree of uniformity of method and style which makes their presentations identifiable as 'preaching'. We need not assume that it was any different in the time of the second temple. The 'preachers' of the Haggai and Zechariah traditions clearly remain faithful to the prophets' own teaching and even, to some extent, to their vocabulary. The variety of witness is not reduced to a bland 'official' party line. Yet the other fact remains and, indeed, becomes all the more remarkable. Across all these peculiarities of substance of the tradition so many characteristics of the homiletical style recur in all the traditions we have been examining. This feature argues all the more powerfully for some such living background which has helped to shape all the material. Nor should the differences in substance be magnified too much. Haggai calls for faithfulness in the rebuilding of the temple, Malachi for faithfulness in its upkeep. The addresses issue similar calls. Yet each represents the application of similar theology in different circumstances, namely that loyalty to God results in practical expression of care for the temple and its worship and that such loyalty is rewarded by the faithfulness of God in providing their material needs. Nor should the 'eschatological' divide between prophetic and Chronicler traditions be seen as impossible to bridge in any way. What the prophets saw as the signs of the new age, yet to come in its fullness, the Chronicler, and those who pass on the prophetic traditions, see as already marking to some degree the present age of the theocracy. And all find hope for the community in the promise of God to overcome his (and their) enemies and call similarly for quiet trust and faith in that power.

This leads to the third question. Even if it can be established that this postexilic material affords evidence for the kind of preaching which took place in the second temple, does this have any but purely historical or even antiquarian interest? Does it affect our reading of the text in any important way?

An answer has to be two-fold. In the first place we have to recognise the existence of the 'tradition–element' in much of this material. It is especially clear in the Books of Haggai and Zechariah 1–8, but some process of development or reflection, exegesis and reapplication of the original words is probably not absent from the Book of Malachi, Ezra and Nehemiah or even the work of the Chronicler. We recognise such tradition material in the written texts only by the use of literary evidence and close attention to the text. In the second place, the suggestion that such material is the result not only of a purely literary activity but springs from and reflects the living process of 'preaching the tradition' surely does bring it to life and show something of its importance in the life and faith of a living community. It is all too easy for academic biblical scholars, using the techniques of literary criticism, to present the development of the biblical material in purely literary terms. It is almost as though we discern our counterparts sitting at some oil-lit desk in an ancient prototype of the Bodleian Library engaged in a purely intellectual exercise of up-dating the text, ironing out its difficulties or reinterpreting it so as to uphold its truth when its predictions have not been seen to materialise. But preachers are engaged on a more immediate and urgent task. They are concerned from a sense of pastoral need for a community of faith. They must meet the constant threats of loss of faith or, at least, of apathy towards that faith and its observance through disappointment and disillusion. In the difficult and often depressing days of the post-exilic period such threats must have been felt particularly acutely. Our study has suggested some of the concerns of those preachers. They want to assure their hearers of their authentic heritage from the great days of Israel's past. They want to assure them of the constant vitality of God's promises from the past and of his purposes for them in the present and the future. To them falls the immense task of reinterpreting Yahwism, which had been the establishment religion of the Davidic nation-state, in an entirely different situation of loss of national independence, of political vassalage and military impotence. They have to take the great prophetic promises and show their hearers that they are already experiencing a true and valid fulfilment of them in their present life as a temple-based theocracy, with God's presence among them mediated through its leadership and cultic worship. At the same time they must hold out a living hope of a greater and complete fulfilment of God's purposes in the future. They must explain why the break with the past took place while assuring them of the true continuity of God's plans. They must call for faithfulness and obedience in both cultic and ethical realms for, when their existence as a nation can no longer be guaranteed in political terms, the continuity of the outward forms and institutions of their faith and their separated life as a community of that faith become all-important. These, as we have seen, are the many concerns of the addresses in Chronicles, Ezra and Nehemiah and the post-exilic prophetic books.

To realise that this is not a purely academic exercise but a living process, forged in the furnace of life and experience by those charged with the well-being of a community of faith, is to bring all this material much closer to the people of God in every age. To see how at least some 'preached the tradition' at this critical period in the life of that community is both to recall that such a task is one which continues in every age of the descendants of that post-exilic community and, perhaps, to learn just a little of how it can de done faithfully, creatively and effectively.

Notes

Introduction

1. G. von Rad, 'Die Levitische Predigt in den Büchern der Chronik', first published in *Festschrift für Otto Proksch* (Leipzig, 1934), pp. 113–24, and republished in *Gesammelte Studien zum Alten Testament* (Munich, 1958), pp. 248–61. The English translation, 'The Levitical Sermon in the Books of Chronicles', by E. W. Trueman Dicken, appeared in *The Problem of the Hexateuch and Other Essays* (Edinburgh and London, 1966), pp. 267–80.

2. 'Levitical Sermon', p. 12. (Unless otherwise stated, quotations are from the English translation.) The passages he cites are: I Chr. 28:2–10; II Chr. 15:2–7; 20:14–17; 20:20; 29:5–11; 30:6–9; 32:7f.

3. E.g. J. M. Myers, *II Chronicles*, The Anchor Bible (New York, 1965); P. R. Ackroyd, *I & II Chronicles, Ezra, Nehemiah*, Torch Bible Commentaries (London, 1973); R. J. Coggins, *The First and Second Books of the Chronicles*, The Cambridge Bible Commentary on the New English Bible (Cambridge, 1976); H. G. M. Williamson, *1 and 2 Chronicles*, The New Century Bible Commentary (London, 1982); R. B. Dillard, *2 Chronicles*, Word Bible Commentary (Waco, 1987).

4. Particularly by D. Mathias, 'Die Geschichte der Chronikforschung im 19 Jahrhundert unter besonderes Berücksichtigung der exegetischen Geschichtswerker. Ein problemsgeschichtlicher und methodenkritischer Versuch auf der Basis ausgewählter Texte', unpublished dissertation, Leipzig, 1977, and '"Levitische Predigt" und Deuterismus', *ZAW*, 96 (1984), 23–49; see

also the reservations of R. L. Braun, *1 Chronicles*, Word Bible Commentary (Waco, 1986), pp. xxivf.

5. E.g. W. M. Beuken, *Haggai–Sacharja 1–8* (Assen, 1967), pp. 88ff.; P. R. Ackroyd, *Exile and Restoration* (London, 1963), p. 201; R. A. Mason, *The Books of Haggai, Zechariah and Malachi*, Cambridge Bible Commentary on the New English Bible (Cambridge, 1977), p. 32; 'The Prophets of the Restoration', in *Israel's Prophetic Tradition*, ed. R. J. Coggins *et al.* (Cambridge, 1982), pp. 146ff., and 'Some Echoes of the Preaching in the Second Temple?', *ZAW*, 96 (1984), 221–35.

6. Further significant studies of the speeches in Chronicles since the time of von Rad include: O. Plöger, 'Reden und Gebete im deuteronomistischen und chronistischen Geschichtswerk', in *Festchr. für Gunther Dehn*, ed. W. Schneemelcher (Neukirchen, 1957), pp. 35–49 = *Aus der Spätzeit des Alten Testaments* (Göttingen, 1971), pp. 50–66; C. Westermann, *Basic Forms of Prophetic Speech* (London, 1967) (ET by H. C. White of *Grundformen prophetischer Rede* (Munich, 1967); I. L. Seeligman, 'Die Auffassung von der Prophetie in der deuteronomistischen und chronistischen Geschichtsschreibung (mit einem Exkurs über des Buch Jeremia)', *SVT* XXIX, Congress Volume (Göttingen, 1977), pp. 254–84; J. P. Weinberg, 'Die "ausser kanonischen Prophezeiungen" in den Chronikbüchern', *Acta Antiqua*, 26 (1978), 387–404; Y. Amit, 'The Role of Prophecy and Prophets in the Book of Chronicles', *Beth Mikra*, 93/2 (1983), 113–33; M. A. Throntveit, *When Kings Speak: Royal Speech and Royal Prayer in Chronicles*, SBL Dissertation Series, 93 (Atlanta, 1987).

7. M. Fishbane, *Biblical Interpretation in Ancient Israel* (Oxford, 1985), *passim*, but esp. p. 77 ('rhetors and teachers'); see also pp. 15–18.

1 Introduction to Part 1

1. *Das erste Buch der Chronik KAT* (Leipzig, 1927). See further, J. Hänel, 'Das Recht des Opferschlachtens in der chronistischen Literatur', *ZAW* (1937) 46–67. A survey of nineteenth-century critical study of the Chronicler is given by D. Mathias. See n. 4 to the Introduction above.

2. *Die Bücher der Chronik, Esra, Nehemia, ATD* (Göttingen, 1954).

3. 'Problems in the Books of Chronicles', *VT*, 4 (1954) 401–9. Both citations occur at p. 402.

4. E.g. A. C. Welch, *Post-Exilic Judaism* (Edinburgh & London, 1935), pp. 185f.: 'When they (i.e. I Chr. cc. 1–9) are removed, the unity of design in the Chronicler's work becomes apparent.' See also C. R. North, *The Old Testament Interpretation of History* (London, 1946), p. 116.

5. E.g. J. Botterweck, 'Zur Eigenart der Chronistischen Davidgeschichte', in *Festschrift für Prof. Dr. Viktor Christian* (Vienna, 1956), pp. 12–26, and Galling, *Die Bücher der Chronik, Esra, Nehemiah.*

6. See Ch. 1, n. 147 below and Williamson, *1 and 2 Chronicles*, pp. 320f.

7. F. M. Cross, 'A Reconstruction of the Judean Restoration', *JBL*, 94 (1975), 4–18, and S. L. McKenzie, *The Chronicler's Use of the Deuteronomistic History*, Harvard Semitic Monographs, 33 (Atlanta, 1985).

8. 'Old Testament Historiography', in *Tradition & Interpretation*, ed. G. W. Anderson (Oxford, 1979), pp. 125–62. The citation is from p. 160.

9. 'The Chronicler as Exegete', *JSOT*, Issue 2 (1977), 2–32. The citation is from n. 7, p. 25.

10. *Post-Exilic Judaism*, pp. 186f.

11. 'The Supposed Common Authorship of Chronicles and Ezra–Nehemiah Investigated Anew', *VT*, 18 (1968), 330–71.

12. *Israel in the Books of Chronicles* (Cambridge, 1977), esp. pp. 5–86.

13. R. L. Braun, 'The Message of Chronicles: Rally Round the Temple', *CTM*, 42 (1971), 502–13; 'A Reconstruction of the Chronicler's Attitude toward the North', *JBL*, 96 (1977), 59–62; 'Chronicles, Ezra and Nehemiah: Theology and Literary History', in *Studies in the Historical Books of the Old Testament*, *SVT* 30, ed. J. A. Emerton (Leiden, 1979), pp. 52–64.

14. See his review of Williamson's *Israel in the Books of Chronicles*, *JSOT*, Issue 14 (1979), 68–72.

15. 'Book-Size and the Device of Catch-Lines in the Biblical Canon', *JJS*, 36 (1985), 1–11.

16. R. Polzin, *Late Biblical Hebrew: Toward an Historical Typology of Biblical Hebrew Prose* (Missoula, 1976), pp. 54f.

17. M. A. Throntveit, 'Linguistic Analysis and the Question of Authorship in Chronicles, Ezra and Nehemiah', *VT*, 32 (1982), 201–16.

18. Traditionally, the Chronicler has been dated between 400 and 250 BCE according to whether the later names in the lists were seen to be original to the Chronicler, or the additions of a hand later than his.

19. 'The Chronicler's Purpose', *CBQ*, 23 (1961), 436–42. The citation appears on pp. 439f.

20. 'Old Testament Historiography', p. 154.

21. See F. M. Cross, *The Ancient Library of Qumran*, 2nd edn (New York, 1961), pp. 188–91; 'The History of the Biblical Text in the Light of Discoveries in the Judean Desert', *HTR*, 58 (1964) 281–99; 'The Contribution of the Qumran Discoveries to the Study of the Biblical Text', *IEJ*, 16, 81–95, esp. pp. 84f. W. E. Lemke has pursued this further: 'The Synoptic Problem in the Chronicler's History', *HTR*, 58 (1965), 349–63.

22. Some reserve has to be expressed over the major conclusions of McKenzie's work that the first editor of Chronicles knew the work only of the first editor of the Deuteronomistic History. Indeed, Chronicles, it is argued, can help us to identify the extent of the two editions of the Deuteronomistic History. At such a point, hypothesis is being reared upon hypothesis, conjecture compared with conjecture. What was suggested above about the structure of I & II Chronicles holds

good for the Deuteronomistic History. The various 'stages' in the development of both works are too uncertain to permit of such precision. See further the detailed review of McKenzie by H. G. M. Williamson, *VT*, 37 (1987), 107–14.

2 The addresses in Chronicles

1. This rendering is to be preferred to the reading intended by the vowel pointing of the Massoretes (so giving us the *Qere*, what is to be read, in place of the *Kethib*, the written consonantal text), which wants us to read, 'chief of the thirds' (see II Kgs. 1:13 etc.).
2. *I & II Chronicles, Ezra, Nehemiah*, p. 55.
3. No doubt these chapters are composite in origin and may well be secondary (see n. 21), but their effect, as they now stand, is of full and energetic activity by the king.
4. Since M. Noth's work *Überlieferungsgeschichtliche Studien* (Halle, 1943) (ET *The Deuteronomistic History*, JSOT Supplement Series, 15 (Sheffield, 1981)), it has been widely accepted that Deuteronomy–II Kings forms a unified work which has been finally edited during the period of the Babylonian exile by Deuteronomistic editors. A number of scholars have now questioned Noth's view that it was all the work of one author, however. See, e.g., F. M. Cross, 'The Themes of the Book of Kings and the Structure of the Deuteronomistic History', in *Canaanite Myth and Hebrew Epic* (Cambridge, Mass., 1973); R. D. Nelson, *The Double Redaction of the Deuteronomistic History*, JSOT Supplement Series, 18 (Sheffield, 1981); A. D. H. Mayes, *The Story of Israel between Settlement & Exile* (London, 1983); Porter, 'Old Testament Historiography', pp. 125–62, esp. 132–52.
5. The other two such passages are held to be I Kgs. 8:15ff., 25, 9:3–9. The best exposition of the Deuteronomistic work as 'preaching' to the exiles remains that of E. W. Nicholson. See *Deuteronomy & Tradition* (Oxford, 1967), esp. ch. VI, and, for the material relating to the Deuteronomistic tradition in the Book of Jeremiah, *Preaching to the Exiles* (Oxford, 1970).
6. So Williamson, *1 and 2 Chronicles*, p. 154.
7. *I & II Chronicles, Ezra, Nehemiah*, p. 79.
8. See Josh. 1:13, 15; and see also Deut. 3:20, perhaps a Deuteronomistic section of the Book of Deuteronomy: see A. D. H. Mayes, *Deuteronomy*, NCB (London, 1979), pp. 144ff.
9. See R. E. Clements, *God and Temple* (Oxford, 1965).
10. Exod. c. 33 has proved notoriously difficult to assign to the traditional Pentateuchal sources, and there is no consensus of opinion. See B. S. Childs, *Exodus*, OTL (London, 1974), pp. 584ff.; J. P. Hyatt, *Exodus*, NCB (London, 1971), pp. 312ff.
11. Since this is the main theological concern of the words of David recorded in I

Chr. 23:4f., 25–32, and the purpose of the passage otherwise seems to be to give Davidic sanction for the Levitical orders and certain cultic provisions, they are not treated as a separate 'address'. They reiterate the function of the words already discussed in I 13:2f., 15:2, 12f., and here in 22:6–16.

12. This has been emphasised by R. L. Braun, 'Solomon, the Chosen Temple Builder: The Significance of I Chronicles 22, 28 and 29 for the Theology of the Chronicler', *JBL*, 95 (1976), 581–90. M. A. Throntveit may be right to see I Chr. 23:25 as coming from another hand because it misunderstands the nature of this 'rest' (*When Kings Speak*, p. 87). Generally, however, it follows the idea of David giving the conditions of 'peace' in which Solomon could build the temple.

13. Contra Amit, 'The Role of Prophecy and Prophets', 113–33, and D. J. McCarthy, 'Covenant and Law in Chronicles–Nehemiah', *CBQ*, 44 (1982), 25–44, esp. p. 30.

14. So H. G. M. Williamson, 'The Accession of Solomon in the Books of Chronicles', *VT*, 26 (1976), 351–61, and *1 and 2 Chronicles*, pp. 155f. Williamson sees Deut. 31:7f. and Jos. 1:2–9 especially as passages which the Chronicler has followed closely. So, also, Braun, 'Solomon, the Chosen Temple Builder', 586–8.

15. Since this appears to be the only function of Hiram's words and the reason they are attributed to him by the Chronicler, II 2:12/11 is not dealt with here as a separate 'address'.

16. See references in n. 14. Also D. J. McCarthy, 'An Installation Genre?' *JBL*, 90 (1971), 31–41.

17. 'The Accession of Solomon', 351–61.

18. *1 and 2 Chronicles*, p. 155.

19. See also, e.g., I Kgs. 17:9, 19:5, Jer. 13:4, 6, 18:2, Ezek. 3:22, Jonah 1:2, 3:22 etc.

20. A number of commentators have suggested that vv. 17–19 are a later addition. Rudolph, for example, following Benzinger, sees it as a doublet of cc. 28f., *Chronikbücher*, *HAT* (Tübingen, 1955), pp. 152f. Ackroyd refers to the passage as 'a duplicating statement', *I & II Chronicles, Ezra, Nehemiah*, p. 83. Williamson, however, disagrees, *1 and 2 Chronicles*, p. 157.

21. Among commentators who see these chapters as secondary are Rudolph, *Chronikbücher*, pp. 152ff. Others argue for a mixture of additional sources, some added by the Chronicler himself, the rest by other hands, e.g. Ackroyd, *I & II Chronicles, Ezra, Nehemiah*, p. 81, and J. Myers, *I Chronicles*, The Anchor Bible (New York, 1965), pp. 158f. Williamson sees a double layer, one which was pro-Levitical, from the Chronicler, and the other, which was pro-priestly, added by someone else, *SVT*, 39 (1979), 251–68 (cf. Botterweck, 'Zur Eigenart').

22. So Ackroyd, *I & II Chronicles, Ezra, Nehemiah*, p. 88.

23. So Coggins, *The First and Second Books of the Chronicles*, p. 137.

24. So Williamson, *1 and 2 Chronicles*, p. 136.

25. So Ackroyd, *I & II Chronicles, Ezra, Nehemiah*, p. 90.

26. *1 and 2 Chronicles*, p. 181.

27. It is strange that different renderings of תַּבְנִית occur in most modern English

Versions. NEB has 'design' in Exodus and 'plan' in I Chronicles: RSV, 'pattern' in Exodus and 'plan' in Chronicles; JB follows RSV. No doubt different translation panels are at work, but it obscures the Chronicler's intentional reading of the Exodus material here.

28. Myers sees Deut. 31:6, 8 and Josh. 1:5 being quoted here: *I Chronicles*, p. 193. Cf. Rudolph, *Chronikbücher*, p. 189.

29. André Caquot, 'Peut-on parler de messianisme dans l'œuvre du Chroniste?', *Revue de théologie et de philosophie*, 16 (1966), 110–20. See especially p. 118.

30. Caquot, 'Peut-on parler de messianisme', refers to I Kgs. 11:13, 32, 36, II Kgs. 19:34, 20:6, all of which are omitted in Chronicles. An exception is II Kgs. 8:19 = II Chr. 21:7.

31. As argued by Freedman, 'The Chronicler's Purpose', 436–42; G. von Rad, *Das Geschichtsbild des Chronistischen Werkes, BWANT*, 4th vol., No. 3 (Stuttgart, 1930), 'ist ein starker zug messianischer Erwartung nicht zu verkennen', p. 135; A. M. Brunet, 'La Théologie du Chroniste: théocratie et messianisme', in *Sacra Pagina*, I, ed. J. Coppens *et al.* (Gembloux, 1959), pp. 384–97, argues that for the Chronicler (he includes the books of Ezra/Nehemiah in his work) the Davidic dynasty is an essential element of the theocratic community, p. 388.

32. Caquot, 'Peut-on parler de messianisme', p. 118.

33. *Ibid.*, p. 119. He is speaking of II Chr. 6:41f., with its quotation from Ps. 132; see also I Kgs. 8:50–3.

34. E. L. Curtis, *The Books of Chronicles, ICC*, (Edinburgh, 1910), p. 34 (n. 120).

35. *Ibid.*, p. 303.

36. Rudolph, *Chronikbücher*, p. 189, rightly sees here an allusion to Exod. 36:1. It is another instance of the parallelism which the Chronicler sees between the Mosaic tabernacle and the Solomonic temple, just as he sees the building of the Solomonic temple as a model for the post-exilic reconstruction.

37. E.g. Exod. 1:14; 2:23, 33 etc.; see also Num. 4:23; Exod. 36:2–7.

38. E.g. Josh. 22:27.

39. *I & II Chronicles, Ezra, Nehemiah*, p. 132.

40. Williamson, *Ezra, Nehemiah*, World Bible Commentary (Waco, 1985), pp. lif., shows how the Books of Ezra and Nehemiah bring together acceptance of present political realities and future hope. He bases his observations in part on the prayers of Ezra c. 9 and Neh. c. 9.

41. For the same device in other addresses see, e.g., II Chr. 15:2; 24:20, and also Zech. 1:3; 7:13.

42. Rudolph observes, 'With these prophetic words the Chronicler wishes equally to instruct his own contemporaries' ('Mit diesen Prophetenworten will der Chr. zugleich seine eigenen Zeitgenossen belehren'), *Chronikbücher*, p. 233, while Williamson says, 'It is hard to avoid the impression that the Chronicler is aligning this whole account as closely as he can with the situation of his own readers' (*1 and 2 Chronicles*, p. 248). I have tried to show that is done in the very specific

theological diagnosis he is making of the situation of those contemporaries rather than in the general way in which Rudolph and Williamson speak of it.

43. Such a conclusion runs entirely counter to those arrived at by Weinberg, 'Die "ausser kanonischen Prophezeiungen"', 387–404. Weinberg conducts a most interesting and informative statistical analysis of the prophetic addresses, although he fails to note the close parallels between these extra-canonical prophecies and the very similar passages attributed to those who are not prophets. He argues that the names of the prophets, their titles, the call formulae, the themes, the form of the prophecies and the use of oral formulae all point to a date in the pre- or early monarchic period of Israel. A typical example of the argument is that the use of the catchword 'peace' (שָׁלוֹם) in I Chr. 12:18/19 points to this period because we know that the term belongs to the ancient Jerusalem tradition (pp. 398ff.). It did, but that cannot determine the date of each use of the term in subsequent stages through which the material passed. Such an argument could be used, for example, to show that Isa. 26:3 originated in the pre- or early monarchic period, which is unlikely. Only a full examination of the form and content of these addresses in their relation to the work of the Chronicler as a whole, and to other examples of post-exilic biblical literature, can offer adequate criticism of Weinberg's position. His suggestion that the oracles stemmed from Levitical priestly circles from northern Judah and especially from Jerusalem might not be so wide of the mark if the Chronicler himself came from some such tradition and either composed, or echoed, the kind of material and theological viewpoint which was current among them.

44. Plöger, 'Reden und Gebete', pp. 57f.

45. *When Kings Speak*, pp. 36f., 115f. See also Williamson, *Israel in the Books of Chronicles*, pp. 110–18.

46. See J. Gray, *I & II Kings*, 2nd edn (London, 1970), pp. 347f.

47. So Rudolph, who says, 'If the Chronicler is to allow the king to appear here as the representative of the true Israel then he must naturally omit the adverse verdict passed on him in I Ki. 15:3' ('Lässt der Chronik hier den König als den Anwalt des wahren Israel auftreten, so muss er natürlich das schlechte Urteil dass I Rg. 15:3 über ihn fällt, ausscheltern'). *Chronikbücher*, p. 238.

48. See Caquot, 'Peut-on parler de messianisme', p. 119.

49. There has been considerable discussion about the historicity of this battle. Rudolph says of it that in outline it 'must be historical' (*Chronikbücher*, p. 235), but agrees that the details are the Chronicler's invention (p. 237). Williamson, who cites wide references from those who have discussed the issue, agrees in substance with this, allowing that the account 'bears all the marks of the Chronicler's own ideology and style based on some information additional to the books of Kings' (*1 and 2 Chronicles*, pp. 250f.). Since then an important article by R. W. Klein has appeared, 'Abijah's Campaign against the North (II Chr. 13) – What Were the Chronicler's Sources?', *ZAW*, 95 (1983), 210–17. Klein argues

that II Chr. 13:19 is based on a list of towns in Josh. 18:21–4 which includes Zemaraiam, Bethel and Ephron, while Jeshanah can be reconstructed in Josh. 18:21 with the help of the LXX.

50. Williamson argues that the address offers mitigating circumstances for the North's defection from the Judaean kings and that this gives added force to Abijah's call to them to return. *Israel in the Books of Chronicles*, pp. 110ff.

51. Even the site of Zemaraim remains a mystery. Klaus Koch said in 1962, 'The issue of the location of Zemmaraim has to remain open', 'Zur Lage von Semarajim', *Zeitschrift des Deutschen Palästina-Vereins*, 78 (1962), 29. Sites either in the Jordan valley or in the vicinity of Bethel have been suggested, Dalman favouring the latter, 'Einiger geschichtliche Statten im Norden Jerusalems', *JBL*, 48 (1929), 354–61, esp. pp. 360f.

52. The variation between the bull and two rams mentioned in the Exodus text and the bull and seven rams of II Chr. 13:9 is not easily explicable. It is perhaps always possible that it appears to the Chronicler as yet another perversion of the law by the people of the apostate North.

53. Rudolph takes it that there was some extra-canonical source for this available to the Chronicler, 'Der Aufbau der Asa-Geschichte (2 Chr. xiv–xvi)', *VT*, 2 (1952), 367–71, esp. p. 368.

54. See P. Welten, *Geschichte und Geschichtsdarstellung in den Chronikbüchern*, *WMANT*, 421 (Neukirchen, 1973), esp. pp. 18, 44, 50f.

55. So Ackroyd, *I & II Chronicles, Ezra, Nehemiah*, p. 136.

56. Israel Ben-Shem has attempted to show some historical background to this incident, 'The War of Zerah the Cushite (II Chron. 14:8–14, 16:8)', in *Bible & Jewish History: Studies in Bible and Jewish History Dedicated to the Memory of Jacob Liver*, ed. B. Uffenheimer (Tel-Aviv, 1971), pp. 51–6. See Williamson for further discussion of the issue, *1 and 2 Chronicles*, pp. 263f.

57. Rudolph, *Chronikbücher*, pp. 239ff.

58. Mic. 3:8 is an exception, but it is often regarded as a gloss. See J. L. Mays, *Micah*, OTL (London, 1976), p. 86.

59. E.g. II 20:14; 24:20.

60. Actually the MT reads, 'When Asa heard these words *and* the prophecy, Oded the prophet, he encouraged himself and removed the idols from all the land of Israel.' The *waw* is not a problem since it can be taken as *waw* explicative, giving the sense, 'these words, *that is* the prophecy . . .'. But the absolute form of the noun 'prophecy' remains a difficulty when followed by the proper name 'Oded'. Perhaps some words have dropped out such as 'the prophecy which *Azariah the son of Oded* spoke': cf. Syr. Vulg.

61. See the references to the Chronicler's idea of the nature of prophecy in T. Willi, *Die Chronik als Auslegung. Untersuchungen zur literarischen Gestaltung der historischen Überlieferung Israels*, *FRLANT*, 106 (Göttingen, 1972), pp. 216–19, who says that the practice of citing earlier prophetic material in the addresses

gives them greater authority. He describes Azariah's address in this respect as a typical 'Rabbinic method' (p. 226). Similarly Seeligman, 'Die Auffassung', says, 'For the Chronicler the prophets possess such great authority, that he undertakes a midrashic actualising of their words' (p. 273, 'Die Propheten besitzen also für den Verfasser der Chronik eine so grosse Autorität, dass er eine midraschartige Aktualisierung ihre Worte vornimmt'). He adds that even the plural form of address, 'Hear me!' (שְׁמָעוּנִי), follows the prophetic practice of addressing the whole community (p. 274.). For the views of C. Westermann, see n. 71.

62. See Nicholson, *Preaching to the Exiles*, pp. 97ff.
63. Rudolph, for example, finds a number of close parallels here to Judges:

    3b = Judg. 2:11–14
    3b = Judg. 17:16; 21:25
    5a = Judg. 5:6; 6:2ff.
    5 = Judg. 8:5–9, 15–17; 9:1, 2, 4ff.; cc. 20f.
    4 = Judg. 2:18; 3:9, 15; 6:6bff.; 10:9bff.

64. J. Weingreen, 'The Title Moreh Sedek', *JJS*, 6 (1961), 171.
65. 'Thora in den biblischen Chronikbüchern', *Judaica*, 36 (1980), 102–5, 148–51, esp. p. 104.
66. See the discussion referred to in Chapter 1, pp. 9f. above.
67. We are a long way here from Ben Sirach. See Ecclus. 38:1–15.
68. Rudolph, 'Der Aufbau der Asa-Geschichte', 367–71.
69. Welten, *Geschichte und Geschichtsdarstellung*, esp. p. 140.
70. *I & II Chronicles, Ezra, Nehemiah*, pp. 135f.; see also pp. 162, 166f. etc.
71. See Westermann, *Basic Forms of Prophetic Speech*, pp. 142–58, 170–6. Nevertheless, this is one of the prophetic oracles of which Westermann says they 'have practically nothing in common with the original forms of the individual judgement speech and are no more than the forms used to express the Chronicler's interpretation of history' (p. 163), while of the oracles of Shemaiah and Azariah he says, 'the prophets express the thesis of the Chronicler's view of history so plainly ... that one must at least reckon with a transformation by the Chronicler, but probably with his own construction' (p. 164).
72. See J. Day, 'Asherah in the Hebrew Bible and North West Semitic Literature', *JBL*, 105 (1986), 385–408.
73. So, for example, Williamson, *Israel in the Books of Chronicles*, p. 67; Japhet, 'The Supposed Common Authorship', 330–71.
74. So D. J. McCarthy, 'The Ancient Near Eastern Background of the Love of God in Deuteronomy', *CBQ*, 29 (1967), 77–87; *Old Testament Covenant: A Survey of Current Opinions* (Oxford, 1973), p. 15; N. Lohfink, 'Hate and Love in Osée 9:15', *CBQ*, 25 (1963), 417.
75. The VSS suggest a slight emendation of MT so as to give, 'The LORD loves those who hate evil.' While this may offer a better parallel to the following lines in

which Yahweh is the subject, the effect of the lines, even so, is that of an imperative call to avoid evil if the love of Yahweh (subjective or objective) is to be real.

76. Williamson has emphasised this theme in the chapter in relation to David's choice as king by Yahweh. See '"We are Yours, O David" (1 Chr. 12:1–23)', *OTS*, 21 (1981), 164–76.

77. R. Micheel says, 'קצף conforms to the Chronicler's vocabulary. Of the twenty-seven times this term appears in the OT, seven occur in the Chronicler's writing' ('קצף entspricht dem chronistischen Sprachgebrauch. Von den 27 mal, die diese Vokabel im AT vorkommt, entfallen allein sieben Stellen auf die Chronik'). *Die Scher- und Propheten-Überlieferungen in den Chronik, Beiträge zur biblischen Exegese und Theologie*, No. 18 (Frankfurt & Bern, 1983), p. 108 (n. 3).

78. McCarthy, 'Covenant and Law', 25–44, esp. pp. 27f.

79. This characteristic of the Chronicler's writing has often been discussed. See, e.g., G. von Rad, ET D. G. M. Stalker, *Old Testament Theology* (Edinburgh & London), 1 (1962), pp. 348ff. Von Rad is, however, wrong to say that this means 'that the Chronicler has lost sight of the understanding of Israel's history as a unity' (p. 350). He fails to see the binding theological structure which has been stressed by Mosis and Ackroyd, among others.

80. *Gesammelte Studien*, pp. 252f.; *Problem of the Hexateuch*, pp. 271f.

81. M. A. Throntveit also notes this. 'The speeches of Jehoshaphat ... do not fit as neatly into our categories as the Chronicler's other speeches' (*When Kings Speak*, p. 48). He divides the royal speeches into three types: (a) 'Edicts', in which a specific audience is addressed and an imperative or its equivalent calls for immediate action; (b) 'Rationales', which lack those characteristics but give a reason for some cultic action, and (c) 'Orations', which address a specific audience, employ an imperative or equivalent, but are longer than the Edicts. Unlike the other forms they do not mark significant turning-points in the Chronicler's structure of history. Jehoshaphat's address is assigned to the Orations. The general argument is discussed on p. 135 below.

82. There are many problems associated with the account of Jehoshaphat's reforms narrated here, but not in the Deuteronomistic History, and their relation to Exod. 18:19ff. and Deuteronomy. Wellhausen dismissed any historical truth to them, seeing the whole episode as based on the king's name, *Prolegomena zur Geschichte Israels* (Berlin, 1883), p. 186. Others, while questioning v. 4 and seeing the Chronicler's own hand in the parenetic material of vv. 6f., 9f., and 11b, with its close paralleling of some Deuteronomic material, yet believe that some of the details in vv. 5, 8 and, for some, v. 11a, suggest a situation earlier than that of Deuteronomy, so going back to an actual legal reform from Jehoshaphat's time. These include R. Knierim, 'Exodus 18 und die Neuordnung der Mosaischen Gerichtsbarkeit', *ZAW*, 73 (1961), 146–71. He argues that the details envisaged in Exod. 18:21b, 25b were earlier than the time of Josiah's reform and represent an attempt to give an aetiological explanation for a situation which had prevailed

for a long time. G. C. Macholz, 'Zur Geschichte der Justizorganisation in Juda', *ZAW*, 84 (1972), 314–40, argues that II Chr. 19:5–11 is a reliable witness to an actual reform by Jehoshaphat in the mid nineteenth century, which brought all earlier judicial organisation into a single, centrally organised 'state' system, while Deut. 16:19, 17:8–12 represents attempts to reform the system excluding the king's influence. Also supporting the general case for historicity are A. J. Phillips, *Ancient Israel's Criminal Law* (Oxford, 1970), pp. 18ff.; A. D. H. Mayes, *Deuteronomy*, New Century Bible, London, 1979, pp. 261–269; K. G. Whitelam, *The Just King* (Sheffield, 1979), 185–206; Myers, *II Chronicles*, p. 108; Williamson, *1 and 2 Chronicles*, pp. 287–91; Rudolph, *Chronikbücher*, pp. 257f. It is, however, difficult to avoid the impression, as I argue below, that, at least in v. 11a, the Chronicler is depicting a situation which obtained in the post-exilic period, for we have no other evidence of a division of responsibility between 'chief priests' and 'governor' earlier.

83. There is a general discussion of this theme in H. D. Preuss, '. . . ich will mit dir sein!', *ZAW*, 80 (1986), 139–73. He argues that the phrase is used mainly in post-exilic times. As we observe in these addresses, however, their application is extended well beyond the theme of war, which Preuss sees as of most importance.

84. J. M. Myers says that 'the strong religious emphasis is throughout testifying once more to the principle of social solidarity governed by the cultic interests of the writer' (*II Chronicles*, p. 108).

85. So M. Noth, *Exodus*, OTL (London, 1962), p. 150; G. Beer, *Exodus*, *HAT* (Tübingen, 1939), p. 95.

86. 'Exodus', IB, 1 (1966), 966; cf. Hyatt, *Exodus*, p. 193.

87. The exact relationship between Exod. 18 and the reforms of Jehoshaphat is complex (see n. 73 above). While those like Macholz who see the Exodus passage as being dependent on a knowledge of an historical reform by Jehoshaphat may be right, equally the Chronicler could be using it in an hermeneutic, expository fashion to give authority for his picture of the reforms.

88. Beuken, *Haggai–Sacharja 1–8*, pp. 46, 50–60.

89. 'An Installation Genre?', pp. 31–41.

90. This is one of the oracles which Westermann, in spite of his claim that the oracles owe much to the Chronicler's own composition (see n. 71), believes to contain a good, genuine prophetic tradition (*Basic Forms of Prophetic Speech*, p. 163). He quotes with approval von Rad's words that 'the promise of success in the holy war is preserved here in a manner astonishingly close to the very old speech forms from the holy war'. Apparently neither sees that the old speech forms may be imitated by a later writer to claim the authenticity of antiquity for his teaching.

91. Assuming this a reasonable emendation of the twice-repeated 'Ammonites' in the MT. Williamson sees the reference as to people living west of the Arabah. *1 and 2 Chronicles*, p. 294.

92. II Kgs. c.3 cannot be deemed in any way a *Vorlage* for this: the differences are too great.

93. M. Noth, 'Eine palästinische Lokalüberlieferung in 2 Chr. 20:20', *Zeitschrift des Deutschen Palästina-Vereins*, 67 (1945), 45–71, asserts that the formal characteristics, the dependence on the Deuteronomistic History and the play on words from the prophetic books and the Psalms all show this to be 'from beginning to end the Chronicler's composition' (p. 47). He rejects Benzinger's suggestion (*Die Bücher der Chronik*, HKAT (Tübingen & Leipzig, 1901), p. 107) that v. 19, with its reference to the Levites, meant that the Chronicler had a written *Vorlage*, yet he believes that the Chronicler did get his material from somewhere. He believes that it must have been associated with an incursion of Nabataean tribes in the latter half of the fourth century or the beginning of the third. This must remain entirely hypothetical.

94. S. J. de Vries, 'Temporal Terms as Structural Elements in the Holy War Tradition', *VT*, 25 (1975), 80–105.

95. Ackroyd, *I & II Chronicles, Ezra, Nehemiah*, p. 148.

96. B. S. Childs, '*A Study of the Formula "Unto This Day"*', *JBL*, 82 (1963), 279–92.

97. Perhaps this theological theme is also familiar from the liturgy. Ps. 84:6/7, speaking of the pilgrimage to Zion, reads:

> As they go through the valley of Baca [perhaps
> 'valley of weeping' if the MT is pointed
> differently]
> they make it a place of springs;
> the early rain also covers it with blessings [or
> 'pools'. Yet the VSS already read, by a different
> pointing, 'blessings', and at the least this may
> represent a play on words or early exegesis of the
> Psalm.]

98. *I & II Chronicles, Ezra, Nehemiah*, p. 148. Further, we have to note that the genealogy traces Jahaziel's descent back to the time of David. See D. L. Petersen, *Late Israelite Prophecy: Studies in Deutero-Prophetic Literature and in Chronicles* (Missoula, 1977), p. 73.

99. See A. R. Johnson, *The Cultic Prophet in Ancient Israel*, 2nd edn (Cardiff, 1962), pp. 72f.

100. A. Schmitt, 'Das prophetische Sondergut in II Chr. xx 14–17', in *Künder des Wortes: Festschrift für J. Schreiner*, ed. L. Ruppert *et al.* (Würzburg, 1982), pp. 273–83. Cf. Williamson, *1 and 2 Chronicles*, pp. 297f., who sees this in terms of 'an oracle of salvation' associated with the holy war, rather than a 'Levitical Sermon' in the strict sense.

101. Petersen argues for an imitation of an ancient 'holy war' priestly oracle here. *Late Israelite Prophecy*, pp. 73–7.

102. In *Biblical Interpretation*, pp. 386f., Fishbane sees the words of Jahaziel as an echo of Isaiah's oracle to Ahaz in Isa. 7:4, 7.

103. Fishbane usefully draws attention to v. 8, which reflects the Chronicler's emphasis that 'the people' (all Israel) built the temple, whereas Kings stresses that Solomon built it (*Biblical Interpretation*, p. 386, n. 12).

104. See above, pp. 38ff. on Abijah's address, II 13:4.

105. See above, p. 23.

106. See Fishbane, *Biblical Interpretation*, pp. 386f., 408: 'prophetic oracles such as that enunciated by Isaiah in 7:9b reappear transformed in the mouth of laymen giving exhortation (cf. 2 Chron. 20:20b)' (p. 414).

107. Seeligman, 'Die Auffassung', p. 273.

108. Williamson, *1 and 2 Chronicles*, p. 303: Willi, *Die Chronik als Auslegung*, p. 219.

109. It now seems generally agreed that 'Tarshish' in such references is an adjective describing a type of large, sea-going vessel rather than a proper noun denoting a destination. See Gray, *I & II Kings*, p. 267.

110. Coggins says of this address, 'It may be that there were those in his [i.e. the Chronicler's] own day who wished to pursue a more active policy than the quietism which seems to have characterized the Jewish community', *The First and Second Books of the Chronicles*, p. 226. Rather more literally, R. B. Dillard says that enemies from the past (e.g. the Nabataeans) may have been posing a new threat in the Chronicler's day. Nevertheless, Dillard sees in the 'holy war' motif of such passages an eschatological hope in the Persian period for Yahweh's eventual intervention. *2 Chronicles*, p. 161.

111. E.g. Jer. 1:16; Pss. 115:4; 135:15; Hos. 14:3/4. See P. R. Ackroyd, 'Yad', in *Theologisches Wörterbuch zum Alten Testament*, ed. G. J. Botterweck u. H. Ringgren, Band II, Lieferung 4, Spalt 455 (Stuttgart, 1975); ET D. E. Green, *Theological Dictionary of the Old Testament* (Grand Rapids, MI, 1986), Vol. V, p. 426.

112. *Basic Forms of Prophetic Speech*, p. 167.

113. See II Kgs. 1:17. It seems that the reference to the accession of Jehoram to the throne of Israel in 'the second year of Jehoram, the son of Jehoshaphat, king of Judah', if it has any historical validity at all, can only refer to the second year of a co-regency of the Judaean Jehoram with his father, Jehoshaphat. See Gray, *I & II Kings*, pp. 66f.

114. R. Kittel, *Die Bücher der Chronik und Esra, Nehemia und Esther*, HAT (Göttingen, 1902), p. 143.

115. So Ackroyd, *I & II Chronicles, Ezra, Nehemiah*, p. 153.

116. So Myers, *II Chronicles*, p. 120.

117. Rudolph, *Chronikbücher*, p. 267.

118. *Ibid.*, p. 267. Williamson, however, maintains that this cannot refer to an assault on Jerusalem since v. 3 has shown it was Jehoram's policy to station his family in the various fortified cities of Judah. *1 and 2 Chronicles*, p. 308.

119. We have also the strange variation in the name of the younger son. Apparently the Chronicler used the name 'Ahaziah' (22:1). Does the use of the name 'Jehoahaz' (21:17) suggest an earlier source (so Williamson, *1 and 2 Chronicles*, p. 308), or that Ahaziah was a throne name?

120. Other passages claiming 'sons' as signs of God's blessing include I Chr. 14:3–7; II 11:18–23; 13:21.

121. Williamson comments similarly that the device of a 'letter' sent by Elijah 'will have been attractive to him because in the books of Kings, Elijah stands as the champion of Yahwism against the inroads of Baalism into the northern kingdom', *1 and 2 Chronicles*, p. 306.

122. Rudolph rightly refers to the letter as a *Drohwort* ('threat of judgement'), *Chronikbücher*, p. 267.

123. See Ackroyd, *I & II Chronicles, Ezra, Nehemiah*, p. 154.

124. Shaul Zalevski, 'The Change of Policy of Joash and the Prophecy of Zechariah, Son of Jehoida (II Chronicles xxiv 17–22)', *Bar-Ilan*, 13 (1976), 31–57, sees the Chronicler's account of Joash's reign as a unity, rightly refusing to accept any attempt to explain the 'unfavourable' elements as being due to a secondary source. But he attributes the change to historical causes, possibly growing tension between the king and the priestly line or, more probably, prophetic opposition to a change of foreign policy to one of alliance with Israel against Syria. The historical evidence on which such a change of policy is based is slight, however, and Ackroyd (*I & II Chronicles, Ezra, Nehemiah*, p. 158) and Coggins (*The First and Second Books of the Chronicles*, p. 238) more persuasively see theological factors at work in the Chronicler's presentation of a judgement/salvation motif. R. Micheel (*Die Seher- und Propheten-Überlieferungen*, pp. 57f.) argues that the whole account of Joash's reign is the work of the Chronicler and not due to an alternative source. This in reaction to Bright, who argued for the possibility of such a source (*History of Israel* (London, 1960), p. 237n.). However, in subsequent editions of his work (2nd edn (1972), p. 252; 3rd edn (1980), p. 255), Bright withdrew the footnote making this suggestion, while still maintaining that there was probably some historical truth behind the Chronicler's account.

125. See also the comments of Williamson at this point, *1 and 2 Chronicles*, p. 319 and Dillard, *2 Chronicles*, p. 164.

126. So *BHS*.

127. *The Books of Chronicles*, pp. 142f. Ackroyd says that perhaps there should be a change of subject understood in v. 13: 'they (the mercenaries) fell upon the cities of Judah . . . but they (the Judeans) killed three thousand of them' (*I & II Chronicles*, p. 164). R. B. Dillard leaves the text unamended and takes the sense, as I have done, as ironic (*2 Chronicles*, pp. 196f.).

128. E. Junge, *Der Wiederaufbau des Heerwesens des Reiches Juda unter Josia* (Stuttgart, 1937), although he assigns this incident to the time of Josiah. See Williamson, *1 and 2 Chronicles*, pp. 261ff.

129. Micheel sees no real inconsistency between the account of the attack by the mercenaries on the cities of Judah on the one hand, and the victory over the Edomites on the other. This 'mixed bag' of blessing and judgement from Yahweh is the divine response to the 'mixed' attitude of Amaziah already shown towards Yahweh even before the mention of his bringing back the Edomite gods with him. *Die Seher- und Propheten-Überlieferungen*, p. 63.

130. We should note the view of Welten that such 'sources' were the Chronicler's invention. Welten, *Geschichte und Geschichtsdarstellung*, pp. 79–114. But see also the objections raised by Williamson, *1 and 2 Chronicles*, pp. 262f.

131. E.g. I Chr. 5:10, 19; 20:4; II Chr. 11:4; 13:12 (where there is a direct contrast between God being 'with' his people so that others must not fight 'with', i.e. 'against' God); 17:10 etc.

132. Rudolph, *Chronikbücher*, p. 283.

133. P. R. Ackroyd, 'A Judgement Narrative Between Kings and Chronicles? An Approach to Amos 7:9–17', in *Canon & Authority*, ed. G. W. Coats and B. O. Long (Philadelphia, 1977), p. 81. Williamson (*1 and 2 Chronicles*, p. 330) is not impressed by the points of contact between these passages which, he says, are so general as to make direct dependence unlikely: 'it may simply be that, perhaps even unconsciously, these earlier narratives have themselves exerted some influence on his [i.e. the Chronicler's] shaping of the narrative'. But is not this a way in which familiar and authoritative material exercises its influence and so gives rise to 'exegesis' in the broadest sense? For example, much prayer is full of echoes of biblical phrases and applies those phrases in a new situation without the speaker consciously calling particular passages to the forefront of his mind.

134. As Rudolph does, *Chronikbücher*, p. 287.

135. E.g. II Sam. 6:16–19; I Kgs. 8:14; 12:25–33.

136. See the discussion of Zech. 3:6ff. below, pp. 205ff. It is significant that in his version of II Sam. 6:16–19 the Chronicler omits reference to David sacrificing the burnt offerings and peace offerings, I Chr. 16:1.

137. For a fuller discussion of the treatment of Hezekiah see P. R. Ackroyd, 'The Biblical Interpretation of the Reigns of Ahaz and Hezekiah', in *In the Shadow of Elyon: Essays in Honour of G. W. Ahlström*, JSOT Supp. 31 (Sheffield, 1984), pp. 247–59.

138. Coggins, *The First and Second Books of the Chronicles*, p. 258.

139. So, e.g., Gray, *I & II Kings*, pp. 635, 638.

140. So J. Robinson, *The Second Book of Kings*, The Cambridge Bible Commentary (Cambridge, 1976), p. 150.

141. *I & II Chronicles, Ezra, Nehemiah*, p. 175.

142. *1 and 2 Chronicles*, p. 345. Williamson, however, allows that the Chronicler 'has used it [i.e. the historical source] freely to convey his particular interpretation of the reign of Ahaz'. *Ibid.*, p. 345.

143. *Chronikbücher*, p. 289.

144. Micheel says of this, 'Only because Yahweh is angry with Judah does he permit Israel to be victorious over it' ('Nur weil Jahwe zornig ist über Judah liess er Israel über es siegen'), *Die Seher- und Propheten-Überlieferungen*, p. 61.

145. Throntveit attributes this to the fact that Hezekiah's reign sees a return to the united Davidic Kingdom, ruling over North and South, although the speech in II 32:7f. is the one which marks this, following his call to the people of the North

to come to the central Passover. This periodisation of history is shown by the close parallels between Abijah's appeal to the people of the North (II 13:4–13) and Hezekiah's (II 30:6–9), *When Kings Speak*, pp. 113–20. Williamson had also seen this 'structuring' in the Chronicler's view of history, *Israel in the Books of Chronicles*, pp. 97–131, as did Plöger, 'Reden und Gebete', pp. 37f.

146. For a comparison of this account with those in II Kings and elsewhere, see B. S. Childs, *Isaiah and the Assyrian Crisis*, SBT, II, 3 (London, 1967), pp. 104–11. See also P. R. Ackroyd, 'Historians and Prophets', in *Svensk Exegetisk Aarsbok*, 33 (Lund, 1968), pp. 18–54 = *Studies in the Religious Tradition of the Old Testament* (London, 1987), pp. 121–51; also 'An Interpretation of the Babylonian Exile: A Study of II Kings 20, Isaiah 38–39', *SJT*, 27 (1974), 329–52.

147. So, e.g., A. C. Welch, *The Work of the Chronicler, its Purpose and its Date* (London, 1939), pp. 103ff. On the other hand, Büchler, *ZAW* (1899), 109ff., has argued that it was the Levites who added to the original narrative. Substantially the same view has been advanced by M. Noth, *Überlieferungsgeschichtliche Studien I. Die sammelnden und bearbeitenden Geschichtswerke im Alten Testament* (Halle, 1943); ET H. G. M. Williamson, *The Chronicler's History*, JSOT Supplement Series, 15 (Sheffield, 1987), esp. p. 33, where cc. 23–7 are seen as additions whose purpose was 'to trace back to David the origins of the late post-exilic divisions of the various cultic servants'. T. Willi makes a similar point, *Die Chronik als Auslegung*, esp. pp. 194–204.

148. So, for example, Rudolph, who says that the stress on the Levites shows where the Chronicler's heart is (*Chronikbücher*, p. 293). Nevertheless, it is clear that the priests offer the sacrifice (v. 24) so that in the address (v. 5) 'Levites' must stand for 'priests and Levites'. See also Kittel, *Die Bücher der Chronik*, p. 160: 'by the use of the term "Levites" v. 5 thinks naturally of both groups, Priests and Levites' ('v. 5 denkt natürlich mit den Leviten an beide Teile, Priester und Leviten, vgl. 30:27'). The fact that in v. 12 the Levites are mentioned first 'means nothing more than that the author had a special preference for them' ('beweist nicht mehr als die besondere Vorliebe des Verfassers für sie, vgl. v. 34'), p. 160.

149. Learned speculation on whether this is the first month after his coming to the throne, or the first of his full regnal year, seems unnecessary. Coggins is much nearer the mark when he says, 'of all those whom the Chronicler especially praises – David, Hezekiah, the returning exiles [he might well have added Josiah to the list, 34:3] – it is stressed that they began their work at the first opportunity', *The First and Second Books of the Chronicles*, p. 266.

150. See R. Mosis, *Untersuchungen zur Theologie des chronistischen Geschichtswerkes*, (Freiburg & Basle, 1973), pp. 29f., and Ackroyd, 'The Chronicler as Exegete', 7.

151. It is interesting to note that the term is divided almost equally among the prose and poetic passages in the Book of Jeremiah, whatever deduction we may draw from this for the very interesting question of the relation between the two.

152. Ackroyd, *I & II Chronicles, Ezra, Nehemiah*, p. 181.

153. See Williamson, *1 and 2 Chronicles*, pp. 353ff.

154. See Z. W. Falk, 'Gestures Expressing Affirmation', *JSS*, 4 (1959), 268f.

155. See Rudolph, *Chronikbücher*, pp. 299f., who contrasts this with the somewhat 'Pharisaic' address of Abijah in 13:4ff. Others, however, point to the strong parallels between the two addresses and the importance of this for the structuring of the Chronicler's history. See n. 145 above.

156. The issues concern the historicity of such a Passover in Hezekiah's reign or whether it may not represent a projection of Josiah's Passover back into the reign of a king who is such a hero for the Chronicler; whether this was originally an account of a Feast of Unleavened Bread, and the dating of the festival in the 'second month'. See the discussion in the commentaries.

157. This is well demonstrated by Carol Meyers, 'Jachin and Boaz in Religious and Political Perspective', *CBQ*, 45 (1983), 167f.

158. E.g. Williamson, *Israel in the Books of Chronicles*, pp. 119–25. Throntveit argues that the figure of Hezekiah in Chronicles is an ideal amalgam of David *and* Solomon, *When Kings Speak*, p. 124.

159. W. L. Holladay, *The Root Sûbh in the Old Testament with Particular Reference to its Usage in Covenantal Contexts* (Leiden, 1958).

160. These passages are often assigned to the Priestly Writing. However, many have argued that Exod. cc. 35–40 represents a secondary strand in P. So Noth, *Exodus*, pp. 274f.: Hyatt, *Exodus*, p. 27. Earlier commentators to note this included Baentsch, *Exodus–Leviticus–Numeri*, *HAT* (Göttingen, 1903), pp. 286f.; Holzinger, *Exodus*, *KAT* (Tübingen, 1900), p. 148. See also Childs, *Exodus*, pp. 529–37.

161. 'Das Barometer für den religiösen Eifer einer Gemeinde ist stets die Willigkeit und Pünktlichkeit im Bezahlen der nötigen Abgeben' (*Chronikbücher*, p. 307).

162. Childs, *Isaiah and the Assyrian Crisis*, pp. 104–11.

163. 'This process functions in terms of a dialectic movement which proceeds from the interpreter to the text and *vice versa*, from the text to the interpreter.' *Ibid.*, p. 107. Ackroyd has argued that the Chronicler's treatment of these incidents in Hezekiah's life can be understood only as the interpretation of a text already familiar to writer and reader (*I & II Chronicles, Ezra, Nehemiah*, pp. 189f. See also the references in n. 127). Wilkinson thinks it unlikely that the Chronicler had access to any other source, 'Ancient Jerusalem: Its Water Supply and Population', *PEQ* (1974), 33ff.

164. See above, pp. 24ff.

165. See A. R. Johnson, *The Vitality of the Individual in the Thought of Ancient Israel*, 2nd edn (Cardiff, 1964), pp. 50ff.

166. So Myers, *II Chronicles*, p. 212; Williamson, *1 and 2 Chronicles*, p. 404; Rudolph, *Chronikbücher*, p. 235. See also 29:34; 30:3.

167. The two references often cited to show that the Levites had such a role in this time must be treated with caution. In II 17:7–9 'princes' (שָׂרִים) are mentioned as being assigned a special role by Jehoshaphat in teaching, while the Levites (including two 'priests') are spoken of in a way which suggests a somewhat

subsidiary role. Similarly, Neh. 8:7f. need not imply that this was the general practice of all Levites. It may have been a more specific task assigned to a few for the one occasion. See Mathias, '"Levitische Predigt" und Deuterismus', esp. pp. 40f. Equally, II 35:3 might suggest that only some Levites 'taught all Israel'. However, the three references, taken together, make it likely that there was *some* Levitical 'preaching' known in the period of the second temple, even if not all Levites necessarily fulfilled such a role, and if others besides Levites also engaged in it.

168. So Ackroyd, *I & II Chronicles, Ezra, Nehemiah*, p. 204.
169. *Israel in the Books of Chronicles*, p. 9; *1 and 2 Chronicles*, p. 419.
170. 'The Supposed Common Authorship', 338–41.
171. So Coggins, *The First and Second Books of the Chronicles*, p. 309; Ackroyd, *I & II Chronicles, Ezra, Nehemiah*, p. 210.
172. So, e.g. Myers, *II Chronicles*, p. 224; Rudolph, *Chronikbücher*, p. 338.
173. See Braun, 'Chronicles, Ezra and Nehemiah', pp. 52–64, and especially these words on p. 62: 'It is possible that material significant for the understanding of the Chronicler's conception of the monarchy and to some extent the conclusion of his history is to be found in the writer's depiction of Cyrus... Is it possible that the Chronicler, like Second Isaiah (Isa. xlv 1, lv 3) has reinterpreted the "everlasting covenant" with David, and now views the Persian Cyrus as the founder of the rebuilt temple and the guarantee of Israel's existence in Palestine?'

3 Summary of the addresses

1. See above, pp. 78f.
2. See above, pp. 24f.
3. See above, p. 48.
4. See above, pp. 98f.
5. See S. Japhet, *Das Land Israel in biblischer Zeit: Jerusalem-Symposium 1981 der Hebräischen Universität und der Georg-August-Universität*, ed. G. Strecker, Göttinger Theologische Arbeiten, 25 (1983), pp. 103ff.
6. See, for example, *Studies in Deuteronomy*. SBT, 9 (London, 1953), pp. 66f., an English translation by D. Stalker of *Deuteronomium-Studien* (Göttingen, 1948).
7. See above, n. 167, pp. 279f.
8. See D. Mathias, '"Levitische Predigt" und Deuterismus', 23–49, esp. pp. 29f.
9. D. L. Petersen, *Late Israelite Prophecy*, pp. 68–77.
10. See especially the address of Abijah, II Chr. 13, discussed above on pp. 38ff.
11. A useful study of the way in which the prophets came to be regarded in the postexilic and later eras of Judaism and Christianity is supplied by J. Barton, *Oracles of God* (London, 1986).
12. D. L. Petersen, *The Roles of Israel's Prophets*, JSOT Supp. 17 (Sheffield, 1981).
13. R. R. Wilson, *Prophecy and Society in Ancient Israel* (Philadelphia, 1980), pp. 191f., 292–4.

14. See comments on Ackroyd's arguments, p. 65.
15. Although Westermann allows that there may be some genuine remnants of old judgement oracles in the words of the 'prophets' in Chronicles, he is clear that the real intention of the Chronicler in including the prophetic speeches was to give divine authority to his interpretation of history. *Basic Forms of Prophetic Speech*, p. 166.
16. See the discussion of this genre in the addresses, pp. 24f.
17. See 'The Levitical Sermon', p. 278.
18. 'Some Echoes of the Preaching?', 221–35.
19. D. Mathias, in particular, has strongly, and with justice, criticised von Rad for failing to do this. '"Levitische Predigt" und der Deuterismos', 43ff.
20. See above, p. 2.
21. Fishbane, *Biblical Interpretation*, p. 77.
22. J. Blenkinsopp, *Prophecy and Canon* (Notre Dame, 1977), pp. 132ff.
23. See M. Dibelius, 'The Speeches in Acts and Ancient Historiography', in *Studies in the Acts of the Apostles*, ed. H. Greeven (London, 1956), pp. 138–45.

4 The 'speeches' in the Books of Ezra and Nehemiah

1. The meaning of the phrase 'some of all his place' is discussed by H. L. Ginsberg, 'Ezra 1:4', *JBL*, 79 (1960), 167–9. He believes it means that any Jew who could not afford to return would be helped by his Babylonian neighbours. This is rejected by Williamson, *Ezra, Nehemiah*, pp. 14f., although he believes that an editor has extended the meaning of the decree in v. 6 (see n. 2 below).
2. See G. W. Coats, 'Despoiling the Egyptians', *VT*, 18 (1968), 450–7. The typology of this has also been used by Second Isaiah. See B. W. Anderson, 'Exodus Typology in Second Isaiah', in *Israel's Prophetic Heritage*, ed. B. W. Anderson and W. Harrelson (London, 1962), pp. 177, 195. Williamson, *Ezra, Nehemiah*, p. 16, believes that the use of the phrase 'all their neighbours' in v. 6 extends the sense of the original decree to bring this motif in.
3. J. M. Myers, *Ezra, Nehemiah*, The Anchor Bible (New York, 1965), pp. 7f.
4. The break in historical order in Ezr. c. 4 from the rebuilding of the temple under the inspiration of Zerubbabel and Joshua in the time of Cyrus (vv. 2–4), through opposition in the reign of Xerxes (v. 6) to the time of the rebuilding of the wall in the time of Artaxerxes (vv. 7–23), only to conclude with the stopping of the rebuilding of the temple between the reigns of Cyrus and Darius, in v. 24, used to be paraded as an example of the 'Chronicler's' hopelessly confused understanding of the history of the period. More often now, however, it is recognised that these are examples of opposition at all stages of the people's fortunes, and Rudolph suggests that the original Hebrew of the Aramaic כְּזֹאת was בֵּאדַיִן, and was to be translated '*In the same way* work on the house of God was stopped ...' (*Ezra und Nehemia samt 3 Esra* (Tübingen, 1949), pp. 35f.). Recent discussion is summarised by Williamson (*Ezra, Nehemiah*, pp. 56f.), who similarly argues that

the 'whereupon' of v. 24 is an example of 'repetitive resumption'. The possibility of a wide survey of Israel's history after the exile being presented in Ezra 1–6 is argued by A. H. J. Gunneweg, 'Zur Interpretation der Bücher Esra–Nehemia: Zugleich ein Beitrag zur Methode der Exegese', *SVT*, 32 (1981), 146–61. Gunneweg argues that the whole account of the return in Ezr. 1–6 with the restoration of the temple, in spite of all opposition from 'the opponents of Judah and Benjamin', is the focal point of the narrative, which he attributes to the Chronicler. The completion of both temple and walls is the work of the 'true and entire Israel', a point underlined by the close resemblance between the list of those who returned with Ezra and those who built the walls with Nehemiah (Ezr. 2:2ff. = Neh. 7:7ff.). This is not so far from the view of Williamson, who sees the final arrangement of the Books of Ezra and Nehemiah as a narrative in four 'chapters' which illustrate external opposition to the initial rebuilding sanctioned by the Persian king (Ezr. 1–6); internal opposition to the ministry of Ezra, also sanctioned by the Persian authorities (Ezr. 7–10); the parallel ministry of Nehemiah, sanctioned by the Persian king, together with external opposition (Neh. 1–7); and the triumphant restoration of the temple, city and people, in which 11:1–20, closely parallel to Ezr. 6, brings the united work of Ezra and Nehemiah to its conclusion. Neh. 13, however, is a reminder that this work, which has had the powerful support of the Gentile overlords, suffers also not only from external opposition, but from the continuing failure of the people. These combined notes of 'victory' and 'weakness' present a theological picture of the 'Now, but not yet . . .' part-fulfilment of the divine purpose which the community experience in the present.

5. Such issues are discussed in the commentaries, but are peripheral to our interests here.

6. For the symbolic value of the temple vessels to this theme of 'continuity' see P. R. Ackroyd, 'Continuity and Discontinuity: Rehabilitation and Authentication', in *Tradition and Theology in the Old Testament*, ed. G. Knight (Philadelphia & London, 1977), pp. 215–34 = *Studies in the Religious Tradition of the Old Testament* (London, 1987), pp. 31–45.

7. A recent variation of this view is that of Williamson, who believes that the remarkable details of the decree could occur because it came in response to a detailed Jewish petition (*Ezra, Nehemiah*, pp. 11, 80, 82). See n. 8 below for further references relevant to the issue.

8. This was suggested by E. Meyer, *Die Entstehung des Judentums* (Halle, 1896), p. 65; H. H. Schaeder, *Esra der Schreiber* (Tübingen, 1930), p. 55; Rudolph, *Esra und Nehemia samt 3 Esra*, pp. 73, 76. Gunneweg, 'Zur Interpretation', 151, argues from the suggestion that the author was Ezra that this decree is 'authentically Chronistic', and cites C. C. Torrey on this point with approval. Torrey wrote, 'The letter of Artaxerxes to Ezra (7:12–26) was created entirely by the Chronicler' (*Ezra Studies* (Chicago, 1910), p. 157). D. J. Clines says that

'short of suggesting large-scale revision by a Jewish editor or outright fabrication', only composition by a Jewish official would explain the detailed knowledge of Jewish liturgical matters shown in the decree (*Ezra, Nehemiah, Esther*, NCB (London & Grand Rapids, 1984), p. 102). Williamson cites epigraphical evidence to show that the royal decrees in the book of Ezra are authentic (*Ezra, Nehemiah*, pp. 60, 82). This may be to claim too much. The parallels with the Ezra material are far from exact.

9. The literature on the topic is voluminous. The essential elements in the discussion remain depressingly the same with seemingly endless permutations. The arguments between the rival claims of Ezra's mission in 458 BCE (the seventh year of Artaxerxes I), 428 BCE (assuming two corruptions in the text of Ezr. 7:7f. which, it is claimed, originally read 'the *thirty*-seventh year of Artaxerxes I) and 398 (assuming that the reference is to the seventh year of Artaxerxes *II*) are well set out by G. Widengren in 'The Persian Period', in *Israelite and Judean History*, ed. J. H. Hayes and J. M. Miller (London, 1977), pp. 503–15, with the literature cited there. Recent writers who have urged the more traditional view that Ezra preceded Nehemiah, returning in 458 BCE, are Clines, *Ezra, Nehemiah*, p. 23; and Williamson, *Ezra, Nehemiah*, p. xliv. My own approach is that much of this argument is sterile because it asks the wrong questions of the text as we have it. There it is clear that the 'Nehemiah memoirs' of cc. 1–7 have been secondarily inserted in the Ezra narrative of Ezr. 7–10, Neh. 8. There must be a *theological* reason for the attempt to present them as contemporaries. Answers to this theological question may prove just as elusive as the historical ones, but it offers a more fruitful line of enquiry. Such a call for a *theological* reading of the text is made powerfully by Gunneweg, 'Zur Interpretation', and also by P. R. Ackroyd, *The Age of the Chronicler* (Auckland, 1970), 'History and Theology in the Writing of the Chronicler', *CTM*, 38 (1967), 501–15 and 'The Chronicler as Exegete', 2–32. Williamson also argues for a theological pattern in the final arrangement of the books: see n. 4 above.

10. Again, it this theological motif which offers the easier and more plausible explanation for this element in the decree than attempts like Williamson's to find a likely historical explanation for the role of these appointees (*Ezra, Nehemiah*, pp. 104f.).

11. See Ch. 6, n. 45 below.

12. Williamson is right to see the stress on the 'separation' of the people in the books of Ezra and Nehemiah as a major theme in the circumstances of the post-exilic era when the definition of the community had to be made more by race and religion than by nationality (*Ezra, Nehemiah*, p. 1). Braun, 'A Reconstruction of the Chronicler's Attitude toward the North', 59–62, suggested that, in the Books of Chronicles, the Chronicler was more open to people from the North than the attitude suggested in the Books of Ezra and Nehemiah and questioned whether the same writer could be responsible for both (p. 62). Williamson also argued

strongly for this difference in attitude as one argument for a difference of authorship between Chronicles and these two books. *Israel in the Books of Chronicles*, pp. 60f.

13. So Myers, *Ezra, Nehemiah*, p. 99, who sees it as an 'evasion' to divert the suspicions of their purpose in rebuilding the temple expressed by the Samaritans. See also L. W. Batten, *The Books of Ezra and Nehemiah*, *ICC* (Edinburgh, 1913), p. 193 and Clines, *Ezra, Nehemiah*, p. 141.

14. Clines made this point (*Ezra, Nehemiah*, p. 142), as had Kellermann earlier: *Nehemiah: Quellen, Überlieferung und Geschichte*, *BZAW* (Berlin, 1967), pp. 156–9. The reply of Emerton (*JTS*, 23 (1972), 177, supported by Williamson, *Ezra, Nehemiah*, p. 179), that the text does not state explicitly that the graves were *inside* the city, seems a rather desperate shift in the name of a literal historicism.

15. Gunneweg stresses such a note of continuity as being part of a deliberate design of these works, 'Zur Interpretation', 155f. 'The cleansed community completes the building of the wall of the sacred city. The . . . repetition of the list of Ezra ii in Neh. vii appears from this conception which is significant throughout. The community which constituted itself in joy and celebration after the building of the temple and walls . . . is none other than that which was purified through the judgement and has returned home from the exile . . .' ('Die reine Gemeinde vollbringt den Bau der Mauer der heiligen Stadt. Auch noch die viel diskutierte Wiederholung der Liste von Esra ii in Neh. vii erscheint von dieser Konzeption aus als durchaus sinnvoll: Die Gemeinde, welche nach dem Wiederaufbau von Tempel und Stadtmauer sich feierlich und festlich konstitutiert, wie in Esra viii–x berichtet wird, ist personell keine andere als die durch das Gericht geläuterte und aus dem Exil heimgekehrte . . .').

16. *I & II Chronicles, Ezra, Nehemiah*, pp. 272, 278.; see Pss. 2, 46, 48, Isa. 29:1–8, II Kgs. 19:32–4 = Isa. 37:33–5, Zech. 2:1–4 (5–9) etc.

17. See P. R. Ackroyd, *Israel under Babylon and Persia*, New Clarendon Bible (Oxford, 1970), pp. 168f.

18. N. P. Lemche rightly points out the difficulty of knowing whether this is based on the law of manumission in Lev. c. 25: 'The Manumission of Slaves: The Fallow Year; The Sabbatical Year: The Jobel Year', *VT*, 26 (1976), 38–59. This goes for much of the legal practice referred to in the Books of Ezra and Nehemiah. It is notoriously difficult to pinpoint which 'law-code' is the precise authority for any one incident. The interests here also seem to be more general and theological than historical.

19. Fishbane, *Biblical Interpretation*, pp. 130f.

20. See A. L. Ivri, 'Neh. 6:19', *J. Stud. of Judaism*, 3 (1972) 35–45. Ivri argues that this is a reference to commandeering the whole temple/palace, thus assuming *royal* prerogatives. 'Nehemiah, if he had followed Shemaiah's advice, would have been challenging the authority of the High Priest . . . He would, in short, be acting like a king' (p. 43).

21. A number of commentators see this as a covenant following Ezra's reading of the law, so forming a fitting climax to Ezra's work. So L. E. Browne, 'Ezra and Nehemiah', in *Peake's Commentary on the Bible* (London, 1962), p. 376. P. R. Ackroyd (*I & II Chronicles, Ezra, Nehemiah*, p. 307), notes verbal parallels between this chapter and the account of Ezra's reading of the law. Others link this chapter more with Neh. 13. So Myers, *Ezra, Nehemiah*, p. 174; L. H. Brockington, *Ezra, Nehemiah and Esther*, NCB (London, 1969), p. 187; Batten, *Ezra and Nehemiah*, pp. 372f.

22. D. J. Clines, 'Nehemiah 10 as an Example of Early Jewish Biblical Exegesis', *JSOT*, 21 (1981), 111–17. Clines sees the chapter as recording an event which followed Nehemiah's second period of governorship (Neh. 13). Laws identical with those in the Pentateuch form the basis of it. It is a 'pledge' rather than a 'covenant', since this is not an account of any bilateral agreement. It provides an example of the exegesis of Pentateuchal laws in the post-exilic community. Fishbane sees Neh. 10 as 'a subsequent ratification and codification of the *ad hoc* measures discharged by Nehemiah during the course of his procuratorship', *Biblical Interpretation*, p. 130.

23. So J. Myers, *Ezra, Nehemiah*, p. 217.

24. See Williamson, *Israel in the Books of Chronicles*, pp. 60f.

5 The Book of Haggai

1. Since in the prophetic books we are no longer dealing with clearly demarcated units such as the 'addresses' or the 'speeches', the passages are no longer set out in translation.

2. The best treatment of the Book of Haggai from this point of view remains that of Beuken, *Haggai–Sacharja*. See also R. Mason, 'The Purpose of the "Editorial Framework" of the Book of Haggai', *VT*, 27 (1977) 413–21. It is unfortunate that Beuken's work has not been translated into English because, at least until comparatively recently, it has received far less popular attention than it deserved. Some writers have continued to ignore the clear distinction of material in the book. Such neglect distorts the assessment of Haggai given by P. D. Hanson, *The Dawn of Apocalyptic* (Philadelphia, 1975), pp. 240–62. Of commentators who have taken note of Beuken's work, Rudolph rejects his view that the editors came from a 'Chronistic milieu' and claims that they were a group of Haggai's disciples who wanted to show that the real impulse for the rebuilding of the temple came from Haggai. The messianic hopes about Zerubbabel show that the book must have achieved its final form almost immediately after the close of the prophet's ministry before events had falsified such hopes. *Haggai, Sacharja 1–8, Sacharja 9–14, Maleachi* KAT (Gütersloh, 1976), p. 39. D. L. Petersen (*Haggai & Zechariah 1–8* (London, 1985)) appears to find closer links with the Deuteronomistic than the Chronicler tradition, and sees the book as bearing stronger similarities to certain short prose historical compositions of the sixth

century than to pre-exilic prophetic collections (p. 37). Petersen does not seem to be wholly unsympathetic to my conclusions in 'The Purpose'. C. L. Meyers and E. M. Meyers (*Haggai, Zechariah 1–8*, The Anchor Bible (New York, 1987)) agree that there is an editorial framework, but find it near in date to the prophet himself. The whole book, together with Zech. 1–8, formed a composite work for presentation at the rededication of the temple in 515 BCE (p. xlviii). R. J. Coggins, *Haggai, Zechariah, Malachi*, Old Testament Guides (Sheffield, 1987), believes that both Haggai and Zechariah were brought into their final form in temple circles (p. 29).

3. *Haggai-Sacharja 1–8*, pp. 29f.

4. Heb. חָרֵב. This is usually translated 'ruined' or 'desolated', but here it stands in antithetic parallelism to the people's living (/ישׁב) in their own cared-for houses. Since the Niph'al of the verbal root can be paralleled with 'uninhabited' in reference to a city (Tyre, Ezek. 26:19), we should probably see here a reference not only to its ruined state in comparison with their own decorated houses but to its desertion as a place of activity. 'Neglect' seems to catch both facets of this parallelism.

5. A. R. Johnson, 'Ps. 23 and the Household of Faith', in *Proclamation & Presence: Old Testament Essays in Honour of Gwynne Henton Davies*, ed. J. I. Durham and J. R. Porter (London, 1970), pp. 255–71.

6. It is possible to see a unity in the present arrangement of vv. 2b, 4–6, for all their variety of form and formulae, constituting a 'prophetic disputation'. V. 2b describes the people's present attitude and excuses; v. 4 represents a challenging question by the prophet, drawing out the true enormity of their behaviour, and this is climaxed by a pronouncement of Yahweh, challenging the people to see their present condition in traditional terms of divine judgement. It is strange that this is generally paralleled with vv. 7, 9–11. Some have argued that the two were spoken to different audiences (so Rudolph, *Haggai, Sacharja 1–8, Sacharja 9–14, Maleachi*, p. 35; O. Steck, 'Zu Haggai 1:2–11', *ZAW*, 83 (1971), 355–79). Such an approach is questioned by J. Whedbee, 'A Question–Answer Schema in Haggai 1: The Form and Function of Haggai 1:9–11', in *Biblical and Near Eastern Studies: Essays in Honour of William Sandford LaSor* (Grand Rapids, 1978). T. Chary sees vv. 7b–11 as 'a second wave of the prophetic attack' or, perhaps, even the summary of a second sermon (*Agée-Zacharie, Malachie*, Sources Bibliques (Paris, 1969), p. 21). We can probably agree that v. 8 is intrusive where it stands, while seeing it as an authentic call by the prophet. Amsler sees it as the climax of the passage (S. Amsler *et al.*, *Agéee, Zacharie Malachie*, commentaire de l'Ancient Testament, XIc, 2nd edn (Neuchâtel & Paris, 1988), p. 21). Least likely is Beuken's contention that the original words of the prophet about the temple (vv. 4, 8, 9b) have been joined to words about the hardship of the times (cc. 5f., 9a, 10f.). The connection between 'temple' and 'prosperity' is a marked feature of the Zion tradition (see, e.g. Rudolph, *Haggai, Sacharja 1–8, Sacharja 9–14, Maleachi*, pp. 34f., and the references cited there).

We should probably heed the warning of Amsler, who says that, while such reconstructions may follow the dictates of logic, they miss the vehemence of the discourse which is marked by certain repetitions of thought (Amsler *et al.*, *Agée*, p. 21). D. R. Jones similarly says, 'All attempts by commentators to rearrange this passage in order to achieve a more logical sequence of thought and avoid repetition, are precarious. The present order is due not to editorial clumsiness, but to reverence for the tradition in the forms it has already assumed by the time the editor handles it' (*Haggai, Zechariah and Malachi*, TBC (London, 1962), p. 38).

7. Johnson, *The Cultic Prophet*, in p. 65; *The Cultic Prophet and Israel's Psalmody* (Cardiff, 1979), pp. 64, 198, 29.

8. So *BHS*, and see the discussion by Ackroyd, *Exile and Restoration*, p. 155n.

9. D. Hillers, *Treaty Curses and the Old Testament Prophets* (Rome, 1964), pp. 28f., describes both the lists in Deut. c. 28 and Hag. 1:6 as 'futility curses'. He describes the form of these as consisting of a protasis which describes the activity, and an apodosis which describes the frustration of the activity, the latter often being introduced by the formula 'but not'.

10. In addition to the discussions in the commentaries, see D. J. Clark, 'Problems in Haggai 2:15–19', *The Bible Translator*, 34 (1983), 432–9, who agrees that the main thrust of this passage is one of hope and promise.

11. See my discussion in 'The Prophets of the Restoration', pp. 143f., and references cited there.

12. Petersen, *Haggai and Zechariah 1–8*, pp. 71–85; Meyers and Meyers, *Haggai, Zechariah 1–8*, p. 57.

13. This general interpretation is now accepted by Coggins, *Haggai, Zechariah, Malachi*, pp. 36–8.

14. For an examination of the relation between the two passages, see P. R. Ackroyd, 'Some Interpretative Glosses in the Book of Haggai', *JJS*, 7 (1956), 163–7, esp, p. 167.

15. Mason, 'The Purpose', 413–21.

16. *Haggai–Sacharja 1–8*, pp. 27–83.

17. *Haggai and Zechariah 1–8*, pp. 32–9. See also n. 1 above.

18. See Beuken, *Haggai–Sacharja 1–8*, p. 38 for references.

19. I Kgs. 12:15; 15:29; 16:12, 17, 34; 17:16; II Kgs. 9:36; 14:25; 17:13, 23; 21:10.

20. II Chr. 33:8; 34:14; 35:6 (Neh. 9:14).

21. Exod. 9:35; 35:29; Lev. 8:36; 10:11; 26:46; Num. 4:37, 45; 9:23; 10:13, 23; 21:10.

22. See the article 'Remnant' by G. F. Hasel, in *IDB* (Supp. Vol.), Abingdon, 1976), pp. 735f., and literature cited there, together with *The Remnant: The History and Theology of the Remnant Idea from Genesis to Isaiah* (Michigan, 1972; 2nd edn, 1974).

23. I Chr. 28:20f., 29:9. See above, pp. 31f., 34.

24. I Chr. 22:13; 28:10, 20. See above, pp. 24f., 30.

25. See also Exod. 13, 21f.; 14:19f., 24. See the discussion by Ackroyd, 'Some Interpretative Glosses', 163. See also K. Elliger, *Die Propheten Nahum, Habakuk, Zephanja, Haggai, Sacharja, Maleachi, ATD*, 25 (Göttingen, 1964), p. 92.
26. *Haggai–Sacharja 1–8*, pp. 51f.
27. Apart from David's charge to Solomon and the leaders of the people, and the particular groups addressed by Jehoshaphat, Hezekiah and Josiah, Shemaiah addresses Rehoboam and the princes of Judah (II 12:5);
Ahijah addresses Jeroboam and all Israel (13:4);
Azariah addresses Asa and all Judah and Benjamin (15:2);
Hanani addresses Asa, king of Judah (16:7);
Jehu addresses Jehoshaphat (19:2);
Jahaziel addresses all Judah, the inhabitants of Jerusalem and Jehoshaphat (20:15);
Eliezer addresses Jehoshaphat (20:37);
Elijah addresses Jehoram (by letter, 21:12);
Zechariah addresses the people (24:20), but Asa and the princes of Judah are clearly included (vv. 17f.);
A 'man of God' addresses Amaziah (25:7);
A 'prophet' addresses Amaziah (25:15).

6 Zechariah 1–8

1. It is now generally agreed that Zech. cc. 9–14 come from (a) different and later hand(s) than cc. 1–8, although there are some interesting connecting lines of tradition which suggest that the merging of the two sections was not entirely arbitrary. See R. Mason, 'The Relation of Zechariah 9–14 to Proto-Zechariah', *ZAW*, 88 (1976), 227–39. In his criticism of this paper, John Day has misunderstood the quite general thematic continuity for which I argued there rather than direct and specific literary dependence: 'Prophecy', in *It is Written: Scripture Citing Scripture: Essays in Honour of Barnabas Lindars*, ed. D. A. Carson and H. G. M. Williamson (Cambridge, 1988).
2. *Haggai & Zechariah 1–8*, pp. 120–2. The fullest treatment of the oracles is that of A. Petitjean, *Les Oracles du proto-Zacharie. Un programme de restauration pour la communauté juive après l'exile* (Paris, 1969). Beuken's treatment is also detailed and illuminating, *Haggai–Sacharja 1–8*. Petersen is almost certainly right to suggest that the present form of the oracles is the result of a fairly complex process of comment upon and exegesis of the visions (p. 122).
3. *Die zwölf kleinen Propheten, HAT* (Tübingen, 1964), p. 216.
4. See Petersen, *Haggai & Zechariah 1–8*, p. 129.
5. In the addresses in Chronicles, Ahijah uses the phrase in this more favourable sense (II 13:12); and also Hezekiah (II 29:5).

6. *Haggai–Sacharja 1–8*, p. 85.
7. The construction is discussed in GK, §117 p, q.
8. *Haggai–Sacharja 1–8*, pp. 88–103.
9. *Haggai & Zechariah 1–8*, pp. 135f.
10. Petersen takes too literally the language and imagery of 2:1–5/5–9 as implying that Zechariah rejected Ezekiel's and Haggai's view of God returning to reside in the temple, or as being in any way limited to the confines of the sanctuary (see, e.g., the argument on p. 117). The error is to fail to realise how much, especially for Ezekiel, the temple was the symbol of God's presence in the whole land and community (see, for instance, the 'mountains' motif as discussed by J. D. Levenson, *Theology of the Programme of Restoration of Ezekiel 40–48* (Missoula, 1976), esp. pp. 7–19: 'It [Mount Zion] is the focus of all the land of Israel, the "objective correlative" . . . of the fortunes of the people of Israel' (p. 17). One ought to add that the imagery of Ezek. 47 shows that God's healing presence in the temple reaches out to embrace the whole land. There is no reason to suppose that Haggai, who uses so much of Ezekiel's language and imagery, thought any differently. The purpose of the vision in Zech. 2:1–5/5–9 is to assure the community of God's presence and power to defend, and of the fulfilment of Second Isaiah's promises about the miraculous enlarging of population (Isa. 54:1–3), rather than to repudiate the notion of God's presence in temple and city.
11. Westermann has dealt with the widespread use of the 'accusing question' in the prophetic judgement speeches (*Basic Forms of Prophetic Speech*, pp. 142–5) and of its particular use in the speeches in Chronicles (pp. 163f.). This testifies to its suitability as a rhetorical device in spoken address. In the addresses in Chronicles, however, as well as warning, it serves as a summons to belief in the good purposes of God for his people.
12. *Les Oracles du proto-Zacharie*, p. 43.
13. A.S. van der Woude, '"Seid nicht wie eure Väter!" Bemerkungen zu Sacharja 1:5 und seinem Kontext', *BZAW*, 150 (1980), 163–73; also *Zacharia, De Prediking van het Oude Testament* (Nijkerk, 1984), pp. 23–5.
14. So Beuken, *Haggai–Sacharja 1–8*, pp. 112f. The view goes back to Jerome. See H. G. Mitchell, *Haggai, Zechariah, Malachi, Jonah, ICC* (Edinburgh, 1912), p. 112 for references. More recently van der Woude has argued for this ('"Seid nicht wie eure Väter!"'). But this entails a rather desperate re-reading of the text as הַנְּבִיאִים הֲלָעוּ לָמוֹ , 'and the prophets who [taking ה as relative] spoke nonsense (/לעע) to them'.
15. Meyers and Meyers find this placing of the prophets over against the word of God curious, for they are normally at one with it. They argue that the point is that the prophets share the *mortality* of their ancestors in contrast to the eternal divine word. *Haggai, Zechariah 1–8*, p. 95.
16. See Nicholson, *Preaching to the Exiles*, pp. 49–51, and especially the statement that the prophets function 'as preachers of the law', a feature which is 'exempli-

fied in the many instances in which they are described as having confronted those who transgressed it with its demands and inveighed against the constant failure to obey them . . .' (p. 50).

17. 'But while the fathers, the object of the preaching, and the prophets, the subject of the preaching, no longer exist, the content of the preaching does, i.e. the prophetic word of God to which the present generation can and must pay heed. With these words the concept of an Old Testament Canon is heralded.' ('Aber mögen die Väter, das Objekt der Verkündigung und die Propheten, das Subjekt der Verkündigung, nicht mehr vorhanden sein, so ist doch der Inhalt der Verkündigung noch da, das prophetische Wort Gottes, nach dem sich also auch die gegenwärtige Generation noch richten kann und muss. In diesen Worten kündigt sich der Kanon des Alten Testament an.' *Die Propheten*, p. 101.

18. This is spiritedly argued by van der Woude, '"Seid nicht eure Väter!"', p. 171 and *Zacharia*, pp. 27f.

19. Among those who see v. 6b as description of the response of Zechariah's hearers are Beuken, *Haggai-Sacharja 1–8*, pp. 104ff., who stresses particularly the parenetic function of this *Gerichtsdoxologie*; Elliger, who maintains that it shows that repentance is a pre-requisite for the time of salvation, *Die Propheten*, p. 217; and Meyers and Meyers, *Haggai, Zechariah 1–8*, p. 96.

20. *Les Oracles du proto-Zacharie*, pp. 50f.

21. *Haggai & Zechariah 1–8*, p. 136n.

22. *Die Propheten*, pp. 120ff.

23. Horst, *Die zwölf kleinen Propheten*, p. 227.

24. I Kgs. c. 22. See N. L. A. Tidwell, 'Wā'ōmar (Zech. 3:5) and the Genre of Zechariah's Fourth Vision', *JBL*, 94 (1975), 343–55, who argues, on the basis of I Kgs. 22, Isa. 6 and other such passages, for a specific genre of narrative scenes in the Council of Heaven.

25. Petersen, *Haggai & Zechariah 1–8*, pp. 195f., says that it was the exile which had made the high priest's atoning role invalid and it was for this reason, rather than for any personal guilt on Joshua's part, that he needed to be restored. Meyers and Meyers agree that the exact grounds of the charge are left unspecified but assume that it is because of God's past judgement on Jerusalem, temple and people and, by their role in that temple, the priestly line of which Joshua is here the representative (*Haggai, Zechariah 1–8*, pp. 185f.). Others, less probably, have seen indications here of some rivalry between different priestly groups, particularly between the Zadokites who had been in Babylon and the Levites who had stayed behind (so Hanson, *The Dawn of Apocalyptic*, p. 254).

26. A number of commentators argue for such 'prophetic' status being granted to Joshua here: e.g. Petersen, *Haggai & Zechariah 1–8*, p. 208.

27. See, e.g., Clements, *God and Temple*, esp. pp. 1–15.

28. For a discussion of the great number of different interpretations, see Petitjean, *Les Oracles du proto-Zacharie*, pp. 173–85.

29. Ackroyd, *Exile and Restoration*, p. 187.

30. Mitchell, *Haggai, Zechariah*, p. 154.
31. So, most recently, Petersen, *Haggai & Zechariah 1–8*, p. 238; Meyers and Meyers, *Haggai, Zechariah 1–8*, see this passage, together with 3:8–10 and 6:9–15, as three oracular units whose concern was to present and justify 'the new Yehudite political restructuring to the restoration community' (p. 265). However, their view that the insertion of vv. 6b–10a in the framework of the fourth vision 'which espouses so explicitly the dyarchic pattern of leadership' shows the originality of the passage to Zechariah is difficult to accept. It is more likely that it argues for a different pattern of leadership, as the argument in these pages maintains.
32. *Haggai & Zechariah 1–8*, p. 239.
33. See Horst, *Die zwölf kleinen Propheten*, p. 233.
34. So Petitjean, *Les Oracles du proto-Zacharie*, pp. 215ff. This ancient Near Eastern building practice as a background to Zech. 4:7 is argued for by Petersen, *Haggai & Zechariah 1–8*, pp. 240–44, who bases his conclusions on the work by R. Ellis, *Foundation Deposits in Ancient Mesopotamia* (New Haven, 1968).
35. So L. Rignell, *Die Nachtgesichte des Sacharja* (Lund, 1950), p. 231; Ackroyd, *Exile and Restoration*, pp. 198ff.
36. Th. Chary, *Agée-Zacharie, Malachie*, p. 112.
37. So Ackroyd, *Exile and Restoration*, p. 197; see also Rignell, *Die Nachtgesichte des Sacharja*, pp. 188f.
38. A point made in another connection by J. Eaton, 'The Psalms & Israel's Worship', in *Tradition & Interpretation*, ed. G. W. Anderson (Oxford, 1979), pp. 268f.
39. All the commentaries discuss the various interpretations. See, e.g., Mason, *The Books of Haggai, Zechariah and Malachi*, pp. 65f., and, more recently, Petersen, *Haggai & Zechariah 1–8*, p. 281; R. L. Smith, *Micah–Malachi*, World Bible Commentary (Waco, 1984), p. 221; van der Woude, *Zacharia*, pp. 124–7; Meyers and Meyers, *Haggai, Zechariah 1–8*, pp. 382ff.
40. Meyers and Meyers see the term 'Regem-Melech' as the title of an official, while Petersen takes it as a personal name.
41. So Ackroyd, *Exile and Restoration*, p. 209.
42. See above, Ch. 5 n. 7.
43. So, e.g., D. Winton Thomas, 'Zechariah', IB, 6, pp. 1082f. Horst raises this as one possible interpretation, *Die zwölf kleinen Propheten*, p. 239.
44. Notably, E. Würthwein, *Der 'Amm Ha'arez' im Alten Testament. BWANT*, 17 (Stuttgart, 1936), pp. 51–7, 60f. So also Smith, *Micah–Malachi*, p. 223.
45. So E. W. Nicholson, 'The Meaning of the Expression "am ha'ares" in the Old Testament', *JSS*, 10 (1965), 59–66. Amsler is emphatic: '*people of the land* is an expression which designates the whole population grouped around Jerusalem, both those who stayed in the land during the exile and those who had returned from the deportation' ('*peuple du pays*, expression qui désigne l'ensemble de la population groupée autour de Jérusalem, restée au pays pendant l'exil ou revenue de déportation'), *Agée*, p. 115. The same view is shared by Petitjean, *Les Oracles*

du proto-Zacharie, p. 307; J. Baldwin, *Haggai, Zechariah, Malachi*, Tyndale Old Testament Commentaries (London, 1972), p. 144; Rudolph, *Haggai, Sacharja 1–8, Sacharja 9–14, Maleachi*, p. 144; Elliger, *Die Propheten*, p. 135f.

46. D. Winton Thomas sees v. 8 as breaking a sequence which continues from v. 7 in v. 9, 'Zechariah', p. 1084, a view expressed earlier by H. G. Mitchell, *Haggai and Zechariah*, pp. 200f. So also Petitjean, *Les Oracles du proto-Zacharie*, pp. 321f.; and Smith, *Micah–Malachi*, p. 225. Smith believes that v. 7 refers to vv. 9f. since the prophets did not teach about fasting but about social justice. Those who see vv. 8–10 as intrusive include P. R. Ackroyd, 'Zechariah', in *Peake's Commentary on the Bible* (London, 1962), p. 650, *Exile and Restoration*, p. 210; Elliger, *Die Propheten*, p. 137; Th. Chary, *Agée-Zacharie, Malachie*, pp. 117, 123; van der Woude, *Zacharia*, pp. 131f.; Petersen, *Haggai & Zechariah 1–8*, pp. 290f.; Meyers and Meyers, *Haggai, Zechariah 1–8*, p. 398.

47. See GK, §113a 2. This says that its use following a finite verb to continue the sequence of action occurs 'in the later books'.

48. *Ibid.*, §113h, which actually cites Zech. 7:5 as an instance of this.

49. See GK §117x, where it is suggested it may derive from popular language. Cf. §135e.

50. G. H. Guthrie, 'Fast, Fasting', *IDB* II, pp. 241–4.

51. D. R. Jones implies this interpretation, *Haggai, Zechariah and Malachi*, pp. 97f.

52. So Ackroyd, 'Zechariah', in *Peake's Commentary*, p. 650.

53. So Mitchell, *Haggai, Zechariah*, p. 200.

54. LXX reads καὶ εὐθηνία τοῖς ἀγαπῶσίν σε perhaps suggesting a Hebrew text וְשַׁלְוָה לְאֹהֲבָיִךְ. See E. G. Briggs, *The Psalms, II*, ICC (Edinburgh, 1907), p. 450.

55. Isa. 56–66 has not been included in the material treated in this book because of the extreme uncertainty which attaches to the date, authorship and composition of the chapters. In spite of widespread agreement among many scholars that these represent the work of a 'Trito-Isaiah' who wrote just after the period of the exile, I remain unconvinced. Doubtless some of the oracles do belong to this period and doubtless themes of Isaiah of Jerusalem and 'Second Isaiah' are picked up here. But the material remains so disparate in subject, style and theme that it seems hazardous to speak of the thought of one author, even allowing that such thought would have been the subject of a continuing tradition, in anything like the way in which we may speak of the thought of Haggai or Zechariah or even of the Chronicler, for all the later tradition-elements to be found in the books which bear their names.

56. Fohrer cites Hos. 8:1 (v. 1); Mic. 3:8 (v. 1); Isa. 52:12 (v. 8), *Das Buch Jesaja, III*, Zürcher Bibelkommentare (Zurich & Stuttgart, 1964), p. 208.

57. R. N. Whybray, *Isaiah 40–66*, NCB (London, 1975), p. 212.

58. C. Westermann, *Isaiah 40–66*, OTL (London, 1969), p. 333.

59. Mason, 'Some Echoes of the Preaching?' p. 230n.

60. The MT here has 'he', but we must surely follow the Syriac and read the first person.

61. *Exile and Restoration*, p. 211.
62. *Haggai, Zechariah*, pp. 202f.
63. An admittedly slightly Targumic rendering of 'eschatologische Höchstspannung nicht zur Schwärmerei verleitet, sondern erst recht sittlichem Handeln antreibt'. Nevertheless, we shall see that something of the 'dream' element does surface in c. 8, although well subordinated to the call for ethical conduct in the light of such hopes.
64. 'Some Echoes of the Preaching?', p. 231.
65. Meyers and Meyers find seven distinct oracles in vv. 1–17 and say, 'In every instance, the formula serves to introduce a discrete oracular unit', *Haggai, Zechariah 1–8*, p. 410. D. J. Clark argued for a very tight literary structure to Zech. cc. 7f. on the basis of the repetition of varying introductory and concluding formulae marking the opening of major paragraphs and smaller subsections. 'Discourse Structure in Zech. 7:1–8:23', *The Bible Translator*, 36 (1985), 328–35. It will be seen from the text that I have some sympathy for his hint that this literary structure forces us to ask questions about thematic structure in the chapters, although I find it difficult to accept as tight a structure as he finds.
66. *Haggai & Zechariah 1–8*, p. 298. Petitjean gives a wider range of examples, *Les Oracles du proto-Zacharie*, p. 367.
67. So, e.g., Meyers and Meyers, *Haggai, Zechariah 1–8*, p. 411.
68. See BDB, p. 511.
69. Such a process is seen by R. P. Carroll to be a feature of later prophecy generally, whose purpose is to explain why the promises of earlier prophets had not been fulfilled. *When Prophecy Failed* (London, 1979).
70. So G. Fohrer, *Das Buch Jesaja*, *III*, p. 266; C. Westermann, *Isaiah 40–66*, p. 409; Whybray, *Isaiah 40–66*, p. 277. All follow the idea that חטא is used here, not in the sense of 'sinner', but as one who 'misses the mark' of 100 years of life. Because of this he may be deemed to have done something wrong to live for such a short time!
71. Some problems of interpretation attach to the Hebrew text of v. 6 (10), but the sense is clear. As Meyers and Meyers say of the rare verb פרשן, 'its meaning is not in doubt' (*Haggai, Zechariah 1–8*, p. 163).
72. It would be pleasant to think it might echo the promise of Ps. 103:12 that God has removed his people's sins 'as far as the east is from the west'.
73. The MT does not phrase the words of v. 6b as a question. We have either to suppose the interrogative 'he' (ה) has dropped out, assume that it was a question by 'tone of voice' or assume the words to be ironic – 'If it seems a marvel in the eyes of the remnant of the people, then [it must of course] also seem a marvel in my eyes!' See also D. R. Jones, *Haggai, Zechariah and Malachi*, pp. 105f. Fortunately the sense is clear. The words are of divine reassurance of God's ability to do the seemingly impossible.
74. So Meyers and Meyers: 'This oracle here and in verse 10 following, echoes the language and sentiments of Haggai.' *Haggai, Zechariah 1–8*, p. 419. Meyers and

Meyers see the relationship of Zech. cc. 7f. to the material in Haggai as further evidence for their view that Zechariah forms a composite work with the two chapters of Haggai (p. ix).

75. *Haggai & Zechariah 1–8*, p. 304.

76. *Haggai–Sacharja 1–8*, pp. 156–71. R. L. Smith also sets out the comparison between these two passages in tabular form. *Micah–Malachi*, p. 235.

77. As so often, Petitjean is most thorough and comprehensive. *Les Oracles du proto-Zacharie*, pp. 322–41.

7 The Book of Malachi

1. These are usually divided as follows: 1:1–5; 1:6–2:9; 2:10–16; 2:17–3:5; 3:6–12; 3:13–4:3 (Heb. 3:13–21). The book ends with two appendices, 4:4 and 5f. (Heb. 3:22 and 23f.).

2. So Smith, *Micah–Malachi*, p. 300; Baldwin, *Haggai, Zechariah, Malachi*, pp. 213f. H. J. Boecker, 'Bemerkungen zur formgeschichtlichen Terminologie des Buches Maleachi', *ZAW*, 78 (1966), pp. 68–80, prefers the term 'Discussion Addresses' (*Diskussionsworte*) to *Disputationsworte*, but the latter term is defended by Beth Glazier-McDonald, *Malachi: The Divine Messenger*, SBL Diss. Series, 98 (Atlanta, 1987), pp. 19–23.

3. Westermann, *Basic Forms of Prophetic Speech*, p. 210.

4. Chary, *Agée–Zacharie, Malachie*, p. 226 ('A l'époque de Malachie, le prophétisme était encore assez vivant pour se manifester par la prédication effective').

5. J. A. Fischer, 'Notes on the Literary Form and Message of Malachi', *CBQ*, 34 (1972), 315–20, although he too thinks the device is literary. The question and answer scheme is 'obviously a literary device' (p. 316). Fischer believes the main thrust of Malachi's message is to be found in the opening statement of each section: 'Yahweh loves Jacob' (1:2); 'he is Israel's father' (1:6); 'he is the father of all Israelites' (2:10); 'he wants honesty rather than words' (2:13, 17); 'he is faithful to his word' (3:6).

6. G. Wallis, 'Wesen und Struktur der Botschaft Maleachis', in *Das Ferne und Nahe Wort, Festschr. für Leonard Rost*, *BZAW*, 105 (1967), pp. 229–37.

7. Most recently, Glazier-McDonald, *Malachi: The Divine Messenger*, pp. 27–9.

8. A. S. van der Woude, 'Der Engel des Bundes: Bemerkungen zu Maleachi 3:1c und seinem Kontext', in *Die Botschaft und die Boten, Festschr. für H. W. Wolff*, ed. J. Jeremias u. L. Perlitt (Neukirchen-Vluyn, 1981), pp. 289–300.

9. 'Wesen und Struktur', p. 230.

10. See discussion above, p. Ch. 4.

11. A point made long ago by H. H. Rowley, *The Growth of the Old Testament* (London, 1950), p. 123.

12. Beth Glazier-McDonald has protested against the view that these verses are not from Malachi on the grounds of their thematic and linguistic relationship with

the other oracles (*Malachi: The Divine Messenger*, pp. 245ff.). Such links, if they exist, do not close the argument, since a glossator may imitate a prophet's style. The startling difference in form and their appropriateness as conclusion not only to Malachi, or even to the 'Book of the Twelve', but to the whole prophetic canon, speak for their being editorial.

13. S. L. McKenzie and H. N. Wallace, 'Covenant Themes in Malachi', *CBQ*, 45 (1983), 549–63. The attention the writers draw to the prominence of the 'covenant' theme in the Book of Malachi is a most valuable one, however.

14. Wallis, 'Wesen und Struktur'.

15. See n. 13 above.

16. For something of the background to 'love' and 'hate' as covenant vocabulary, see W. L. Moran, 'The Ancient Near Eastern Background of the Love of God in Deuteronomy', *CBQ*, 25 (1963), 77–87.

17. *Die Propheten*, p. 90.

18. B. C. Cresson, 'The Condemnation of Edom in Post-Exilic Judaism', in *The Use of the Old Testament in the New and Other Essays*, ed. J. F. Efird (Durham, NC, 1972), pp. 125–48. Cresson quotes Stinespring's rather delightful description of this theme as the 'Damn-Edom Theology'.

19. The sources cited by Beth Glazier-McDonald to show that 1:2–5 is rooted in some near contemporary destruction of Edom are too remote to make the argument other than hypothetical (*Malachi: The Divine Messenger*, pp. 35f.).

20. J. M. P. Smith, *Malachi*, ICC (Edinburgh, 1912), p. 23. See also Jones, *Haggai, Zechariah and Malachi*, p. 184.

21. For the significance of Jacob for the Chronicler, see Williamson, *Israel in the Books of Chronicles*, pp. 62–4.

22. So Rudolph, *Haggai, Sacharja 1–8, Sacharja 9–14, Maleachi*, p. 256.

23. McKenzie and Wallace ('Covenant Themes in Malachi') take 1:6–14 and 2:1–9 as two separate units because of the fresh heading at 2:1 and because of the 'shift' of argument from general cultic abuses in 1:6–14 to the breach of the covenant of Levi in 2:1–9 (p. 550n.). It is true that there is a shift of emphasis in 2:1–9, but since the authors themselves rightly indicate the covenant overtones of the father/son relationship, it seems better to regard this as a unified section dealing with the priests and their breach of their covenant, both in general and in specific forms. F. C. Fensham also stresses the 'covenant' aspect of the father/son terminology in 'Father & Son as Terminology for Treaty & Covenant', in *Near Eastern Studies in Honour of William Foxwell Albright*, ed. H. Goedicke (Baltimore & London, 1971), pp. 121–35.

24. 'Covenant Themes in Malachi', p. 558.

25. This is not the place to examine the many views which have been advanced to explain v. 11. Some see it as a reference to the worship of the Jews of the Diaspora; others to heathen worship; others, again, to an eschatological expectation of a universal acknowledgement of Yahweh. The quotation of the opening of Ps. 50 is surely significant: 'From the rising of the sun to its setting . . .', for that is a psalm

which rejects animal sacrifice but calls for the 'sacrifice of thanksgiving' to God the creator as well as for right ethical living. Since there is no reference to blood sacrifice in Mal. 1:11, the thought may be that of sheer gratitude expressed by all peoples for the gifts of creation. Whether they know it or not they are acknowledging Yahweh's goodness, and the genuineness and the gratitude of their offerings are a rebuke to the indifferent Jerusalem priesthood. For a full discussion and citation of references see Smith. *Micah–Malachi*, p. 312ff.

26. If, as seems most plausible, we follow LXX here and read at v. 3a, 'I will cut off your arm' (Heb. גֹּדֵעַ לָכֶם אֶת־הַזְּרֹעַ) in place of the reading of MT (גֹּעֵר לָכֶם אֶת־הַזֶּרַע) 'I will rebuke your offspring', this would strengthen the idea of rendering unfit for cultic duties. The arm could no longer be raised in blessing.

27. In this case the amendment of מְהִיוֹת to לִהְיוֹת (as proposed, among others, by Chary, *Agée-Zacharie, Malachie*, p. 250) is not really necessary, nor would MT represent a later attempt to efface such adverse comments against the priesthood, as Chary maintains.

28. Beth Glazier-McDonald (*Malachi: The Divine Messenger*, p. 80) argues that a distinction between 'priest' and 'Levite' is presupposed in this passage, even if it be a distinction of attitude rather than function.

29. R. Vuilleumier, *Agée, Zacharie, Malachie*, Commentaire de l'Ancient Testament (Neuchâtel & Paris, 1981), p. 239 ('Le grand nombre d'explications proposées par différents exégètes nous invite à la prudence').

30. The issues and recent scholarly contributions are well presented and discussed by Smith, *Micah–Malachi*.

31. Note the use of the word בָּרָא for the act of divine creation, the term used by the Priestly Writer in Gen. c. 1 and by Second Isaiah.

32. Elliger, *Die Propheten*, p. 201.

33. So *ibid.*, p. 201.

34. *Micah–Malachi*, p. 323.

35. C. C. Torrey, 'The Prophecy of Malachi', *JBL*, 17 (1898), 1–15. An article by G. S. Ogden, 'Figurative Language in Malachi', *The Bible Translator*, 39 (1988), 223–30, resurrected the figurative explanation of this section by which 'intermarriage' is seen as a symbol of religious apostasy. His article suffers from an assumption (which he does not justify) that the passage refers exclusively to the priests. Glazier-McDonald, *Malachi: The Divine Messenger*, sees the two themes of intermarriage with foreigners and religious apostasy as indissolubly linked. I argue in the text that this is mistaken.

36. W. Rudolph, 'Zu Mal. 2:10–16', *ZAW*, 93 (1981), 85–90, appears to have very much the better of the argument with S. Schreiner, 'Mischehen-Ehebruch-Ehescheidung: Betrachtungen zu Maleachi 2:10–16', *ZAW*, 91 (1979), 207–28, who had argued that this rested on Deuteronomic law and did not forbid divorce but was, rather, a strong plea for monogamy.

37. So Smith, *Malachi*, p. 56. Smith cites Ezek. 16:8, Deut. 22:30, Ruth 3:9.

38. The suggestion of Beth Glazier-McDonald that the two words have sexual overtones of the one who stimulates desire and the one who responds is interesting and certainly possible given the context. 'Malachi 2:12: *'ēr we' ōneh* – Another Look', *JBL* (1981), 295–8; *Malachi: The Divine Messenger*, pp. 95–9.

39. So Vuilleumier, *Agée, Zacharie, Malachie*, pp. 243f.

40. A. S. van der Woude, 'Der Engel des Bundes . . .', argues that 'angel of the covenant' in this passage, which he also sees as a secondary addition, is Israel's guardian angel, a heavenly vision of Yahweh.

41. The frequent occurrence of such 'smelting' imagery in the exilic and post-exilic prophets (e.g. Ezek. 22:17–22) suggests that it may have become a general symbol for judgement aimed at purifying. If this is so, the treatment of the theme by A. Robinson, 'God, the Refiner of Silver', *CBQ*, 11 (1949), 88–90, with its quest for a period when silver was more highly valued than gold, may be just a little too literal in a heavy-handed way.

42. There appears to be an allusion to such an understanding of the Jacob tradition in Hos. 12:2f.

43. Chary points to II Chr. 8:3 and 27:5 to show that this could be rendered, 'Your words have been too much [strong] for me', *Agée-Zacharie, Malachie*, p. 272.

44. D. J. McCarthy argued that only in Hosea is the fatherhood of God depicted in a tender, compassionate sense. Elsewhere, the emphasis is on the reverential 'fear' and obedience owed to a father by his children. 'Notes on the Love of God in Deuteronomy and the Father–Son Relationship between Yahweh and Israel', *CBQ*, 27 (1965), 144–7. But Mal. 3:17 must be placed alongside the Hosea texts as one which stresses more the love and compassion.

45. See A. R. Johnson, *Sacral Kingship in Ancient Israel*, 2nd edn (Cardiff, 1967), pp. 93f., 108f.

Select bibliography

Ackroyd, P. R. 'Zechariah', in *Peake's Commentary on the Bible*, London, 1962, pp. 646–55.

Exile and Restoration, London, 1963, p. 201.

'History and Theology in the Writing of the Chronicler', *CTM*, 38 (1967), 501–15.

'Historians and Prophets', *Svensk Exegetisk Årsbok*, 33, Lund, 1968, 18–54 = *Studies in the Religious Tradition of the Old Testament*, London, 1987, pp. 121–51.

The Age of the Chronicler, Auckland, 1970.

Israel under Babylon and Persia, New Clarendon Bible, Oxford, 1970.

I & II Chronicles, Ezra, Nehemiah, Torch Bible Commentaries, London, 1973.

'An Interpretation of the Babylonian Exile: A Study of II Kings 20, Isaiah 38–39', *SJT*, 27 (1974), 329–52.

'The Chronicler as Exegete', *JSOT*, Issue 2 (1977), 2–32.

'Continuity and Discontinuity: Rehabilitation and Authentication', in *Tradition and Theology in the Old Testament*, ed. G. Knight, Philadelphia & London, 1977, pp. 215–34 = *Studies in the Religious Tradition of the Old Testament*, London, 1987, pp. 31–45.

'A Judgement Narrative Between Kings and Chronicles? An Approach to Amos 7:9–17', in *Canon & Authority*, ed. G. W. Coats and B. O. Long, Philadelphia, 1977.

'The Biblical Interpretation of the Reigns of Ahaz and Hezekiah', in *In the Shadow of Elyon: Essays in Honour of G. W. Ahlström*, *JSOT* Supp. 31, Sheffield, 1984, pp. 247–59.

Amit, Y. 'The Role of Prophecy and Prophets in the Book of Chronicles', *Beth Mikra*, 93/2 (1983), 113–33.

Amsler, S. A., Lacocque and R. Vuilleumier, *Agée, Zacharie, Malachie*, Commentaire de l'Ancient Testament, xic, 2nd edn, Neuchâtel & Paris, 1988.

Anderson, B. W. 'Exodus Typology in Second Isaiah', in *Israel's Prophetic Heritage*, ed. B. W. Anderson and W. Harrelson, London, 1962, pp. 177–95.

Baentsch, B. *Exodus–Leviticus–Numeri, HAT*, Göttingen, 1903.

Baldwin, J. *Haggai, Zechariah, Malachi*, Tyndale Old Testament Commentaries, London, 1972.

Barton, J. *Oracles of God*, London, 1986.

Batten, L. W. *The Books of Ezra and Nehemiah, ICC*, Edinburgh, 1913.

Beer, G. *Exodus, HAT*, Tübingen, 1939.

Ben-Shem, I. 'The War of Zerah the Cushite (II Chron. 14:8–14, 16:8)', in *Bible & Jewish History: Studies in Bible and Jewish History Dedicated to the Memory of Jacob Liver*, ed. B. Uffenheimer, Tel-Aviv, 1971, pp. 51–6.

Benzinger, I. *Die Bücher der Chronik, HKAT*, Tübingen & Leipzig, 1901.

Beuken, W. M. *Haggai–Sacharja 1–8*, Assen, 1967.

Blenkinsopp, J. *Prophecy and Canon*, Notre Dame, 1977.

Boecker, H. J. 'Bemerkungen zur formgeschichtlichen Terminologie des Buches Maleachi', *ZAW*, 78 (1966), 68–80.

Botterweck, J. 'Zur Eigenart der Chronistischen Davidgeschichte', in *Festschrift für Prof. Dr. Viktor Christian*, Wien, 1956.

Braun, R. L. 'The Message of Chronicles: Rally Round the Temple', *CTM*, 42 (1971), 502–13.

    'A Reconstruction of the Chronicler's Attitude toward the North', *JBL*, 96 (1977), 59–62.

    'Chronicles, Ezra and Nehemiah: Theology and Literary History', in *Studies in the Historical Books of the Old Testament, SVT* 30, ed. J. A. Emerton, Leiden, 1979, pp. 52–64.

    1 Chronicles, Word Bible Commentary, Waco, 1986.

Bright, J. *History of Israel*, London, 1960; 2nd edn, 1972; 3rd edn, 1980.

Brockington, L. H. *Ezra, Nehemiah and Esther*, NCB, London, 1969.

Browne, L.E. 'Ezra and Nehemiah', in *Peake's Commentary on the Bible*, London, 1962.

Brunet, A. M. 'La Théologie du Chroniste: théocratie et messianisme', in *Sacra Pagina*, i, ed. J. Coppens *et al.*, Gembloux, 1959, pp. 384–97.

Caquot, André. 'Peut-on parler de messianisme dans l'œuvre du Chroniste?', *Révue de théologie et de philosophie*, 16 (1966), 110–20.

Carroll, R. P. *When Prophecy Failed*, London, 1979.

Chary, T. *Agée–Zacharie, Malachie*, Sources Bibliques, Paris, 1969.

Childs, B. S. 'A Study of the Formula "Unto This Day"', *JBL*, 82 (1963), 279–92.

    Isaiah and he Assyrian Crisis, SBT, ii, 3, London, 1967.

Exodus, OTL, London, 1974.

Clark, D. J. 'Problems in Haggai 2:15–19', *The Bible Translator*, 34 (1983), 432–9.
    'Discourse Structure in Zech. 7:1–8:23', *The Bible Translator*, 36 (1985), 328–35.

Clements, R. E. *God and Temple*, Oxford, 1965.

Clines, D. J. 'Nehemiah 10 as an Example of Early Jewish Biblical Exegesis', *JSOT*, 21 (1981), 111–17.
    Ezra, Nehemiah, Esther, NCB, London & Grand Rapids, 1984.

Coats, G. W. 'Despoiling the Egyptians', *VT*, 18 (1968), 450–7.

Coggins, R. J. *The First and Second Books of the Chronicles*, The Cambridge Bible Commentary on the New English Bible, Cambridge, 1976.
    Haggai, Zechariah, Malachi, Old Testament Guides, Sheffield, 1987.

Cresson, B. C. 'The Condemnation of Edom in Post-Exilic Judaism', in *The Use of the Old Testament in the New and Other Essays*, ed. J. F. Efird, Durham, NC, 1972, pp. 125–48.

Cross, F. M. *The Ancient Library of Qumran*, 2nd edn, New York, 1961.
    'The History of the Biblical Text in the Light of Discoveries in the Judean Desert', *HTR*, 58 (1964), 281–99.
    'The Themes of the Book of Kings and the Structure of the Deuteronomistic History', in *Canaanite Myth and Hebrew Epic*, Cambridge, Mass., 1973.
    'A Reconstruction of the Judean Restoration', *JBL*, 94 (1975).

Curtis, E. L. *The Books of Chronicles*, ICC, Edinburgh, 1910.

Dalman, G. 'Einiger geschichtliche Statten im Nordern Jerusalems', *JBL*, 48 (1929) 354–61.

Day, J. 'Asherah in the Hebrew Bible and North West Semitic Literature', *JBL*, 105 (1986).

Dibelius, M. 'The Speeches in Acts and Ancient Historiography', in *Studies in the Acts of the Apostles*, ed. H. Greeven, London, 1956, pp. 138–45.

Dillard, R. B. *2 Chronicles*, Word Bible Commentary, Waco, 1987.

Eaton, J. 'The Psalms & Israel's Worship', in *Tradition & Interpretation*, ed. G. W. Anderson, Oxford, 1979.

Elliger, K. *Die Propheten Nahum, Habakuk, Zephanja, Haggai, Sacharja, Maleachi*, ATD, 25, Göttingen, 1964.

Falk, Z. W. 'Gestures Expressing Affirmation', *JSS*, 4 (1959), 268.

Fensham, F. C. 'Father & Son as Terminology for Treaty & Covenant', in *Near Eastern Studies in Honour of William Foxwell Albright*, ed. H. Goedicke, Baltimore & London, 1971, pp. 121–35.

Fischer, J. A. 'Notes on the Literary Form and Message of Malachi', *CBQ*, 34 (1972), 315–20.

Fishbane, M. *Biblical Interpretation in Ancient Israel*, Oxford, 1985.

Fohrer, G. *Das Buch Jesaja*, III, Zürcher Bibelkommentare, Zurich & Stuttgart, 1964.

Freedman, D. N. 'The Chronicler's Purpose', *CBQ*, 23 (1961), 436–42.

Galling, K. *Die Bücher der Chronik, Esra, Nehemia*, ATD, Göttingen, 1954.

Ginsberg, H. L. 'Ezra 1:4', *JBL*, 79 (1960), 167–9.

Glazier-McDonald, B. 'Malachi 2:12: *'ēr we'ōneh* – Another Look', *JBL* (1981), pp. 295–8.

　　Malachi: The Divine Messenger, SBL Diss. Series, 98, Atlanta, 1987.

J. Gray, *I & II Kings*, 2nd edn. London, 1970.

Gunneweg, A. H. J. 'Zur Interpretation der Bücher Esra–Nehemia: Zugleich ein Beitrag zur Methode der Exegese', *SVT*, 32 (1981), 146–61.

Guthrie, G. H. 'Fast, Fasting', *IDB*, ii, pp. 241–4.

Hänel, J. 'Das Recht des Opferschlachtens in der chronistischen Literatur', *ZAW* (1937), 46–67.

Hanson, P. D. *The Dawn of Apocalyptic*, Philadelphia, 1975.

Haran, M. 'Book-Size and the Device of Catch-Lines in the Biblical Canon', *JJS*, 36 (1985), 1–11.

Hasel, G. F. *The Remnant: The History and Theology of the Remnant Idea from Genesis to Isaiah*, Michigan, 1972; 2nd edn, 1974.

　　'Remnant', *IDB* (Supp. Vol.), Abingdon, 1976, pp. 735f.

Hillers, D. *Treaty Curses and the Old Testament Prophets*, Rome, 1964.

Holladay, W. L. *The Root Sûbh in the Old Testament with Particular Reference to its Usage in Covenantal Contexts*, Leiden, 1958.

Holzinger, H. *Exodus*, *KAT*, Tübingen, 1900.

Horst, G. *Die zwölf kleinen Propheten*, *HAT*, Tübingen, 1964.

Hyatt, J. P. *Exodus*, NCB, London, 1971.

Ivri, A. L. 'Neh. 6:19', *JSJ*, 3 (1972), 35–45.

Japhet, S. 'The Supposed Common Authorship of Chronicles and Ezra– Nehemiah Investigated Anew', *VT*, 18 (1968), 330–71.

　　Das Land Israel in biblischer Zeit: Jerusalem-Symposium 1981 der Hebräischen Universität und der Georg-August-Universität, ed. G. Strecker, Göttinger Theologische Arbeiten, 25, 1983.

Johnson, A. R. *The Cultic Prophet in Ancient Israel*, 2nd edn, Cardiff, 1962, pp. 72f.

　　The Vitality of the Individual in the Thought of Ancient Israel, 2nd edn, Cardiff, 1964.

　　Sacral Kingship in Ancient Israel, 2nd edn. Cardiff, 1967.

　　'Ps. 23 and the Household of Faith', in *Proclamation & Presence: Old Testament Essays in Honour of Gwynne Henton Davies*, ed. J. I. Durham and J. R. Porter, London, 1970, pp. 255–71.

　　The Cultic Prophet and Israel's Psalmody, Cardiff, 1979.

Jones, D. R. *Haggai, Zechariah and Malachi*, TBC, London, 1962.

E. Junge, *Der Wiederaufbau des Heerwesens des Reiches Juda unter Josia*, Stuttgart, 1937.

Kellermann, U. *Nehemiah: Quellen, Überlieferung und Geschichte*, *BZAW*, Berlin, 1967, pp. 156–9.

Kittel, R. *Die Bücher der Chronik und Esra, Nehemia und Esther*, *HAT*, Göttingen, 1902.

Klein, R. W. 'Abijah's Campaign against the North (II Chr. 13) – What Were the Chronicler's Sources?', *ZAW*, 95 (1983), 210–17.

Knierim, R. 'Exodus 18 und die Neuordnung der Mosaischen Gerichtsbarkeit', *ZAW*, 73 (1961).

Koch, K. 'Zur Lage von Semarajim', *Zeitschrift des Deutschen Palästina-Vereins*, 78 (1962).

Lemche, N. P. 'The Manumission of Slaves: The Fallow Year; The Sabbatical Year: The Jobel Year', *VT*, 26 (1976).

Lemke, W. E. 'The Synoptic Problem in the Chronicler's History', *HTR*, 58 (1965), 349–63.

Levenson, J. D. *Theology of the Programme of Restoration of Ezekiel 40–48*, Missoula, 1976.

Lohfink, N. 'Hate and Love in Osée 9:15', *CBQ*, 25 (1963).

McCarthy, D. J. 'Notes on the Love of God in Deuteronomy and the Father–Son Relationship between Yahweh and Israel', *CBQ*, 27 (1965), 144–7.

'The Ancient Near Eastern Background of the Love of God in Deuteronomy', *CBQ*, 25 (1967), 77–87.

'An Installation Genre?', *JBL*, 90 (1971), 31–41.

Old Testament Covenant: A Survey of Current Opinions, Oxford, 1973.

'Covenant and Law in Chronicles–Nehemiah', *CBQ*, 44 (1982), 25–44.

Macholz, G. C. 'Zur Geschichte der Justizorganisation in Juda', *ZAW*, 84 (1972), 314–40.

McKenzie, S. L. *The Chronicler's Use of the Deuteronomistic History*, Harvard Semitic Monographs, 33, Atlanta, 1985.

McKenzie, S. L. and H. N Wallace, 'Covenant Themes in Malachi', *CBQ*, 45 (1983), 549–63.

Mason, R. A. 'The Relation of Zechariah 9–14 to Proto-Zechariah', *ZAW*, 88 (1976), 227–39.

The Books of Haggai, Zechariah and Malachi, Cambridge Bible Commentary on the New English Bible, Cambridge, 1977.

'The Purpose of the "Editorial Framework" of the Book of Haggai', *VT*, 27 (1977), 413–21.

'The Prophets of the Restoration', in *Israel's Prophetic Tradition: Essays in Honour of Peter Ackroyd*, ed. R. J. Coggins *et al.*, Cambridge, 1982.

'Some Echoes of the Preaching in the Second Temple? Tradition Elements in Zechariah 1–8', *ZAW*, 96 (1984), 221–35.

Mathias, D. 'Die Geschichte der Chronikforschung im 19 Jahrhundert unter besonderes Berücksichtigung der exegetischen Geschichtswerker. Ein problemsgeschichtlicher und methodenkritischer Versuch auf der Basis ausgewählter Texte', unpublished dissertation, Leipzig, 1977.

'"Levitische Predigt" und Deuterismus', *ZAW*, 96 (1984), 23–49.

Mayes, A. D. H. *Deuteronomy*, NCB (London, 1979).

The Story of Israel between Settlement & Exile, London, 1983.

Mays, J. L. *Micah*, OTL, London, 1976.

Meyer, E. *Die Entstehung des Judentums*, Halle, 1896.

Meyers, C. 'Jachin and Boaz in Religious and Political Perspective', *CBQ*, 45 (1983), 167f.

Meyers, C. L. and E. M. *Haggai, Zechariah 1–8*, The Anchor Bible, New York, 1987.

Micheel, R. *Die Seher- und Propheten-Überlieferungen in den Chronik, Beiträge zur biblischen Exegese und Theologie*, No. 18, Frankfurt & Bern, 1983.

Mitchell, H. G. *Haggai, Zechariah, Malachi, Jonah*, ICC, Edinburgh, 1912.

Moran, W. L. 'The Ancient Near Eastern Background of the Love of God in Deuteronomy', *CBQ*, 25 (1963), 77–87.

Mosis, R. *Untersuchungen zur Theologie des chronistischen Geschichtswerkes*, Freiburg & Basle, 1973.

Myers, J. M. *I Chronicles*, The Anchor Bible, New York, 1965.

II Chronicles, The Anchor Bible, New York, 1965.

Ezra, Nehemiah, The Anchor Bible, New York, 1965.

Nicholson, E. W. 'The Meaning of the Expression "am ha'ares" in the Old Testament, *JSS*, 10 (1965), 59–66.

Deuteronomy & Tradition, Oxford, 1967.

Preaching to the Exiles, Oxford, 1970.

North, C. R. *The Old Testament Interpretation of History*, London, 1946.

Noth, M. *Überlieferungsgeschichtliche Studien I. Die sammelnden und bearbeitenden Geschichtswerke im Alten Testament*, Halle, 1943 (ET *The Chronicler's History*, JSOT Supplement Series, 15, Sheffield, 1981).

'Eine palästinische Lokalüberlieferung in 2 Chr. 20:20', *Zeitschrift des Deutschen Palästina-Vereins*, 67 (1945), 45–71.

Exodus, OTL, London, 1962.

Ogden, G. S. 'Figurative Language in Malachi', *The Bible Translator*, 39 (1988), 223–30.

Petersen, D. L. *Late Israelite Prophecy: Studies in Deutero-Prophetic Literature and in Chronicles*, Missoula, 1977.

The Roles of Israel's Prophets, JSOT Supp. 17, Sheffield, 1981.

Haggai & Zechariah 1–8, London, 1985.

Petitjean, A. *Les Oracles du proto-Zacharie. Un programme de restauration pour la communité juive après l'exile*, Paris, 1969.

Phillips, A. J. *Ancient Israel's Criminal Law*, Oxford, 1970.

Plöger, O. 'Reden und Gebete im deuteronomistischen und chronistischen Geschichtswerk', in *Festschr. für Gunther Dehn*, ed. W. Schneemelcher, Neukirchen, 1957, pp. 35–49 = *Aus der Spätzeit des Alten Testaments*, Göttingen, 1971, pp. 50–66.

Polzin, R. *Late Biblical Hebrew: Toward an Historical Typology of Biblical Hebrew Prose*, Missoula, 1976.

Porter, J. R. 'Old Testament Historiography', in *Tradition & Interpretation*, ed. G. W. Andersen, Oxford, 1979, pp. 125–62.

Preuss, H. D. '. . . ich will mit dir sein!', *ZAW*, 80 (1968), 139–73.

Rad, G. von *Das Geschichtsbild des Chronistischen Werkes*, *BWANT*, 4th vol., No. 3, Stuttgart, 1930.

 Deuteronomium-Studien, Göttingen, 1948 (ET D. Stalker, *Studies in Deuteronomy*, SBT, 9, London, 1953).

 Theologie des Alten Testaments, Munich, Bd. i, 1957, Bd. ii, 1960 (ET D. G. M. Stalker, *Old Testament Theology*, Edinburgh & London, Vol. i, 1962, Vol. ii, 1965).

 'Die Levitische Predigt in den Büchern der Chronik', in *Festschrift für Otto Proksch*, pp. 113–24, = *Gesammelte Studien zum Alten Testament*, 1958, pp. 248–61 (ET E. W. Trueman Dicken, 'The Levitical Sermon in the Books of Chronicles', in *The Problem of the Hexateuch and Other Essays*, Edinburgh and London, 1966, pp. 267–80).

Rignell, L. *Die Nachtgesichte des Sacharja*, Lund, 1950.

Robinson, A. 'God, the Refiner of Silver', *CBQ*, 11 (1949), 88–90.

Robinson, J. *The Second Book of Kings*, The Cambridge Bible Commentary, Cambridge, 1976.

Rothstein, J. W. and J. Hänel, *Das erste Buch der Chronik*, *KAT*, Leipzig, 1927.

Rudolph, W. 'Der Aufbau der Asa-Geschichte (2 Chr. xiv–xvi)', *VT*, 2 (1952), 367–71.

 'Problems in the Books of Chronicles', *VT*, 4 (1954), 401–9.

 Chronikbücher, *HAT*, Tübingen, 1955.

 Haggai, Sacharja 1–8, Sacharja 9–14, Maleachi, *KAT*, Gütersloh, 1976.

 'Zu Mal. 2:10–16', *ZAW*, 93 (1981), 85–90.

Rylaarsdam, J. C. 'Exodus', IB, 1 (1966).

Schaeder, H. H. *Esra der Schreiber*, Tübingen, 1930.

Schmitt, A. 'Das prophetische Sondergut in II Chr. xx 14–17', in *Künder des Wortes: Festschrift für J. Schreiner*, ed. L. Ruppert *et al.*, Würzburg, 1982, pp. 273–83.

Schreiner, S. 'Mischehen-Ehebruch-Ehescheidung: Betrachtungen zu Maleachi 2:10–16', *ZAW*, 91 (1979), 207–28.

Seeligman, I. L. 'Die Auffassung von der Prophetie in der deuteronomistischen und *SVT*, xxix, Congress Volume, Göttingen, 1977, pp. 254–84.

Smith, J. M. P. *Malachi*, *ICC*, Edinburgh, 1912.

Smith, R. L. *Micah–Malachi*, Word Bible Commentary, Waco, 1984.

Steck, O. 'Zu Haggai 1:2–11', *ZAW*, 83 (1971), 355–79.

Thomas, D. W. 'Zechariah', IB, 6, pp. 1053–88.

Throntveit, M. A. 'Linguistic Analysis and the Question of Authorship in Chronicles, Ezra and Nehemiah', *VT*, 32 (1982), 201–16.

 Ezra and Nehemiah', *VT*, 32 (1982) 201–16.

 When Kings Speak: Royal Speech and Royal Prayer in Chronicles, SBL Dissertation Series, 93, Atlanta, 1987.

Tidwell, N. L. A. 'Wāʾōmar (Zech. 3:5) and the Genre of Zechariah's Fourth Vision', *JBL*, 94 (1975), 343–55.

Torrey, C. C. 'The Prophecy of Malachi', *JBL*, 17 (1898), 1–15.

Ezra Studies, Chicago, 1910.

Vries, S. J. de 'Temporal Terms as Structural Elements in the Holy War Tradition', *VT*, 25 (1975), 80–105.

Wallis, G. 'Wesen und Struktur der Botschaft Maleachis', in *Das Ferne und Nahe Wort, Festschr. für Leonard Rost*, BZAW, 105 (1967), pp. 229–37.

Weinberg, J. P. 'Die "ausser kanonischen Prophezeiungen" in den Chronikbüchern', *Acta Antiqua*, 26 (1978), 387–404.

Weingreen, J. 'The Title Moreh Sedek', *JJS*, 6 (1961).

Welch, A. C. *Post-Exilic Judaism*, Edinburgh & London, 1935.

The Work of the Chronicler, its Purpose and its Date, London, 1939, pp. 103ff.

Wellhausen, J. *Prolegomena zur Geschichte Israels*, Berlin, 1883.

Welten, P. *Geschichte und Geschichtsdarstellung in den Chronikbüchern*, WMANT, 421, Neukirchen, 1973.

Westermann, C. *Grundformen prophetischer Rede*, Munich, 1964 (ET H. C. White, *Basics Forms of Prophetic Speech*, London, 1967).

Isaiah 40–66, OTL, London, 1969.

Whedbee, J. 'A Question–Answer Schema in Haggai 1: The Form and Function of Haggai 1:9–11', in *Biblical and Near Eastern Studies: Essays in Honour of William Sandford LaSor*, Grand Rapids, 1978.

Whitelam, K. G. *The Just King*, Sheffield, 1979.

Whybray, R. N. *Isaiah 40–66*, NCB, London, 1975.

Widengren, G. 'The Persian Period', in *Israelite and Judean History*, ed. J. H Hayes and J. M. Miller, London, 1977, pp. 489–538.

Willi, T. *Die Chronik als Auslegung. Untersuchungen zur literarischen Gestaltung der historischen Überlieferung Israels*, FRLANT, 106, Göttingen, 1972.

'Thora in den biblischen Chronikbüchern', *Judaica*, 36 (1980).

Williamson, H. G. M. 'The Accession of Solomon in the Books of Chronicles', *VT*, 26 (1976), 351–61.

Israel in the Books of Chronicles, Cambridge, 1977.

'"We are Yours, O David" (1 Chr. 12:1–23)', *OTS*, 21 (1981), 164–76.

1 and 2 Chronicles, The New Century Bible Commentary, London, 1982.

Ezra, Nehemiah, Word Bible Commentary, Waco, 1985.

Wilson, R. R. *Prophecy and Society in Ancient Israel*, Philadelphia, 1980.

Woude, A. S. van der '"Seid nicht wie eure Väter!" Bemerkungen zu Sacharja 1:5 und seinem Kontext', *BZAW*, 150 (1980), 163–73.

'Der Engel des Bundes: Bemerkungen zu Maleachi 3:1c und seinem Kontext', in *Die Botschaft und die Boten, Festschr. für H. W. Wolff*, ed. J. Jeremias u. L. Perlitt, Neukirchen-Vluyn, 1981, pp. 289–300.

Zachariah, De Prediking van het Oude Testament, Nijerk, 1984.

Würthwein, E. *Der 'Amm Ha'arez' im Alten Testament*, BWANT, 17, Stuttgart, 1936.

Zalevski, S. 'The Change of Policy of Joash and the Prophecy of Zechariah, Son of Jehoida (II Chronicles xxiv 17–22)', *Bar-Ilan*, 13 (1976), pp. 31–57.

Index of modern authors

Rudolph, W., 8, 46f., 53, 75, 76f., 88, 93,
    108f., 115, 187, 267, 268, 269, 270, 271,
    273, 275, 276, 277, 278, 279, 280, 281,
    282, 285, 286, 292, 295, 296, 305
Rundgren, F., 156
Rylaarsdam, J. C., 62, 305

Schaeder, H. H., 282, 305
Schmitt, A., 66ff., 274, 305
Schreiner, S., 296, 305
Seeligman, I. L., 70, 264, 271, 275, 305
Smith, J. M. P., 295, 305
Smith, R. L., 246, 248, 291, 292, 294, 295,
    296, 305
Steck O., 286, 305

Thomas, D. W., 220, 291, 292, 305
Throntveit, M. A., 9, 39, 135, 264, 267,
    277f., 279, 305
Tidwell, N., 290, 305
Torrey, C. C., 248, 282, 296, 305f.

Vries, S. J. de, 65, 67, 274, 306
Vuilleumier, R., 245, 296, 297

Wallace, H. N., 238f., 242, 295
Wallis, G., 235, 236, 238, 294, 295, 306
Weinberg, J. P., 264, 306
Weingreen, J., 48, 269, 271, 306
Welch, A. C., 9, 264, 278, 306
Wellhausen, J., 203, 272, 306
Welten, P., 53, 270, 271, 277, 306
Westermann , C., 74, 217, 235, 264, 271,
    273, 281, 289, 292, 293, 294, 306
Whedbee, J., 286, 306
Whitelam, K. G., 273, 306
Whybray, N., 217, 292, 293, 306
Widengren, G., 283, 306
Willi, T., 48, 72, 270f., 275, 278, 306
Williamson, H. G. M., 9, 17, 20, 22, 30, 35,
    39, 47, 72, 92, 93, 101, 116, 119, 263,
    265, 266, 267, 268, 269, 270, 271, 272,
    273, 274, 276, 277, 278, 279, 281f., 282,
    283f., 285, 295, 306
Wilson, R. R., 136, 280, 306
Woude, A. S. van der, 202, 236, 289, 290,
    291, 292, 294, 297, 306
Würthwein, E., 291, 306

Zalevski, S., 276, 306

Subject index

Abijah, 38ff., 85, 100, 124, 130, 133, 139, 173, 202, 247
Ahaz, 91f., 99f., 131
Ahijah, 163
Amasai, 13ff., 134
Amaziah, 83ff., 87ff., 127, 276
Ark of the covenant, 17, 19, 22, 26, 98, 115f.
Artaxerxes, 155ff., 181
Asa, 43ff., 45ff., 51ff., 127, 129, 133, 135, 230
Azariah, the 'high' priest, 108ff., 134, 135, 139, 155, 188, 253
Azariah, the priest, 89f., 134, 139, 173, 208
Azariah ben Oded, 45ff., 128, 130, 134, 135, 137, 141, 230

Branch, 207, 210, 211f.

Chronicler
    date of, 7ff., 131ff., 265
    'messianism' of, 32
Chronicles
    relation to Ezra/Nehemiah, 9f., 56, 182f.
    sources of, 8f.
    unity of, 7ff., 267

Covenant, 38, 40f., 242ff., 250f., 255, 295, 297
Cyrus, 118f., 133f., 147ff., 152ff., 181

Darius I, 152ff., 181
David, 13ff., 61, 65, 69f., 97, 103f., 111f., 124f., 128, 130, 163, 164, 166, 168, 171f., 194, 225
    addresses of, 16ff., 18f., 19ff., 25ff., 27ff., 31f., 32ff., 138, 164, 165, 168, 206f.
    zeal for temple and worship, 17, 19, 27, 29f., 31f., 35, 39, 69f., 97, 108, 114, 148, 163, 187, 192f.
Davidic covenant, 21, 24, 40, 123f., 130, 135, 206f., 240, 280
Davidic dynasty, 32, 34, 42f., 123
Deuteronomistic History, 17, 21ff., 32, 36, 39, 41, 44, 46, 49, 52f., 56, 75ff., 80, 82, 84, 97, 99, 126, 180, 192, 265f.
Divorce, 245ff.

Edom, 239ff., 295
Eliezer, 71ff., 134, 150, 190, 249
Elijah, 73ff., 86, 87f., 127, 130f., 134, 137, 140f., 276

Index of biblical references

The Apocrypha

Ecclesiasticus

The New Testament

Matthew

Mark